BUTLER'S
LIVES OF THE SAINTS

NEW

FULL EDITION

NOVEMBER

BUTLER'S
LIVES OF THE SAINTS

NEW FULL EDITION

Patron
H. E. CARDINAL BASIL HUME, O.S.B.
Archbishop of Westminster

EDITORIAL BOARD

General Consultant Editor
DAVID HUGH FARMER

General Consultant, U.S.A.
ERIC HOLLAS, O.S.B.

Specialist Consultants
PHILIP CARAMAN, S.J.
JOHN HARWOOD
KATHLEEN JONES
DANIEL REES, O.S.B.
RICHARD SHARPE, MA, PhD
AYLWARD SHORTER, W.F.
ALBERIC STACPOOLE, O.S.B., MA, FRHS
HENRY WANSBROUGH, O.S.B., MA, STL
BENEDICTA WARD, SLG, MA, DPhil

Managing Editor
PAUL BURNS

BUTLER'S LIVES OF THE SAINTS

NEW
FULL EDITION

NOVEMBER

Revised by
SARAH FAWCETT THOMAS

BURNS & OATES

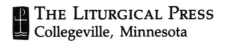

THE LITURGICAL PRESS
Collegeville, Minnesota

First published 1997 in Great Britain by
BURNS & OATES
Wellwood, North Farm Road,
Tunbridge Wells, Kent TN2 3DR

First published 1997 in North America by
THE LITURGICAL PRESS
St John's Abbey, Collegeville,
Minnesota 56321

Butler's *Lives of the Fathers, Martyrs and other principal Saints* ... first published
1756-9. First revised edition, *Butler's Lives of the Saints*, ed. Herbert Thurston, S.J.,
1926-38, copyright © Burns, Oates & Washbourne Limited. Second revised edition,
ed. Herbert Thurston, S.J., and Donald Attwater, 1954-8, copyright © Burns &
Oates Limited.

ISBN 0 86012 260 3 Burns & Oates
ISBN 0-8146-2387-5 The Liturgical Press

The emblems appearing at the foot of some pages are taken from W. Ellwood Post,
Saints, Signs and Symbols: A Concise Dictionary. © Copyright 1962, 1974 by
Morehouse Publishing, with the permission of the publishers. The Scotus Logo on
p. 60 is from H. Schneider (ed.), *Blessed John Duns Scotus: Thought and Prayer* (Duns
Scotus Committee of the Archdiocese of St Andrew's and Edinburgh, 1993), used
with permission.

Library of Congress Catalog Card Number: 95-81671

Typeset by Search Press Limited
Printed in the United States of America

CONTENTS

(Entries in capital letters indicate that the feast or saint is commemorated through-out the Roman Catholic Church with the rank of Solemnity, Feast, Memorial, or Optional Memorial, according to the 1969 revised Calendar of the Latin [Roman] Rite of the Catholic Church, published in the Roman Missal of 1970, or that the saint is of particular importance for the English-speaking world. These entries are placed first on their dates. All others are in chronological order.)

Contents

PREFACE

November opens with the Solemnity of All Saints—the great festival of all who have made it through the vicissitudes of this present phase of our human existence and have reached the "City of God." It is a festival that encapsulates and celebrates the infinite variety of the saints and gives us the key we need to understand and appreciate them. The mere 200 or so recorded here demonstrate that there is no blueprint for holiness—apart from Christ's general injunction, "love one another as I have loved you." Looking at the lives of these men and women, we see how each, in particular circumstances, with particular gifts, strove to unpack the meaning in those deceptively simple words and put them into practice.

One of the interesting things about approaching their lives in condensed form and in quick succession is that it brings the historical dimension to the fore. Besides comparing different manifestations of holiness, we have the opportunity to see how attitudes to it change over time, in terms both of how the individuals themselves perceive what they are aiming at and of how others perceive what they have achieved. In other words, what seemed in one age an admirable sign of holiness might, in another, disqualify a person from being canonized—for example, would St James of the March (28), who dealt so rigorously with the members of a dissident group that several bishops complained of his methods, be canonized today? And how do we feel today about the ideal of holiness followed by those women saints of the thirteenth to fifteenth century (see, for example, Bd Helen of Arcella on the 7th) who indulged in extreme forms of penance—fasting, in some cases, literally to death?

Many people, usually not Catholic but there are exceptions, apparently find the concept of saints and holiness off-putting. They are not necessarily hostile to it, but they seem to nurture a prejudice that it must be inherently boring. I came across this attitude several times while I was working on this volume, and it set me wondering why it should be and what if anything can be done about it. People will avidly read a biography of Virginia Woolf or John F. Kennedy or Prince Rupert of the Rhine, even of Hitler (perhaps especially of Hitler). But stick the little abbreviation St in front of someone's name and their eyes glaze over. Part of the answer must be that because we are all flawed, we find it reassuring to learn about people who are as flawed as, or preferably more flawed than, we are. And people decide the saints are beyond their range on the erroneous assumption that they are less flawed and therefore less interesting. For this, some hagiographers must definitely take part of the blame. In their fear of saying anything negative, they remove the challenge of the saints. But I think that blame must also be laid at the door of the Church. Since 1634, when Pope Urban VIII systematized it, the process has become so formal that it seems to place the individual concerned on another plane of being, with nothing to say to the rest of us.

This is a shame. Because, if you make the imaginative effort, even the most distant in time can come alive, with something relevant to say about living the Christian life. St Hugh of Lincoln died over seven centuries ago, but it is impossible not to be attracted by his humanity and impressed by his courage; and there is something very appealing about the zeal of St Malachy, who, a century earlier, made the long journey from Ireland to Rome in order to discuss the problems of the Irish church with the pope, and struck up a friendship with St Bernard on the way back. Then there is St Brice. He clearly had a very difficult personality and came to holiness rather late in life. Yet the people of Tours, where he had succeeded St Martin as bishop, venerated him as a saint when he died in 444.

This volume includes also quite a number of men and women who were beatified or canonized after the previous revision of Butler's *Lives* and are therefore included for the first time. Notable among these are Bd Rupert Mayer (1 Nov.), Bd Elizabeth of the Trinity (8), St Raphael Kalinowski (15), and Bd Michael Pro (23). They have an advantage in being so much closer to us in time than many of their predecessors. Not only do the sources tend to be richer in terms of letters, memoirs, and reliable first-hand accounts, but we also have access to photographs, which, with their power to reveal, to confirm, and sometimes to surprise, tell their own story—look, for example, at the touching full-length picture of Elisabeth Catez (Bd Elizabeth of the Trinity) dressed up to go to a ball, or at that of her hands on the piano keyboard, or else at the powerful portrait of Raphael Kalinowski, taken without his realizing it in March 1897.

These new saints still include relatively few laypeople among their number, which again prompts the question, why? and possibly provides at least a partial answer to my earlier question, why do people find the saints difficult to cope with? It is certainly true that lay saints have always been in the minority, and those that there have been, splendid as they are—St Margaret of Scotland (16) and St Elizabeth of Hungary (17) come immediately to mind—have tended to be royal (or martyrs). St Homobonus (13), the simple citizen of twelfth-century Cremona, is a glorious and too-little-known exception.

The main November casualty of the 1969 revision of the Roman Martyrology was St Catherine of Alexandria, research having finally proved to the Vatican's satisfaction that she never existed. However, it is difficult to let her go without a mention. For centuries her feast was celebrated on the 25th, and even those unfamiliar with the details of her legend could pick her out quickly in works of art. Since she is no longer in the Martyrology you will not find her in these pages, but you can still see her with her wheel and her sword in art galleries throughout the world (she appears in at least twenty-eight paintings in London's National Gallery alone), and she crops up frequently in wall paintings, stained-glass, and other media.

I would now like to thank everyone who has helped me in any way, and in particular Paul Burns, who persuaded me to take part in what has turned out to be a revelatory and fascinating project and was consistently helpful and encouraging; David Farmer, who read the entire manuscript at the half-way stage, and was so generous with his time, his knowledge, and his books; Helen Forshaw, S.H.C.J., who provided background material, expert knowledge, and much-valued comments for the entry on St Edmund of Abingdon; Dr Richard Sharpe, who took time to read and comment on the Celtic entries; Dom Henry Wansbrough, O.S.B., who also made time to read and comment on the New Testament entries; Dame Máire Hickey, O.S.B., who provided useful material on SS Gertrude and Mechtildis; Michael Walsh, who gave me access to the library of Heythrop College; Desmond Sullivan; Dr Joan Padro; and above all Tony, who gave such constant and good-humoured support, and by this stage deserves an entry himself.

---

1 March 1996, St David's Day

Sarah Fawcett Thomas

Abbreviations and Short Forms

AA.SS.   *Acta Sanctorum*. 64 vols. Antwerp, 1643– .

AA.SS. O.S.B.   L. D'Achéry and J. Mabillon. *Acta Sanctorum Ordinis Sancti Benedicti.* 9 vols. 1668–1701.

Anal.Boll.   *Analecta Bollandiana* (1882–).

Bede, *H.E.*   The Venerable Bede, *Historia Ecclesiastica* (ed. L. Sherley-Price and D. H. Farmer). London, 1955; revised ed. 1990.

Bibl.SS.   *Bibliotheca sanctorum*. 13 vols. Rome, 1960–70; Suppl. 1, *Prima Appendice*. Rome, 1987.

C.M.H.   H. Delehaye. *Commentarius Perpetuus in Martyrologium Hieronymianum* (*AA.SS.*, 65). 1931.

C.S.E.L.   *Corpus Scriptorum Ecclesiasticorum Latinorum*. Vienna, 1866– .

D.A.C.L.   H. Cabrol and H. Leclerq (eds.). *Dictionnaire d'Archéologie Chrétienne et de Liturgie*. 15 vols. Paris, 1907-53.

D.C.B.   W. Smith and H. Wace (eds.). *Dictionary of Christian Biography*. 4 vols. London, 1877-87.

D.H.G.E.   A. Baudrillart *et al.* (eds.). *Dictionnaire d'Histoire et de Géographie Ecclésiastiques*. Paris, 1912– .

Dict.Sp.   M. Viller, S.J., *et al.* (eds.). *Dictionnaire de Spiritualité*. 1937– .

D.T.C.   A. Vacant, E. Mangenot, and E. Amman (eds.). *Dictionnaire Théologie Catholique*. 15 vols. Paris, 1903–50.

E.E.T.S.   Early English Text Society.

E.H.R.   *English Historical Review* (1886–).

Eusebius   Eusebius. *Historia Ecclesiastica* (ed. K. Lake). 1927.

H.S.S.C.   F. Chiovaro *et al.* (eds.). *Histoire des Saints et de la Sainteté Chrétienne*. Paris, 1972-88.

I.E.R.   *Irish Ecclesiastical Record* (1864–).

J.T.S.   *Journal of Theological Studies* (1900–).

K.S.S.   A. P. Forbes (ed.). *Kalendars of Scottish Saints*. 1872.

L.E.M.   E. H. Burton and J. H. Pollen (eds.). *Lives of the English Martyrs*. 2d series, London, 1915.

M.G.H.   *Monumenta Germaniae Historica*. The *Scriptores* series is split into several sub-series, including *Auctores antiquissimi, Scriptores rerum merovingicarum*, and *Scriptores*.

M.M.P.   R. Challoner. *Memoirs of Missionary Priests*. London, 1741–2; new ed. by J. H. Pollen, London, 1924.

N.A.	*Neues Archiv der Gesellschaft für ältere deutsche Geschichts-kunde.*
N.C.E.	*New Catholic Encyclopedia.* 14 vols. New York, 1967.
O.D.C.C.	F. L. Cross and E. A. Livingstone (eds.). *The Oxford Dictionary of the Christian Church.* Oxford, New York and Toronto, 2d ed., 1974.
O.D.P.	J. N. D. Kelly. *The Oxford Dictionary of Popes.* Oxford, 1986.
O.D.S.	D. H. Farmer. *The Oxford Dictionary of Saints.* 3d ed., Oxford and New York, 1993.
P.B.A.	*Proceedings of the British Academy* (1903–).
P.G.	J. P. Migne (ed.). *Patrologia Graeca.* 162 vols. Paris, 1857-66.
P.L.	J. P. Migne (ed.). *Patrologia Latina.* 221 vols. Paris, 1844-64.
Propylaeum	*Propylaeum ad Acta Sanctorum Decembris.* Brussels, 1940.
R.H.E.	*Revue d'Histoire Ecclésiastique* (1900–).
R.S.	Rolls Series (1858–).
S.C.	*Sources Chrétiennes.* Paris, 1940– .
Tillemont	L-S. Le Nain de Tillemont. *Mémoires pour servir à l'histoire écclésiastique des six premiers siècles.* Paris, 1693-1712.
T.R.H.S	*Transactions of the Royal Historical Society* (1871–).
Vies des Saints	J. Baudot and P. Chaussin (eds.). *Vies des Saints et des Bienheureux.* 13 vols. Paris, 1935-59—J. Dubois and P. Antin, vols. 7ff.
V.S.H.	C. Plummer (ed.). *Vitae Sanctorum Hiberniae.* 2 vols. 1910; 2d ed., 1968.

ATLANTIC OCEAN

New Spain
(V)

Mexico ⚓
(1546)

Cuba (c)

⚓ Santo Domingo
(1546)

Guatemala
(c)

PACIFIC OCEAN

Caracas (c)
⚓ BOGOTA (1564)
New Granada
(V)

Lima ⚓ Peru
(1546) (V)

Brazil
(V)

⚓ Charcas
de la Plata
(1609)

La Plata
(V)

Chile
(c)

▨ Principal mission areas in the
sixteenth century

⚓ Archdioceses with dates of
establishment

Viceroyalties (V) and Captaincies (C)
in the eighteenth century

1. THE NEW WORLD

Source for maps 1 and 2: E. Dussel (ed.) The Church in Latin America, 1492–1992 *(Tunbridge Wells and Maryknoll, N.Y., 1992)*

See St Martin de Porres, *pp. 18–20*

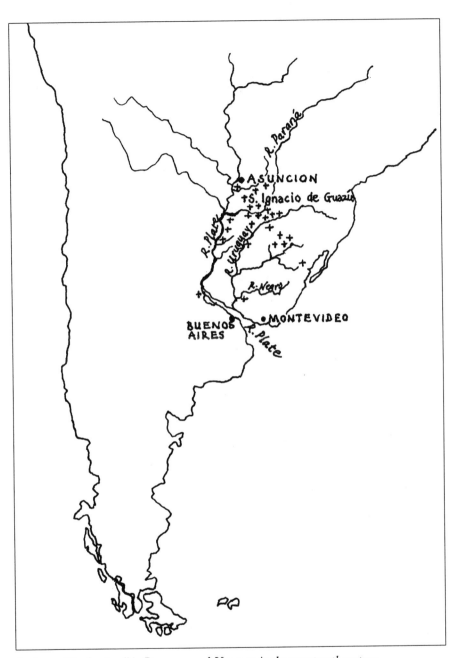

2. Areas of "reductions" in Paraguay and Uruguay in the seventeenth century
See St Roque González and Companions, *pp. 125–7, and next page for an eighteenth-century map*

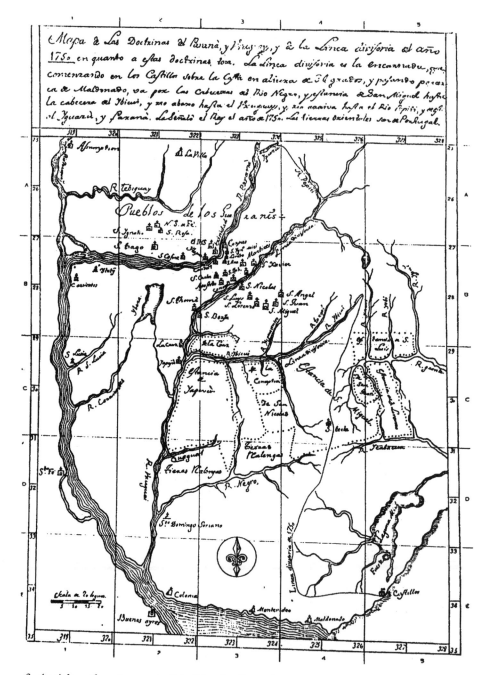

3. *An eighteenth-century map of the "doctrines" or reductions*

The line running west from the coast and then north shows the division between the "doctrines" administered
by Spain (west) and Portugal (east), signed by the king of Spain in 1750.

1

SOLEMNITY OF ALL SAINTS

Today the Church celebrates the fulfillment of Pentecost, and its own hope, in those men and women known and unknown, who, whenever and wherever they lived and whatever the circumstances of their lives, are now "with God." In honouring them it acknowledges that salvation is open to all—the idea St John was striving to express when he spoke of "a great multitude which no man could number, from every nation, from all tribes and peoples and tongues, standing before the throne and before the Lamb."

The origins of the feast are not entirely clear. However, there is evidence that from quite early times the Eastern Church had a collective celebration for the martyrs (only martyrs were recognized as saints in those days)—St Ephrem of Syria (9 June), for example, writing in his *Carmina Nisibena* in the middle of the fourth century, mentions a feast held in honour of "the martyrs of all the earth." This seems to have been celebrated on 13 May in Edessa, although from 411 or possibly earlier a feast of "all the martyrs" was celebrated elsewhere in Syria on the Friday of Easter week (as it still is by Catholics of the Chaldean rite and by the Nestorians); and the Byzantine churches kept, and still keep, a festival of all the saints on the Sunday after Pentecost (Trinity Sunday in the West).

Matters are even less clear in the West. Maximus of Turin, in the fifth century, is known to have preached a sermon in honour of all the martyrs on that same Sunday, but on the face of it that was an isolated incident. On 13 May 610 the Pantheon in Rome, which had been given by the emperor Phocas (602-10) to Pope St Boniface IV (608-15; 8 May) for use as a church, was dedicated to "St Mary and all the Martyrs," and some have taken this to mark the origin of the feast in the West. However, the *Comes of Wurzburg*, a seventh-century lectionary, was already referring to a feast of all the saints, rather than just the martyrs—the reference being to a Sunday, *domi. in nat. scorum.* In the following century sometime between 731 and 741, during the reign of Pope St Gregory III (10 Dec.), a chapel in St Peter's basilica was dedicated to Christ, the Virgin Mary, and all the saints.

Some manuscripts of the ninth-century *Félire*, or martyrology, of St Oengus the Culdee (11 Mar.) and the *Martyrology of Tallaght* (*c.* 800), which have a commemoration of the martyrs on 17 April, a feast of "all the saints of the whole of Europe" on 20 April, and a feast of All Saints of Africa on 23 December, also refer to a celebration of all the saints on 1 November, although there are indications that this was a mistake. In any case, the first firm mention of 1 November seems to come from England, where the feast was introduced in the first quarter of the

1

eighth century, probably by St Egbert of York (24 Apr.). The primitive text of Bede's martyrology contains no reference to the feast, but in copies dating from the end of the eighth century and the beginning of the ninth, the entry for 1 November reads: "Natale sancti Caesarii et festivitas omnium sanctorum...." What is certain is that in 799 Alcuin of York, then abbot of Tours, wrote to his friend Arno, bishop of Salzburg, about the *solemnitas sanctissima* of All Saints, which he was in the habit of celebrating on 1 November, preceded by a three-day fast. And a ninth-century calendar from the north of England, now in the Bodleian Library, Oxford, lists All Saints as a major feast on 1 November. The implication seems to be that Rome adopted the English-Gallican practice, and not vice versa. According to John of Beleth (*c.* 1165), Pope Gregory IV (827-44) transferred the feast definitively from May to November because Rome could not accommodate the number of pilgrims who came for the feast during the summer months—an explanation sufficiently practical to ring true. What is certain is that in the Western Church there was a long tradition of celebrating a feast, first of all the martyrs and then of all the saints, and that by the twelfth century 1 November was the date.

In England—where there are no less than 1,255 ancient church dedications to all the saints—the feast was formerly known as All Hallows. Hence Halloween (All Hallows' Eve), which, because they connect it with ghosts, many people mistakenly associate with the feast of All Souls (2 Nov.).

Propylaeum, pp. 488-9. For the origins of the feast see Tertullian, *De corona*, c.3; *P.G.*, 46, 953; 50, 705; Ephrem of Syria, *Carmina Nisibena*, ed. Bicknell, pp. 23, 84. See also *N.C.E.*, pp. 38-9; *O.D.S.*, p. 16; F. Cabrol in *D.A.C.L.*, 5, 1418-9; J. Hennig, "The Meaning of All the Saints," in *Medieval Studies* 10 (1948), pp. 147-61; M. Walsh, *A Dictionary of Devotions* (1993).

St Benignus of Dijon, *Martyr* (? Third Century)

According to one tradition St Benignus was a disciple of St Polycarp (23 Feb.) in Smyrna and was martyred in Dijon during the reign of Marcus Aurelius (161-80). Another tradition, to which Alban Butler subscribed, held that he was a Roman missionary who suffered near Dijon, "probably in the reign of Aurelian" (270-5). It is also possible that he was a disciple not of St Polycarp but of St Polycarp's disciple, St Irenaeus, bishop of Lyons (28 June), and he may have been martyred in Epagny rather than Dijon.

What is certain is that, although his nationality is doubtful and little seems to have been known about him locally, St Benignus was traditionally held to have spread the gospel throughout Burgundy, and his cult did develop and flourish in and around Dijon. St Gregory of Tours (17 Nov.), writing in the sixth century, confirmed that in his time people were venerating Benignus at a particular tomb which his own great-grandfather, St Gregory, bishop of Langres (4 Jan.), believed was that of a pagan until he was warned in a dream, backed up by a miracle, that the martyr St Benignus was buried there.

The existence and history of this tomb throw interesting light on what happened when the burial place of a martyr—it was most likely to be a martyr at this period—

attracted a cult. Benignus would have been buried in the vast cemetery outside the walls of Gallo-Roman Dijon. His sarcophagus was located by Gregory of Langres, who restored it and built a basilica over it, and it was sufficiently significant for a monastery to be established nearby. Gregory's building was superseded by a Romanesque basilica, which collapsed in 1272 and was replaced by the present cathedral. And meanwhile a new town had grown up round it, and what had been outside the walls in Gallo-Roman times was now the centre of the city.

When he was doing his restoration, Gregory of Langres had no details about Benignus' life and death, though eventually some pilgrims returning from Italy passed on to him a *passio Sancti Benigni*. Unfortunately this document, which in its present form seems to be contemporaneous with Gregory and is unlikely to have originated in Rome, was at least edited in Dijon and is undoubtedly spurious.

According to the *passio*, St Polycarp had a vision of St Irenaeus (already dead, although in fact he died fifty years after Polycarp himself), which inspired him to send two priests, Benignus and Andiochus, and a deacon, Thyrsus, to preach the gospel in Gaul. On the way they were shipwrecked in Corsica, and there St Andoleus joined them. Having reached Marseilles at last, they travelled on to the Côte d'Or and in Autun were received into the house of one Faustus, whose son St Symphorian (22 Aug.) was baptized by Benignus. When the missionaries separated soon after this, Benignus went first to Langres and then on to Dijon, where he preached compellingly and performed miracles. But it was a time of persecution for Christians, and Benignus was denounced to the emperor Aurelian (who did indeed visit Gaul but not until about one hundred years after the death of St Polycarp). Shortly after this he was arrested at Epagny, near Dijon, and there, after much ill treatment, to which he responded with new miracles, his head was crushed with an iron bar and his heart pierced. He was buried in a tomb which was made to look like a pagan monument in order to deceive the persecutors.

So ends the account in the *passio*. In his *Fastes Episcopaux* Mgr Duchesne shows that the latter was in fact the original link in a chain of religious romances which were written in the first half of the sixth century to describe the origins of the churches at Autun, Besançon, Langres, and Valence in eastern France. They are historically unreliable, and the very existence of some of the martyrs connected with these places is doubtful.

Five texts of the *passio* are to be found in *AA.SS.*, Nov., 1, pp. 152-62. See also G. Bardy, "Les actes des martyrs bourguignons et leur valeur historique," in *Annales de Bourgogne 2* (1930), pp. 235-53; L. Duchesne, *Fastes Episcopaux*, 1, pp.51-62; H. Leclerq in *D.A.C.L.*, 4, 835-49.

SS Caesarius and Julian, *Martyrs* (?)

The extant "acts" of these martyrs are not authentic. Nevertheless, whatever their true story, Caesarius and Julian are mentioned in the early martyrologies, and there has been a church of San Cesareo on the Palatine in Rome since the sixth century— it is now a cardinalatial church. Alban Butler stripped the extant accounts of various formula marvels and summarized them as follows.

The town of Terracina sits on the Adriatic between Rome and Naples. Here, during the first centuries of the Christian era, it was the custom on certain significant occasions for a young man voluntarily to sacrifice himself to Apollo, the tutelary god of the city. For some months beforehand he would be pampered by his fellow-citizens. Then when the festival day arrived, having first offered sacrifice to Apollo, he would throw himself from a precipice into the sea. Caesarius, a deacon from Africa, happened to be in Terracina on one occasion when this was going on. Unable to contain his indignation at such an abominable practice, he spoke out openly against it. The temple priest immediately had him apprehended and accused him before the governor, who sentenced him to death. After nearly two years' imprisonment, Caesarius was put into a sack, together with a Christian priest called Julian, and cast into the sea.

See H. Delehaye, *Les Origines du culte des martyrs* (1933), pp. 308, 409; L. Duchesne in *Nuovo bollettino di arch. crist.* (1900), pp. 17ff.; J. P. Kirsch, *Der stadtrömische Fest-Kalender*, p. 208.

St Austremonius, *Bishop* (? Fourth Century)

All that is known for certain about this saint is that he was a missionary in the Auvergne, where, as St Stremoine, he is venerated as the apostle and first bishop of Clermont. Even the time during which he flourished is disputed—the fourth century is a possibility, but St Gregory of Tours (17 Nov.) names him as one of seven bishops who were sent to Gaul from Rome in the middle of the third century. The legendary accounts of Austremonius' life evolved during the sixth and following centuries after a deacon had a vision at his reputed tomb at Issoire, and a cult developed. According to these accounts, he was one of the seventy-two disciples of the Lord; and he died when a Jewish rabbi, whose son he had converted, cut off his head and threw it into a well. Because of the supposed circumstances of his death, Austremonius was revered as a martyr in Clermont. But there is no reason to believe that he was a martyr, and he is not recognized as one by the Roman Martyrology.

See L. Duchesne, *Fastes Episcopaux*, 2, pp. 119-22; A. Poncelet in *Anal.Boll.* 13, pp. 33-46; H. Leclercq in *D.A.C.L.*, 3, 1906-14; L. Levillain in *Le Moyen-Age* (1904), pp. 281-337.

St Mary, *Martyr* (? Fourth Century)

The surviving text of the *passio* which provides details of Mary's life contains extravagant borrowings from other fictional hagiography and has clearly been re-written to suit the taste of a later period. What is more, it dates the martyrdom to the reign of Marcus Aurelius (161-80), which is most unlikely. Nevertheless, some authorities find in it the traces at least of an authentic story. According to this account Mary was a slave of Tertullus, a Roman senator. She was baptized at birth and remained a committed Christian, but she was the only Christian in the household, and her constant praying and fasting, especially on pagan festivals, annoyed Tertullus' wife. However, both of them valued her for her loyalty and her hard work, and when persecution broke out Tertullus tried to persuade her to renounce her faith. She refused, so fearing he would lose her once she fell into the hands of the prefect, he had her whipped and then hidden in a dark room. Eventually news of this leaked out, and Tertullus, who was charged with concealing a Christian in his house, handed her over. When she bore witness to Christ in court, the crowd demanded that she be burned alive. Undeterred, Mary prayed for constancy, telling the judge: "The God I serve is with me. I am not afraid of your torments, which can only take away a life I am willing to lay down for Jesus Christ." She was sentenced to be tortured, but this was carried out with such cruelty that the crowd, unable to stand the sight, now pleaded for her release. The judge handed her over to a soldier, who took pity on her and allowed her to escape. Although she eventually died a natural death, Mary is ranked as a martyr in the Roman Martyrology because of all she suffered for Christ.

See H. Quentin, O.S.B., *Les Martyrologes historiques* (1908), p. 180.

St Maturinus (Fourth Century)

Nothing is known for certain about the life of St Maturinus (Mathurin). According to the legend, he was the son of pagan parents and grew up at Larchant in the territory of Sens in northern France. Unlike his father, who was actively anti-Christian, Maturinus was attracted to the gospel and by the time he was twelve was judged ready for baptism. This seems to have impressed his parents, who eventually became his first converts. He became a priest when he was twenty, and he was so trusted by the local bishop that he was left in charge of the diocese when the latter had to go to Rome. Maturinus, who was gifted with an extraordinary power to cast out evil spirits, took the gospel to the Gâtinais, where he made many converts; but his reputation as an exorcist spread, and he was sent to Rome to help a young noblewoman who was being tormented by an evil spirit. It was in Rome, according to the legend, that he died. His remains were brought back to Sens and from there to Larchant; they were subsequently destroyed by the Huguenots. His cult seems not to have been very widespread, and he is best remembered in the colloquial name of the Trinitarian friars, who are known in France as "Mathurins" after the church of St Mathurin in Paris, which was given to them sometime after 1228.

On the local significance of the cult, see E. Thoison, articles in *Annales de la Société hist.-archéol. Gâtinais* (1886-8).

St Marcellus, *Bishop* (*c.* 410)

St Marcellus is one of the many whose biographies were written by St Venantius Fortunatus (14 Dec.) in the late sixth century. However, in his case at least, the Life is little more than a collection of miracles. According to Venantius Fortunatus, Marcellus was born in Paris in relatively humble circumstances and devoted himself so completely to prayer and the practice of virtue that he became "disengaged from both the world and the flesh." His serious character and the progress he made in his theological studies drew him to the attention of Prudentius, bishop of Paris, who ordained him a reader (the second of the traditional minor orders) and made him his archdeacon. When Prudentius died he was chosen unanimously to be bishop of Paris. Venantius Fortunatus tells how he defended his people against the barbarians and attributes to him some surprising marvels (including victory over a great dragon). On this, Alban Butler comments somewhat tersely that "the circumstances depend upon the authority of one who wrote over a hundred years after the time, and who, being a foreigner [a bit unfair since, although he was born in Italy, Venantius Fortunatus lived in Poitiers from the age of thirty], took them upon trust and probably upon popular reports." Marcellus died on 1 November (the only precise piece of information provided by Venantius Fortunatus) early in the fifth century. He was buried in a catacomb known by his name in an area on the left bank of the Seine, which today is the Paris suburb of Saint-Marceau.

For Venantius Fortunatus' Life, see *M.G.H, Auctores antiquissimi*, 4, 2, pp. 49–54. See also *Bibl.SS.*, 8, 668–70; L. Duchesne, *Fastes Episcopaux*, 2, p. 470.

St Vigor, *Bishop* (*c.* 537)

Vigor was born in Artois, in northern France, and was active during the reign of the Frankish king Childebert I (511-58). According to a short Latin Life dating from the eighth century, he was educated in Arras by St Vedast (6 Feb.), after which he decided to become a priest. Fearing that his father would disapprove of this and inspired by the then popular concept of monastic *peregrinatio*, he and a companion ran away and lived concealed at the village of Ravière, near Bayeux. Insofar as their concealment allowed it, the two men preached and instructed the people. Once ordained, however, Vigor greatly extended the range of his missionary work, and in 513, when the bishop of Bayeux died, he was appointed to succeed him. The story is told of how, finding that some people were still worshipping a stone figure on a hill near the city, he cast down the idol and replaced it with a church, renaming the place the Hill of Anointing. Angered by this, one Count Bertulf tried to take the site back, but he broke his neck in a fall from his horse, which was taken as God's judgment on an ill-advised attempt to reclaim the newly-sanctified hill. Vigor died in about 537 and was buried at the monastery he built near Bayeux. Later the body was sold surreptitiously to the abbot of Saint-Riquier, whose successor was responsible for publicizing the Life. Saint-Vigor-le-Grand, where he built the monastery, is named after him; and two or three churches in England were dedicated to him by the Normans.

J. Corblet, *Hagiographie du diocèse d'Amiens* (1868-75), 4, pp. 657-64; L. Duchesne, *Fastes Episcopaux*, 2, p. 220.

St Cadfan, *Abbot* (Sixth Century)

During the second half of the fifth century immigrants began to establish new settlements in north and west Wales. They came from Letavia, or what is now known as Brittany. One of the groups was led by Cadfan, grandson of Emyr Llydaw, who travelled with his cousin, St Padarn (15 Apr.). When they reached the west coast Padarn set up his monastic headquarters near present-day Aberystwyth. Cadfan himself went further up the coast to Tywyn, where he established a church and founded a monastery; this persisted into the Middle Ages as a *clas*, or collegiate church, in which married priests were the norm. His name is connected also with Ynys Enlli (Bardsey Island), where according to tradition, he founded the monastery that eventually took over the entire island. In its heyday it flourished as a "resort of 20,000 monks"; and as a Celtic settlement outside the normal pattern of medieval monastic foundations, it seems to have survived the dissolution of the monasteries. Even in the late eighteenth century it was held in such reverence that, as they approached, local fishermen "made a full stop, pulled off their hats, and offered up a short prayer." Cadfan is usually said to have died and been buried on Ynys Enlli, though Tywyn also claims to be his place of burial. His other principal foundation was at Llangadfan, near modern Welshpool, in Powys.

No formal Life of Cadfan has come down to us. However, a twelfth-century poem throws light on—and raises a few problems about—his cult. It speaks of "Cadfan's high church near the shore of the blue sea," in which "three magnificent altars, famous for miracles," were dedicated to the honour of Our Lady, St Peter, and St Cadfan himself. "The glory of Meirionnydd," this church was a place of sanctuary, to which many fled for protection.

The poem also calls Cadfan "protector in battle," and it is true that in Quimper there is a statue, said to be of him, dressed as a soldier, with a sword. From this it has been inferred that before he was a missionary and a monk he distinguished himself as a soldier. However, this may all be a misunderstanding. Cadfan was probably confused either with his cousin and fellow-missionary, St Tydecho, who is described in a fifteenth-century poem as "one of heaven's warriors," or else with his father, Cadfan, king of Gwynedd, who was a Welsh leader in the wars against Ethelfrith, king of Northumbria.

See R. Rees, *An Essay on the Welsh Saints* (1836), pp. 213-5; A. W. Wade-Evans, *Welsh Christian Origins* (1934), pp. 161-4. See also G. H. Jones, "Celtic Britain and the Pilgrim Movement" in *Y Cymmrodor*, 12 (1912), pp. 354-62; E. G. Bowen, *Settlements of the Celtic Saints in Wales* (1954); E. R. Heaken, *Tradition of the Welsh Saints* (1987); *D.C.B.*, pp. 363-4.

Bd Nonius (1360-1431)

Nun' Alvares de Pereira is one of the great heroes of Portuguese history. His story is told in the sixteenth-century *Crónica do Condestável*, one of the classics of early Portuguese literature. Born at Sernache de Bomjardim, near Lisbon, on 24 June 1360, he was the son of Don Alvaro Gonçalves de Pereira, grand master of a branch of the Order of the Knights of St John of Jerusalem. When he was thirteen, he went to the court of the Portuguese king, Ferdinando (1383), to train for a military career. As a boy he had read the Arthurian legends and dreamed of remaining celibate and serving his king, like Galahad; but in fact, when he was not quite seventeen, he married Dona Leonora de Alvim, with whom he had three children before she died in 1387.

At twenty-three Nonius was made constable in command of the armed forces of Portugal by the grand master of the Knights of Aviz, who became king two years later as João I (1385-1433). As constable he was greatly respected by his men and eventually led them to victory at the battle of Atoleiros, where the army of Castile was defeated and Portugal definitively established as a sovereign state.

Then, in 1422, to the astonishment of the court, Nonius became a lay brother in the Carmelite friary he had founded in Lisbon and remained there for the rest of his life. On All Saints' Day 1431, he was reading the Passion according to St John, and had just come to the words, "Behold thy mother!" when he died. The funeral was attended by the entire court, and he was buried in the Carmelite church in Lisbon. His cult was approved for Portugal and for the Carmelite Order in 1918. Because of the marriage of his daughter Beatriz and Alfonso, the eldest son of João I, who was also duke of Braganza, Nonius is regarded as the founder of that house; and Manuel II, the last king of Portugal, who abdicated in 1910, was one of his descendants.

Crónica do Condestável de Portugal (1526); biographies by J. P. de Oliveira Martins (1893); R. Chianca (1914); E. Battaglia (1918); V. A. Cordeiro (1919). For an account in English, see J. M. Haffert, *The Peacemaker Who Went to War* (1945).

Bd Rupert Mayer (1876-1945)

One of the six sons and daughters of Rupert Mayer and Maria Schwörer, Rupert was born on 23 January 1876 in Stuttgart, where his father had a business. Both parents were deeply committed Christians, concerned that their children should develop morally and spiritually as well as intellectually and physically. They asked much of them at all levels and were not disappointed—in later years Rupert would often thank God for his education, and in particular for its solid moral and spiritual foundation. He had a lively, generous disposition with an ability to enjoy life and make the most of the experiences it offered. And he was physically strong and good at sports, as well as being gifted intellectually.

In 1894, having achieved brilliant results in the school-leaving certificate, he told his father that he wanted to become a Jesuit. Surprisingly perhaps, his father said that he would like him to become a secular priest first and enter the Society of Jesus later, if he still wanted to. To this Rupert agreed, though he made clear that the decision was his father's. Following the pattern then current in Germany, he did not go immediately to the seminary. He first studied philosophy and theology in the respective faculties at the universities of Fribourg, Munich, and Tübingen, and only in his final year did he enter the seminary at Rottenburg. He was ordained in

Rottenburg cathedral on 2 May 1899 and spent the next year as a curate in the parish of Spaichingen (in Baden-Württemberg, south of Stuttgart). His ultimate goal did not change, however, and in 1900 he finally entered the Jesuit novitiate at Feldkirch in Austria.

For the next five years he prayed and studied, there and at Valkenburg in The Netherlands, preparing for his future apostolic work. This began formally in 1906, and from then to 1912 he preached missions throughout Rhineland-Westphalia. Then, in 1912, he was transferred to Munich to look after the welfare of immigrants from the surrounding villages and country areas. Although he made sure that they were not in want materially, his main task was to help them adjust to an intellectual and moral climate very different from the one they had left behind—less traditionally religious, more open to freethinking and atheistic ideas, and with a distinctly easy-going attitude to morality. To this end he visited them in their homes personally and recruited assistants who could share the task with him. He also spoke frequently at the meetings of workers' associations, supported organizations involved in the welfare of children, and reached out to the students at the university through the *Marianischen Männer Kongregation* (M.M.K.—Sodality of Our Lady).

When the First World War broke out in 1914, he enlisted as a volunteer and was sent immediately to one of the camp hospitals. Soon, however, he was appointed chaplain of the Eighth Bavarian Division, which took him to the front in France, Galicia, and Romania. It was in Romania, in 1917, that he was seriously wounded and had to have his left leg amputated, which cut short his active service. But while he was at the front he worked tirelessly wherever he went for the spiritual welfare of the soldiers, sometimes holding as many as eight religious services on a Sunday, and bringing personal comfort to countless of the wounded and dying. His reputation for courage and heroic selflessness was legendary. He was the first German priest in this war to receive one of the highest military honours, the Iron Cross (first class). When it was all over, he went back to Munich, where he turned his attention to alleviating the miseries caused by the war itself and by the political unrest that followed it—he would even turn up unannounced at Socialist and Communist meetings and, ignoring threats, refute the arguments of the scheduled speakers.

Rupert's teaching does not seem to have been especially progressive or original, but he was absolutely convinced that Christians must be prepared to declare their beliefs openly and without fear and to involve themselves somehow in the charitable mission of the Church. These were the precepts he lived by himself, and they were the core of the message he passed on to the young men of Munich who belonged to the university branch of the M.M.K., of which he became director in 1921. He brought to this new task the same indefatigable commitment that he gave to everything he did. The members of the sodality, whom he organized in groups in all fifty-three parishes in the city, had the benefit of numerous sermons, lectures, and conferences—up to seventy a month—which he used, among other things, to help them form their views on the difficult moral issues of the day. By the end of ten years the membership had doubled in size.

Two other things stand out from this period of his life. In 1925 he persuaded the authorities that, for the convenience of travellers, it would be a good idea to have regular Sunday Masses in the city's central railway station. A huge room was made available, and every Sunday and holyday of obligation six Masses were celebrated, starting at 3.10 in the morning (Rupert usually celebrated the first two, despite the fact that he had spent a long evening the day before hearing confessions). The Nazis put a stop to the custom in 1937, but it was resumed for a while in 1945. The other venture in which Rupert was involved was a new religious Congregation for women. In 1914, with another priest, A. Pichlmair, he founded the *Schwestern der Heiligen Familie* (Sisters of the Holy Family), whose mission was to care for the needs of workers and their families. He wrote the ascetical chapters of their Rule, and remained their spiritual director for the rest of his life.

Rupert inevitably came to the attention of the Nazis, who had already moved to close church-affiliated schools and were uneasy at the thought that a priest should have so much influence in a major city. Obstacles were placed in the way of his preaching and teaching until finally, on 16 May 1937, he was banned from speaking in public; then, on 5 June, he was arrested and given a suspended sentence. His superiors advised him to remain silent, which he did until the Nazis publicly defamed him, at which point his superiors gave him permission to resume his preaching. He was re-arrested on 5 January 1938 and served his suspended sentence. When, on his release, he resumed his work with small discussion groups in Munich, this was too much for the Nazis. In December he was arrested once again and sent to the concentration camp at Oranienburg-Sachsenhausen. But he had been there for only seven months when his health began to give way. Fearing that he might die and be hailed as a martyr, the Nazis released him and interned him in the Benedictine monastery at Ettal, near the German-Swiss border, for the remaining years of the war. This was undoubtedly the most difficult and lonely period of his life. For years he had expressed his love for God and found his sense of self in active giving to the thousands of people whose needs he had tried to meet in one way or another; now he was completely isolated and condemned to inactivity. He endured it with quiet dignity, and although he kept no diary, a brief remark made in a letter he wrote from Ettal to his mother suggests that the source of the inner strength that people had always observed in him had not dried up: "Now I truly have nothing and no one but God, but that is enough—indeed, it is more than enough."

American troops entered Ettal on 6 May 1945, and within a few days Rupert was back in Munich, helping people to put their lives together again and urging them to set aside their hatred and forgive. He also found time to mobilize the men's branch of the M.M.K., giving it a new orientation and a new and younger director. But the experiences of the previous eight years had done permanent damage to his health. On 1 November 1945, he had a stroke while preaching at the morning Mass on our need to imitate the saints if we are to enter the kingdom of heaven. He died that same day and was buried in the cemetery of the Jesuit college at Pullach outside

Munich. But on 23 May 1948 the apostle of Munich came home. To general rejoicing, his remains were transferred to the crypt of the Bürgersaal (the church next to St Michael's, where the M.M.K. used to meet) in the centre of the city. Thirty-five thousand people followed the procession from Pullach and another 100,000 waited in the square outside the church. He was beatified in Munich on 3 May 1987.

Biographies by R. Bleisten (1993); P. Molinari (1988); H. Staffner (1993); W. Rupp and H. Vieregg (1987); W. Sandfuchs (1984); P. Riesterer (1978); A. Korbling (1950; trans. Ital. 1958, Sp. 1959, Eng. 1961, Du. 1965). See also J. N. Tylenda, *Jesuits Saints and Martyrs* (1984); P. Molinari in *La Civiltà Cattolica* 111/2 (1960), pp. 254-63, 588-603; *Bibl.SS.*, 9, 244-8.

ALL SAINTS (pp. 1-2)

2

SOLEMNITY OF ALL SOULS

Death fills human beings sometimes with dread, always with awe. So it is only natural that, whatever their culture, they have surrounded it with rituals. Many of these express some sort of belief that there is a life after the present one and that the individual needs to undergo a process of purification in order to enter it—and further, that the process can be helped by those left behind.

In the Judaeo-Christian tradition, prayers for the dead are specifically recommended in 2 Maccabees 12:44-5: "For if he [Judas Maccabeus] were not expecting that those who had fallen would rise again, it would have been superfluous and foolish to pray for the dead. But if he was looking to the splendid reward that is laid up for those who fall asleep in godliness, it was a holy and pious thought. Therefore he made atonement for the dead, that they might be delivered from their sin." And from the earliest Christian times there is evidence—inscriptions in the Roman catacombs, for example—that prayers were offered for individual Christians who had died. However, it was some time before the Church set aside a day on which to remember and pray for the dead in general, to help them on their journey through what later came to be known as purgatory to the presence of God. This reluctance on the Church's part may have had something to do with the fact that pre-Christian superstitious beliefs and practices associated with death persisted well into the Christian era.

The first instance of such a commemoration dates from the time of St Isidore of Seville (d. 636; 6 Oct.), although this may have been confined to Spain; the date assigned to it was the Monday after Pentecost. By the first half of the ninth century monasteries were in the habit of formally commemorating their own deceased monks and benefactors. There does not seem to have been a fixed day for this, but in 800 two monasteries, Saint-Gall and Reichenau, made a formal agreement to pray for the dead of both monasteries on 14 November each year. At about the same time Amalarius, writing in his *De ordine antiphonarii*, made a definite connection between the feast of All Saints and the commemoration of All Souls: "After the office of the saints I have inserted the office for the dead; for many pass out of this world without at once being admitted into the company of the blessed."

This text may well have been in the mind of St Odilo, abbot of Cluny (d. 1049; 1 Jan.), when he directed his congregation to observe 2 November as a day of prayer for the dead: "As the feast of all the blessed saints was already celebrated throughout the Church of God, so it seemed desirable that at Cluny they should also keep with joyous affection the memory of the faithful departed who have lived from the beginning of the world until the end."

Such was the influence of Cluny that the practice spread rapidly. However, there is no trace of any papal decree extending it to the Church in general, and two or three centuries were to pass before the *Commemoratio animarum* was at all common in calendars and martyrologies under 2 November. All Souls' Day is definitely mentioned in a martyrology compiled in Besançon in the middle of the eleventh century. But in England, where, as early as 1075, Lanfranc, in his *Monastic Constitutions*, enjoined his monks to celebrate a solemn Mass for the dead on 2 November, there are four or five Canterbury calendars of the twelfth and thirteenth centuries which do not mention such a commemoration at all.

The practice of celebrating three Masses on All Souls' Day seems to have originated at the Dominican priory in Valencia, in response to local demand for special Masses, early in the fifteenth century. Pope Benedict XIV sanctioned it for the whole of Spain in 1748, and in 1915 Pope Benedict XV extended the privilege to the whole Western Church on account of the number of war dead.

In England there are at least four known dedications, the most famous being All Souls College, Oxford, founded by Archbishop Henry Chichele in 1437, and All Souls Church, Langham Place, London, built by John Nash between 1822 and 1824. Some of the more popular beliefs associated with All Souls' Day—for example, that the souls of the dead could return on this day as ghosts or witches to haunt people who had done them wrong during their lives—are now more commonly associated with Halloween (31 Oct.).

N.C.E., 1, p. 319; *O.D.S.*, p. 16; H. Delehaye, *Sanctus* (1927); H. Thurston, *The Memory of Our Dead*, pp. 101-34, 224-41; D. Knowles (ed.), *The Monastic Constitutions of Lanfranc* (1951), pp. 63-4. For folklore customs, see Bächtold-Stäubli, *Handwörterbuch des deutschen Aberglaubens*, 1, pp. 267-73.

St Victorinus, *Bishop and Martyr* (303)

The *passio* of St Victorinus, who was bishop of Poetavium in Upper Pannonia (Pettau, now Ptuj in Slovenia) and a distinguished exegete, is no longer extant. This means that little is known about him apart from what can be gleaned from casual references in the writings of St Jerome (30 Sept.), Optatus of Milevis, and Cassiodorus. From these it emerges that, having been a rhetorician, he became bishop of Pettau and wrote commentaries on several books of the Old and New Testaments. St Jerome quotes from these and generally speaks well of him as a scholar, observing, in the words of Alban Butler, that "his works were sublime in sense, though the Latin style was low, the author being by birth a Grecian." Jerome's views about him as a bishop are more qualified—although he spoke out against certain of the heretical views that were circulating at the time, Victorinus himself was thought to lean toward Millenarianism (the belief that Christ would return in person to reign on earth for a thousand years). At one time, owing to a mistaken Latinization of the name of his see, Victorinus was wrongly supposed to have been the first bishop of

Poitiers. He is thought to have died a martyr during the severe persecution of Christians that took place at the end of the reign of Diocletian (284–305).

AA.SS., Nov., 1; Jerome, *De Viris Illustribus*, 74. See also H. Quentin, O.S.B., *Martyrologes historiques*, pp. 310, 380; O. Bardenhewer, *Geschichte der altkirchlichen Literatur* (2d ed.), 2, pp. 657-63.

St Marcian (*c.* 387)

According to Theodoret, who provides all the information we have about him, Marcian was born into a patrician family in the city of Cyrrhus in Syria. Wishing to give himself exclusively to the service of God and determined not to do anything by halves, he left his family and his friends and retired to a remote area of the desert of Calchis, between Antioch and the Euphrates. There he made a small enclosure, in which he cultivated a little garden and built a cell so narrow and so low that it was impossible for him to stand or lie in it without bending. In this solitude, which to him was a paradise, he spent his days singing the psalms, reading, praying, and working. All he ate was bread, in small quantities but always enough to give him the strength to do what God required of him. Despite his concern not to attract attention to himself, news of his wisdom and holiness began to travel. Eventually he was prevailed upon to accept two disciples, Eusebius and Agapitus, and before long he had a large body of followers, over whom he appointed Eusebius as abbot.

On one occasion, St Flavian, patriarch of Antioch (18 Feb.), arrived, together with some other bishops, and begged to be allowed to attend Marcian's regular spiritual conference. Marcian was completely overawed and unable, at first, to reply. Recovering himself, he said: "God speaks to us every day through his fellow-creatures, and through the world around us. God speaks to us through the gospel, from which we learn what we ought to do both for ourselves and for others. What more can Marcian say that can be of use?"

According to Theodoret, Marcian worked a number of miracles but was greatly embarrassed by the reputation of wonder-worker which he acquired as a result. He refused to listen when people made specific requests for miraculous intercession—when a hermit asked him to bless some oil for a man whose daughter was sick, Marcian's answer was a peremptory "no" (although the girl allegedly recovered at that same moment).

During his last years, Marcian, who lived to a considerable age, had to put up with the importunity of rival individuals who looked forward to having custody of his dead body—several, including his nephew Alipius, even built chapels in which it could be buried. In view of this, Marcian made Eusebius promise to bury him secretly. Eusebius complied, and fifty years passed after the saint's death before people learned where his burial place was. When they did, his relics were solemnly translated and became an object of pilgrimage.

For Theodoret's Life, see *AA.SS.*, Nov., 1, pp. 535-8; *Bibl.SS.*, 8, 687-8.

Bd Thomas of Walden (*c.* 1375-1430)

Thomas Netter was born at Saffron Walden in Essex in about 1375. At a relatively young age he joined the Carmelites in London, spent his first years in the Order at Hitchin, in Hertfordshire, went on to study for a doctorate in theology at Oxford University, and was ordained priest in about 1400. He made a name for himself as a teacher of theology and in 1409 was sent to the Council of Pisa, where he is said to have been one of those who supported the election of Pope Alexander V (1409-10) as part of an attempt to end the Great Western Schism.

Returning to England, he threw himself into opposing the Lollards and other followers of John Wyclif, who among other things denied the doctrine of transubstantiation, condemned war and capital punishment, and argued that ecclesiastical property should be put to charitable use. Thomas was regarded as the most able of their opponents, and people would say of him: "Never was there such a netter of heretics." He took part in the trials of their leaders, amongst whom was Sir John Oldcastle (one of the few members of the nobility to join the Lollards, who was hanged as a traitor in 1417), and in his principal writings, notably his *Doctrinale fidei*, concentrated on refuting their teachings. He was elected prior provincial of his Order, probably when he was still under forty years old, and at about the same time King Henry V chose him as his confessor—it was then fashionable among the nobility to have a Carmelite confessor. From 1414 to 1417 he was one of the English representatives at the Council of Constance, which, among other things, brought the schism to an end and condemned the teachings of Wyclif and Hus. From the council, Thomas went on to Poland as a member of an embassy from the pope and the emperor to get new recruits for the papal army. He is said to have established Carmelite friaries in Lithuania and Prussia. In 1422, Henry V, whom Thomas had accompanied to France, died in his arms at Vincennes. The guardians of the then infant Henry VI subsequently appointed him as the young king's tutor.

Although he spent so much of his life caught up in conflict, Thomas was a kindly man and affectionate in his relations with others. He died in Rouen, where he had gone with Henry, on 2 November 1430, leaving behind him a reputation for learning and holiness; miracles were reported at his tomb. His writings, which were admired by Pope Martin V (1417-31), earned him the titles *doctor praestantissimus* (pre-eminent teacher) and *doctor authenticus* (authoritative teacher). His treatise *De sacramentalibus* includes a discussion of canonization which is of some historical significance.

B. Zimmerman, *Monumenta historica Carmelitana* (1907), pp. 442-82; *idem*, in *Catholic Encyclopaedia*, 10, pp. 764-5. See also *O.D.P.*, p. 236; R. L. Hine, *History of Hitchin* (1927), 1, pp. 133-8.

Bd Margaret of Lorraine (1521)

René I le Bon, duke of Anjou, had two daughters, Marguerite, who married Henry VI of England, and Yolande, who married Ferri de Lorraine. Marguerite de Lorraine was the daughter of the latter, and she herself married René, duke of Alençon, when she was twenty-five. Four years later René died, leaving her with three very young children and responsibility, on their behalf, for the Alençon estates. The first thing she did was to secure her right to the guardianship of her children, which the French king, Charles VIII (1483-98), wanted to take from her. Having done this, she settled down in her castle at Mauves, where she brought them up. Margaret was as solicitous for the spiritual and temporal welfare of her vassals as she was for that of her sons; she showed herself to be a most capable administrator—when her son Charles came of age and married, his inheritance was in a state considerably better than that in which his father had left it.

Marguerite had come under the influence of St Francis of Paola (2 Apr.) and since her husband's death had been leading a genuinely ascetic life. In about 1513, when her responsibility for her children came to an end, she withdrew to Mortagne, south-east of Argentan. Here there was a convent, which gave her the opportunity to look after the poor and the sick. She subsequently took some of the nuns from this convent and established them, under the rule of the Poor Clares, at Argentan, where she herself took the habit in 1519 but refused to accept the office of abbess. She died at Argentan on 2 November 1521. In 1793 the Jacobins removed her body from its tomb and threw it into a common burying ground—she herself might have found a certain aptness in this act of desecration in that it united her with the poor and nameless people to whom she had been so devoted.

AA.SS., Nov., 1, pp. 418-9. Lives include those by P. de Hameau (1628), E. Laurent (1854), R. Guérin (1926).

Bd John Bodey, *Martyr* (1549-83)

John Bodey, the son of a wealthy merchant, was born in Wells, where his father had been mayor, in 1549. He was educated at Winchester and then at New College, Oxford, of which he became a fellow when he was only nineteen. In 1577, a year after he and seven other Roman Catholics had been deprived of their fellowships by the bishop of Winchester, he went over to the recently-founded college in Douai, where he studied law. On his return to England it is possible that he married—Bd William Hart, also of Wells (15 Mar.), in a letter written to his mother before his own execution in 1583, mentions that "John Body" is in prison and a little further on asks to be recommended to "Mrs Body and all the rest" (though the Mrs Body he speaks of could equally well have been John's mother). When William Hart wrote this letter, John Bodey had already been in prison in Winchester for three years. In the spring assizes of 1583 he was convicted, with Bd John Slade (30 Oct.), of denying the royal supremacy. There was a re-trial in Andover in August of the same year, but the conviction and sentence were upheld. On 16 September John

Bodey wrote to Dr Humphrey Ely assuring him of his constancy and that of his fellow-prisoner and asking "the good prayers of you all for our strength, our joy, and our perseverance unto the end." Professing to the last his innocence of all treason, he was hanged, drawn, and quartered in Andover on 2 November. His mother is said to have celebrated the glory of her son's martyrdom by giving a dinner for their friends.

M.M.P.; J. H. Pollen, *Acts of the English Martyrs* (1891), pp. 49-65; Publications of the Catholic Record Society, 5, pp. 39-50; *L.E.M.*, 1, pp. 8-21.

ST HUBERT (p. 23)
The legend of the stag. Silver stag
and cross on blue field.

3

ST MARTIN DE PORRES (1575-1639)

Martin was the first *mulatto* to be recognized by the Church for his heroic practice of Christian virtue. He was born in Lima, Peru, on 9 December 1575, the natural son of Don Juan de Porres, a Spanish hidalgo, and Ana Velázquez, a freed black slave from Panama. Juan was disappointed to find that his son had inherited his mother's features and complexion, and when Martin was eventually baptized on 9 November 1579, he was entered in the register as "son of an unknown father." In thus refusing publicly to acknowledge Martin or his younger sister as his own, Juan was consigning them to the category of "illegitimate," a formidable disadvantage in the hierarchically-structured society of Lima at that time. But although he left his children by and large to the care of their mother, Juan did not abandon his responsibilities entirely. He took both children with him to Ecuador, where they received some education. Although he sent them back to their mother when he was appointed governor of Panama in 1567, he did have Martin, who was by then twelve, apprenticed to a barber-surgeon in Lima, Dr Marcelo de Ribera.

From Dr Ribera Martin got a good grounding in the medical knowledge of the day and learned among other things how to let blood, deal with wounds and fractures, and prescribe medicines. The combination of this theoretical and practical knowledge with what he learned from his mother, who was a recognized practitioner of herbal medicine, was to stand him in good stead. There were many times over the years when he successfully treated conditions for which conventional medicine alone had no answer.

When he was sixteen, Martin, who was already a member of the Third Order of St Dominic, was accepted by the Dominicans at the Convento del Santo Rosario in Lima as a *donado*—a member of the Third Order, a layman who received food and lodging at the friary in return for work of a particularly menial sort. His father, who was still governor of Panama, is said to have taken this as an affront to his own dignity only to be told, when he tried to get Martin accepted as a full member of the Order of Preachers, that the idea had already been put to the boy himself, who had rejected it. In fact, it was a little more complicated than that. There was a law at the time that prevented "Indians, blacks and their descendants" from joining religious Orders. The prior at the Convento del Santo Rosario, Juan de Lorenzana, was prepared to disregard it in Martin's case and accept him as a lay brother, but Martin resisted; it was not until 1603, when he was twenty-four, that he finally made his profession as a lay brother.

What we know of Martin's life as a Dominican comes from the detailed eyewitness accounts submitted during the beatification process. One member of the community, Fernando de Aragonés, gave an overall picture: "Many were the offices to which the servant of God, Fray Martín de Porres, attended, being barber, surgeon, wardrobe-keeper and infirmarian. Each of these jobs was enough for any one man, but he filled them all alone with great generosity, promptness and attention to detail, without being weighed down by any of them. It was most striking, and it made me realize that, in that he clung to God in his soul, all these things were effects of divine grace." Others described more specific instances of his charity and his extraordinary power to heal. Fernando del Aguila, for example, told how Gerónimo Batista, one of the priests in the community, had such bad ulcers on one of his legs, despite the care taken by the doctor, that arrangements were made to amputate it. The surgeon was about to begin the operation when Martin came in and asked what was going on. When he heard that the friar was about to lose his leg, he told the surgeon to stop and said that he would heal it. In a few days the patient was completely cured.

It was not only within the community that Martin cared for the sick and others in need. He extended his attention to the sick of the city and was instrumental in the establishment of an orphanage and foundling hospital, which had other charitable institutions attached to it. He was given the task of distributing to the poor the convent's daily alms of food (which he is said to have increased miraculously on occasion), and he took it upon himself to care for the slaves who were brought to Peru from Africa. His great ambition was to be sent abroad to some foreign mission where he could earn the crown of martyrdom. But this was impossible, so he practised rigorous penances instead—much was said during the beatification process not only of his penances but also of his extraordinary supernatural gifts, which included an apparent ability to move through locked doors. His love for God's creatures extended to all animals—he became known as the St Francis of the Americas—and there are many accounts of his devotion to these *criaturas* of God. He even excused the depredations of rats and mice on the grounds that the poor little things were inadequately fed, and he kept a "cats' and dogs' home" at his sister's house.

According to his protégé, Juan Vasquez Parra, Martin was eminently practical in his charity. He used the money and goods he collected carefully and methodically, raising a dowry for his niece in three days while at the same time collecting as much and more for the poor. He showed Parra how to sow camomile in the well-manured hoof prints of cattle; he bought a black servant to work in the laundry; he looked after anyone who needed anything, be it blankets or candles, or shirts or sweets, or miracles or prayers. Martin's sensitivity about his colour is revealed in two incidents. A lawyer, Don Baltasar Carrasco, wanted to be his "adopted son," and to call him "father." Martin objected: "Why do you want a *mulatto* for a father? That would not look well." "Why not?" retorted Don Baltasar. "It would rather be said that you have a Spaniard for a son." And on another occasion, when his priory was having trouble repaying a debt, Martin offered himself in payment: "I'm only a poor *mulatto*, and I'm the property of the Order. Sell me."

19

Martin was a friend of St Rose of Lima (23 Aug.) and also of Bd John Macías (18 Sept.), who was a lay brother at the Dominican priory of Santa María Magdalena in the city. When he died, aged sixty, on 3 November 1639, he was carried to his grave by prelates and noblemen, and people from all walks of life and all levels of society claimed him as "their" saint. He was beatified in 1837 and, after long delays, canonized on 6 May 1962. He is the patron of social justice and race relations, simply because of his own all-embracing charity.

Proceso de Beatificación de Fray Martín de Porres (Sp. trans. 1960 of orig. ed. 1660-71). For the earliest biography, by Bernardo de Medina, see *AA.SS.*, Nov., 3 (Latin trans. of 1663 orig., republished 1964 as *San Martín de Porres: biografía del Siglo XVII*). More recent biographies include G. Cavallini, *St Martin de Porres: Apostle of Charity* (1963); H. McBride, *Vida Breve de Fray Martín de Porres* (1968). See also Alex García-Rivera, *St Martin de Porres* (1995), a cultural study with useful bibliography.

St Winifred, *Martyr (c. 650)*

Of all the Welsh saints, St Winifred (Gwenfrewi) was and is the most widely venerated outside her own country. Yet the earliest written records of her life and the traditions concerning her—a Latin Life by pseudo-Elerius, the so-called *Vita prima*, although it is in fact the later of the two, and a Life by Robert of Shrewsbury—date from about 500 years after her death, and she does not figure in Welsh calendars before the fourteenth century. This means that, while it is probably going too far to say that she never existed, the information we have is too late to establish anything about her with certainty. From the two Lives mentioned, Alban Butler set out her legend as follows.

Winifred's father, Teuyth, was a courageous soldier and wealthy resident of Tegeingl in present-day Clwyd, her mother a sister of St Beuno (21 Apr.). The latter came and settled for a time near his relatives, and when Teuyth gave him some land at Sychant he built a chapel on it. While he was there Winifred listened eagerly to his teachings about God. When Caradog, a young chieftain from Hawarden, fell in love with her she persistently rejected his advances—until one day, enraged beyond endurance, he pursued her as she fled to Beuno's chapel and cut off her head. According to Robert of Shrewsbury, Caradog was immediately swallowed up by the earth, while at the place where Winifred's head fell a stream sprang forth with fragrant moss growing from its sides and pebbles and rocks streaked with red in its bed. Winifred herself was raised to life by the prayers of Beuno, who set her severed head back on her shoulders, where it regrew immediately, leaving only a scar. The beheading, on account of which she is regarded as a martyr, took place and was commemorated on 22 June.

At this point the two accounts diverge. According to the *Vita prima*, Winifred went to Rome, returning only in time to attend a synod on the matter of hermits coming together in monasteries. The *Vita secunda*, on the other hand, says that Beuno went off to found a church at Clynnog Fawr, south of Caernarfon. Later, either after Beuno's departure or after his death, Winifred herself left home and joined a nunnery at Gwytherin, where there was also a monastery of monks, presided over by a holy abbot named Eleri. When the abbess, Tenoi, died, Eleri invited Winifred to succeed her. This she did, and it was here, fifteen years after her miraculous resuscitation, that she died. She was buried by Eleri, and her relics remained enshrined at Gwytherin until 1138, when they were conveyed with much ceremony to the Benedictine abbey in Shrewsbury. According to an eighteenth-century study of the relevant calendars, it was decreed in 1348 that her feast should be kept throughout the province of Canterbury.

Subsequent events connected with Winifred's name are more easily checked than the events of her life. The miraculous spring has given the place its English name (Holywell) as well as its Welsh name (Tre Ffynnon)—springs like this are a common feature of Celtic and other legends, but this is certainly the most famous in the British Isles. Both Robert of Shrewsbury and pseudo-Elerius speak of miracles associated with the relics and shrines of St Winifred, and Alban Butler describes five individual cures (at least two involving Protestants) which took place at Holywell in the seventeenth century—these he selected from a number mentioned in detail, with evidence, by Philip Metcalf, S.J., in his *Life of St Winifred* (1712). It seems that over the centuries, up to the present day, pilgrimages have been made to St Winifred's Well and cures have been reported there without interruption, and both receive frequent mention in public and private records. Henry V came, for example, to give thanks for his victory at Agincourt; an estimated 14,000 people, with 150 priests, gathered there on the saint's feast-day in 1629, in the middle of the penal times; and Dr Johnson recorded that he saw people bathing there on 3 August 1774. Even in the penal times the faith did not die out in Holywell, which became a centre for Jesuit missionary activity—in 1930 the Jesuits handed the parish over to the diocesan authorities, who still hold the well on lease from the town. The buildings which enclose it were built by Henry VII's mother, Lady Margaret Beaufort, and members of the Welsh nobility. There was a tense moment in 1917, when, despite restrictions placed on them by Parliament, mining operations in the Holywell area caused the well to run dry. Fortunately it was possible to draw on water from the original subterranean reservoir, and the well is still flowing today.

In 1991, a triangular section of an oak reliquary box or shrine for St Winifred, dating perhaps from the eighth or ninth century, was discovered at Gwytherin; and a stone, mentioned in a rural dean's report in 1729 as St Winifred's gravestone, is now in the church there. Meanwhile, in Shrewsbury there are statues of St Winifred and St Beuno on the pulpit of the abbey refectory. And finally, Gerard Manley Hopkins began a verse tragedy on her in 1879, but completed only fragments.

The feast of St Winifred is observed in the dioceses of Menevia and Shrewsbury, and she appears—as a virgin-martyr in England (*sic*)—in the Roman Martyrology, one of the few Welsh saints to be so honoured. The others are Asaph (11 May), Samson (28 July), and Maglorius (Maelor, 24 Oct.), but curiously not David (Dewi Sant), the patron saint of Wales (1 Mar.).

For the Latin Life by pseudo-Elerius and the Life by Robert of Shrewsbury in translation, see I.F. (trans.), *The Admirable Life of Saint Wenefride, Robert of Shrewsbury* (1976). A. W. Wade-

Evans, *Vitae Sanctorum Britanniae* (1944). Other Lives: English Life, printed by Caxton (*c.* 1485); translation from Latin by J. Falconer, S.J. (1635); Philip Metcalf, S.J., *The Life of Saint Winifred* (1712; reprinted 1917, ed. Herbert Thurston S.J.). For interest in the well and miracles recorded there, see *The Month* (Nov. 1893, Feb. 1895, July 1916); *Anal. Boll.* 6, pp. 305-52. On the calendar, see D. Wilkins, *Concilia Magnae Britanniae et Hiberniae*, 3 (1737), pp. 234, 376. On the shrine and gravestone, see L. A. S. Butler and J. Graham Campbell in *Antiquaries' Journal* 70 (1990), pp. 40-8; N. Edwards and T. Gray Hulse in *Antiquaries' Journal* 72 (1992), pp. 91-101; *loc. cit.*, p. 101. The Hopkins fragment is in *Poems of Gerard Manley Hopkins*, ed. W. H. Gardner (3d ed., 1948), pp. 153-9.

St Rumwold (Seventh Century)

The legend surrounding the birth, death, and burial of St Rumwold (Rumwald, Rumbald, Rumbold) is something of a hagiographical oddity. He is supposed to have been a member of the royal house of Mercia who was buried at Buckingham—where there was indeed a shrine before the Norman Conquest. However, the legend, the earliest written mention of which is in a manuscript at Corpus Christi College, Cambridge (John of Tynemouth and Capgrave merely reproduced it), supplies some quite extraordinary details.

He was, it says, the son of King Alcfrid of Northumbria and St Cyneburga (6 Mar.) and was born at Sutton (later known, on this account, as King's Sutton) in Northamptonshire. When he was baptized on the third day after his birth by a bishop named Widerin and a priest named Edwold, he made his own profession of faith in a clear voice, and then died, having first preached a sermon on the Holy Trinity for the benefit of his parents, and given directions for his burial. He was buried first at King's Sutton, where, because of the prodigy attributed to him, a cult grew up. His relics were then translated, first to Brackley, two months after his death, and then, two years later, to Buckingham. The cult continued to flourish in all three places, as it also did, before the Conquest, in at least six monasteries in Mercia and Wessex. His name appears in the *Bosworth Psalter* (*c.* 1000), but not in monastic calendars that date from after 1100. On the other hand, there are churches dedicated to him in Dorset, Essex, Kent, Lincolnshire, Northants, and North Yorkshire (in the last-named at Romaldkirk, which was named after him). At Boxley in Kent, up until the Reformation, when it was burned, there was a statue of him; the fishermen of Folkestone were still invoking him in Camden's time. And in the Northamptonshire hamlet of Astrop there is a well, known, according to Leland, as "St Rumoaldes Welle, wher they say that, within a fewe dayes of his birth, he prechid." Rumwold, who was virtually unknown in the rest of Europe, is thought to have died on 3 November.

The legend is in *AA.SS.*, Nov., 1, pp. 682-90; *O.D.S.*, p. 424. On the so-called rumbal feast of the Folkestone fishermen, see *Victoria County History of Kent*, 3 (1932), p. 428.

St Hubert, *Bishop* (727)

Nothing is known about the early life of St Hubert, nor anything certain about what Alban Butler called "the extraordinary manner" in which he was called to the service of God. The legendary account of the event is as follows. As a young man Hubert was very fond of hunting. One Good Friday, instead of going to church with everyone else, he rode off in pursuit of a stag. As they reached a clearing in the woods, the stag turned round. Hubert was astonished to see a crucifix between its horns and to hear a voice coming from the animal. "Unless you turn to the Lord, Hubert," it said, "you shall fall into hell." He dropped to his knees, asking what he should do, and was told to seek out Lambert, the bishop of Maastricht, who would give him guidance. The same legend is, of course, told about St Eustace (who did not survive the 1969 revision of the Roman Calendar).

Whatever the circumstances in which it happened, Hubert did enter the service of St Lambert (17 Sept.). He was ordained priest and, when the bishop was murdered in Liège in about 705, was chosen to succeed him. Some years later he took Lambert's remains, which had been buried in Maastricht, back to Liège and re-buried them in the church he built over the spot where Lambert had met his death. He made this church his cathedral, moving the episcopal see from Maastricht to Liège, which grew into a flourishing city. St Lambert is honoured there as the principal patron of the diocese and St Hubert as the city's founder and first bishop.

During the twenty or so years he spent as bishop, Hubert preached Christ tirelessly throughout his diocese, particularly in those areas of the Ardennes forest—which at that time stretched from the Meuse to the Rhine—where the gospel had never taken root. The author of a short contemporary memoir of the saint attributes to him the gift of miracles, and he is said to have been warned of his death a year before it happened. In May 727 he went into Brabant to consecrate a church and was taken ill immediately after the ceremony at Terveuren, near Brussels. Six days later, on 30 May, he died peacefully, and his body was taken to the church of Saint-Pierre in Liège for burial. His relics were enshrined there on 3 November 743 (which explains the date chosen for his feast), and then, in 825, they were translated to the abbey of Andain (since renamed Saint-Hubert) on the Luxembourg border. The miracles attributed to Hubert, and the story of the stag in particular, made his cult popular beyond the confines of The Netherlands. Two Orders of chivalry, one in Lorraine and one in Bavaria, were founded under his patronage. Representations of his conversion include a painting from the studio of the fifteenth-century Master of the Life of the Virgin in the National Gallery, London. St Hubert is the patron saint of hunters, and he is also invoked against rabies.

AA.SS., Nov., 1, pp. 759-930. For the folklore aspects, see Bächtold-Stäubli, *Handwörterbuch des deutschen Aberglaubens*, 4, pp. 425-34; E. Van Heurck, *Saint Hubert et son culte en Belgique* (1925). See also A. Poncelet in *Revue Charlemagne* (1911), pp. 129-45; H. Leclercq, in *D.A.C.L.*, 9, 630-1, 655-6; T. Réjalot, *Le culte et les reliques de S. Hubert* (1928); M. Coens (ed.), "Une relation inédite de la conversion de S. Hubert," in *Anal.Boll.* 45, pp. 84-92; *idem*, "Notes sur la légende de S. Hubert" in *Anal.Boll.* 45 (1927), pp. 345-62; studies by F. Peny (1961), A. Paffrath (1961), F. Baix in *Mélanges F. Rousseau* (1958), pp. 71-80.

St Pirminus, *Bishop* (753)

The early evangelization of what became the Grand Duchy of Baden and is today part of Baden-Württemberg was achieved principally by a handful of monasteries. Prominent among the founders of these monasteries was St Pirminus, who probably came to the region from southern Gaul or Spain as a refugee from the Moors. According to a short Latin Life, written in the ninth century by a monk of Hornbach, Pirminus went to Rome relatively early on to obtain the pope's blessing on his mission. He had a reputation as a preacher, and became even more famous as a founder of monasteries, in Germany, where they were seen as a powerful means of spreading Christianity, and in Alsace, where there were political interests involved as well. He also rebuilt the abbey of Dissentis in the Grisons (Switzerland), which had been destroyed by the Avars.

He is best known as the first abbot of Reichenau, the oldest Benedictine monastery on German soil. Pirminus founded Reichenau in 724 on an island in Lake Constance, and for a time it rivalled the abbey of Saint-Gall in influence. For political reasons he was subsequently exiled and went to Alsace, where he founded the monastery at Murbach, between Trier and Metz. He also founded the Benedictine monastery at Amorbach in Lower Franconia; and a manual of popular instruction, the *Dicta Pirmini*, or *Scarapsus*, which was widely circulated during the Middle Ages, was attributed to him. Pirminus was never bishop of Meaux, as the Roman Martyrology states, though he was a regional bishop. He died in 753. A cult soon developed, even before the end of the eighth century, and it enjoyed a revival in the nineteenth century, when the dioceses of Hornbach and Speyer were amalgamated.

The Latin Life is in *M.G.H., Scriptores*, 15. See also *Bibl.SS.*, 10, 927-32; J. Clauss, *Die Heiligendes Elsass* (1935), pp. 246-7; G. Jecker in *Die Kultur der Abtei Reichenau*, 1 (1925), pp. 19-36; *ibid., Die Heimat des hl. Pirmin* (1927); J. E. Congumus in *Pfalzer Lebensbilder*, 1 (1964), pp. 9-22.

St Amicus (1045)

All we know of St Amicus comes from two medieval Latin Lives, one apparently written by a contemporary. Both are largely taken up with his miracles. He seems to have come from a good family in the neighbourhood of Camerino in the March of Ancona and was a secular priest of that town. At some point he became a hermit, and subsequently a monk. The force of his example was such that it is said to have inspired his father, mother, brothers, and nephews to enter the religious life. Amicus himself found the discipline at his monastery insufficiently austere, so he took himself off again, this time to the Abruzzi. There he lived entirely alone for three years, until disciples began to gather round him. It was said that on one occasion he miraculously relieved a famine—though perhaps he simply persuaded people to produce what they were hoarding. He died, reportedly at the age of 120, at the monastery of Fonteavellana, recently founded by St Dominic of Sora (22 Jan.), where he spent the last years of his life. He is not to be confused with the monk Amicus mentioned by St Peter Damian (21 Feb.) in one of his letters.

Both the Latin Lives are printed in *AA.SS.,* Nov., 2. pp. 89–102.

St Malachy, *Bishop* (1094-1148)

At the beginning of the eleventh century social and religious conditions in Ireland had reached a low ebb. This was still true in the northern half of the country when Mael Maedóc Ua Morgair (anglicized to Malachy O'More) was born there in 1094. He was brought up in Armagh, where his father taught in the school. After the death of his parents he became the disciple of a hermit named Eimar, but St Celsus (Ceallach), the archbishop of Armagh (1 Apr.), recognized his quality and obliged him to accept ordination to the priesthood. Malachy, who was twenty-five at the time, was also commissioned to preach and to introduce reforms in the Irish church. He approached his task with great zeal and vigour. His one fear was that he would have insufficient knowledge of canon law to carry out a thorough reform of discipline and worship, so he went for instruction to St Malchus, bishop of Lismore, who had been educated at Winchester in England and was known for his learning and his holiness.

At about the same time, in 1123, one of Malachy's uncles, who as lay abbot and coarb (or heir) of St Comgall held the great abbey of Bangor, Co. Down, and its revenues, decided to hand over his title to his nephew. His idea was that Malachy would repair the fabric of the monastery and then reintroduce the religious life. With ten members of Eimar's community, Malachy rebuilt the house and church, using wood in the traditional Irish manner, but the land he handed over, amidst protest, to another abbey. While praising his spirit of poverty, St Bernard, on whom we have to rely for most of our knowledge of Malachy, commented that he "carried disinterestedness or spirit of holy poverty too far, as subsequent events proved."

Malachy had been governing the rebuilt monastery for only a year when, at the age of twenty-nine, he was appointed bishop of Connor. The people here were Christian in little more than name, but this did not deter him. He preached with a mixture of firmness and kindness, and when the people would not come to church to hear him, he went to find them at home or in the fields. As a result of his efforts, people began to come frequently to the sacraments, the diocese had zealous pastors, and the canonical hours were regularly observed. Then, in 1127, a chieftain from the north swept through Antrim and Down, and the community was driven from Bangor. Malachy, who was still living there himself, withdrew with some of his monks first to Lismore and then to Iveragh in Kerry, where he settled down once more to the monastic life.

In 1129, Celsus of Armagh died, and for several years Malachy was involved in a conflict with the archbishop's relatives. For generations the see of Armagh had been hereditary within Celsus' family, but he, in order to discontinue what he regarded as a deplorable custom, decreed on his deathbed that he should be succeeded by Malachy of Connor, to whom he sent his pastoral staff. When Celsus died, his kinsmen immediately installed his cousin Murtagh, and for three years Malachy would not even try to occupy the see. Then his objections were overruled by a number of people, including St Malchus and the papal legate. Insisting that once he had restored order he would resign, he took over the government of the diocese as far as he could, although he would not enter his cathedral or even the city in case his presence provoked bloodshed. By the time Murtagh died in 1134, having named Celsus' brother Niall to succeed him, both sides were backed by armed force, and Malachy's supporters were determined to see him enthroned in his cathedral. As they were gathering to this end, they were surprised by a band of Niall's supporters, but the latter were scattered by a violent thunderstorm, during which twelve of them were struck dead by lightning.

After this Malachy did take possession of his see, but he was still unable to rule it in peace. For when Niall was finally forced to leave Armagh, he took with him two important relics—a book, probably the Book of Armagh, a ninth-century New Testament bound together with Lives of St Patrick (17 Mar.) and St Martin (11 Nov.), which served as insignia of the archbishop, and a crozier known as the Staff of Jesus, both supposed to have belonged to St Patrick. He also took the loyalty of some of the people, who assumed that the relics were in the hands of the rightful archbishop. Malachy was persecuted as a result, especially by Niall's relations, one of whom invited him to a meeting with a view to murdering him. Against the advice of his friends, Malachy accepted, thinking that his death might lead to peace. But in the event, his calm dignity so disarmed his adversaries that peace was concluded without it. He nevertheless felt the need for an armed bodyguard until, having recovered the book and the crozier, he was acknowledged as archbishop by all. Then, in 1137, with the hereditary succession broken and peace restored, he carried out his promise to resign, ordaining Gelasius, the abbot of Derry, in his place.

Malachy returned to his former see, which he proceeded to divide into two. He consecrated another bishop for Connor, and reserved Down for himself, living, as far as his duties would permit him, in the community of regular canons he established either at Downpatrick or, which is more likely, on the ruins of the old monastery at Bangor.

Two years later, to obtain the pope's general blessing on the many things he had done and specifically to procure the *pallium* for the archbishops of Armagh and Cashel (established as Ireland's second metropolitan see in 1111), he undertook the long journey to Rome. From Ireland he crossed to Scotland, went down to York, where he met St Waltheof of Melrose (3 Aug.), who gave him a horse, and then crossed to France. On his way through Burgundy he stopped at Clairvaux, where he met St Bernard, who became his devoted friend and admirer and subsequently wrote his Life. When Malachy finally reached Rome, far from allowing him to resign from his see, Pope Innocent II confirmed all that he had been doing in Ireland, made him his legate there, and promised the *pallia* if they were formally applied for.

Malachy went back via Clairvaux, where, as St Bernard put it, "he gave us his blessing a second time." And because he could not stay there himself, he left behind four of his companions, who took the Cistercian habit and later, in 1142, returned to Ireland and founded the abbey of Mellifont. Malachy, meanwhile, continued on his way through Scotland, where King David (1124–53) asked him to heal his son, Henry, who was dangerously ill.

In 1148, a great synod was held at Inishpatrick, off Skerries. The bishops and other clergy who attended decided to apply formally for *pallia* for the two metropolitan sees, and Malachy himself set out to find Pope Eugenius III, who was then in France. Unfortunately, he was delayed by the political suspicions of the English king, Stephen (1135–54), and by the time he reached France, the pope had already returned to Rome. He nevertheless took the opportunity to visit Clairvaux again, where he was welcomed enthusiastically by Bernard and the other monks. On the feast of St Luke (18 Oct.) he was taken seriously ill with a fever, and he died in Bernard's arms on All Souls' Day (2 Nov.). During the funeral service—he was buried at Clairvaux—Bernard boldly sang the post-Communion prayer from the Mass for a confessor-bishop. This "canonization of a saint by a saint" was confirmed in 1190 by Pope Clement III (1187-91), the first papal canonization of an Irishman. St Malachy's feast is kept by the Cistercians and the Canons Regular of the Lateran.

It is impossible to talk about St Malachy without mentioning the so-called prophecies about the popes connected with him. Using symbolic titles and mottoes, these attribute certain characteristics to the popes, starting with Celestine II (1143-4) and ending, at the end of the world, with "Peter the Roman." They were first mentioned in 1595, by a Benedictine, Dom Arnold de Wyon, who attributed them to St Malachy but did not say why, or, indeed, where they had been found. In the seventeenth century a Jesuit maintained that they had been forged by a supporter of Cardinal Simoncelli during the conclave of 1590, but in 1871 Abbé Cucherat was arguing in favour of St Malachy's authorship. The truth is that these "prophecies" are certainly spurious and that St Malachy had nothing to do with them.

For St Bernard's Life, see J. Leclercq and A. Gwynn (eds.), *Opera S. Bernardi*, 3; H. J. Lawlor, *St Malachy of Armagh* (1920). More recent Lives: A. J. Luddy (1930); J. O'Boyle (1931), A. B. Scott (1976). See also *Bibl. SS.*, 8, 576-82; A. Gwynn in *Irish Ecclesiastical Review* 71 (1949), pp. 134-48; L. Gougaud, *Christianity in Celtic Lands* (1933), pp. 401-8; R. Sharpe, *Medieval Irish Saints' Lives* (1991); A. Gwynn, *The Irish Church in the Eleventh and Twelfth Centuries* (1992). On the "prophecies," see E. Vacandard in *Revue apologétique* (1922), pp. 657-71; H. Thurston, *The War and the Prophets* (1915), pp. 120-61. For other spurious prophecies attributed to St Malachy, see P. Grosjean, "La prophétie de S. Malachie sur l'Irlande" in *Anal. Boll.* 51, pp. 318-24; 54, pp. 254-7.

Bd Alpais (c. 1150-1211)

The account that has been preserved of Alpais' life is particularly interesting for three reasons. It was written while she was still alive, the author was a Cistercian monk of Les Echarlis who knew her well, and it is confirmed both in contemporary chronicles and in certain records that still exist. She was the eldest child of a peasant family at Cudot, now in the diocese of Orleans, and worked in the fields from a very young age, until she was stricken by a serious disease, possibly leprosy. According to her biographer, she had a vision of Our Lady, probably in 1170, during which she was cured of her illness. But she lost completely the use of her limbs, and from then on was confined to her bed, helpless but perfectly well. He adds that for a long while she took no food or drink—in fact that nothing passed her lips but the Blessed Sacrament, which she received once a week, on Sunday. This was brought to the attention of Guillaume, the archbishop of Sens, who appointed a commission to look into it. The commission reported that her fast was genuine (she is the earliest person of whom it was said that she lived for years on the Eucharist alone). The archbishop then had a church built next to her home in Cudot, which meant that she was able, through a window, to take part in the religious services celebrated there by an Order of Canons Regular. It also meant that Alpais' holiness as well as her reputation for miracles and ecstatic states made Cudot a place of pilgrimage, and the church there benefitted financially, as many people, including prelates and members of the nobility, came from far and wide to see her. In 1180, Queen Adela, wife of King Louis VII of France, made a benefaction to the canons "for love of Alpais." Alpais died on 3 November 1211 and was buried in the choir of the church in Cudot. Her cult, which flourished from the time of her death, was confirmed in 1874.

For a text of the Life, taken from a collation of four manuscripts, with relevant passages from the chronicles of Robert of Auxerre and Ralph Coggeshall, see *AA.SS.*, Nov., 1, pp. 174-209. See also *Bibl.SS.*, 1, 884-6; L. H. Tridon, *La vie merveilleuse de Ste Alpais de Cudot* (1886); M. Blanchon, *Vie de la bienheureuse Alpais* (1899). On fasting saints, see Rudolph M. Bell, *Holy Anorexia* (1985); Walter Vandereycken, *From Fasting Saints to Anorexic Girls* (1994).

Bd Ida of Fischingen (1226)

We know only three things for certain in connection with this saint: that there was a holy woman called Ida, that she died and was buried at Fischingen in Switzerland, and that a popular cult began to flourish immediately after her death. The rest is legend, colourful in its detail, from which she emerges as a cross between Desdemona and Geneviève de Brabant. To a literal-minded and fact-obsessed age this may seem absurd or even shocking, but it is important to remember that the legend was written not to inform, but to explain and justify a cult.

The legend presents Ida as the childless wife of Count Henry of Toggenburg (unknown to history), a man as feared and disliked as she was loved and respected. In response to her alleged but unverified infidelity, he threw Ida from a window. Some bushes broke her fall, and, having recovered, she escaped into the hills. Count Henry was filled with remorse and went to search for the body. Of course he failed to find it. The Iago-like counsellor who had alleged her infidelity gave him no comfort but insisted that Ida was a guilty woman who had justly been put to death. For seventeen years Ida made her home in a cave. Then one of her husband's servants stumbled across the cave and recognized her. Hearing how full of remorse Count Henry was, she asked the man to fetch him. When he arrived she forgave him but refused to return with him as his wife, asking him instead to build her a cell near the castle chapel. Here she lived until she was driven, by the sheer number of people who flocked to see her, to take refuge in a Benedictine monastery at Fischingen. So much for the legend. The holy woman called Ida died in Fischingen in 1226 and was buried in the church there. Her cult was confirmed by Pope Benedict XIII (1724–30) in 1724.

See Leo M. Kern in *Thurgauische Beitrage zur vaterlandische Geschichte*, 63–5 (1928), pp. 1–136.; H. Delehaye in *Anal. Boll.* 47 (1929), pp. 444–6; *idem* in *Nova et Vetera* 4 (1929), pp. 359–65; *Bibl. SS.*, 7, 637.

Bd Simon of Rimini (1319)

When he was twenty-seven, Simone Ballachi joined the Dominican friary in his native Rimini as a lay brother. Not content with this lowly position, he humbled himself still further by volunteering to do all the meanest tasks in the house, and he disciplined his body with an iron chain, offering his pain for the conversion of sinners. He is said to have suffered greatly from diabolical visitations. He was employed principally in the garden, but he also concerned himself with the spiritual growth of children and would go through the streets with a cross in his hand calling them to catechism. At the age of fifty-seven he went blind, and for the last few years of his life he was completely bedridden. But he bore his afflictions with great courage, remaining consistently cheerful. On account of this, and of the miracles he was said to have performed, he was venerated as a saint from the day of his death. This cult was confirmed in 1821.

J. Procter (ed.), *Short Lives of Dominican Saints* (1901), pp. 306–9.

Bd Pius Campidelli (1868–89)

Luigi Campidelli was born in Trebbio, a village south of Florence, on 29 April 1868 and taken that same day by his parents, Giuseppe Campidelli and Filomena Belpani, to be baptized in nearby Poggibonsi. His father died while he was still very young, and he was brought up by his mother, to whose active faith and strong religious conviction he was very responsive. As he grew up he felt called to the priesthood, but because his family could not afford to pay the seminary fees he applied, at the age of fourteen, to join the Passionists. He was scarcely seventeen when he made his vows, taking the name Pio, and he lived his short religious life in the Passionist houses at Santa Maria di Casale and San Eutizio, near Viterbo. He was pursuing his philosophical and theological studies, had received the tonsure, and was about to be ordained to the subdiaconate when he contracted tuberculosis. He died on 2 November 1889 and was beatified by Pope John Paul II on 17 November 1985.

4

ST CHARLES BORROMEO, *Bishop* (1538-84)

Charles (Carlo) Borromeo was a great pastoral theologian and one of the out-standing figures of the Catholic Reformation. He was born in the castle at Arona on Lake Maggiore, on 2 October 1538, the second of two sons in a family of six. His father, Count Gilberto Borromeo, was a good as well as a talented man; his mother, Margherita, who died when Charles was nine, was a Medici from Milan, not Florence, whose younger brother, Gianangelo, became Pope Pius IV (1559-65).

Charles himself was a serious and devout boy. He suffered throughout his life from some kind of speech impediment, probably a stammer, which some misinter-preted as a sign of dullness. In fact he was highly intelligent, and his disability was offset by determination and an extraordinary capacity for hard work. When he was only twelve he received the clerical tonsure; and the Benedictine abbey at Arona, which for some time had been held by members of his family *in commendam*, was passed on to him by his uncle, Giulio Cesare. It was typical of Charles that he reminded his father that, apart from what was spent on his own clerical education, the revenues of the abbey were the patrimony of the poor and should not be put to any secular use. Gilberto seems to have taken him at his word: Charles' letters show that when he went to study, first in Milan and then in Pavia, keeping up a house-hold on a strictly limited allowance from the income of his abbey left him continu-ally short of cash. By the time he obtained his doctorate in 1559, both his parents had died. He returned to Milan, only to hear that his uncle had been elected pope in the conclave that followed the death of Pope Paul IV (1555-9).

At the start of the following year, when Carlo was not yet twenty-two and still only in minor orders, the new pope made him a cardinal. Then, on 8 February, he appointed him administrator of the vacant see of Milan—which was not a little odd, given that he immediately proceeded to load him with a number of other responsibilities (head of the Consulta, which meant Carlo was the pope's secretary of state; papal legate in Bologna, Romagna, and the March of Ancona; and cardinal-protector of Portugal, the Low Countries, the Catholic cantons of Switzerland, the Friars Minor, the Carmelites, the Knights of Malta, and others). All this kept him in Rome and meant he had to find deputies to govern his new diocese.

Charles set about his new tasks with enormous energy but in such a methodical way that he never gave the impression of being hurried. He always found time to see to the affairs of his family and to seek recreation in music and physical exercise. From the start he was a patron of learning, which he wished to encourage among the clergy. To this end he set up several organizations, including, in the Vatican, a literary academy, which had lay as well as clerical members. Having decided that it was necessary, in his position, to follow the style of the papal court, he kept up a large palace with a household to match and provided the customary sorts of entertainment. But within himself, having taken "a near view of its emptiness," he managed to remain detached from this way of life. His main concern was the archdiocese of Milan, and his enforced absence combined with the difficulties presented by his life in Rome made him uneasy. When the archbishop of Braga, Bartolomeo de Martyribus, visited the city, Charles confided to him these misgivings: "You see my position. You are aware of what it means to be the pope's nephew—his much-loved nephew. The dangers are infinite. I am young, and I have no experience. What should I do? God has given me a love of penance, and I sometimes think of entering a monastery and living as if there were only God and myself in the world." The archbishop managed to reassure him that God had given him a task for the service of the Church and that he should not abandon it. But he did add that Charles should find a way of getting to Milan as soon as possible.

This was easier said than done. Shortly after his election Pius IV announced his intention of reconvening the Council of Trent, which had been suspended in 1552, during the reign of Pope Julius III (1550-5). Fortunately for Pope Pius, the idea fired Charles' imagination. It was in great measure thanks to his energy and influence that the council was reopened, in January 1562, for its final and most important session, and thanks even more to his diplomacy and vigilance that it kept going for the two years that it needed to complete its work. Two areas in which he was particularly active personally were the drafting of the Catechism and the reform of liturgical books and church music (he was a supporter of Palestrina, from whom he commissioned the *Missa "Papae Marcelli"*). But it can safely be said that he was the mastermind and ruling spirit of the last period of this reforming council, during which many of its most significant doctrinal and disciplinary decrees were passed.

While the council was still in session, Charles' elder brother, Federigo, died, and Charles found himself head of the family. This provoked another crisis for him— some people assumed that, because he was not yet ordained, he would give up all thoughts of the priesthood and marry. Charles, however, had other ideas. He resigned his position in the family to his uncle Giulio and in 1563 was at last ordained to the priesthood. Two months later he was consecrated bishop. But he was still not allowed to go to his diocese, which, after eighty years without a resident bishop, was in a deplorable state. His vicar, helped by a group of Jesuits, had done what he could to implement a programme of reform, but this had been far from successful. Eventually the pope gave Carlo permission to visit the diocese himself and to hold a provincial council, which in the event was attended by ten suffragan bishops. Carlo took the opportunity to promote regulations which embodied the decrees of the recent council, especially those which related to the discipline and training of the clergy and the celebration of the liturgy. It was while he was on his way back to Rome, via Tuscany, where he had duties as legate *a latere*, that word reached him that Pius IV was dying. He hurried back, reaching Rome in time to be there, along with St Philip Neri (26 May), when the pope actually died. The new pope, St Pius V (1566-72; 30 Apr.), persuaded Charles to remain in Rome for a time, but Charles, who saw his uncle's death as being in this sense the opening he was looking for, pressed the case for his return to his diocese.

With the pope's blessing, he arrived in Milan at last in April 1566 and immediately set about implementing his programme of reform. There was much to do: in general people no longer went to Mass or frequented the sacraments, the clergy were uneducated, lazy, and loose-living, and corruption and superstition were widespread. But partly through the firmness with which he enacted his decrees without respect for persons, partly through his own obvious goodness and spirit of prayer, and partly through sheer hard work, Charles eventually turned things round. He began with his own household, insisting that each of its hundred or so members receive a proper salary and forbidding them to accept gifts. He lived particularly simply himself—although he had the sense not to let his austerities sap the strength he needed for his work. He had a considerable income from various sources, but he seems to have been extraordinarily generous with it, reserving the absolute minimum for his use and giving the rest to families in need and to a variety of good causes (the English College in Douai was one of the foundations that benefitted from his generosity).

He was particularly concerned that priests should be properly educated and founded seminaries for the purpose, an idea which was much copied elsewhere. He also arranged retreats for his priests, and he himself went on retreat twice a year, and to confession every morning before Mass. His confessor was Dr Griffith Roberts, a Welsh priest from the diocese of Bangor, author of a famous Welsh grammar, and he appointed another Welshman, Dr Owen Lewis (afterwards bishop of Calabria), to be one of his vicars general. He had a particular love of the liturgy and never rushed it, however busy he might be. His own preaching was inevitably made more difficult by his speech impediment, but he succeeded in overcoming it sufficiently to reach the hearts of his people. A friend, Achille Gagliardi, commented: "I have often wondered how it was that, without any natural eloquence or anything attractive in his manner, he was able to work such changes in the hearts of his listeners. He spoke but little, gravely, in a voice barely audible—but his words always had an effect."

Equally anxious that children should be properly instructed, Charles directed parish priests to provide public catechism classes on Sundays and holydays. He also set up the Confraternity of Christian Doctrine, through which some three thousand catechists reached as many as 40,000 pupils. In all this work of reform, Charles was supported by a number of religious Orders, including the Jesuits and the Clerks Regular of St Paul, or Barnabites, whose Constitutions he had helped to revise. Later, in 1578, faced with the refusal of the cathedral canons to cooperate with some of his reforms, he instituted a society of secular priests, the Oblates of St Ambrose, who, having made a simple vow of obedience to the bishop, could then be employed by him as he saw fit. The society still exists as the Oblates of St Ambrose and St Charles (Ambrosians), and Cardinal Manning used it as a model when he founded the Oblates of St Charles in London in 1857.

Inevitably, Charles met with opposition and at least twice, in 1567 and 1569, came into serious conflict with the civil authorities, essentially over questions of jurisdiction. On both occasions the matter was referred to Pope Pius V and to King Philip II of Spain (Milan was under Spanish rule at the time), and on both occasions it was settled in favour of the archbishop. He, meanwhile, remained undeterred, and personally started taking his reforms to Alpine valleys north of the city, where the people, as good as abandoned by his predecessors as well as by their local clergy, had begun to turn to Zwinglian Protestantism. These missions were interrupted briefly in 1569, when an attempt was made on his life by a member of an Order called the *Humiliati*, which he was trying unsuccessfully to reform.

Charles' devotion to his people was more than usually evident in 1570, when the harvest failed and there was a serious famine in the city. He was tireless in procuring relief supplies for the poor, and himself fed about three thousand people daily for three months. Then, in 1576, he was absent from Milan when the city was struck by the plague, which was to last for almost two years. He hurried back, to find that the governor and those who could afford to do so had left as quickly as possible. Although the former did eventually return at his request, it was Charles who organized care for the sick, burial for the dead, and daily food supplies for up to 70,000 people. He exhausted all his resources and incurred large debts on behalf of those who suffered in any way as a result of the plague. Even in these circumstances, the Milanese magistrates were making complaints about him to the pope—possibly not entirely ill-founded, since he did have a reputation for expressing himself extremely in his zeal to get things done.

In the spring of 1580 Charles entertained a group of young men who were on their way from Rome to the English mission, among them St Ralph Sherwin and St Edmund Campion (both 1 Dec.), both of whom would give their lives for the faith in the following year. But by this stage frequent travel, lack of sleep, and the strain of work and worry were beginning to undermine his health. In October 1584, after a particularly busy two years, he went to Monte Varallo to make his annual retreat. On the 24th he was taken ill, and on the 29th he set off for Milan, stopping at his birthplace on the way to celebrate Mass. When he reached Milan on 2 November, he went straight to bed and asked for the last sacraments. These he received from the archpriest of the cathedral, and he died peacefully during the night of 3 to 4 November. He was only forty-six years old.

Charles Borromeo was buried in Milan cathedral and immediately became the object of a cult. This spread rapidly, and he was canonized by Pope Paul V (1605-21) in 1610. Artists began to paint him, alone or as one of a group of saints, even before he was canonized. Among several fine portraits is one by Giovanni Battista Crespi in the church of Santa Maria della Passione in Milan. And in the church of San Carlo in Arona there is a reliquary with a copy of his death mask on it.

See C. Bascapè, *De vita et rebus gestis Caroli cardinalis* (1592); Lives by A. Valiero (1586); J. P. Giussano (1610, Eng. trans. 1884); L. Celier (1912); C. Orsenigo (1929; Eng. trans. 1943); M. Yeo (1938); A. Deroo (1963); J. M. Headley and J. B. Tomaro, eds. (1988); E. Tiefenthaler (1988). See also *O.D.S.*, pp. 63-4; *N.C.E.*, 2, pp. 710-12; *Bibl.SS.*, 3, 812-50; *H.S.S.C.*, 8, pp. 77-87.

St Pierius (*c.* 310)

Pierius was head of the catechetical school in Alexandria at the time when St Theonas was bishop there. He was the teacher of St Pamphilus (1 June), a brilliant biblical scholar and defender of Origen (*c.* 183-252), who died a martyr in 309. Pierius himself was so distinguished for his love of work and learning, and his homilies were so popular and instructive, that he was known as the Younger Origen. He is praised both by Eusebius of Caesarea and by St Jerome (30 Sept.), and we know from the latter that he survived the persecution of Diocletian (284-305) and spent his last years in Rome. Others mention his temperance and poverty as well as the clear, brilliant, and spontaneous quality of his writings; there is a long *elogium* of him in the Roman Martyrology.

See L. B. Radford, *Three Teachers of Alexandria* (1908); *D.T.C.*, 12, 1744-6.

SS Vitalis and Agricola, *Martyrs* (date unknown)

Writing at the end of the sixth century, St Gregory of Tours (17 Nov.) complained that there was no proper *passio* of Vitalis and Agricola available. That, it turns out, was not absolutely true, and what we know of the two men is based on an authentic statement made by St Ambrose (7 Dec.) in 392, another made by St Paulinus of Nola (22 June) in 403, and two fictitious accounts unwarrantably attributed to Ambrose—all of which are included in the *Acta Sanctorum*. In fact, almost no one had heard of Vitalis and Agricola until 392, when it was revealed to Bishop Eusebius of Bologna that the bodies of two Christian martyrs with those names had been buried in the Jewish cemetery in the city. Eusebius had the remains located, and they were given a Christian burial. Ambrose, who was present on this occasion, referred to the martyrs in his sermon and urged the congregation to respect their relics, which had been laid under the altar. That there was a widespread cult of the two saints in the West for some time after this is, in fact, largely due to Ambrose, who not only wrote about them but brought some of their relics to his own see of Milan and sent some to Florence, which encouraged other bishops to request some for their own cathedrals. The cult remained strong in Bologna: a basilica was built over the relics, which were later translated to an adjacent chapel when the cathedral fabric was in danger.

As for the details of their lives, it seems that Agricola was a citizen of Bologna and a Christian and that Vitalis was his slave. Vitalis, who had followed his master into the Church, was the first to suffer for his faith. He was taken to the amphitheatre and there, in the presence of Agricola, was tortured in every part of his body until he died. It had been hoped that the sight of his faithful servant's sufferings would weaken Agricola's resolution, but it had quite the contrary effect. When the judges and the people saw that he had been fortified and encouraged by Vitalis' death, their sympathy turned to anger. Agricola was hung on a cross and his body was pierced with nails.

See H. Delehaye, *Origines du culte des martyres*; *C.M.H.*, pp. 623-4; G. Morin in *Revue Bénédictine* 19 (1902), p. 355; H. Quentin, O.S.B., *Martyrologes historiques*, pp. 251, 627; G. Cantagalli, *I martiri bolognesi SS Vitale e Agricola* (1927); J. Dubois, *Le Martyrologe d'Usuard* (1965), p. 349; *Bibl.SS.*, 12, 1225-8.

St John Zedazneli and Companions (Sixth Century)

Although the title Apostle of Iberia (Georgia) is given to St Nino (15 Dec.), the country was in fact evangelized from more than one direction and over a considerable period of time. In about the middle of the sixth century a band of monks, led by John Zedazneli, came to the Caucasus from Syria and established the monastic life that flourished so intensely in Georgia during the early centuries of Christianity there. One of John's disciples, St Scio Mghvimeli, is reputed to have had two thousand monks living under his direction; another, St David Garejeli, also had a large community in the mountains above Tiflis, where for a time he lived as a hermit in a cave; while St Antony the Recluse, said to have been a disciple of St Simeon Stylites the Younger (3 Sept.), became a stylite himself and lived on or in a pillar. Two of the missionaries became bishops, and one of these, St Abibus of Nekressi, was stoned to death by the Persians because he opposed the fire-worshipping cult of Mazdaism. The monks did their work so well that soon native Georgians were founding monasteries not only in their own land but in Palestine, Syria and Sinai, and as far west as Salonika and Crete. In Georgia, each of the thirteen is honoured individually as a saint, but on this day they are also venerated together as the Fathers of the Iberian Church.

M. Tamarati, *L'Eglise Georgienne des origines jusqu'à nos jours* (1910), esp. pp. 211-20. See also P. Peeters, "L'Eglise Georgienne du Clibanion" in *Anal. Boll.* 46, pp. 254, 283; "Georgie" in *D.T.C.*, 5 (esp. 1255); M. F. Brosset, *Histoire de la Georgie*, 1 (1918); *Bibl.SS.*, 6, 295.

St Clarus, *Martyr* (Eighth Century)

There is little satisfactory information available about the life of St Clarus. He was introduced into the Roman Martyrology from that of the French Benedictine Usuard, who mentions him briefly; and then there is a short Latin Life, but that dates from the twelfth century at the earliest and contains features which suggest that it is not historically reliable. On the other hand, there is no doubt that St Clarus was the object of a considerable cult—he was greatly honoured in France during the century after his death, and until recently at least his feast was being observed in some French dioceses. He was said to have been English by birth, a native of Rochester in Kent. He crossed over to Normandy, where he led the life of a hermit and preached Christianity by word and by example, settling eventually in the Vexin, at Naqueville, near Rouen. Here, a woman with some standing in the town became so obsessed with him that, in order to escape her advances, he fled to a nearby forest. By way of revenge, the woman sent two ruffians after him, who ferreted him out and cut off his head. St Clarus was among the English saints represented in wall-paintings in the chapel of the English College in Rome, and he gave his name to Saint-Clair-sur-Epte, near the place of his martyrdom. St Clarus the martyr should not be confused with the St Clarus "whose epitaph Paulinus wrote." He was a priest of the Tours diocese under St Martin (11 Nov.) and is mentioned in the Roman Martyrology on 8 November.

AA.SS., Nov., 2, pp. 102-25; 3, pp. 784-6, gives a full account of what sources there are.

St Joannicus (*c*. 754-846)

There are three extant Lives of St Joannicus, two of them written in Greek by monks who lived under his Rule (the one by Sabas is the better executed and more complete of the two); the third was possibly compiled by St Simeon Metaphrastes (28 Nov.). The story they tell is of a man who, after a dissolute youth, underwent a profound religious conversion and came to be honoured by the Greek church with the title "the Great." Joannicus was born in Bithynia (part of modern Turkey), where he spent his boyhood working as a swineherd. At the age of nineteen he became a soldier in the guard of the Byzantine emperor, Constantine V Copronymus (740-75), and for more than a decade led a dissolute life, while following the fashion of the time in supporting the Iconoclasts. In his mid-thirties, as a result of conversations he had with a monk, he reformed his ways and for six years led an exemplary life while remaining within the army. When he turned forty he quit the service and went to a monastery on Mount Olympus in Bithynia, where he learned the rudiments of the monastic life and went through a process described by himself as the "seasoning of his heart." He subsequently led an eremitical life, becoming famous for his gifts of miracles and prophecy and for his wisdom as a spiritual director.

Eventually he went back to Mount Olympus and received the tonsure at Eraste, near Brusa, where he was closely associated with St Theodore Studites (11 Nov.) and St Methodius of Constantinople (14 June). He lived for a while in a cell on Mount Tricherlice but re-emerged in 815 to defend orthodoxy against the emperor Leo V (813-20) and other Iconoclasts during the second Iconoclast crisis. At the same time he called for flexibility and restraint in the case of priests ordained by Iconoclast bishops, and when some of Methodius' supporters wanted to have the orders of such priests declared invalid, Joannicus reminded him: "They are erring brethren. Treat them as such while they persist in their errors, but when they repent receive them into their proper rank, unless they have been notoriously violent heretics and persecutors." He was particularly fearless in rebuking the emperor Theophilus (829-42), who not only banned sacred images but banned the use of the word "holy" before the names of saints. But his prophecy that Theophilus would eventually restore images was fulfilled only by the latter's widow, Theodora, who had remained orthodox throughout.

Toward the end of his long life, during which he witnessed the second triumph of orthodoxy over the heresy he himself had once professed, Joannicus retired to a hermitage. There he died, aged over ninety, on 3 November 846.

J. Pargoire, "Quel jour St Joannicus est-il mort?" in *Echos d'Orient* 4 (1900), pp. 75-80; *Bibl.SS.*, 6, 1066-7.

Bd Emeric (*c*. 1000-31)

Although the ninth centenary of the death of Bd Emeric (Imre) was marked with some solemnity in Hungary in 1931, few reliable details of his short life have come down to us. According to the Latin Life which has survived, and which was compiled when he had already been dead for nearly a century, Emeric was the only son of St Stephen, king of Hungary (16 Aug.), who ruled from 997 to 1038, and Gisela, sister of another saint, the Holy Roman Emperor Henry II (13 July). He was born sometime between 1000 and 1007 and educated by St Gerard Sagredo. Apart from this, we are told only that when Henry's successor, Conrad II (1024-39), proposed that Emeric should benefit from his planned disendowment of the diocese of Bamberg, Stephen refused to allow this. The authenticity of Stephen's "instruction" to his son has been denied, as has the assertion that he resigned his crown to him, although it does seem that he wanted to hand over at least some of his responsibilities to him. In any case, before anything could be done about this, Emeric died in a hunting accident at the age of twenty-three. When Stephen heard the news he said, "God loved him, and so took him away early." Emeric was buried in the church at Székesfehérvár, south-west of Budapest, and many miracles were recorded at his tomb. His relics were enshrined, together with those of his father, in 1083, by order of Pope Gregory VII. Although he is generally referred to as St Emeric, he is listed as *beatus* in the Roman Martyrology.

Bibl.SS., 4, 116; *Annales Hildesheimenses*; *Life of St Stephen*; C. A. Macartney, *The Medieval Hungarian Historians* (1953).

Bd Frances of Amboise (1427-85)

There is no early biography of Frances (Françoise). What have survived are some enthusiastic narratives, published later by Albert Le Grand of Morlaix and others, which come with a warning from the Bollandists that they should not be accepted too readily as historical fact. One thing is certain: in 1431, when Jean V, duke of Brittany, arranged a matrimonial alliance between his house and that of Thouars, Louis d'Amboise sent his four-year-old daughter, Frances, to be brought up at the ducal court. At the age of fifteen, Frances married Jean V's second son, Pierre, and found herself with a difficult husband—jealous, sulky, and sometimes violent. She bore her troubles without complaint, did what she could to restore peace among the incessantly feuding members of the family, and eventually, through her patience and prayers, brought about a marked improvement in her husband. In 1450, when he succeeded his father, she took full advantage of her position to do good—founding a convent of Poor Clares in Nantes, for example, interesting herself in the canonization of St Vincent Ferrer (5 Apr.), and spending large sums on relief for the poor and other charitable works.

The couple had no children, and when Pierre died in 1457 his successors were wary of the influence and popularity of the young duchess—she was still only thirty. Resisting an offer of marriage from Louis XI of France, she withdrew increasingly from public life to spend time with the Poor Clares in Nantes and later with the Carmelites, whom she established and endowed in Vannes in 1463. In this she was helped and encouraged by the prior general of the order, Bd John Soreth (30 July). It was to a great extent thanks to Frances that John Soreth was able to introduce the Carmelites into France, and in that sense she can rightly be described as the co-founder of the women's branch of the Order there. Like many people in her position, Frances was unable to resist completely the temptation to interfere in the affairs of her foundation; unlike many who do so interfere, she did not hesitate to admit that she was in the wrong: once, when she found an extraordinary confessor for one of the nuns without consulting the prioress and was rebuked by the latter, she apologized immediately and asked for a suitable penance.

In 1468, Frances herself decided to become a nun. She received the habit from John Soreth at the Vannes convent, where, after spending four years as infirmarian, she was elected prioress for life. When the convent in Vannes became too small, she opened another in Couets, near Nantes, and it was here that she died in 1485. Because of her goodness, and the miracles reported at her tomb, Frances was quickly venerated as a saint, although the cult was not confirmed until 1863, after Abbé François Richard (later archbishop of Paris) had put the case for her beatification. He published a two-volume biography in 1865.

For a full treatment, see F. Richard, *Vie de la bse Françoise d'Amboise* (1865). See also B. Zimmerman, *Monumenta historica Carmelitana* (1907), pp. 520-1.

ST CHARLES BORROMEO (pp. 30-4)
Born to wealth, venerated for humility. Gold crown,
silver inscription on blue field.

5

SS Zechariah and Elizabeth (First Century)

Zechariah and Elizabeth were the parents of St John the Baptist (24 June). All that we know of them is in the first chapter of St Luke's Gospel; and St Peter Damian (21 Feb.), in his third sermon on the birth of Our Lady, took the view that further inquiry into things the evangelists chose not to tell us was a sign of "an improper and superfluous curiosity." St Luke says that Zechariah was a priest belonging to "the division of Abijah," that Elizabeth was a descendant of Moses' brother, Aaron, and that both were "in all the commandments and ordinances of the Lord blameless." They had no children, and Elizabeth may well have been past the childbearing age when Zechariah had the vision recorded by St Luke. It was the turn of his section of the priesthood to officiate in the Temple, and it had fallen to him by lot to enter the sanctuary and burn incense there. While he was performing this duty, he had a vision of the angel Gabriel, who told him that his prayer had been heard and that Elizabeth was to bear a son. The child, who was to be called John, would be filled with the Holy Spirit, "even from his mother's womb," and he would "bring back many of the sons of Israel to the Lord their God." Because he questioned the possibility of this, Zechariah was struck dumb and told he would remain so until the child was born.

Luke then relates how, at Ain-Karim, as a seventh-century calendar of the church of Jerusalem specifies, Elizabeth was visited by her kinswoman, Mary, in whose presence "the babe in [her] womb leapt for joy"; how Elizabeth was delivered of a son; and how Zechariah's tongue was loosed in prophecy as soon as he "asked for a writing-tablet and wrote, 'His name is John.'" After that, nothing more is heard of Zechariah and Elizabeth, although some Fathers of the Church, among them St Epiphanius (12 May), St Basil (2 Jan.), and St Cyril of Alexandria (27 June) believed that Zechariah died a martyr. According to one apocryphal text, he was killed in the Temple, "between the porch and the altar," by order of Herod, because he refused to disclose the whereabouts of his son at the time of the massacre of the Innocents; but the Roman Martyrology says nothing of martyrdom when it mentions Zechariah and Elizabeth on 5 November.

Zechariah was venerated throughout the East, and in 415 his supposed relics were taken to Constantinople—an event celebrated by the Greeks on 11 February; there is also said to be a relic of his at the Vatican. He is one of the saints mentioned in the Canon of the Mass in the Mozarabic rite. Elizabeth has never been celebrated on her own, but a church was built in her honour a little west of Jerusalem in 1939. The iconography is very rich, and although neither Zechariah nor Elizabeth has any particular attribute, Elizabeth is usually shown as an older, if not yet old, woman.

Luke 1, *passim.* See also O. Bardenhewer, *Biblische Studien*, 6, pp. 187 (1901); *H.S.S.C.*, 1, pp. 206-7.

St Bertilla (*c.* 705)

The extant Latin Life of St Bertilla (or Bertila) was probably not compiled until about 800. Owing to a mistake made by Bede, a number of false deductions have been made regarding the chronology; the account is nevertheless based on earlier material that is known to have been authentic. Bertilla was born in the territory of Soissons and while still young made up her mind that she would become a nun. She was encouraged in this decision by St Ouen, bishop of Rouen (24 Aug.), and her parents eventually sent her to Jouarre, a monastery near Meaux, which had been founded not long before under the rule of St Columbanus (23 Nov.). Bertilla was warmly welcomed into the community and soon completed her strict novitiate. Her prudence and tact were remarkable in someone of her age, and before long the community's care of strangers, of the sick, and of children had been successively committed to her charge.

When St Bathildis (30 Jan.), the English wife of Clovis II, the Merovingian Frankish king of Neustria and Burgundy (639-57), restored the abbey of Notre-Dame-de-Chelles, south-west of Meaux, she asked the abbess of Jouarre to send a small group of her most experienced and exemplary nuns to form the nucleus of the new community. The abbess agreed, and Bertilla, who was chosen to lead the group, became the first abbess there. Her own reputation and the discipline she established attracted a number of women from abroad, including Hereswitha, widow of Aethelhere, king of East Anglia, and sister of St Hilda (17 Nov.), while among those who joined the abbey from nearer at hand was Bathildis herself. The presence in the community of two former queens made no difference to Bertilla. She always seemed to be the humblest and most fervent of the sisters and led well because she had learned to obey. In her old age, far from relaxing her fervour, Bertilla strove continually to increase it, and she died, much loved by everyone, after forty-six years as abbess of Chelles. Her relics are venerated at Chelles-Saint-André.

W. Levison in *M.G.H., Scriptores Merov.*, 6. St Bertilla is mentioned in the trustworthy Merovingian Life of St Bathildis. See also C. Torchet, *Histoire de l'abbaye royale de Notre-Dame-de-Chelles*, 1 (1889), pp. 43-58.

Bd Gomidas Keumurgian (*c.* 1656-1707)

At the end of the seventeenth century Islamic Constantinople passed through something of an upheaval. The city was a hotbed of secular and ecclesiastical politics, and the movement within Christian circles in favour of reunion with Rome was quite strong. However, thanks in part to the over-zealous activity of the French ambassador, what began as an anti-Catholic reaction soon led to persecution, and Gomidas was one of its victims.

He was born in Constantinople in about 1656, the son of an Armenian priest, and was educated by a priest of the same communion. When he was about twenty he married, and later, having completed his studies, was ordained and appointed to the parish of St George in the south of the city. Here he gained a reputation for eloquence as well as for genuine spirituality and lack of self-interest. He was soon prominent in the reunion movement, and when he was forty converted, with his family, to Rome. As was customary at the time, he continued to minister at St George's, and within a few years five of the twelve priests there had followed his example. After 1695, things were made more difficult for Catholics, and Gomidas went into exile at the Armenian monastery of St James in Jerusalem. Here he supported the pro-Catholic party and incurred the enmity of one John of Smyrna.

When he returned to Constantinople in 1702, on the death of the persecuting Armenian patriarch, Gomidas found that the new patriarch had appointed John of Smyrna as his vicar. He went into hiding until the new patriarch was exiled for political reasons nine months later; but he had not long come out of hiding when the patriarch returned, was accused of being a "Frank" (a Latin Catholic or foreigner), and was deported to Cyprus. There the French ambassador had him kidnapped and taken to France. This unwise move aroused strong anti-Catholic feeling in Constantinople, and the Turkish authorities soon took action against the Catholics. Gomidas, who was physically impressive and no coward, was arrested in the Lent of 1707 and charged before Ali Pasha, who condemned him to the galleys. Friends bought him a brief period of freedom, but on 3 November that year he was re-arrested and brought to trial on the charge that he was a Frank and had stirred up trouble in the Armenian nation within the Turkish realm. The case was referred to the chief *kadi*, Mustafa Kamal, who, as a Muslim canonist, was inclined to judge in favour of Gomidas, but finally bowed to pressure from the Armenians, led by their patriarch, and allowed him to be taken to prison. There, having said goodbye to his wife and children, he remained in prayer until the next day, when he was taken to the Old Seraglio in Constantinople. Here, after an unsuccessful attempt to persuade him to convert to Islam, Ali Pasha sentenced him to death. He was led off to the place of execution—the sequence of events throughout is extraordinarily similar to that of the passion of Christ—and, having refused one last chance to save his life, was beheaded.

Since no Catholic priest came forward to bury him, this task was undertaken by Greek Orthodox priests. But his courage had a profound effect in the longer term, and a century later there were so many Catholic Armenians in Constantinople that "Catholic" was understood to mean one of the Armenian rite. Gomidas was beatified in 1929—the most illustrious martyr since the days of the Iconoclast persecution and probably the first recorded priest martyr whose wife and children followed him to the place of execution. One of his sons, also Gomidas, entered the service of the kingdom of Naples, calling himself Cosimo do Carbognano—a name which is sometimes given to his father.

H. Randall, *Une page tragique de l'histoire religieuse du Levant* (1929)—cf. *Anal. Boll.* 48, pp. 450-1. See also V. Inglisian, *Der Diener Gottes Mechitar von Sebaste* (1929); D. Attwater, *A Book of Eastern Saints* (1938), pp. 109-21.

Bd Bernard Lichtenberg (1875-1943)

Bernhard Lichtenberg was born in Ohlau in Silesia, now in Poland, into a middle-class family. He studied theology at Innsbruck and was ordained at the age ot twenty-four. He was sent to Berlin, where he was to spend most of the rest of his life as a parish priest in the rapidly-growing capital. He was eventually elected to the chapter of St Helwig's Cathedral.

He was a typical German conservative of his generation, with strict views on morals and obedience, strongly supportive of hierarchy, and emphatic on the obedience owed to the pope. For a time after the First World War he sat in the Berlin regional parliament as a member of the Catholic Centre Party. At the same time he was passionate for justice and charity in action, and he supported the pacifist "Peace League of German Catholics" in 1931. This and other actions attracted the wrath of the Nazi paper *Der Angriff*, then edited by Josef Goebbels.

When Hitler came to power in 1933, Bernard tried in vain to persuade Cardinal Bertram, the temporizing president of the German bishops' conference, to protest against the boycott imposed on Jewish shops. In 1935 he protested to Hermann Goering about the treatment of Jews in concentration camps: Goering denied everything and demanded that he be taken into protective custody for spreading lies about the German State. The Concordat signed between Germany and the Holy See in 1935 effectively deprived Catholics of effective organization in the Third Reich, and resistance became a matter for individuals. Bernard helped to distribute clandestine copies of Pope Pius XII's encyclical *Mit brennender Sorge*, banned in Germany. After the *Kristallnacht* of 10 November 1938 he addressed his congregation, telling them that a temple was burning—"and that, too, is a house of God"—and asking for prayers for the Jews.

He was exceptional in concentrating his condemnation on Hitler's treatment of the Jews. For this he was imprisoned in 1941 and on his release two years later was handed over to the Gestapo for "re-education." By this time he was old and ill. The Gestapo sent him to Dachau, but he collapsed on the way and was taken to hospital in Hof in Bavaria, where he died on 5 November 1943. His body was taken to Berlin for burial, and a crowd of 4,000 followed the coffin, despite constant air raids. One onlooker said: "I wonder if they know they have buried a saint?" He was beatified, together with a fellow-resister against the Nazis, Fr Karl Leisner, by Pope John Paul II on his second visit to Germany in June 1996.

There is a biography in German: Erik Kock, *Er widerstand* ("He resisted"; 1996). The above is based on the review article by Roland Hill in *The Tablet*, 26 Oct. 1996, pp. 1401-2.

6

St Illtud, *Abbot* (Sixth Century)

The earliest surviving information about Illtud, one of the most celebrated of the Welsh saints, is in a seventh-century Life of one of his pupils, St Samson (28 July). Here we are told that Illtud was a disciple of St Germanus (Germain) of Auxerre (3 Aug.), by whom he was ordained priest, and that he presided over the monastic school at Llanilltud Fawr (now Llantwit Major, in South Glamorgan). The author emphasizes both his learning and his wisdom: "This Illtud was the most learned of all the Britons, both in the Old Testament and in the New, and in all kinds of philosophy—poetry and rhetoric, grammar and arithmetic. . . . Were I to begin to relate all his wondrous works I should be led to excess." There are further references in a ninth-century Life of another pupil, St Paul Aurelian (12 Mar.), which mentions the fact that Illtud established a monastery on an island "within the borders of Dyfed, called Pyr"—usually identified as Caldey Island, off Tenby. The Life of Gildas tells how Paul, Samson, and two other pupils, St Gildas (29 Jan.) and St David (1 Mar.—though it is unlikely that the latter was Illtud's pupil), suggested that Illtud increase the size of this "very limited area hemmed in by the sea." Illtud took the young men into the church to pray for this, and when they had answered "Amen!" they came out, "and behold, the island made bigger on every side and bright flowers blossoming everywhere." The Life of Paul gives a more circumstantial account.

The only Life we have of Illtud himself is in Latin and dates from about 1140. This tells us that his father was a Briton who lived with his wife in Brittany. When he grew up, Illtud travelled by water to visit "his cousin King Arthur" and married a woman called Trynihid. On leaving Arthur, he entered the military service of a chieftain in Glamorgan, thus earning for himself the title Illtud the Knight. The story goes on to say that after a hunting accident, in which some of his friends lost their lives, Illtud decided to enter the monastic life and that St Cadoc (23 Sept.), who was scarcely born at this point, encouraged his resolve. Initially, Illtud went to live with Trynihid in a reed hut by a stream called the Nadafan, but he was warned by an angel to leave her. This he did, very roughly, early in the morning, and then went off to St Dyfrig (14 Nov.) to receive the tonsure. After that, he lived austerely as a solitary on the banks of another stream, the Hodnant, until disciples began to gather round him. The land was good and they worked hard, with the result that they flourished materially as well as spiritually. Eventually, the monastery at Llanilltud Fawr became the first great monastic school in Wales. The only person who was unwelcome there seems to have been Trynihid, who came to see her husband one day while he was working in the fields, but he took offence and would not speak to her. This, however, may be the hagiographer's way of saying that he had turned his back on the world.

The Life is to a great extent taken up with anecdotal accounts of wonders performed by the saint—accounts which provoked a seventeenth-century Benedictine, Dom Serenus Cressy, to complain about "fables and unsavoury miracles" when he came across them in Capgrave's *Nova legenda Angliae*. We learn, for example, that when Illtud was driven from his monastery for a while by a local chieftain and took refuge in a cave near the river Yfenni, he lived on food received from heaven, and that he miraculously made good a wall which the monks had tried but failed to repair after its collapse left their lands under threat from the sea. But we also learn that he introduced his monks, and therefore the people, to an improved method of ploughing and that he went with corn-ships to relieve a famine in Brittany (places and churches bearing his name are found there as well as in Wales).

According to the Life, Illtud crossed the sea again in his old age and died at Dol in Brittany. On the other hand, the Life of Samson gives a moving account of his last days at Llanilltud; while a local tradition in Powys says that he died at Defynnog and was buried at the place still called Bedd Gwyl Illtud (Grave of Illtud's Feast). In one of the Welsh triads Illtud is named as one of the three knights of Arthur—the others being Cadoc and Peredur—who had charge of the Holy Grail, and attempts have been made to identify him with the Galahad of the Arthurian legends. He does not seem to have been mentioned in any calendar, martyrology, or litany earlier than the eleventh century.

For the Latin Life, see A. W. Wade-Evans (ed.) in *Vitae sanctorum Britanniae* (1944)—with translation. For the best account in English, see G.H. Doble, *Lives of the Welsh Saints* (1971). See also R. Fawtier (ed.), *Vita Samsonis* (1912; Eng. trans. T. Taylor, 1925); A. W. Wade-Evans, *Welsh Christian Origins* (1934), pp. 132-7 and *passim*; F. Duine, *Mémento des sources hagiographiques . . . de Bretagne* (1918), pp. 129-31; Rachel Bromwich (ed.), *Trioedd Ynys Prydain* (1961).

St Melaine, *Bishop* (*c.* 530)

Melaine (Melanius) was born at Placet, in the Breton parish of Brain, sometime during the second half of the fifth century. Of three Lives that have survived, none dates from earlier than the ninth century, but Melaine's popularity is mentioned by St Gregory of Tours (17 Nov.) later in the sixth. He had already spent a number of years as a monk when the clergy and people of the diocese of Rennes persuaded him to accept the see left vacant by the death of St Amand (6 Feb.). As bishop, Melaine played a leading role in the drawing up of the canons of the Council of Orleans (511), and in 519 or 520, together with others, he wrote a letter of rebuke to two Breton priests who were wandering from place to place and scandalizing the laity by their behaviour. But he was known above all for his genuine humility and for his spirit of continual prayer, and the author of his Life reports that he performed many miracles. The Frankish king, Clovis I (481-511), who became a

Christian in 497 or 498, is said to have held him in great esteem. Melaine died at the monastery he had built in Placet, but he was buried at Rennes, where his feast is still observed (it used also to be observed at Mullion in Cornwall, where he had supplanted an earlier St Mollien or Moellien as the local patron). He should not be confused with St Mellon (22 Oct.), who was venerated in Normandy and seemingly gave his name to the Welsh town of St Mellons, between Newport and Cardiff. Melaine is one of the saints invoked in times of drought.

M.G.H., Scriptores merov., 3; L. Duchesne, *Fastes Episcopaux*, 2, pp.340-1. See also Gregory of Tours, *De Gloria Confessorum*, in *M.G.H., Scriptores*, 1; G. H. Doble, *St Melaine* (1935); *Bibl.SS.*, 9, 286-7.

St Leonard of Noblac (? Sixth Century)

During the later Middle Ages St Leonard of Noblac was one of the most popular saints in western Europe, yet almost nothing definite is known about him. Most of the details in a Latin Life written in the first half of the eleventh century come from Lives of St Remigius (13 Jan.) and others, and there is no trace of a cult earlier than this. What seems certain is that Leonard was a hermit who lived near Limoges sometime between the sixth and the tenth century. According to the Life, he was born in Gaul of a noble Frankish family during the reign of the emperor Anastasius (491-518) and was converted to Christianity by St Remigius. It was expected that he would join the army, but he surprised his family by entering the monastery of Micy, near Orleans.

Refusing the bishopric subsequently offered him by his godfather, the Frankish king, Clovis I (481-511), he looked instead for greater solitude, building a cell in a forest near Limoges and living there for some time entirely alone. One day, the Life continues, Clovis was hunting in the forest, when his wife, who was of the party, went into labour. Thanks to Leonard's help and prayers, she was safely delivered of her child, and Clovis, to express his gratitude, promised Leonard as much land as he could ride round on his donkey in one night. On this land Leonard set up an oratory in honour of Our Lady and called the place Nobiliacum. A community grew up around him and eventually became the abbey of Noblac (now identified as the town of Saint-Léonard). He took the gospel to the people of the neighbourhood, and by the time he died, allegedly in the middle of the sixth century, he was revered for his holiness and his miracles—particularly in connection with the release of prisoners.

Cardinal Baronius, who introduced St Leonard into the Roman Martyrology, appealed to Bede and Ado as witnesses, but he was mistaken. As far as we know, St Leonard was mentioned for the first time just before 1028, when a priest in Limoges, on behalf of his bishop, asked Fulbert of Chartres if he knew anything about him; he appeared in writing for the first time in 1028 in the *Historiae* of Adémar de Chabannes; and it was only after that, in about 1030, that the anonymous Life was published—"*fabularum plena*" according to the Bollandists. The remarkable burgeoning of the cult was contemporaneous with the publication of the Life, which suggests that, if the Life did not create the cult, it certainly transformed it. The church at Noblac became a centre of pilgrimage, and St Leonard was invoked not only by women in labour but by prisoners of war (partly because, according to the legend, Clovis promised to free every captive St Leonard visited, and partly because, in 1103, Bohemund, prince of Antioch, who was captured during the first Crusade, visited the shrine at Noblac after his release from a Muslim prison, leaving there some silver chains patterned on those he wore in prison). From France the cult spread to Bavaria, where in one town alone four thousand cures and other answers to prayer were attributed to St Leonard's intercession between the fourteenth and the eighteenth century; to Italy; and to England, where there are two towns and 177 churches dedicated to him, including one as far west as St Ives, in Cornwall.

AA.SS., Nov., 3, pp. 139-209; *O.D.S.*, pp. 296-7; *Bibl.SS.*, 7, 1198-1208; A. Poncelet "Boémond et S. Léonard," in *Anal.Boll.* 31, pp. 24-44. See also F. Arbellot, *Vie de S. Léonard* (1863); J. A. Aich, *Leonard, der grosse Patron des Volkes* (1928); G. Schierghofer, *Alt-Bayerns Umritte und Leonhardifahrten* (1913).

St Winnoc, *Abbot* (*c.* 717)

If Winnoc was indeed British, as one tradition suggests, his direct connection with Britain is slight—another tradition has it that he was born at Plouhinec in Brittany. In either case it is curious that, in contrast to St Illtud (6 Nov.), he is commemorated in nearly all the English calendars of the tenth and eleventh centuries, as well as in the Old-English Martyrology (*c.* 850). Of three Latin lives that have survived, only the earliest, which may have been written in the eighth century, is of any account, the others being obviously based on it. They tell how, as a young man, Winnoc was travelling with three companions and came to the newly-founded monastery of Saint-Pierre at Sithiu (Saint-Omer). The four were so impressed by the fervour of the monks and the wisdom of their abbot, St Bertin (5 Sept.), that they agreed to take the habit together. Soon, as the monastery chronicler puts it, Winnoc "shone like a morning star among the hundred and fifty monks who inhabited that sanctuary."

When the monks decided to found a daughter house in a remoter part of the country of the Morini in the hope of spreading the gospel, Heremar, a man who had recently become a Christian, gave Bertin a suitable plot of land at Wormhout, near Dunkerque. Bertin sent Winnoc and his three British companions, who worked tirelessly to build a church, cells for the monks, and a hospital. Before long the new monastery had become a thriving missionary centre. Winnoc was as devoted in the service of his monastic brethren as he was in that of the heathen peoples amongst whom they lived, and many miracles were attributed to him. According to one story, even in his old age he regularly ground corn for the poor of the neighbourhood. Some who doubted that a man of his age would have the strength to turn the hand-mill himself looked through a chink in the barn wall to see what was going on, and saw the quern turning by itself, without being touched.

Winnoc died on 6 November, according to the fourteenth-century tradition, in 716 or 717. Count Baudouin IV of Hainaut subsequently founded a new abbey at Bergues, to which he invited a colony of monks from Sithiu and translated the relics of St Winnoc. The lands of the monastery of Wormhout were settled on this house, and the town is called Bergues-Saint-Winnoc. St Winnow in Cornwall apparently gets its name from St Winnoc, which has led to the suggestion that Winnoc was a Welshman who founded the Cornish church and subsequently went to Sithiu, probably via Brittany.

Latin Lives in *M.G.H., Scriptores Merov.*, 5. See also tenth- and eleventh-century calendars, ed. F. Wormwald for Henry Bradshaw Society; Van der Essen, *Etude critique sur les Saints Mérov.*, 5; Flahaut, *Le culte de St Winnoc à Wormhout* (1903); F. Duine, *Mémento*, p. 64.

St Demetrian, *Bishop* (*c.* 912)

St Demetrian is venerated as one of the greatest bishops and saints of Cyprus. Yet all we know of him is contained in an early Greek Life, the only surviving manuscript of which is mutilated toward the end. He was born sometime in the ninth century at Sika, a village in Cyprus, where his father was a much-respected priest. He married while he was still very young, but he and his wife had been together for only three months when she died. Demetrian took the habit in the monastery of St Antony, and after a while, during which he became known for his piety and his powers of healing, he was ordained priest. Eventually he was elected abbot, and he ruled for many years with great wisdom and holiness, until the see of Khytri became vacant and he was appointed to it.

As he had by this time been a monk for nearly forty years, Demetrian was disinclined to involve himself with the responsibilities and distractions of the episcopate. So he fled to a friend of his, one Paul, who hid him in a cave. Paul then had scruples about what he had done and told the authorities where the fugitive was, and Demetrian had to submit to consecration. Toward the end of his twenty-five-year episcopate Cyprus was ravaged by the Saracens, and many Christian Cypriots were taken off into slavery. Demetrius is said to have followed and interceded with the raiders, who were so impressed by his venerable age and his selflessness that they allowed the prisoners to return to their homes.

For the Greek Life, see *AA.SS.*, Nov., 3, pp. 300–8; H. Grégoire (ed.), *Byzantinische Zeitschrift*, 16 (1907), pp. 217–37.

St Barlaam of Khutyn, *Abbot* (1193)

Barlaam, whose baptismal name was Aleksei, was born into a wealthy family in Novgorod. When his parents died he sold his property, gave away much of what he earned to the poor, and went to live as a solitary at a place called Khutyn on the banks of the Volga. Here he built a wooden chapel and, as his reputation for holiness spread, was joined by others. When he was no longer able to accommodate the numbers who came, he organized them as a monastic community, ruling over them as abbot with the name of Barlaam (Varlaam). The wooden chapel was rebuilt in stone and dedicated to Christ's transfiguration. Among the pilgrims and other visitors who flocked to the new monastery was Duke Yaroslav of Novgorod, who became its benefactor. But Barlaam did not live for long once the community was finally established. Having provided for its upkeep and nominated a monk named Antony to succeed him, he died on 6 November 1193. Miracles were reported at his burial-place, and his relics were solemnly enshrined in 1452. His Life was written by a Serbian monk named Pachomius, and he is commemorated in the Russian liturgy during the preparation of the bread and wine.

J. Martynov, "Annus ecclesiasticus Graeco-Slavicus" in *AA.SS.*, Oct., 11, p. 263; cf. note under St Sergius (25 Sept.).

Bd Christina of Stommeln (*c.* 1242-1312)

In her native village of Stommeln, near Cologne, and at Julich, where she was eventually buried, Christina Bruso was venerated as a saint during her lifetime as well as after her death. This local veneration, which continued without interruption through six centuries, was confirmed by Pope St Pius X (1903-14; 26 Aug.) in 1908. However, without the contemporary testimony, much of it from eyewitnesses, either she would have been dismissed as a devout but mentally sick young woman or her biographers would have been regarded as dupes or liars. As it is, scholars remain divided, some sharing the view of one modern scholar who contended that it was easier to regard the whole thing, including Christina's existence, as "a romance concocted . . . by Petrus of Dacia" than to believe the extravagances recorded in her letters.

Christina's father was a prosperous peasant who made sure his daughter received some sort of education, and although she could not write, she could read the Psalter. In the short account of her early life, which she dictated to her parish priest, Johannes, she says that at the age of ten she was betrothed to Christ, who appeared to her in a vision, and when she was thirteen she ran away to become a *Béguine* in Cologne. This did not last long: her extravagant devotions and austerities led her sisters to conclude that she was a hysteric, and she returned home. When she was twenty-five, she met a young Dominican, Petrus of Dacia, and there was an immediate rapport between them. At their first meeting, in the presence of others, she was thrown about the room and her feet were pierced by an invisible agent. For the next two years, Fr Petrus kept a record of all he witnessed in her regard, which ran the gamut from ecstasy to frankly repulsive manifestations.

Fr Petrus left Cologne in 1269, so Christina corresponded with him through the parish priest, Fr Johannes, who sometimes added comments of his own. From the letters it seems that the bizarre and sometimes violent manifestations continued— nor were they confined to Christina but affected those close to her, and she herself attributed them to the devil. And they continued after Fr Johannes died eight years later, when the role of *amanuensis* was taken on by the local schoolmaster, also called

Johannes. But now the accounts became even more extreme. As the article already quoted puts it: "The accounts of Christina's experiences between 1279 and 1287, which reached her Dominican friend through the intermediary of Magister Johannes, are so preposterous that, if they really emanated from herself, one can only regard them as hallucinations of a brain which, for the time being at least, was completely unhinged." There is no corroborative evidence for anything described in the letters. However, two significant passages suggest that, unless the schoolteacher invented the extravagances, which in the circumstances is regarded as unlikely, Christina communicated them when she was in a trance or some other abnormal state and he filled in the detail.

Christina's known history ends in 1288, when Fr Petrus died, but she lived for another twenty-four years. She died in 1312 at the age of seventy and was immediately venerated as a saint. Her relics were translated first to Niedeggen and then, in 1569, to Julich, where they remain. Some have argued that in a case like Christina's veneration is misplaced. But holiness is something quite independent of the types of supernatural favour and abnormal physical phenomena she experienced. In confirming her cult, the Church had nothing to say about these, recognizing instead the evidence in her life of genuine holiness.

For material collected by Petrus of Dacia for his projected book *The Virtues of the Bride of Christ Christina*, see *AA.SS.*, June, 4, pp. 270–454; J. Paulson (ed.), *Vita Christinae Stumbelensis, Petrus of Dacia* (1985). See also H. Steffens, *Die hl. Christina von Stommeln* (1912); J. Colijn (ed.), *Vita b. Christinae Stumbelensis* (1936); C. Ruhrberg, *Der literarische Körper der Heiligen, Leben und Viten der Christina von Stommeln* (1995); H. Thurston in *The Month*, Oct. 1928, pp. 289–301, Nov. 1928, pp. 425–37; *Douleur et stigmatisation* (1936), pp. 44–9, in series "Etudes Carmelitaines"; *Anal. Boll.* 57 (1939), pp. 187–9.

Bd Joan de Maillé (1332-1414)

Joan (Jeanne Marie) was born at Roche-St-Quentin in Touraine on 14 April 1332. She was the daughter of Baron Hardouin VI de Maillé (or Maillac) and his wife, Jeanne de Montbazon. As a child, she was exceptionally devout, and on one occasion her prayers are said to have saved the life of a little neighbour, Robert de Sillé, who had fallen into a pond. The boy became deeply attached to her, and when they grew up Joan's grandfather arranged a marriage between them—her father by this time had already died. Joan herself had hoped to become a nun, a hope intensified by her recovery from a serious illness, but she could not disobey her grandfather (who, as it happened, died on the day of the wedding). The young couple, who decided to live as brother and sister, seem to have been very happy together for sixteen years. They adopted three orphaned children, and their *château*, in which no gambling or bad language was permitted, became a refuge for the poor of the neighbourhood.

This peaceful existence was shattered by the Hundred Years War. Robert followed the French king, Jean II le Bon (1350–64), to defend France against the English, and in 1356 was left for dead at the disastrous battle of Maupertuis (Poitiers).

The *château* of Sillé was pillaged by the enemy troops who overran the land after the battle, and a ransom of 3,000 florins was demanded for the release of Robert, who had been found alive and taken prisoner. Joan sold her jewels and horses and borrowed what was still needed to make up this huge sum—all of which meant a delay of about nine days, during which Robert was virtually starved by his captors. His release, when it came, he attributed to Our Lady, who was said to have appeared to him and broken his chains, thus enabling him to escape. From this moment until Robert's death in 1362, Joan and her husband became, if possible, even more self-denying in their own lives, and added the ransom of prisoners to their list of charitable causes.

After Robert's death, Joan's grief was compounded by the unkindness of his family, who accused her of impoverishing the estate by encouraging Robert to give alms, deprived her of her dowry, and drove her from her home. Initially, she took refuge with an old servant, but she found herself treated with contempt once it became obvious that she had come empty-handed. She then returned to her mother at Luynes, where she learned to make up medicines and salves. But she was still young, and suitors, encouraged by her mother and brother, began to bother her. To escape their attentions, she withdrew to a little house next to the church of St Martin in Tours and there spent her time praying, attending the divine office and caring for the sick and the poor. She was praying in the church one day when a deranged woman threw a stone at her, seriously injuring her back. Even the surgeon sent by Anne de Bretagne said he could do nothing to help her, but she then experienced what she interpreted as a miraculous cure, which enabled her to resume her austere way of life. It is possible that she became a Franciscan tertiary at this point. Her life was punctuated by bouts of serious ill health, after one of which she decided to give up all her possessions, including the Château des Roches, which had been restored to her by her husband's family. She made everything over to the Carthusians at Liget and formally renounced any property that might come to her in the future. This succeeded in alienating her own relations, and when she returned to Tours completely destitute, no one would house her. She was forced to beg from door to door for food, and sometimes slept in disused pigsties and kennels. At one point she was taken in as a servant at the hospital of St Martin, but her obvious holiness aroused jealousy, and she was calumniated and forced to leave. At last she found peace in the solitude of Planche-de-Vaux near Cléry and lived there for some time. She restored a ruined chapel, which was named the chapel of the Good Anchoress after her and became a place of pilgrimage.

In 1389, when she was fifty-seven, she returned to Tours, where she found accommodation in a tiny room near the Franciscan church. Although some people still thought she was mad or a witch, others now recognized that they had a saint living among them. Conversions and miracles were reported as a result of her intercession, and she received unwelcome recognition as a result of her gift of prophecy. She retained to the end a deep compassion for all prisoners, criminals as well as captives in war. She would visit them in prison, assist and instruct them, and she once persuaded the king to free all the prisoners in Tours. She died on 28 March 1414. Her cult was approved in 1871, and the Friars Minor keep her feast on 6 November.

Léon, *Auréole Séraphique* (Eng. trans.), 2, pp. 106-30; A. de Crisnoy, *La bienheureuse Jeanne de Maillé* (1948); *Vies des Saints*, 3, pp. 601-5; *Bibl.SS.*, 589-90.

7

ST WILLIBRORD, *Bishop* (658-739)

As the first to take the Northumbrian Christian tradition to the continent, inaugurating a century of English influence there, Willibrord was one of the most compelling figures of the seventh- to eighth-century Church. We rely almost entirely on Bede for our knowledge of him and his work. Sadly none of his own letters survives, and although Alcuin wrote two Lives, one in verse for use in teaching children in the monastic schools, there is too much about miracles and not enough about Willibrord's work in both.

Willibrord was born in Northumbria in 658, and he was still very young when his father, Wilgils, decided to become a hermit. He was sent, before he was seven, to be educated by St Wilfrid (12 Oct.) at Ripon Abbey—Wilfrid, who was bishop of Northumbria, was also abbot of Ripon. Despite the atmosphere of controversy over such matters as the role of the Roman church and the date of Easter which always surrounded Wilfrid, the two developed a close friendship. Willibrord was described as the *filius* of Wilfrid, and according to St Boniface (5 June) was professed when he was only fifteen.

In 678, when the diocese of Northumbria was divided into four over Wilfrid's head, Willibrord went to join two companions, St Egbert (24 Apr.) and St Wigbert (13 Aug.), in Ireland. Here he spent twelve years studying—possibly at Mellifont Abbey—and was ordained priest. In 690 he returned to England, and from there, inspired by Egbert (who had wanted to go himself but was warned in a vision not to), he set off with twelve companions as a missionary to the Frisians, a Germanic people then occupying the coast of what is now The Netherlands. They landed at the mouth of the Rhine and, via what became Utrecht, made their way into Frankish territory. Here they received the full support of the Frankish king, Pepin of Herstal, who encouraged them to go and preach in Frisia, between the river Meuse and the sea—an area he had won from the fiercely anti-Christian pagan Frisian king, Radbod.

In 692, once the mission was on its feet, Willibrord himself set off for Rome to obtain authority from the pope, St Sergius I (687-701; 8 Sept.), for what he was doing. For the Franks and the Frisians, Rome would have had almost no significance, but for an Englishman, conscious of the Roman origins of his church, this maintaining of relations would have been important. During his absence one of his companions, St Swithbert (1 Mar.), went to England, where he was consecrated bishop with no fixed diocese by St Wilfrid. On his return, Swithbert, possibly because Pepin resented what he saw as interference in his own area of jurisdiction, set off up the Rhine to preach to the Boructuarii. At all events, Willibrord, who came back from Rome with relics for the consecration of churches, continued his successful mission for a while, and then, in 695, returned to Rome, this time carrying letters of recommendation from Pepin that he be ordained bishop. Sergius I received him with honour, ordained him archbishop of the Frisians, and gave him the *pallium* in the basilica of Santa Cecilia on that saint's feast-day, 22 November, giving him the additional name of Clement.

Willibrord spent only fourteen days in Rome this time—a rapid turn-around in a period when the journey itself took so long. He came back to western Frisia with a mandate to organize the church there along the normal lines, taking Canterbury as his model, with one metropolitan see and suffragan sees elsewhere. Pepin gave him the fortress at Wiltaberg, later Utrecht, as a site for his cathedral. But as he zealously built churches, consecrated bishops, and founded monasteries, including Echternach in Luxembourg, which he founded in 698 in collaboration with Pepin's mother-in-law, St Irmina (24 Dec.), Willibrord's overriding concern was the spiritual welfare of the people amongst whom he worked.

Although Willibrord's apostolate enjoyed a good measure of success in western Frisia, elsewhere it was somewhat patchy and seems to have depended on the attitude of temporal rulers. Things did not go well, for example, when he extended his activities into the territory of Radbod. And in Denmark all he appears to have managed to do was purchase thirty Danish boys, whom he instructed, baptized, and brought back with him to western Frisia. According to Alcuin, during the return journey the ship he was travelling in was blown off course and forced to land on Heligoland. This island, which sits in the North Sea near the mouth of the Elbe, was revered at the time as a holy place by both the Danes and the Frisians; and it was considered a sacrilege to kill any living creature, eat anything that grew, or draw water there without observing complete silence. To demonstrate that this was superstition, Willibrord used what appears to have been his customary technique in such situations: direct confrontation. He killed some animals as food for his companions and baptized three people at a fountain, pronouncing the words in a very loud voice. When he neither went mad, as they expected he would, nor dropped down dead, the onlookers were at a loss to know whether this was because their god was patient or because his power had deserted him. Radbod, however, took matters into his own hands: lots were drawn and one of Willibrord's companions, was sacrificed to appease the god. Things went better on the island of Walcheren, where Willibrord made many converts, managed to fend off an outraged pagan priest whose idol he had destroyed, and eventually returned safely to Utrecht.

In 714 Radbod regained the parts of Frisia that he had lost, and much of Willibrord's work was undone—missionaries were killed, churches were destroyed, and he himself was driven from Utrecht. Then, in 719, Radbod was killed, and Willibrord was free to return not only to the western part of Frisia, which he had already evangelized, but to the eastern part as well. Here he was joined by St Boniface, who was on his way to Germany. The two worked fruitfully alongside one another for a while, and Willibrord would have liked Boniface to remain as his eventual successor at Utrecht. But Boniface had received a definite mission from Pope Gregory II (715-31) to go to Germany, and after three years with the by now aging Willibrord, he went on his way.

Throughout his busy life it had been Willibrord's habit to retreat from time to time to his monastery at Echternach. In his old age he retired there permanently, and it was there that he died, on 7 November 739, at the age of eighty-one. He was immediately venerated as a saint, and his tomb in the crypt of the abbey church became a place of pilgrimage. His remains were transferred in 1031 to a position under the main altar of a new abbey church especially built in his honour, where they remained until the French Revolution. They were returned to the abbey church in 1906, but because the new tomb built for them obstructed the view of the main altar, they were returned to their original position in the crypt.

A curious observance known as the *Springende Heiligen* (Dancing Saints) takes place in connection with his shrine every Whit Tuesday. Its origin is unknown, but it is has taken place regularly (except from 1786 to 1802) at least since 1553. Forming a procession four or five abreast, the participants (including bishops, priests, and religious), move forward, hand-in-hand or arm-in-arm, to a three-steps-forward-two-steps-back dancing measure, in time to traditional music. In this way they cross the bridge over the river Sure and enter St Willibrord's shrine, where the ceremony ends with Benediction of the Blessed Sacrament. Whatever its origin, it is now penitential in character and includes special prayers for those suffering from epilepsy and mental illness.

One of the most interesting surviving relics is the calendar of St Willibrord. Compiled for Willibrord's private use, it provides important evidence for the cults of Northumbrian saints and contains a marginal entry in his own hand giving details about his episcopal consecration. As to the sort of man he was, Alcuin describes him as striking in appearance, graceful and cheerful in his manner, wise when it came to offering advice, and unflaggingly energetic in his ministry, which was based on a deep interior life nourished by prayer, meditation, and reading. The conversion of Holland and Luxembourg may not have happened as quickly or as completely as some of the medieval hagiographers would like us to think, and a larger part than is commonly recognized may have been played by St Swithbert, especially in the early days. But St Willibrord has every right to the title Apostle of the Frisians, by which he is known.

Alcuin's Life and a Life by Theofrid, abbot of Echternach, are in *AA.SS.*, Nov. 3, pp. 435-500; see also Bede, *HE*, 3, 13; 5, 10-11, 19. For the calendar of St Willibrord, see the "Epternach MS" of the *Hieronymianum* (now MS Paris Latin 10837); H. A Wilson, *The Calendar of St Willibrord* (Henry Bradshaw Society, 1918). See also A. H. B. Breukelaar, *Historiography and Episcopal Authority in Sixth-Century Gaul* (1994); W. Levison, *England and the Continent in the Eighth Century* (1956), pp. 56-9; G. H. Verbist, *St Willibrord, apôtre des Pays-Bas* (1939); modern biographies by A. Grieve (1923), K. Heeringa (1940), and C. Wampach (1953). For a trans. of Alcuin's Life, see C. H. Talbot, *Anglo-Saxon Missionaries in Germany* (1954).

St Herculanus, *Bishop and Martyr* (547)

In 547 the Ostrogoths, who were resisting the attempts of the Byzantine emperor Justinian I (527-62) to regain Italy, took the city of Perugia, to which they had laid siege on and off for seven years. When they finally entered the city, their king, Totila, ordered that Herculanus, the local bishop, should have a strip of skin torn from the crown of his head to his heels, and then be beheaded. This was done, although the officer entrusted with the task had the humanity to cut off Herculanus' head before he flayed him. Christians hastily recovered both the head and the body, which had been thrown from the walls into the fosse, and gave them temporary burial. Forty days later they disinterred them in order to transfer them to the church of San Pietro, only to find, according to St Gregory the Great (3 Sept.), that the head was attached to the trunk, with no sign of separation. The only other detail of Herculanus' life that has survived is that when the Ostrogoths captured Tifernum (Città di Castello), a young deacon named Floridus took refuge in Perugia. While he was there Herculanus ordained him to the priesthood and he subsequently became bishop of Tifernum. The story of the miracle connected with Herculanus' remains and the frescoes by Benedetto Bonfigli in the Palazzo del Municipio have helped to perpetuate his memory.

The Perugians venerate another Herculanus, bishop of their city, who, they say, was a Syrian who went to Rome and was sent from there to evangelize Perugia. However, the Bollandists, who quote the notice from the *Dialogues* of Gregory the Great, hold that there was only one Herculanus connected with Perugia.

AA.SS., Nov., 3, p. 322.

St Florentius, *Bishop* (Seventh Century)

It is hard to say how much is known for certain about St Florentius. There is a twelfth-century Life, but this has been shown to be of no historical value, and it is not clear whether he died at the end of the seventh century or at the beginning of the eighth. He is said to have been an Irishman—though that, too, has been called in question—who travelled to Alsace and settled as a hermit in a valley at the foot of the Ringelberg. From here he went out to preach in the surrounding regions. He was also believed to have healed the blind daughter of the Frankish king, Dagobert (629-39), who, in gratitude, helped him to found a monastery at Haslach. When he was appointed bishop of Strasbourg in about 678, he was joined by many Irish and other monks. For these, he built a house outside the city walls and dedicated it to St Thomas the Apostle. It subsequently became a monastery under the Irish Rule and later a collegiate chapter of canons.

L. Duchesne, *Fastes Episcopaux*, 3, p. 171; M. Barth, *Der hl. Florentius von Strasbourg* (1952).

St Engelbert, *Bishop and Martyr* (*c.* 1186–1225)

During the Middle Ages it was not uncommon to find youths, and even children, being put forward for church benefices—sometimes more than one at a time. The story of St Engelbert, who probably owed his preferment to the fact that his father was the powerful count of Berg, provides a good illustration of this abuse. While still a boy at the cathedral school in Cologne, he became provost of St Mary's in Aachen, and of St George's, St Severinus', and the cathedral itself in Cologne. As he grew older his way of life did not match up to his obligations, and eventually he was excommunicated for taking up arms against the emperor Otto IV (1198–1218). He also joined the Crusade against the Albigensians (1209–29) for a while. Then, in 1217, when he was only about thirty years old, he skillfully played two rival claimants off one against the other and was consecrated bishop of Cologne.

At the time the diocese was in the throes of a serious political and ecclesiastical upheaval. However, Engelbert, who clearly possessed all the natural qualities needed for the task—commanding presence, strength of will, shrewd judgment, and a deeply-ingrained sense of justice—seems at last to have risen to the occasion. He welcomed both the Dominicans and the Friars Minor to the diocese and held synods to maintain discipline among the clergy, both secular and regular. The people liked his affable, peace-loving personality, and they appreciated his generosity to the poor as well as the firm but fair way in which he dealt with disputes. But he was not concerned with diocesan matters only—in fact, much, if not most, of his time was taken up with affairs of State.

As a trusted supporter of the Hohenstaufen emperor, Frederick II (1212–50), he was appointed regent when Frederick went to Sicily in 1220, leaving behind his ten-year-old son, Henry. The boy loved and respected Engelbert, who, two years later, in Aachen, crowned him king of the Romans. He carried out his duties as guardian with characteristic energy, but in this area the very qualities of vigour, determination, and concern for justice which made him popular in his diocese won him powerful enemies, especially among his own relations.

Sometime later, one of his cousins, Count Frederick of Isenburg, taking advantage of his position as administrator for a convent in Essen, stole the nuns' property and oppressed their vassals. Engelbert called him to order immediately and demanded that he make restitution. Frederick's response was to plot his cousin's murder. Engelbert was warned of the danger, and he did take precautions. But on 7 November 1225, needing to make a journey, he set out with an inadequate escort. At the Gevelsburg, he was attacked by Frederick and other aggrieved nobles, not to mention some fifty soldiers, who left him dead with forty-seven wounds in his body. The young King Henry brought Frederick to justice, and Engelbert was declared a martyr by the papal legate. Although he was never formally canonized—it is possible that his cult would never have arisen at all, had it not been for his violent death in defence of a religious house—his feast was instituted in Cologne, and he was listed in the Roman Martyrology.

The Life by Caesarius of Heisterbach is in *AA.SS.*, Nov., 3, pp. 644-81. See also A. Knipping (ed.) in the *Regesta* of the diocese of Cologne, 3 (1909). German biographies by J. Ficker (1853); H. Foerster (1925); J. Lothmann (1993).

Bd Helen of Arcella (*c.* 1208-42)

In about 1220 St Francis of Assisi (4 Oct.) went to Arcella, near Padua, to establish a convent of Poor Clares. While he was there he gave the habit to a young noble-woman, Elena Enselmini, who cannot have been much more than about twelve at the time. There is no contemporary Life, but it seems that six years later she contracted a painful disease, of which we know nothing except that she suffered from it for the rest of her life. She is said to have borne it with great patience and to have received a number of remarkable spiritual consolations. Toward the end of his own life St Anthony of Padua (13 June) was her spiritual guide. People who knew her also reported that she lived for several months on nothing but the Host. This may or may not be literally true; what is more than likely is that a diet verging on starvation, not uncommon in female saints of the period, exacerbated the blindness and deafness from which she eventually suffered and led to her death on 4 November 1242, at the early age of thirty-four. Some writers believe she died as early as 1230, but the generally accepted date is 1242.

Bartholomew of Pisa (*c.* 1385) in *De Conformitatibus*, 8; *AA.SS.,* Nov., 2, pp. 512-7, for a short biography by Sicco Polentono (1437). See also Léon, *Auréole Séraphique* (Eng. trans.), 4, pp. 36-8. On fasting saints, see Rudolph M. Bell, *Holy Anorexia* (1985); Walter Vandereycken, *From Fasting Saints to Anorexic Girls* (1994).

Bd Margaret Colonna (1280)

The earliest information we have about Margaret (Margherita) Colonna, daughter of Prince Odo Colonna (d. *c.*1256) comes from two sources: the Life written by Giovanni, the eldest of her four brothers, and another Life by a Poor Clare of San Silvestro. Both came out within about twelve years of her death. Margaret lost both her parents while she was still a child, and she grew up in the care of her brothers. When the time came for them to arrange a marriage for her, she refused to cooper-ate. Instead, she retired, with two attendants, to a villa in Palestrina, twenty-four miles east of Rome, where she put all her energy and everything she possessed into serving the sick and the poor.

Prevented by ill health from joining the Poor Clares at their house in Assisi, as she so longed to do, she decided to establish a convent of that order in Palestrina. She was helped in this by her brother Giacomo, who had by then been made a cardinal. (He is described on this account as her *dignior frater*, while Giovanni is referred to as her *senior frater*.) Giacomo obtained the necessary permission from the pope, and the new community was given the Rule of the Poor Clares as modified by Pope Urban IV (1261-4). However, owing to her continuing ill health, Margaret was unable either to join the community or to take an active part in its government. For the last seven years of her life, during which she acquired a reputation for miracles, she suffered from a painful cancer, which she faced with great courage and patience. She died when she was still young and was buried at Palestrina. Later, when the nuns moved from Palestrina to San Silvestro in Capite in Rome, they took the relics of their foundress with them. Some 700 years later, when the house at San Silvestro was turned into a general post office, the relics were moved again, this time to the community's new home at Santa Cecilia in Trastevere. The cult of Bd Margaret Colonna was confirmed by Pope Pius IX in 1847.

B. Mazzara, *Leggendario Francescano* (1680), 2, pt. 2, pp. 775-80; other Franciscan chroniclers. See also L. Oliger, *B. Margherita Colonna* (1935); Léon, *Auréole Séraphique*, 4 (Eng. trans.), pp. 170-3.

Bd Antony Baldinucci (1665-1717)

Antony (Antonio) was born in Florence in 1665 to Filippo Baldinucci, a painter and writer, and his wife, Caterina Scolari. Sometime earlier, Filippo, who already had four sons, had promised to dedicate his next son, should he have one, to St Antony of Padua (13 June), to whose intercession he attributed his cure from a serious illness. When a boy was duly born, he was brought up with the idea that he should become a priest. Far from driving him to do the opposite, as it would have done with most teenage boys, this, and the influence of St Aloysius Gonzaga (21 June), who had lived for a while in the Baldinucci house on via degli Angeli almost a century before, encouraged Antony to seek entry into the Society of Jesus when he was only sixteen.

Despite his somewhat precarious health, he was accepted. His hope that he might be sent abroad as a missionary was not fulfilled, however, and instead he found himself, during his early years as a Jesuit, teaching young men and giving instructions to Confraternities, first in Terni and then in Rome. Then his health started giving him trouble again: he experienced a series of seizures and bad headaches and was sent first to his native Florence and then to various Jesuit houses in the country. This did much to restore his health, and he was able to take up preaching, which he did with considerable success.

He was ordained to the priesthood in 1695, and after he had completed his tertianship he once again sought leave to go to the Indies. Again he was refused, being sent instead to Viterbo and Frascati, where he worked among the poor and uneducated for the remaining years of his life. The methods he adopted to secure their attention, which were modelled on those used by St Peter Claver (9 Sept.) with the black slaves in the New World and St Julian Maunoir (28 Jan.) amongst the Bretons, were nothing if not arresting. He organized processions of penitents in which each participant wore a crown of thorns and beat himself with a discipline; he himself would preach carrying a heavy cross or wearing chains, or else he would go about scourging himself violently in order to strike fear into people's hearts. Once the desired impression had been made and people gathered to listen to him, his approach became less extreme. Marshals were appointed to keep order among the crowds; these were often men of violent or dissolute character who were flattered to be chosen and in many cases mended their ways. In the course of his missions, which frequently ended with a public burning of cards, dice, obscene pictures, and so on, he was constantly confronted with the human misery that can result from violence and brutality, reckless gambling and sexual excess. But he also witnessed many genuine conversions and the organization of good works.

Despite the enormous pressure of his mission work (in twenty years he gave 448 missions in thirteen dioceses in Romagna and the Abruzzi), Antony found time to write down many of his sermons and instructions, and he kept up an extensive correspondence. One is not surprised to learn that he seldom slept for more than three hours a night, and that on a bed of planks; and he fasted for three days out of seven. Pope Clement XI dispensed him from the recitation of the divine office in view of all this activity, but he did not make use of the dispensation.

In 1708 the grand duke of Tuscany, Cosimo III de' Medici (1670–1723), called on him to preach throughout Lent in Livorno. Antony arrived barefooted, in a tattered cassock and carrying his luggage on his back. At first the gentry would not come to his sermons, but eventually he won them round, and after that there was always a major city in which he could be found preaching during Lent. In 1716 there was a serious famine in central Italy, and Antony, who was just over fifty at the time, worked indefatigably to bring people relief. But the strain of this effort in addition to his usual activities was too much for him, and he died on 7 November in the following year. He was beatified by Pope Leo XIII in 1893.

Biographies by F. M. Galluzzi (1720), P. Vannucci (1893), F. Goldie (1894, Eng.), L. Tognetti (1946); and Letters, ed. L. Rosa (1899). See also *D.H.G.E.*, 3, 756–60; *Bibl.SS.*, 722–3.

Bd Vincent Grossi, *Founder* (1845-1917)

Vincent (Vincenzo) Grossi was the youngest of the seven children of Baldassare Grossi and Maddalena Capellini. He was born and brought up at Pizzighettone, in the diocese of Cremona, and entered the diocesan seminary in 1864, when he was nineteen. After his ordination on 22 May 1869, he served successively as assistant priest in the parish of San Rocco, curate and spiritual director at Sesto Cremonese, spiritual director of Ca' de' Soresini, and parish priest in Regona Cremonese. Then, in 1883, he was sent as parish priest to Vicobellignano, where he was to remain for the rest of his life.

As a priest he devoted himself unremittingly to the care of his parishioners, inspiring them by his preaching and by the example of his life. He was a gifted teacher, and his most fruitful idea was to set up in each parish a group of young women who would help the parish priest with the moral and religious guidance of the girls of the parish. The idea caught on and led to the foundation of the Istituto Figlie dell'Oratorio (Institute of the Daughters of the Oratory). Vincent wrote the Rules and Constitutions, which were approved by the bishop of Cremona on 20 June 1901. On 20 May 1915 the new Congregation received provisional approval from the Sacred Congregation for Religious, and on 29 April 1926 it was defini- tively approved by the Holy See. It now has more than 400 religious in about seventy houses.

Vincent himself did not live long enough to know of the Holy See's approval. He died on 7 November 1917, greatly mourned by his parishioners and all who knew him and leaving behind him a reputation for genuine holiness. He was beatified by Pope Paul VI (1963-78) on 1 November 1975.

See Carlo Salvaderi, *Il Servo di Dio D. Vincenzo Grossi, Fondatore dell'Istituto Figlie dell'Oratorio* (1955).

Scotus Logo, designed by Michael Fisk, 1993.

8

BD JOHN DUNS SCOTUS, *Doctor* (*c.* 1265-1308)

The greatest English-speaking philosopher and theologian of his age was born, probably in late 1265 or early 1266, in Duns, a few miles west of Berwick-upon-Tweed, in Scotland. Little is known for certain about the early life of John of Duns, Scotus. There is one local tradition that he received some of his early education on North Uist, in the Western Isles, while according to another tradition he was educated by his paternal uncle at the Franciscan friary in Dumfries, then became a Franciscan himself when he was fifteen and went to study at Oxford. The first certain date is that of his ordination to the priesthood as a Franciscan on 17 March 1291, in Northampton.

After his ordination he went to study for a master's degree in theology in Paris, where he remained until 1296, though at this stage he does not seem to have completed the work required. In any case, by 1297 he was back in Oxford—and also Cambridge—lecturing on the *Sentences* of Peter Lombard, which he continued to do, revising his work continuously until 1301. In 1302 he returned to Paris, though he was forced to leave again in the following year when he refused to support the appeal of the French king, Philippe IV Le Bel (ruled 1285-1314) to a general council against Pope Boniface VIII (1294-1303). This was part of the smouldering dispute between the two that was essentially a power struggle and had to do with the relationship between Church and State. He was not away for long, however, and when he returned he brought with him a letter of recommendation from Gonsalvus Hispanus, who had been his teacher in Paris from 1293 to 1296 and was now minister general of the Order. In the letter, Gonsalvus referred to Scotus' "praiseworthy life" and his "most subtle genius"—he was later dubbed *doctor subtilis*. In 1305 Scotus at last obtained the coveted degree of *magister regens* from Paris University and spent the next two years lecturing there. Then, at the end of 1307, he publicly defended the view, controversial at the time, that the redemption had been applied in anticipation to Mary as mother of God—in other words, the doctrine of the Immaculate Conception. For his own safety, he was moved to the University of Cologne, where he lectured and defended Catholic orthodoxy against the Béghards and the Béguines (members of lay groups which began to form in the twelfth century and were regarded with suspicion by the ecclesiastical authorities) until he died there a year later, on 8 November 1308. We do not know the reason for his early death, but he was only forty-three.

Scotus was buried in the Franciscan church in Cologne—originally near the altar of the three kings and then, toward the end of the sixteenth century, in the position his tomb occupies today, in the middle of the choir, near the main altar. He was venerated immediately as a saint, and as a sign of continuing interest and veneration, in the course of the next six centuries his remains were verified on numerous occasions. Another sign of interest is the number of times over the centuries that Scotus has been represented in art, alone or in the company of other saints. In a portrait by Benozzo Gozzoli (1420-97) in the cloister of the Franciscan friary at Mönchengladbach, Germany, he is shown looking upward, as if listening intently to the source of his inspiration—a stance that is taken up in a modern statue by Tritschler in the leisure park at Duns; a painting attributed to Justus of Ghent, now in the ducal palace in Urbino, shows him with wonderfully eloquent hands and a look of concentration on his face. Gerard Manley Hopkins, in his sonnet "Duns Scotus's Oxford," describes him as "He ... who of all men most sways my spirit to peace." Proceedings for his beatification were held in Cologne in 1706, and in Nola, near Naples, in 1710 and again in 1905-6. On 8 February 1906 the bishop of Nola decreed that his cult was "from time immemorial," although at this stage it was confirmed for the Order of Friars Minor only. But on 20 March 1993, Pope John Paul II declared that he should be honoured with the title Blessed, not by the Franciscans only, but by the Universal Church.

Scotus was a scholar. His life as outlined above was hardly eventful; his great achievement lies in his teaching and his writings, which were to have such an influence on his successors. He was only about twelve when certain of the teachings of St Thomas Aquinas (25 Jan.) were condemned, in 1277, along with aspects of Averroist philosophy. Consciously or not, he set out to construct a new synthesis based on Avicenna, St Paul, St Augustine, and the great Franciscans Alexander of Hales and St Bonaventure. He had an outstandingly acute mind and was open enough to consider any opinion if it could assist him in his objective search for truth. His main concern, however, was to uphold the autonomy of theology. He relied on Avicenna, for example, for philosophy, but only insofar as Avicenna's teaching did not conflict with Christian teaching. The foundation of his philosophy is being as the primary object of the intellect. The foundation of his theology is love—God, the infinite Being's love for himself, God's love expressed in human beings and in the rest of creation, and the Incarnation as the means through which God can be loved adequately in return. From this flows everything else, and in particular his teaching about Mary—which earned him the additional title of *doctor Marianus*. Scotus was a true Franciscan in that he searched out and expressed in words the theological underpinning of the love of and joy in creation that St Francis (4 Oct.) lived so spontaneously and passed on so spontaneously to his followers.

Not all the works published by L. Wadding in the *Opera omnia* (1639) are authentic. The Scotus Commission is in the process of bringing out a definitive critical edition: *Opera omnia, studio et cura Commissionis scotisticae ad fidem codicum edita* (1950-). See G. Esser and G. D'Andrea, *Johannes Duns Scotus* (1986); B. de Saint-Maurice, *Jean Duns Scot. Un docteur des temps nouveaux* (1944; Eng. trans. C. Duffy, 1955); A. Marchesi, *Esperienza religiosa e riflessione filosofica* (1979); E. Gilson, *Jean Duns Scot. Introduction à ses positions fondamentales* (1952); C. Balic, "Quelques précisions fournies par la tradition manuscrite sur la vie, les oeuvres et l'attitude doctrinale de

Jean Duns Scot," in *Revue d'histoire ecclésiastique* 22 (1926), pp. 551-66; J. Bonnefoy, *Le Vénérable Jean Duns Scot. Docteur de l'Immaculée Conception* (1960). See also *N.C.E.*, 4, pp. 1102-6; *Bibl.SS.*, 6, 861-8.

The Four Crowned Martyrs (? 306)

The feast of the Four Crowned Martyrs used to be celebrated throughout the Church. But for reasons that were hinted at rather than spelled out, this was changed when the Roman Calendar was revised in 1969: "Although ancient, the commemoration of the Four Crowned Martyrs is left to individual calendars. There are many difficulties connected with the history of these martyrs, in honour of whom there is still a celebrated basilica on the Coelian Hill." There has certainly been disagreement about the identity of the Four Crowned Martyrs, or Four Holy Crowned Ones. Before 1969, the Roman Martyrology for this day read: "At Rome, three miles from the city, on the via Lavicana, the passion of the holy martyrs Claudius, Nicostratus, Symphorian, Castorius and Simplicius, who were first cast into prison, then terribly beaten with loaded whips, and finally, since they could not be turned from Christ's faith, thrown headlong into the river by order of Diocletian. Likewise on the via Lavicana the birthday of the four holy crowned brothers, namely, Severus, Severian, Carpophorus and Victorinus, who, under the same emperor, were beaten to death with blows from leaden scourges. Since their names, which in after years were made known by divine revelation, could not be discovered, it was appointed that their anniversary, together with that of the other five, should be kept under the name of the Four Holy Crowned Ones; and this has continued to be done in the Church, even after their names were revealed." The difficulty was that while the first group mentioned contained five names instead of four, the four names in the second—which the Roman Martyrology and the Breviary say were revealed as those of the Four Crowned Martyrs—were borrowed from the martyrology of the diocese of Albano, which keeps their feast on 8 August. And there is a further complication: the Four Crowned Martyrs are sometimes referred to as Claudius, Nicostratus, Symphorian, and Castorius, which—together with that of Simplicius—are the names, not of a group of Roman martyrs, but of a group of five who suffered under Diocletian in Pannonia (parts of modern Austria/Croatia/Bosnia). Although all this more than suggests that there were two groups of martyrs, the Bollandist Fr Delehaye, after extremely detailed research (with which the latest research tends to agree) took the view that there was only one, of Pannonian stonemasons, whose relics were subsequently transferred to Rome.

The legend is told in a conventional and unspecific Roman *passio* and in a much more vivid and detailed Pannonian account, in which, among other things, Diocletian emerges not as a one-dimensional monster, but as an unstable and complex character with a passion for building. According to the Pannonian account, while Diocletian was visiting the imperial quarries and workshops in Sirmium (modern Mitrovica), his attention was drawn to the work of five particularly skilled carvers, Claudius, Nicostratus, Simpronian, and Castorius, all of whom were Christians, and Simplicius, who had become a Christian because he thought the skill of the other four was due to their religion. Diocletian immediately ordered the men to execute a certain number of carvings. This they did, leaving out a statue of Aesculapius, the god of medicine and healing, which, they said (somewhat inconsistently, given that they had already made a statue of the sun god) they could not make on religious grounds. Diocletian was indulgent—"if their religion enables them to do such good work, all the better"—and Aesculapius was entrusted to other workmen.

The local people were less tolerant, however, and the five were thrown into prison for refusing to sacrifice to the gods. At first Diocletian and his officer, Lampadius, treated them leniently; but when Lampadius died suddenly, the Christians were blamed by his relatives, who persuaded the emperor to authorize their execution. Each was put in a leaden box and thrown into the river, from which the bodies were retrieved three weeks later.

The story is taken up in the Roman *passio*. In the following year Diocletian was in Rome, where he built a temple to Aesculapius in the baths of Trajan and ordered his troops to sacrifice to the god. Four *cornicularii* who refused were beaten to death with leaded scourges, and their bodies cast into a sewer. They were retrieved and buried on the via Lavicana by St Sebastian (20 Jan.) and Pope Miltiades, who, because their names had been forgotten, said they should be commemorated as Claudius, Nicostratus, Simpronian, and Castorius (which names also occur among the converts of Polycarp the priest, in the legend of St Sebastian).

A basilica was built on the Coelian hill in Rome, probably in the first half of the fifth century, and dedicated to the Four Crowned Ones (*Quatuor Coronati*). There are good reasons for believing that these were four of the Pannonian martyrs (why Simplicius was omitted is not clear), whose relics had been brought to Rome. One explanation for the double tradition is that, as their names and history became known, the fact that there were five instead of four became an embarrassment. The second *passio* was written to show that the *Quatuor Coronati* were four Roman soldiers, not five Pannonian stonemasons—a convenient fiction described by Fr Delehaye as "l'opprobre de l'hagiographie."

The Four Crowned Martyrs were popular from the start in England, and Bede (25 May) notes that as early as the seventh century there was a church dedicated to them in Canterbury. There most of the early churches are dedicated to Roman saints, perhaps because St Augustine (27 May) came from a monastery near the basilica in Rome and/or because their relics were among those sent from Rome in 601. They were particularly honoured by the medieval stonemasons' guilds. In the articles of one of these there is a section entitled *Ars quatuor coronatorum*, which tells the story "of these martyres fowre, that in this craft were of gret honoure," and points to the *Golden Legend* for further information. And the most scholarly journal of the English Freemasons is called *Ars Quatuor Coronatorum*. Representations of the legend of the Four Crowned Martyrs in art include an anonymous triptych in the Musée Municipal in Brussels and carvings by Nanni di Bianco (early fifteenth century) in the church of Orsanmichele in Florence.

H. Delehaye in *AA.SS.*, Nov., 3, pp. 748-84; *idem.*, "Le culte des Quatre Couronnés à Rome" in *Anal.Boll.* 32, pp. 63-71; *idem*, *Etude sur le légendier romain* (1936), pp. 65-73. See also *H.S.S.C.*, 2, pp. 238-46; J. Dubois in *Vies des Saints*, 11, p. 268; L. Duchesne, *Mélanges d'archéologie et d'histoire* 31 (1911), pp. 231-46; P. Franchi de' Cavalieri in *Studi e Testi* 24 (1912), pp. 57-66; J. P. Kirsch in *Historisches Jahrbuch* 38 (1917), pp. 72-97.

St Cybi, *Abbot* (Sixth Century)

As the founder and first abbot of the monastery at Holyhead, in Anglesey, Cybi is one of the most important of the Welsh saints whose feasts occur in November. Written sources of information about him are rather inadequate: there is a Latin Life, written sometime in the thirteenth century, but it is unreliable, not to say fanciful. A good deal, however, can be gleaned from the evidence of place-names, inscriptions, and local traditions.

Cybi is said to have been born in Cornwall, the son of Selyf. This tradition gains credence from the existence of old churches bearing his name in Duloe, Tregoney, and Landulph. According to the Life, he learned to read at seven (which was, of course, unusual enough in those days to arouse comment), went on pilgrimage to Jerusalem at twenty-seven, and then became a disciple of St Hilary, by whom he was consecrated bishop of Poitiers, where he stayed for fifty years. All of this is chronologically impossible, because apart from anything else, Hilary died in 449. (He has been woven into the lives of not a few Celtic saints because he was someone people had heard of.) Nor is there any reason to believe the Life when it says that Cybi spent four years in Ireland with St Enda.

What is much more likely is that he left Cornwall, perhaps because, as one tradition has it, he did not want to be king there, crossed by sea into Wales, and gradually made his way north until he reached Anglesey. There is a place called Llangybi on the Usk; another near the Teifi, about fifteen miles south of Aberystwyth; and a third north-east of Pwllheli on the Lleyn Peninsula. In a valley about a quarter of a mile from the parish church of the latter there is a well with a half-ruined cell nearby. The site is known as St Cybi's Well, and it could date back to his time. In the graveyard by the church there is a very ancient carved cross; and the well, which was used for baptism and healing, is an imposing early Christian monument.

Having arrived in Anglesey, possibly following a route which included these places (all of which are on or near the sea or a river, which suggests that he travelled by water), he crossed to what became known as Ynys Gybi, or Holy Island. There he founded a monastery, around which grew the town of Caer Gybi—or as it is better known, Holyhead. The legend that he was given the site by Maelgwyn, king of Gwynedd, may well be true; at all events, it is an almost unique example in Wales of a church built within the confines of a Roman fort (*caer* means fort). Using the monastery as his centre, Cybi went out with his monks to evangelize the people of the neighbourhood, and when he died there his shrine became a place of pilgrimage. An inscription on the gable of a fifteenth-century church in Holyhead,

Sancte Kebie, ora pro nobis, points to a thriving cult even after nine centuries. Throughout the Middle Ages the monastic community was represented by a college of secular canons.

G. H. Doble, *St Cuby* (Cornish Saints Series no. 22; 1929); A. W. Wade-Evans, *Vitae Sanctorum Britanniae* (1944); *ibid.*, *The Life of St David* (1923), pp. 98-100; E. G. Bowen, *Settlements of the Celtic Saints in Wales* (1954), pp. 118-20; *Bibl.SS.*, 4, 415-6.

St Deusdedit, *Pope* (618)

Pope Deusdedit, or Adeodatus I, was a Roman by birth, the son of a deacon called Stephen. He had already been a priest for forty years at the time of his election, when he was proposed as the candidate of the party opposed to the pro-monastic policies of Gregory I (590-604) and Boniface (608-15), and his pontificate lasted for only three years, from 615 to 618. As a priest, he "greatly loved the clergy": he showed concern for their welfare, instituted for them an evening office patterned on Matins, and tended to promote them rather than monks to positions within the Church. Throughout the period, which was plagued by war, civil unrest, and epidemic illness that included an outbreak of scab disease followed by an earthquake in the area, Deusdedit cared tirelessly for the poor, encouraging his poverty-stricken clergy to do the same. He is thought to have been the first pope to use leaden seals, or *bullae*, on his documents, which, by a process of transference, became known as papal Bulls: one Bull dating back to his own time still exists. On his deathbed he bequeathed to each of his clergy what is believed to have been the equivalent of a year's stipend. Pope Honorius I (625-38) described him as simple, wise, and devout. Although there are old Benedictine calendars which claim him as a Benedictine, there is no evidence to justify the claim.

See L. Duchesne, *Liber Pontificalis*, 1, pp. 319-20; H. K. Mann, *Lives of the Popes*, 1, pp. 280-93; *O.D.P.*, p. 69.

St Tysilio, *Abbot* (? Seventh Century)

Our knowledge of Tysilio is based on a Breton account of his life and on a few surviving Welsh references. According to the Life, he was the son of Brochwel Ysgythrog, prince of Powys, and his wife, Ardunn, cousin of St Asaph (11 May) and St Deinol (11 Sept.). As a young man he went off to be a monk under the abbot Gwyddfarch at Meifod, near Welshpool, and when his father sent for him to return he refused, fleeing instead to the greater security of what became known as Ynys Suliau in the Menai Strait. After seven years he went back to Meifod, where he is said to have found Gwyddfarch, despite his great age, contemplating a pilgrimage to Rome. Tysilio's alleged response to this may well be an indication of his character: "You want to see the churches and palaces there. Dream about them, instead of going all that way." He then took the old man on a walk over the mountains, tiring him out; the journey to Rome, he told him on their return, was much longer than the one they had just completed. The exhausted Gwyddfarch fell asleep and awoke satisfied, having dreamt of Rome and all its glories. When he died, Tysilio succeeded him as abbot.

Another story connected with his name raises the question of whether or not he is the St Suliau who is honoured in Brittany. According to this legend, when the prince of Powys, Tysilio's elder brother Iago, died, his widow, Haiarnwedd, tried unsuccessfully to persuade Tysilio to marry her and become prince. Taking the refusal as a personal insult, she drove him away from Meifod. He fled first to Builth Wells—where Prince Llewelyn would be betrayed to the English six centuries later—and then, with some of his monks, to Brittany. They landed at the mouth of the river Rance, made contact with St Malo (15 Nov.), and settled at a place that is still called Saint-Suliac. Eventually Haiarnwedd died, and a deputation came to bring Tysilio back to Meifod. Although he would not agree to go, he sent a book of the Gospels and his staff as a sign of good will. When he died he was buried in Brittany.

Despite the fact that the Breton saint was believed to have come from a Welsh background—a Breton Life makes a somewhat obvious attempt to combine elements from the lives of at least two people—the likelihood is that he and "the royal saint of Powys," as the twelfth-century poet Cynddelw called Tysilio, are two separate individuals. Meanwhile, there are several places in Wales that seem to have connections with Tysilio. Apart from Meifod and Ynys Suliau, these include Llandyssil, between Newtown and Welshpool, in Powys; Llandissilio, fifteen miles north of Tenby in Dyfed; and Llandysul, about eight miles east of Cardigan. All this suggests that he did not concentrate exclusively on Powys but travelled, possibly as a *peregrinus*, in other parts of the country. He is thought to have written a number of Welsh poems.

See *Myvyrian Archaiology of Wales*, 3 (1807); A. J. W. Wade-Evans, *Welsh Christian Origins* (1934), pp. 200-1; G. H. Doble, *St Sulian and St Tysilio* (1936), which supports the two-person theory.

St Willehad, *Bishop* (789)

Willehad was one of those Englishmen who, like St Boniface (5 June), St Willibrord (7 Nov.), and others, spent his life bringing the Christian faith to the peoples of north-western Europe. What we know of him is contained in a Latin Life written about eighty years after his death, allegedly by St Anskar (3 Feb.) but more probably by a member of the clergy in Bremen—though St Anskar seems to have been responsible for the book of miracles attached to it.

Willehad was born in Northumbria and educated in York, where he became a friend of Alcuin. Inspired by the missionary work of his predecessors, he went to Frisia in about 766, after his ordination to the priesthood. There he launched his own mission at Dokkum, where Boniface was killed in 754. Here he made a number of conversions before moving on to Overijssel and Humsterland. In Humsterland he narrowly escaped death when the local people drew lots to see if he and his companions should be killed. At this point he decided to return to Drenthe in the less hostile neighbourhood of Utrecht, where, despite the hard work and devotion of Willibrord, there were still plenty of potential converts. Unfortunately some of his fellow missionaries became rather overzealous, demolishing places dedicated to idols. According to one account, the people, angered by this, determined to massacre them. Willehad would have been killed by a sword blow, had not a string round his neck, which supported a little box of relics, saved him. (All of which sounds suspiciously similar to the incident involving St Willibrord on the island of Walcheren.)

Seeing that he was not making a great deal of progress among the Frisians, Willehad went to Aix-la-Chapelle (Aachen) to obtain authorization for a new mission from the Frankish king, Charlemagne (768-814). In 780, asked by Charlemagne to evangelize the recently-subdued Saxons, he set off for the region where Bremen now stands. He was the first missionary to cross the river Weser, and some of his companions travelled even further east, beyond the Elbe. All went relatively well until 782, when the Saxons, led by their king, Widukind, rose up in rebellion against the Franks.

During the bloody conflict that followed, any missionaries who fell into the hands of the Saxons were killed, but Willehad himself managed to escape by sea into Frisia. Taking advantage of this suspension of his missionary activities, he went first to Rome to report to Pope Adrian I (772-95) and then, on his way back, to St Willibrord's monastery at Echternach. Here he spent two years assembling his fellow-missionaries, who had been scattered by the war, and transcribing the letters of St Paul. In 785, when Widukind and Charlemagne finally made peace, he returned to his mission in the region between the Weser and the Elbe. The methods used by Charlemagne in his dealings with the Saxons did not make his work any easier, but he managed to found a number of churches, and in 787 Charlemagne had him ordained bishop of the Saxons. He established his see at Bremen, which seems to have been founded at about this time, and built his cathedral church of wood, consecrating it on 1 November 789 in honour of St Peter. A few days later he was taken ill, and one of his companions, seeing how serious his condition was, begged him not to abandon his flock so soon. But Willehad replied: "Do not prevent me from going to God. My sheep I recommend to him who entrusted them to me, and whose mercy is able to protect them." And so he died, the last of the great eighth-century English missionaries, and his successor buried his body in the new stone church which was built in Bremen.

The Latin Life, together with the book of miracles are in *AA.SS.*, Nov., 3, pp. 835-51. See also L. Halphen, *Etudes critiques sur l'histoire de Charlemagne* (1921); H. Timerding, *Die christliche Frühzeit Deutschlands*, 2 (1929); W. Levison, *England and the Continent in the Eighth Century* (1946).

St Godfrey of Amiens, *Bishop* (1115)

The most reliable source of information about Godfrey (Godefroi) is the autobiography of Guibert de Nogent, the Benedictine historian of the Crusades (1053-*c.* 1130). There is a more detailed Latin Life, compiled in about 1138 by one Nicholas, a monk from Soissons; but this, while valuable in many ways, is quite uncritical in its approach, and certain of its statements are demonstrably incorrect. The date of Godfrey's birth is not known, but when he was only five he was entrusted to the care of the abbot at Mont-St-Quentin. Not surprisingly, he became a monk. He was ordained to the priesthood and later appointed abbot of the Benedictine monastery at Nogent, in Champagne. At the time he took office there was only a handful of monks in the community, and the fabric of the place, like their discipline, was sadly neglected. Godfrey soon turned things round, and the monastery began to flourish again—so much so that the archbishop of Reims and his council urged him to take over the government of the great abbey of Saint-Rémi. His response was uncompromising: there were canonical reasons, he declared, against such a move, and anyway, "God forbid that I should ever desert a poor bride by preferring a rich one!"—words quoted later by St Francis de Sales when he was asked by the French king, Henri IV, to leave Geneva for Paris.

When, in 1104, Godfrey was nevertheless appointed bishop of Amiens, he refused to allow this to affect his way of life. Never forgetting that he was a monk, he lived very simply, and if he thought his cook was treating him too well he would take the best food from the kitchen and give it away to the poor and the sick. But his manner of government, although unquestionably just, could be severe and even harsh. One Christmas, for example, while celebrating Mass for the Comte d'Artois at St-Omer, he refused to accept the offerings of the court until the nobles had modified their dress and behaviour. On another occasion the abbess of St-Michel at Doullens had to walk the eighteen miles to Amiens so that he could rebuke her for ill-treating one of the nuns. She spent the day looking for the nun, whom she was led to believe had gone missing but whom Godefroi had in fact concealed in his own house, and then had to walk back to Doullens. The claim of his see to jurisdiction over the monastery of St-Valéry was vigorously disputed by the monks there, who no doubt feared their discipline would be toughened up, and they even refused to let him bless their altar linen. Within his diocese he had to struggle constantly against simony and disregard of the celibacy law among his clergy, and once, in this connection, a disgruntled woman is said to have made an attempt on his life. This inflexibility, sometimes carried to extremes, as when he forbade the eating of meat on Sundays in Lent, made him unpopular among those less given to austerity. He became discouraged and, wishing to to resign and join the Carthusians, set out, in November 1115, to discuss the matter with his metropolitan. He died on the way, at Soissons, where he was buried.

For the Latin Life and passages from Guibert's autobiography see A. Poncelet (ed.) in *AA.SS.*, Nov., 3, pp. 902-44. See also A. de Calonne, *Histoire de la ville d'Amiens* (1899), 1, pp. 123-42; C. Brunel in *Le moyen âge*, 22 (1909), pp. 176-196; J. Corblet, *Hagiographie d'Amiens* (1870), 2, pp. 373-445.

Bd Elizabeth of the Trinity (1880-1906)

Elizabeth Catez was born at Avor military camp near Bourges on 18 July 1880. The family lived for a while in Auxonne, then moved to Dijon, where, on 2 October 1887, M. Catez died. As a child, Elizabeth was lively, impetuous, intense, and difficult—her sister Marguerite described her at one stage as a "little devil." But her First Communion, on 19 April 1891, without altering her personality, had a profound effect on her. This was reinforced by the sacrament of Confirmation, which she received on 18 June of the same year. Young as she was, she began to be aware of a call to interior silence and recollection and of the gift of contemplative prayer, which would eventually overtake her completely. But in the meanwhile her childhood and adolescence continued. Although she had no real schooling, two governesses gave her the rudiments of knowledge, including a cursory introduction to literature. And her considerable musical gift was developed: she studied the piano at the conservatory in Dijon, carrying off several prizes for performance, and found in music a satisfying form of self-expression and prayer.

When she was about fourteen, she felt, as she put it, "irresistibly moved" to choose Christ as her spouse: "Without hesitation, I bound myself to him by a vow of virginity." And soon her one ambition was to enter Carmel. Her widowed mother, who, apart from anything else, had hoped to receive some support from Elizabeth's musical activity, forbade the girl to have any contact with the Dijon Carmel. She began to introduce eligible young men, whom Elizabeth ignored. While obeying her mother's order about the Dijon Carmel, she made it clear that her intention was unchanged. Finally, in 1899, Mme Catez relented, on condition that Elizabeth wait until she was twenty-one. Elizabeth accepted this cheerfully, and for the next two years carried on her life as usual. She catechized children in the parish, concerned herself with the needs of the poor, and attended the dances and other social functions to which her ever-hopeful mother took her—conscious all the while of the presence of the Trinity within her. "Even in the midst of the world," she wrote, "one can listen to God in the silence of a heart that wants only to be his."

Elizabeth entered the Dijon Carmel on 2 August 1901, and her religious life began full of hope and promise. But on 1 July 1903, seven months after she made her vows, she showed the first symptoms of what was later diagnosed as Addison's disease, a rare condition caused by under-functioning of the adrenal glands, for which at the time there was no known treatment. Elizabeth welcomed this new situation with her characteristic serenity, noting how fitting it was to "conform oneself to the Crucified in love," and the next two years passed peacefully. Then, in the summer of 1906, her condition suddenly worsened. On 21 November 1904 she had offered herself spontaneously as a "prey" to the Trinity, and now it seemed to her that she had been taken at her word. In obedience to her prioress, she recorded her thoughts at this time in two notebooks, which were published later.

Her illness gradually consumed her. She wrote to her mother: "The Father has predestined me to be conformed to his crucified Son. My Spouse wishes me to be the surrogate human being in whom he can suffer again for the glory of the Father and the salvation of the Church. This thought makes me so happy." She spoke a great deal about joy, and in fact, the more she suffered physically, the more she seemed to possess in faith the eternal joy for which she hoped. Toward the end, spiritual pain, including feelings of desolation and abandonment and thoughts of suicide, accompanied the physical pain, which by now was excruciating. By the beginning of November 1906 it was obvious that she had not long to live. On the 1st, she exclaimed: "Everything passes. In the evening of life, nothing remains but love. Everything must be done for love." She lingered for eight days, in the course of which she was heard to murmur: "I am going to the light, to love, to life." She died during the morning of 9 November 1906.

Apart from the two collections of notes transcribed in obedience to her prioress and a substantial number of letters, Elizabeth left little in writing. She did not see herself as a teacher, and in a very real sense her life was her teaching. She summed up her vision in a letter to a friend in 1902: "We carry our heaven within ourselves, because he who satisfies the saints with the light of vision gives himself to us in faith and in mystery. It's the same thing. I feel I have found heaven on earth, because heaven is God and God is in my soul. The day I understood this a light went on inside me, and I want to whisper this secret to all those I love, so that they too, in whatever circumstances, will cling increasingly to God." Elizabeth was beatified by Pope John Paul II on 25 November 1984.

For Bd Elizabeth's writings, see M-M. Philipon (ed.), *Ecrits spirituels: lettres, retraites, inédits* (1949); *Scritti* (1967); *Obras Completas* (1969); *J'ai trouvé Dieu* (3 vols., 1979-80); J. Moorcroft (ed., trans.), *Make me your heaven* (1986—letters) Benedictines of Stanbrook, *The "Praise of Glory": Reminiscences …* (1913). Biographies and studies of her teaching by A. M. Allchin and A. Macdonald (1992); J. Moorcroft (1984); M-D. Poinsenet (1969); C. De Meester (1980); M-M. Philipon (1939, 1966); H. Urs von Balthasar (1952); R. Moretti (1984).

9

St Benen, *Bishop* (467)

The extant Life of St Benen (from the Latin Benignus) is a panegyric rather than a biography. Written in Irish, it consists mainly of extravagant miracles interspersed with fragments of verse and is consequently not very informative on its own. There are other documents, however, relating mainly to St Patrick (17 Mar.), with the help of which it is possible to piece together the facts of Benen's life.

He was born in Meath, the son of a chieftain named Sescnéan, and may have been present as a young boy in about 433, when Patrick celebrated Easter for the first time in Ireland. There are several versions of his first real meeting with Patrick: according to the most famous, when Patrick spent a few days at the family's house, Benen was so impressed by what he had to say that he scattered flowers over the visitor as he slept. When the time came for him to leave, Benen begged him to take him along. All versions are agreed that at some point Benen asked to go with Patrick, that Patrick agreed to take him, and that it was Patrick who chose his baptismal name on account of his gentleness and his attractive disposition. Benen, who was also known for his good singing voice (being referred to as "Patrick's psalmodist"), became the older man's closest disciple and eventually his successor. The first evangelization of Clare and Kerry is attributed to Benen, who went from there to Connaught. He is also said to have had charge for twenty years of a church Patrick founded at Drumlease in Kilmore.

According to William of Malmesbury, in 460 Benen resigned his office and went to Glastonbury. There he met Patrick, who sent him off to live as a hermit, telling him to build his cell wherever his staff fell and burst into leaf and bud. This happened at a swampy place called Feringmere. Here Benen died and was buried, until 1091, when his relics were moved to Glastonbury Abbey. It is possible that someone's relics were moved on this occasion, but there is no truth at all in the legend that associates Patrick and Benen personally with Glastonbury.

For a serious attempt to deal with the inconsistencies, see P. Grosjean in *AA.SS.*, Nov., 4, pp. 145-88. For references to St Benen in documents relating to St Patrick, see W. Stokes (ed.), *The Tripartite Life of Patrick* (1887). On the Glastonbury hypothesis, see J. A. Robinson, *Two Glastonbury Legends* (1926). See also P. Grosjean, "An Early Fragment on St Patrick . . . in the Life of St Benen," in *Seanchas Ardmhacha*, 1, no. 1 (Armagh, 1954), pp. 31-44; J. F. Kenney, *The Sources for the Early History of Ireland* (1929), pp. 330-51; *Bibl.SS.*, 2, 1226-31.

St Vitonus, *Bishop* (*c.* 525)

Almost all the details we have about the life of Vitonus (or Vanne) belong to the realm of legend. There is a Latin Life, but it was written about 500 years after his death. Mabillon, who mentions it in the *Acta Sanctorum O.S.B.*, does not regard it as worth printing, although he does publish a short list of miracles worked at the shrine.

The basic facts seem to be that Firminus, bishop of Verdun, died while Verdun was under siege from the Frankish king, Clovis (481-511). When Clovis finally took the city, he nominated an old priest named Euspicius to the vacant see. Euspicius, who wanted to become a monk, refused to take up the appointment but put forward the name of his nephew Vitonus, whom Clovis accepted as an alternative. Vitonus's episcopate lasted for over twenty-five years, during which he is said to have brought into the Church those within his diocese who remained unconverted. He died in about 525 and was buried in the church of SS Pierre et Paul outside the walls of the city.

Vitonus is chiefly remembered today for the Congregation of Benedictines which bore his name. He is believed to have founded a college for clergy outside the walls of Verdun, the buildings of which were handed over in 952 to some Benedictine monks who re-dedicated them in his honour as the Abbaye de St-Vanne. In 1600, the prior of St-Vanne, Dom Didier de la Tour, initiated a thorough-going reform of the monastery, which became, with Moyenmoutier, the centre of a group of reformed houses in Lorraine, Champagne, and Bourgogne. In 1604, these united officially as a new Congregation, *de St-Vanne et St Hydulphe;* then, fourteen years later, a number withdrew to form the Congregation of St-Maur. Both were suppressed at the Revolution, but were nominally revived (with Cluny) in 1837 to form the new Congregation of Solesmes. St Vitonus' feast is celebrated by that Congregation as well as in Verdun.

AA.SS. O.S.B., 6, pt. 1, 496-500; L. Duchesne, *Fastes Episcopaux*, 3, p. 70. On Moyenmoutier and its reform, see *Gallia Christiana*, 13, 1165ff.; L. Jérôme, *L'Abbaye de Moyenmoutier* (1902).

St Radbod, *Bishop* (*c.* 850-917)

This Radbod was the great-grandson of Radbod, the last king of the Frisians, who is alleged to have said that he would prefer hell with his ancestors to heaven without them. Little is known about him, and the Life that was written shortly after his death is inadequate as biography. However, we do know that he belonged to the nobility and that his father was a Frank and his mother a Frisian. He received his early education at the cathedral school in Cologne, where his maternal uncle, Gunther, was the local bishop, and he became a monk when he was about thirty. In 899 or 900, "having been taken, though unworthy, into the company of the ministers of the church of Utrecht," he was chosen to be bishop of the church there. After his consecration he continued to live as a monk (all his predecessors had been monks), became a vegetarian, and fasted frequently. He managed to continue his studies, in spite of a prodigiously demanding pastoral and administrative programme that made him known in particular for his practical concern for the poor. Radbod also wrote hymns, some of which are still extant, including an office of St Martin (11 Nov.) and a hymn in honour of St Swithbert (1 Mar.). During one of the Danish invasions he moved his see to Deventer, where he died peacefully on 9 November 917.

M.G.H., Scriptores, 15, pp. 569-71; *P.L.*, 132; *M.G.H., Poetae Latini*, 4, pp. 160-73. See also Helen Waddell, *Mediaeval Latin Lyrics* (1935), pp. 130-5.

Bd Louis Morbioli (1433-85)

Most of what we know of Bd Louis comes from a metrical Life, written between 1485 and 1489 by a Carmelite friar, Baptista Mantuanus, who lived for many years in Bologna. Although the chronology is thought to be not entirely reliable, the author avoids poetic licence and relies entirely on his own knowledge or that of eyewitnesses.

Louis (Luigi) Morbioli, who was born in 1433, was one of five sons and one daughter of a middle-class couple, Francesco Antonio and Agnese Morbioli. As a young man, he was good-looking and generally out to have a good time. When still young he married Lucia di Giovanni Tora, but instead of settling down continued to pursue his rather frivolous lifestyle. However, in 1462, he was staying at the monastery of the Canons Regular of San Salvatore in Venice when he was taken seriously ill. This threat to his life, coupled with the kindly advice of his hosts, brought about a complete change in him. He returned to Bologna in 1470, and the transformation was immediately obvious to his friends. It was reflected, for example, in his outward appearance: instead of keeping up with current fashion, he wore the same light, plain garments summer and winter, and he no longer curled or dressed his hair. His wife, no doubt surprised by the sudden change in her husband, agreed to a separation once he had made provision for her. From then on, ignoring the ridicule of his former friends and associates, Louis began to go from place to place preaching repentance. He would also beg alms for the poor and give instruction in the Christian faith, particularly to the young. He liked to spend what moments of leisure he had carving images in bone or wood.

During the last years of his life Louis lodged under the stairs in a large house in Bologna. When he contracted what turned out to be his final illness, he resolutely refused to consult a doctor, asking instead for the sacraments. These he received with great devotion and died on 9 November 1485. He was buried in the cemetery of the cathedral in Bologna, but so many miracles were attributed to his intercession that his body was soon moved into the cathedral. Unfortunately his grave was lost during some rebuilding works that took place during the sixteenth century, and it has never been recovered. This did nothing to interrupt his cult, which was confirmed by Pope Gregory XVI (1831-46) in 1843 for Bologna and the Carmelite Order. The Carmelites claim that, after his conversion, Louis became a member of their Third Order. The habit he wore was similar to that of Carmelite tertiaries, but there is no firm evidence that he actually became a member.

The metrical Life is in *AA.SS.*, Nov., 4, pp. 288-97. See also *Anal. Juris Pontificii*, 19, pp. 1043ff.; R. McCaffrey, *The White Friars* (1926), pp. 62-3.

Bd Gratia of Cattaro (1508)

The earliest accounts of Gratia's life were not compiled until more than a century after his death, though they all seem to go back to a common earlier source. According to tradition he was a native of Cattaro (Kotor), on the Dalmatian coast, and made his living as a fisherman. One day, when he was thirty, he happened to walk into a church in Venice while an Augustinian friar, Simone da Camerino, was preaching. Deeply impressed by what he heard, he determined to enter the Augustinian Order himself. He applied and was accepted as a lay brother at Monte Ortono, near Padua. Here he worked in the gardens and soon earned the respect and veneration of the entire community. Later he was transferred to the friary of San Cristoforo in Venice, where it was said that a mysterious light shone above his cell and that miracles took place at his intercession. It was claimed, for example, that when, during an exceptionally dry summer, the friary church was undergoing repairs in which he was involved, a cistern was unfailingly supplied with water, which remained fresh even when sea water got into it. When he was about seventy, Gratia was taken seriously ill, and he died on 9 November 1508. His cult was confirmed in 1889, and his feast is celebrated by the Augustinians.

AA.SS., Nov., 4, pp. 297-304. Lives by S. Lazarini (1643, Italian); Eliseus Polonius (1677, Latin). For more recent Lives, see N. Mattioli (1890); I. Matovic (1910, Serbo-Croat).

Bd George Napper, *Martyr* (1550-1610)

George Napper (or Napier), whose mother was a niece of Cardinal William Peto, was born at Holywell Manor in Oxford in 1550. In 1565 he became a student at Corpus Christi College, Oxford, but was expelled three years later as a recusant. We next hear of him at the end of 1580, when, still a recusant, he was imprisoned. He obtained his release after nearly nine years by recognizing the royal supremacy, but he soon regretted this weakness and went off to join the English College at Douai, where he was ordained in 1596. He was finally sent on the English mission in 1603 and spent the next seven years working in Oxfordshire. Then, in the early morning of 19 July 1610, he was arrested in the fields at Kirtlington, a small village outside Oxford. Although those who searched him failed to discover a pyx containing two consecrated hosts and a small reliquary, both of which he had on him at the time, they did find his Breviary and the holy oils he carried. These were evidence enough to secure his condemnation as a priest at the next assizes.

Napper's friends managed to obtain a stay of execution, and it is likely that he would have been reprieved altogether but for the fact that while he was still in prison he ministered to a condemned criminal, who died declaring himself to be a Catholic. According to a fellow-inmate in Oxford prison, one of whose surviving letters describes what happened to Napper, "the people stormed; the ministers threw all the blame upon the condemned priest, made a heavy rout, called for justice, and went straightway to Abingdon to make complaint to the judges." Under cross-examination, Napper admitted that he had reconciled the man, and offered "to do as much for their lordships." Once again he was reprieved, but when he refused to take the oath of allegiance in the form which described the pope's deposing power as "impious, heretical and damnable," he was condemned to death. His execution took place in Oxford on 9 November 1610, and he died praying publicly for King James I. The same fellow-prisoner wrote of him: "His charity was great, for if any poor prisoner wanted either meat to fill him or clothes to cover him he would rather be cold himself than they should." He added that, while on the mission, Napper was "remarkably laborious in gaining souls for God."

M.M.P., pp. 307-17. See also *N.C.E.*, 9, pp. 319-32; Stapleton, *Oxfordshire Missions*; E. I. Watkin, *Roman Catholicism in England* (1957).

ST LEO THE GREAT
*Physical courage and pastoral care. Silver and gold mitre,
pick with gold head and silver handle,
on blue field.*

10

ST LEO THE GREAT, *Pope* (461)

Leo is the first of only three popes—the others being St Gregory I (590-604; 3 Sept.) and St Nicholas I (858-67; 13 Nov.)—who have earned the title "Great." No details of his early life have survived, but it seems likely that he was born in Rome of Tuscan parents, probably at the end of the fourth century. As a young man he was ordained at least to the diaconate and made a name for himself as a papal adviser during the pontificates of Celestine I (422-32) and Sixtus III (432-40). He also corresponded during this period with St Cyril of Alexandria (27 June), who was opposing the idea that Jerusalem be made a patriarchate and had asked for his support. He persuaded John Cassian to write the treatise *De Incarnatione Domini contra Nestorium*, which Cassian then dedicated to him. He was then sent to Gaul to mediate between Albinus, governor of the region and prefect of the Praetorian Guard, and the commander-in-chief, Aetius, whose quarrel threatened to jeopardize Gaul's defence against the barbarians. It was in 440, while he was in Gaul on this last mission, that messengers arrived to tell him he had been elected Bishop of Rome.

Described by one of his biographers as a man of boundless energy with a large heart and a strong sense of duty, Leo strove throughout his pontificate to enhance the prestige and influence of the see of Rome. He was the first to crystallize and formulate the belief that the Bishop of Rome is the heir of Peter and that his Christ-given authority is supreme and universal. This conviction that the pope is "the primate of all the bishops" is evident in his writings as well as in his actions and is of the greatest significance for the history of the papacy. He returned constantly to the theme in his sermons. The 143 letters that survive reveal his concern for the Church not only in Rome and Italy but in Africa, Gaul, and Spain, where he was anxious to ensure uniformity of practice and to assert the orthodox teaching against Pelagianism, Priscillianism, and Manicheism. He was particularly severe about the latter and even persuaded the government to reintroduce legislation against its adherents.

Leo was particularly insistent that all other bishops had right of appeal to the Bishop of Rome over their metropolitans. Indeed, he twice found it necessary to reprove Hilary, bishop of Arles (5 May), when Hilary overstepped his authority as metropolitan and behaved as though his see were somehow independent of Rome. But he also defended the rights of metropolitans, as when his representative in Illyricum (south-east Balkan peninsula) went over the heads of the local metropolitans, as though he had full papal power.

In one respect, at least, the highlight of Leo's pontificate was the Council of

Chalcedon, convened to counter the Monophysite heresy, which taught that there is only one nature in Christ. In 448 Bishop Flavian of Constantinople dismissed a monk named Eutyches on the grounds that he was spreading this heretical doctrine. Eutyches appealed to Leo, who understood immediately where this teaching would lead. He sent Flavian a letter (the so-called Tome of Leo) in which he had set out, clearly and elegantly, the orthodox teaching on the Incarnation: Jesus Christ is one person in whom two natures, divine and human, are united, "without confusion or admixture." When a council called by the emperor Theodosius II (408-50) at Ephesus in 449 rejected the Tome and reinstated Eutyches, Leo dismissed it as a *latrocinium*—a den of thieves—and spearheaded the move to hold a new council. This took place at Chalcedon (now Kadikoy), on the Bosphorus, in 451. There were 600 bishops present, all of them from the East, apart from two who came from Africa. The three papal legates, also Westerners, were given a place of honour and invited to read out the Tome. When they had finished, the reaction of those present was summed up: "This is the faith of the fathers; this is the faith of the apostles. We ourselves believe this, those whose faith is true believe this. Let anyone who believes otherwise be anathema! Peter has spoken through the mouth of Leo." The letter was adopted as the teaching of the Church.

In another important matter, however, the advice of the papal legates was ignored. Arguing that Constantinople, like Rome, was an imperial city, the council made it a patriarchate, thus enhancing its status and sowing the seeds of future trouble. Once again Leo had the foresight to realize where this would lead, because he understood that the primacy of the Bishop of Rome has nothing to do with Rome as a place but comes from the apostolic succession. Although he withheld his approval of the council proceedings until March 453 and even then refused to endorse the canon relating to the new patriarchate, the deed was done.

Leo's influence extended also to the political sphere. In 452, when Attila the Hun, who had already sacked Milan, started to march on Rome, Leo went out to meet him at the confluence of the Mincio and the Po, near Mantua, and persuaded him not to sack the city but to accept tribute instead. He showed equal courage but was less successful when he tried the same tactic with Gaiseric the Vandal three years later. Rome was plundered on this occasion, and many people were taken captive to northern Africa. Having failed to save the city, Leo sent priests and financial assistance to the captives. The period was altogether a difficult one, as Rome moved toward what would be the break-up of its empire, and the Church itself was troubled by internal problems, such as an ill-educated clergy and heresy in many forms. But Leo managed to remain positive, restoring basilicas, including St Peter's, building new churches, organizing relief in time of famine, and putting his theological knowledge to practical use in his sermons. He profoundly believed in the reality of incarnation as expressed at Chalcedon, with all its implications, and he was concerned, through his preaching, to educate clergy and people in this faith.

Leo's writings are remarkable for their clear, concise, and well-modulated style. In addition to the letters already mentioned, they include almost 100 sermons and possibly a handful of the collects in the Leonine Sacramentary, though most of these are thought to be inspired by his thought rather than written by him. He was most concerned to promote sound liturgical practice, but the Sacramentary itself dates from the sixth or seventh century.

Leo died on 10 November 461. His feast was originally celebrated on 11 April, following the *Liber Pontificalis*, or 28 June in the Sarum calendar; in the West it has now gone back to his *dies natalis*. In 1754 Benedict XIV declared him a doctor of the Church, more for the brilliance with which he formulated the accepted teaching of the Church than for original theological thinking.

AA.SS., Apr., 2, pp. 14–22; *C.M.H.*, pp. 183, 593–4; L. Duchesne, *Liber Pontificalis*, 1, p. 239. See also A. Régnier, *Saint Léon le Grand* (1910); T. G. Jalland, *The Life and Times of St Leo the Great* (1941); S. Brezzi, *S. Leone Magno* (1947); P. Stockmeier, *Leo der Grosse* (1959); W. Ullmann, "Leo I and the Theme of Papal Primacy" in *J.T.S.* 11 (1960), pp. 25–51. Leo's works are in *P.L.*, 54–6 (ed. Ballerini, 1753–7); C. Feltoe, Eng. trans. of letters (1896); R. Dolle, French trans. of sermons (*S.C.*, 1947 ff.). See also E. Dekkers, "Autour de l'oeuvre liturgique de S. Léon le Grand" in *Sacris Eruditi* 10 (1958), pp. 363–98; H. Arens, *Der Christologische Sprache Leos des Grossen* (1982); D. M. Hope, *The Leonine Sacramentary* (1971); *H.S.S.C.*, 3, pp. 209–12; *Bibl.SS.*, 7, 1232–80; *O.D.P.*, pp. 43–5; *N.C.E.*, 8, pp. 637–9.

St Aedh, *Bishop* (589)

No Irish Life of St Aedh (Áed in Irish) has been preserved. However, there are three Lives in Latin, two of them derived from the first, which was written in the eighth or ninth century. From them, we learn that he was the son of Brecc of Clann Cholmáin, a branch of the southern Uí Néill, and that at his birth, said to have been accompanied by marvels, a stranger predicted that he would be great in the eyes of God. At the time, boys not destined by their parents or others for the priesthood or the monastic life received no education, so Aedh spent his childhood and youth working on his father's land. According to the legend, when Brecc died, Aedh's brothers tried to deprive him of his share of the inheritance, but Aedh was persuaded by St Illand, bishop of Rathlihen, in Offaly, to abandon his claim. Aedh remained with Illand, who eventually sent him to establish a monastery in his own district. Aedh's chief settlement was at Cell air, in West Meath, but he was active over a wide area.

Many miracles were attributed to Aedh, some of them rather extravagant. One story, very similar to another told later about St Odo of Cluny (18 Nov.), is interesting as an illustration of the way people at the time looked for supernatural explanations for events they could not understand or explain in natural terms. Aedh, the story goes, saw a young woman washing her hair after Vespers on Saturday (that is, when Sunday, liturgically speaking, had begun); at his word it all fell out, only growing in again after she repented of doing servile work on the Lord's day. When Aedh died, St Columba (9 June), miles away on Iona, is said to have been aware that this had happened and passed the news on to his brethren.

For the original Life, see W. W. Heist (ed.), *Codex Salmanticensis* (1965), pp. 167–81. See also R. Sharpe, *Medieval Irish Saints' Lives* (1991); *V.S.H.*, 1, pp. 26–8; D. Pochin Mould, *The Irish Saints* (1964).

St Justus, *Bishop* (627)

We know nothing of Justus' early life. But in 601, when Pope Gregory the Great (3 Sept.) sent a new band of missionaries from Rome to help St Augustine (27 May) in England, he was among their number. In 604 he was consecrated the first bishop of Rochester: King Ethelbert of Kent (560-616) had built a church there and dedicated it to St Andrew, from whose church on the Coelian hill the Roman missionaries had set out. After the death of Augustine in 605, Justus joined with St Laurence (3 Feb.), Augustine's successor at Canterbury, and the bishop of London, St Mellitus (24 Apr.), in sending the Irish bishops and abbots a letter inviting them to conform some of their ecclesiastical usages to those of Rome. A similar letter was sent to the clergy of the Christian Britons, provoking Bede's tart observation that "what was gained by so doing the present times still declare."

After Ethelbert's death in 616 there was a pagan revival in Kent, and also among the East Saxons. Realizing that there was not much good they could do, given that they did not have the support of the new king of Kent, Ethelbert's son Edbald, the three bishops decided to withdraw for a while. Justus and Mellitus went over to Gaul. After less than a year, however, Laurence sent word that Edbald had been converted, and he asked the two men to return. This they did, and as a result of their efforts Christianity began to spread more rapidly.

In 624 Justus succeeded Mellitus (who as archbishop of Canterbury had succeeded Laurence), and soon after this Pope Boniface V (619–25) sent Justus the *pallium* and a letter delegating to him the power to consecrate bishops in England. Justus clearly deserved the trust placed in him, and in his letter Boniface refers to "the perfection which your work has obtained" and to personal qualities of integrity, patience, and endurance. He died in 624 after only three years as archbishop, though in that time he did use the newly-delegated powers to consecrate as bishop Paulinus, one of the missionaries who had travelled from Rome with him. When Edbald's sister Ethelburga went north to marry King Edwin of Northumbria, who was not then a Christian, Paulinus went with her as her chaplain, and the way was opened for the great flowering of Christianity that took place in that part of the country.

Like the other early archbishops of Canterbury, Justus was buried at St Augustine's monastery, and his relics were moved with theirs to a site behind the high altar when the monastery church was rebuilt in the eleventh century. His name is mentioned along with those of Mellitus and Laurence, the other writers of the letter to the Irish bishops, in the diptychs of the Irish Sacramentary known as the Stowe Missal.

Bede, *H.E.*, 1, p. 29; 2, p. 9; *AA.SS.*, Nov., 4, pp. 533–7 (includes eleventh-century Life by Goscelin). See also W. St John Hope, *Recent Discoveries in the Abbey Church of St Austin at Canterbury* (1916).

St Andrew Avellino (1521-1608)

Lancellotto Avellino was born in 1521 into a wealthy family at Castronuovo, south-east of Potenza, in the kingdom of Naples. Having decided that he wished to be a priest, he went to Naples, where he studied civil and canon law, obtained his degree, and was ordained in 1545. He proved to be a very successful advocate in the ecclesiastical courts. But he was also ambitious, and in about 1552 he began to feel that he was becoming too engrossed in his work—a feeling that was intensified when he caught himself telling a lie one day while he was pleading a cause. From then on he resolved to commit himself exclusively to religious education and pastoral work. He seems to have been as successful in this field as he was in the ecclesiastical courts, and in 1556 he attracted the attention of the vicar general of Naples, Cardinal Scipio Ribiba, who asked him to see what he could do about reforming the convent of Sant' Arcangelo in Baiano. He imposed strict enclosure and tried to foster a better spirit in the community, but he met with such hostility, even violence, both from some of the nuns and from the men who used to visit them, that eventually, despite his efforts, the convent had to be closed.

In the meantime, he had been thinking seriously of putting himself under a rule, and in that same year, 1556, he joined the Theatine congregation, which had been founded by St Cajetan (7 Aug.) in 1524. On changing his way of life, Lancellotto also changed his name, and from then on he was known as Andrea (Andrew). He remained at the Theatine house in Naples for the next fourteen years, and during that time he held the office first of novice-master and subsequently of superior. His personal qualities and his zealous concern for the reform of the priesthood in Italy were recognized by a number of like-minded prelates, notably Cardinal Paolo Aresio and the cardinal archbishop of Milan, St Charles Borromeo (4 Nov.). In 1570, with the agreement of the provost general of the Theatines, Cardinal Borromeo invited him to come to Milan and open a house of his Congregation. This Andrew did, and while he was there he became a close friend and counsellor of the cardinal. He also founded a Theatine house in Piacenza, where a number of noblewomen were converted by his preaching and even inspired to enter the religious life. There was a general feeling that he had "turned the city upside down," and he was summoned before the duke of Parma to explain himself. As things turned out, not only did he completely satisfy the duke, but the duchess asked him to be her spiritual director. In 1582 he returned to Naples, where his preaching continued to bear great fruit. In the spirit of the Catholic Reformation he spoke eloquently against the teachings of the Reformers; he also energetically opposed the sect of Giulia di Mario, who encouraged immorality under the guise of illuminist teaching. He was offered a bishopric by Pope Gregory XIV (1590-91), but he refused it, preferring to continue his preaching apostolate.

On the morning of 10 November 1608, just as he was about to celebrate Mass, Andrew had a massive stroke, from which he died that afternoon. He was eighty-seven. His body was laid out in the crypt of San Paolo, and large crowds of people came to pay their respects. A number of cuts were made in his skin by those who removed locks of his hair as relics, and thirty-six hours later blood was found to have exuded from these. As the body was still warm at this stage, it is reasonable to suppose that he was not really dead. In fact, blood continued to flow for another thirty-six hours from fresh cuts made by doctors. This was, of course, carefully collected and is supposed to have bubbled visibly four days later. One tradition has it that in subsequent years it was seen to liquefy, like that of St Januarius (19 Sept.), on the anniversary of Andrew's death. However, when this was presented as evidence of a miracle during the process for his canonization, which eventually took place in 1712, it was rejected as inadequate: Giambattista Pamfili, who afterwards reigned as Pope Innocent X (1644-55), testified that a phial of Andrew's blood, by then solid, had never liquefied.

An anonymous portrait of Andrew at the Theatine generalate in Rome is one of several portraits; and there are dedications as far afield as Finisterre (Brussels), Long Island (New York), and Denver (Colorado).

AA.SS., Nov., 4, pp. 609-23, incorporates a memoir by St Andrew's close friend, Fr Valerio Pagani. On St Andrew's devotional writings, see G. de Luca in *Dictionnaire de Spiritualité*, 1 (1937), 551-4. See also *Bibl.SS.*, 1, 1118-23; *Anal.Boll.* 41, pp. 139-48; biographies by G. B. Castaldo (1613), F. Bolvito, and others. On the blood question, see *The Month*, May 1926, pp. 437-43.

ST MARTIN OF TOURS
Gold escarbuncle on blue field
(may be due to armorists confusing his name).

11

ST MARTIN OF TOURS, *Bishop* (*c.* 336?-397)

St Martin, described by Butler as "the glory of Gaul and a light to the western Church in the fourth century," was one of the most popular saints of the Middle Ages. Unlike so many saints of the period, he was fortunate enough to have, in the church historian Sulpicius Severus, a biographer who knew him personally and visited him frequently during the last four years of his life. Although the *Vita Martini* has its drawbacks—it is to some extent an idealized account, and there are chronological problems—Sulpicius does not use Martin simply as a peg on which to hang a moral and religious ideal. Rather, he attempts to record the life of this real man, who, he believed, embodied that ideal. That Martin became so famous is due in large measure to this Life, which was significant as one of the first, if not the first, to celebrate a Christian for the way he lived, not the way he died, and would have been read in virtually every medieval monastery in western Europe.

Martin was born, probably in about 336, at Sabaria (now Szombathely, Hungary) in the Roman province of Pannonia (now western Hungary and parts of east Austria, Slovenia, and Vojvodina). Soon, however, the family moved to Pavia in Italy when his father, who was in the army and rose to the rank of tribune, was transferred there. Both his parents were pagan, but Martin developed an interest in Christianity at an early age, and was no more than ten when he first tried to become a catechumen. His father was vehemently opposed to the idea, and five years later made use of a law under which a son had to follow the profession of his father to get Martin drafted into the army.

Although he was temperamentally unsuited to army life and, though not yet formally a Christian, lived more like a monk than a soldier, Martin fought for at least three years in the imperial guard. He was stationed in Amiens when the incident—typical of him and for which he is most famous—occurred. It was winter and the frost was particularly severe. As he approached the city gate, he saw a half-naked man shivering with cold and begging alms from the passers-by. No one seemed to be giving him anything, so, having nothing on him but his arms and his cloak, he drew his sword, cut the cloak in two and gave half to the beggar—much to the amusement of some bystanders, though others were shamed by his action. That night, in a dream, he saw Jesus wearing the piece of cloak he had given the poor man and heard him say, "Martin, still a catechumen, has covered me with this garment." As a result of this dream, according to Sulpicius, he "flew to be baptized."

Martin was about twenty and still in the army when a barbarian invasion of Gaul brought his personal situation to a head. His company was called to appear before Caesar Julian (355-60) to receive a war-bounty. Refusing to accept his, Martin told Julian: "Up to now I have served you as a soldier. Now let me serve Christ. Give the bounty to these others—they are going to fight, but I am a soldier of Christ and it is not lawful for me to fight." The irate emperor accused him of cowardice, to which he replied that, in the name of Christ, he was prepared to face the enemy on the following day, alone and unarmed. He was thrown into prison, but a swift end to the hostilities meant that no further action was taken against him, and he was simply discharged. His first move was to go to Poitiers, where the local bishop, St Hilary (13 Jan.), was glad to welcome a "conscientious objector" among his disciples. When Martin refused to accept ordination as a deacon, Hilary ordained him to the lower order of exorcist—a role for which Martin, who, if Sulpicius is to be believed, had an unusual awareness of good and evil spirits, may have been well suited.

It is at this point that Sulpicius' narrative begins to present a number of chronological problems. It seems, however, that while Martin was in Poitiers he had a dream which made him feel he should visit his home. So he set off on the journey across the Alps. It was long and difficult, and he was attacked by robbers, from whom he had a remarkable escape, eventually reaching Pannonia. Although his father was not inspired by his influence to become a Christian, his mother and a number of other people were converted while he was there.

We know that Martin did not immediately go back to Poitiers when he left Pannonia. Instead, he travelled first to Illyricum, on the Dalmatian coast—where he spoke out against the triumphant Arians and was scourged for his pains—and then to Milan. Here he heard that Hilary, having defended orthodoxy too vigorously for his own good against the Arians, was in exile. He therefore decided to stay in Milan as long as the Arians remained in the ascendancy in Gaul, but soon he too was driven away by the Arian bishop, Auxentius. He retired with a like-minded priest to Gallinara, a small island in the Gulf of Genoa, and remained there until Hilary returned to Poitiers in 360.

Back in Poitiers, Hilary gave Martin some land at a place now known as Ligugé so that he could pursue what he felt was his vocation to solitude. But, inevitably perhaps, others joined him, drawn by his growing reputation as a holy man. Together they formed what has traditionally been regarded as the first monastic community founded in Gaul. (It flourished until 1607 and was revived by the Solesmes Benedictines in 1853.) Martin spent the next ten years teaching his disciples and preaching to the people in the countryside round about. Then, in 371, the people of Tours began to demand his appointment as their bishop. He was unwilling to accept the office, so in 372 they arranged for him to be called to the city to visit a sick person, and when he arrived they declared him bishop instead. Some of the neighbouring bishops, who had been called to assist at the election, argued that his unkempt appearance made him unsuitable for the office, but their objections were quickly overruled by a majority of the local clergy and people. The election of St

Brice (13 Nov.), one of his most outspoken critics, as his successor, suggests that there was almost certainly a minority who regarded Martin as an outsider, felt his asceticism as a reproach, and resented his appointment.

As bishop, Martin continued to live as a monk, first in a cell near the cathedral, and then, after he began to feel overwhelmed by the constant demands of his office and of the people of Tours, at a deserted spot outside the city (Sulpicius' description probably romanticizes the reality). Here he founded the abbey of Marmoutier, which soon had a community of eighty monks and became a focus, as did the other monastic communities he founded, of his attempt to bring Christianity to the rural areas. In this, as in other respects, Martin was a pioneer (though presumably there were other, equally zealous bishops who were not lucky enough to have a Sulpicius Severus to record their achievements for posterity). When Christianity began to spread in Gaul, it did so first among the urban populations, leaving the country areas untouched. (*Pagus*, from which our loaded word "pagan" derives, was a country district, and the *pagani* were simply the people who lived there.) Thanks to the missionary activity of Martin and his monks, Christianity spread quickly in the region round Tours, and Martin's seventh-century successor, St Gregory (17 Nov.), mentions by name six of the "village churches" he founded.

But some of his methods, particularly the zealous way in which he destroyed pagan temples not to mention the trees and other objects held sacred by the people, met with justified resistance. For until Theodosius I (379-95) enacted laws against them in 391-2, pagan temples and objects of worship were tolerated. So strictly speaking, Martin and his monks were breaking the law when they destroyed them. But Martin, who would never have used his position to gain a favour for himself, may have been quite happy to persuade the authorities to turn a blind eye to his destruction of what he genuinely believed was the work of the devil. There is archaeological evidence of this aspect of Martin's activity in several places. At Mont-Beuvray, in the Morvan, south of Avallon, for example, a popular tradition that Martin had destroyed a pagan temple there gained support when the ruins of a pagan temple were found underneath those of a chapel dedicated to Martin.

Quite apart from the sheer hard work he put into it, Martin's missionary work was said to have been accompanied by the power of miracles. Many examples of these, some more extraordinary than others, are cited by Sulpicius—who also mentions Martin's visions and his spirit of prophecy. In this connection Martin was not without his critics, and toward the end of his life Brice would point to his "superstitions, and his hallucinations of visions" as evidence that he had become senile. But Martin was well aware of Brice's criticisms, which he bore with an extraordinary degree of tolerance.

Sulpicius also gives us an idea of the distances Martin covered. Every year with no thought for his own comfort, he travelled on foot, on a donkey, or by boat to outlying "parishes" within his diocese. Sometimes—which may not have endeared him to his fellow-bishops—he went beyond the confines of his diocese to places as far afield as Chartres, Sens, Autun, and even Vienne, where he is said to have cured

St Paulinus of Nola (22 June) of his eye trouble. He was equally unsparing of himself at home in Tours. On one occasion an autocratic and ruthless imperial officer named Avitian arrived in Tours with a batch of prisoners and gave orders that they should be tortured and executed on the following day. Martin, who hurried from Marmoutier to plead their cause, did not reach Tours until nearly midnight, but he nevertheless went straight to Avitian and would not leave until he had persuaded him to reverse his order.

During the twenty-five years he spent as bishop of Tours, Martin found himself involved in a number of doctrinal disputes, the most significant being that with the Priscillianists. This extreme ascetic sect, named after its leader, Priscillian, had already been denounced by Pope Damasus I (366-84; 11 Dec.) and St Ambrose, archbishop of Milan (7 Dec.), when it was condemned at a synod held in Bordeaux under the aegis of the emperor, Maximus Magnus (383-8), in 384. Priscillian appealed to the emperor against the ruling of the synod, but he was attacked by Bishop Ithacius of Ossanova, who called for his execution. Martin, like Ambrose, took a more moderate line, partly because he was against putting heretics to death and partly because he did not like to see the emperor intervening in ecclesiastical matters. Maximus agreed to spare the lives of Priscillian and his followers, but once Martin had left Trier he ceded to pressure from Ithacius and his supporters and committed their case to the prefect. The prefect found them guilty of the capital offence of sorcery and had them executed.

When Martin came back to Trier to appeal on behalf of suspected Priscillianists who were being hunted down in Spain (in fact they increased in number there immediately after the persecutions and survived into the sixth century), he found himself in a difficult position: as long as he continued to refuse to act with Ithacius and the other bishops, Maximus refused to rescind the order of execution. It was only when he agreed to act with them in consecrating one of their number as bishop of Trier that Maximus withdrew his order. The thought that he might have been too complaisant in this matter was something that troubled Martin for the rest of his life—as did the accusation levelled at him by Brice, that he had sinned by continuing to fight as a soldier after his baptism.

Some time in 397 Martin had a presentiment of his approaching death. When he told his followers, they begged him not to leave them, but he prayed: "Lord, if your people still need me I will not abandon the work. May your will be done." Not long after this he fell ill at Candes in a remote part of his diocese. There he died on 8 November 397 and was buried in Tours three days later. As his successor, Brice built over his grave a chapel, which was subsequently replaced by a magnificent basilica. The successor to this basilica was destroyed during the French Revolution, and a modern church now stands over the shrine—which was itself rifled by the Huguenots in 1562.

After Martin's death his cult was not instantaneous, and the election of Brice as his successor may be evidence of an anti-Martin reaction, at least in Tours. But once it began to spread it did so swiftly—thanks not least to Sulpicius' Life, which was completed in 396. Until 1562 the pilgrimage to Tours was among the most popular in Europe, and a very large number of churches were dedicated in Martin's honour—not only in France, but in Italy, Spain, Germany, and the Low Countries as well. The oldest existing church in England, which stands outside the eastern walls of Canterbury, bears his name. If Bede is right in saying that it was built during the Roman occupation, it must originally have been dedicated to some other saint, but it was definitely St Martin's by the time St Augustine (27 May) and his monks came to use it. By the end of the eighth century there were at least five more churches in Britain dedicated to St Martin, including that of St Ninian (16 Sept.) at Whithorn, and by 1800 the count had risen to 173.

St Martin became a very popular figure in art, where his symbols are the ball of fire that was seen above his head while he said Mass or, from the fifteenth century on, a goose (because this bird often migrates round about the time of his feast). The episode most frequently represented is that of his encounter with the beggar. He features in the stained-glass windows of Tours, Chartres, Beauvais, and Bourges in France, and in England, in those of the fifteenth-century church of St Martin in York. There are also wall paintings in the churches at Chalgrave, Bedfordshire, and Nassington, Northamptonshire. A statue in the Henry VIII Chapel in Westminster Abbey shows him in armour, wearing half a cloak.

For the Life by Sulpicius Severus, together with three Letters and other documents, see C. Halm, *C.S.E.L.*, 1, pp. 107-216; Eng. trans. in F. R. Hoare, *The Western Fathers*. The chronology in Gregory of Tours, *Historia Francorum*, 1, pp. 36-8, 43, and in *de Libri IV S. Martini* (*P.L.*, 71, 911-1008) differs from that in Sulpicius Severus: see H. Delehaye, "S. Martin et Sulpice Sévère" in *Anal.Boll.* 38, pp. 1-136. See also *H.S.S.C.*, 3, pp. 213-20; C. Stancliffe, *St Martin and His Hagiographer* (1983); N. J. K. Chadwick, *Poetry and Letters in Early Christian Gaul* (1955), pp. 89-121; J. Fontaine, "Sulpice Sévère, a-t-il travesti S. Martin en martyr militaire?" in *Anal.Boll.* 81 (1963), pp. 31-58; and *Saint Martin et son Temps* (1961); two other Lives by P. Monceaux (1926, Eng. trans. 1928). For St Martin in art, see K. Künstle, *Ikonographie*, 2, pp. 438-44. For popular traditions and phrases associated with the saint, see Bächtold-Stäubli, *Handwörterbuch des deutschen Aberglaubens*, 5, 1708-25.

St Mennas, *Martyr* (*c.* 300)

As St Mennas (or Menas), like St George, enjoyed a localized, early, and widespread cult, his existence cannot reasonably be doubted. On the other hand, because his story was lost, invented at a later date using the story of another martyr, possibly St Gordius, and then embellished with new and sometimes fantastic detail by succeeding generations, it is impossible to sort out the truth from the fiction. Delehaye takes the view that all we can say with any degree of certainty about Mennas is that he was an Egyptian and that he was martyred and buried in Egypt. Much more generous with the details, the legend tells us that he was an Egyptian by birth and a soldier in the Roman army. While he was serving at Cotyaeum in Phrygia, the persecution of Diocletian began, so he decided to desert from the army. Hiding in the the mountains, he led a life of prayer and (presumably enforced) austerity. One day, when some games were held in Cotyaeum, he walked into the amphitheatre and announced that he, too, was a Christian. He was arrested immediately and taken before the president, who ordered that he should be tortured and beheaded. His body was recovered and brought back to Egypt for burial. Miracles were reported at the tomb, and as the cult spread throughout the East, Mennas' true story became so distorted that he was taken into the ranks of the "warrior saints" and credited with absurd wonders. Churches were built in his honour at a number of places, including Cotyaeum—which led to the creation of a number of mythical saints named Mennas specifically connected with individual towns or cities.

The shrine built over Mennas' tomb at Bumma (Karm Abu-Mina), south-east of Alexandria, was a principal place of pilgrimage until the Arab invasion in the seventh century. The ruins of a basilica, monastery, baths, and other buildings were excavated between 1905 and 1908 by Mgr K. M. Kaufmann, who found innumerable traces of the cult of the martyr. These included phials with inscriptions such as "Souvenir of St Mennas," which turned out to be for carrying water away from a well near the shrine. Phials like this had already been found elsewhere in Africa and in Europe, and it had always been assumed that they contained "oil of St Mennas" taken from the lamps in the basilica. Early in 1943, Christopher II, the Orthodox patriarch of Alexandria, issued an encyclical letter in which he attributed the defeat of Rommel's army at El Alamein and the consequent sparing of Egypt to the intercession of "the holy and glorious great martyr Mennas, the wonder-worker of Egypt." At the same time, he proposed that the saint's ruined shrine be restored as a memorial to those who lost their lives in the battle.

See K. M. Kaufmann, *Die Menasstadt und das Nationalheiligtum der altchristlichen Aegypter* (1910); *idem, Ikonographie der Menas-Ampullen*; H. Delehaye, "L'Invention des reliques de S. Menas à Constantinople" in *Anal.Boll.* 29, pp. 117-50; P. Devos, "Un récit des miracles de S. Menas en copte et en éthiopien" in *Anal.Boll.* 76, pp. 154-60; 78, pp. 275-308; M. A. Murray, "St Menas of Alexandria," *Proc. of the Society of Biblical Archaeology* 29 (1907), pp. 25-30, 51-60, 112-22; R. Miedema, *Der heilige Menas* (1913). See also P. Franco de' Cavalieri in *Studi e Testi* 19 (1908), pp. 42-108; H. Leclercq in *D.A.C.L.*, 11, 324-97, which includes a bibliography; *O.D.S.*, p. 337.

St Theodore the Studite, *Abbot* (759-826)

St Theodore is one of the great figures in the history of monasticism and of the Church in general. He was the eldest of three brothers, who went with their father to the family estate at Sakkoudion, near Mount Olympus in Bithynia (north of the Taurus mountains in modern Turkey), and began to lead the monastic life there. Shortly after this, the young men's uncle, St Plato (4 Apr.), was persuaded to resign as abbot of Symboleon, also on Mount Olympus, in order to become abbot of the new monastery. Theodore, who was then about twenty-one or twenty-two, so impressed his uncle that he was sent to Constantinople to study for the priesthood and was ordained in 787. He continued to make such progress spiritually and intellectually that in 794 Plato, with the consent of the community, stood aside so that the younger man could become abbot in his place.

In the years that followed Theodore became one of the Church's great monastic reformers and guides, while at the same time involving himself in the major political and theological crises of the day—particularly the dispute between the Iconoclasts and the upholders of orthodoxy, about the veneration of images, which continued on and off from 726 to 843. The first sign of trouble for Theodore came when the young Byzantine emperor, Constantine VI (ruled 780-97), abandoned his wife in favour of a woman called Theodota, who happened to be a relative of Plato and Theodore. Ignoring the fact that the patriarch of Constantinople had turned a blind eye to the relationship, Plato and Theodore took the emperor to task. Constantine tried to win them over to his side with promises of preferment, but when this proved unsuccessful he gave orders that Theodore and any monks who supported him should be banished to Thessalonika. Plato he had placed in solitary confinement in Constantinople. A letter survives in which Theodore, full of courage and of admiration for his old master, describes for Plato the hardships of his journey to Thessalonika.

As it turned out, Theodore's exile did not last long. In 797 Constantine's formidable mother, Irene, who had been regent and co-empress with her son since 780, had his eyes put out and claimed the throne, thus becoming the first woman to rule the Byzantine Empire (797-802). She also happened to share Theodore's orthodox views in the Iconoclast dispute, so he and his companions were recalled from exile. He went initially to Sakkoudion, where he re-gathered his scattered community around him. However, in 799 the monastery became vulnerable to Arab raids, and the community was forced to move within the walls of Constantinople. Here Theodore was given charge of the monastery of Studios (Stusios)—so called after its founder, the consul Studius, who had it built when he came to Constantinople from Rome in 463. The monks had been expelled by Constantine V Copronymus (741-75), one of the fiercer Iconoclasts among the emperors, so Theodore found it sadly run down, both spiritually and materially, with no more than twelve monks. However, thanks to his natural authority and the wisdom with which he ruled, that community and its dependents soon came to number something more like a thousand. He used his organizational gifts to develop the strand of monasticism founded four centuries earlier by St Basil (2 Jan.), and his rule soon spread to Mount Athos and from there to Russia, Bulgaria, and Serbia. In these countries it continued to form the basis of cenobitical monastic life until the advent of the communist regimes and the suppression of monasticism in the twentieth century.

Theodore's writings, which include instructions, sermons, liturgical hymns, and treatises on monasticism, reveal in a man of his time and place an unusually moderate and balanced attitude to asceticism. He once told a hermit: "Don't cultivate a self-satisfied austerity. Eat bread, drink wine occasionally, wear shoes, especially in winter, and take meat when you need it." And he was particularly anxious to foster a love of learning in his monks and to encourage their practice of the fine arts: he established a school of calligraphy which retained its reputation for a long time.

Life continued peacefully until 806, when the matter of Constantine VI's adultery indirectly reared its head again. The see of Constantinople had become vacant, and the emperor, Irene's successor, Nicephorus, chose a layman, also called Nicephorus and subsequently a saint (13 Mar.), as patriarch. Objecting to the fact that Nicephorus, however admirable, was still a layman, Theodore, Plato, and a number of other monks opposed the appointment and spent twenty-four days in prison as a result. Then the patriarch and a small synod of bishops reinstated a priest who had been suspended for blessing the marriage of Constantine and Theodota. When he refused to celebrate the liturgy with this priest, Theodore, his brother the archbishop of Thessalonika, and Plato were banished to separate prisons on Princes' Island (now Kizil Adalar, in the Sea of Marmara.) From his isolation Theodore wrote explaining matters to Pope St Leo III (12 June), who wrote back commending him for his prudence and loyalty. But because Theodore's enemies had spread rumours in Rome that he was heretical and that he was annoyed that he had not been appointed patriarch, the pope did not take any action. The Studite monks were dispersed, and Theodore and his fellow-abbots remained in prison until the emperor died in 811.

As soon as Theodore emerged from prison, he was reconciled with Patriarch Nicephorus—a reconciliation cemented by their unity on the vexed question of images, which was to occupy him for the rest of his life. The new emperor, Leo V the Armenian (813-20), was a zealous Iconoclast. When he banished Nicephorus, Theodore openly denied his right to interfere in ecclesiastical affairs, and this, together with his encouragement of the veneration of holy images, marked him out as the leader of the orthodox group. He was exiled, first to Mysia and then, when it was discovered that he was writing letters of encouragement to his followers, to Bonita in Anatolia. Here, despite the extremes of temperature and the lack of nourishment, he was well treated by his gaoler and continued to write letters, including one asking for the help of Pope St Paschal I (817-24; 11 Feb.). Unfortunately, the emperor intercepted another letter, in which Theodore urged the faithful to defy "the infamous sect of image-burners," and handed him over to a less indulgent gaoler, who gave him 100 stripes and left him lying on the ground, exposed to the February cold.

Before Theodore had time to recover completely, he and his faithful attendant were taken under guard to Smyrna. Here, the Iconoclast bishop in whose care they were left threatened Theodore with execution. But in 820, before he could act on his word, Leo V was murdered, and the persecution came to an end. The new emperor, Michael II (ruled 820-9), began with a show of moderation: he recalled the exiles and released prisoners, including Theodore, who urged him to be united with Rome and to permit the veneration of images. But the emperor banned images from Constantinople and refused to reinstate the patriarch, the abbot of the Studite monastery, and other orthodox prelates unless they accepted this.

After remonstrating unsuccessfully with the emperor, Theodore went to Bithynia—and effectively into exile—to encourage and strengthen his followers. "The winter is over," he told them, "but spring is not yet come." So great was his influence that monks in general and Studites in particular came to be identified with orthodoxy. A group gathered round him at a monastery on the Akrita peninsula, and it was here that he was taken ill at the beginning of November 826. On the 4th he was well enough to celebrate Mass. But then his condition worsened, and on the 11th, having dictated his last instructions to his secretary, he died. It was not until eighteen years later that his body was translated to the monastery of Studius.

St Theodore is greatly venerated in the East. But he is also, and rightly, described by the Roman Martyrology as "famous throughout the Church." Not only was he a towering figure in the monastic life of the East, he was also a staunch supporter of the authority of the see of Rome, and he resolutely defended the veneration of sacred images. In this connection, it is important to realize that he opposed the Iconoclasts essentially on theological grounds. He did not regard the veneration of images as a necessary devotional exercise and seems to have had little use for it himself. On the other hand, he recognized that for some people images could be an important devotional aid and that to prohibit their display was to deny the validity of theological principles essential to the Christian faith.

For Theodore's writings, see *P.G.*, 99; A. Mai (ed.), *Nova Patrum Bibliotheca*, 5 (1849); J. P. Cozza Luci (ed.), *ibid.,* 8 (1871), 9 (1888). See also A. Gardner, *Theodore of Studium* (1905); H. Martin, *St Theodore* (1906); I. Huascherr, "Saint Théodore Studite, l'homme et l'ascète," *Orientalia Christiana* 6 (1926), pp. 1-87; E. Amann in *D.T.C.*, 15 (pt. 1), 287-98; *N.C.E.*, 14, pp. 19-20; *O.D.C.C.*, 1359-60. For the Iconoclast controversy, and Theodore's role in it, see *D.A.C.L.*, 7 (1926), 272-84; L. Bréhier, *La Querelle des Images* (1904).

St Bartholomew of Grottaferrata, *Abbot (c. 980–c. 1050)*

The Byzantine-rite abbey of Grottaferrata, near Rome, was founded in 1004 by St Nilus of Rossano (26 Sept.), who died before the buildings were completed. He was followed in quick succession by three of his disciples, Paulus, Cirillus, and Bartholomew; but it is Bartholomew, as the one who brought the building work to completion and established the community, who is honoured as the abbey's lesser founder.

Bartholomew was born in about 980 and was sent at the age of seven to be educated by the Byzantine Greek-rite monks at the monastery of St John Catibata (Calabria followed the Greek rite almost exclusively at that time). When he was twelve, he joined Nilus at the monastery of Vallelucio, near Monte Cassino, and would accompany him on visits to other monasteries. He was with Nilus on one such journey when they stopped at Grottaferrata, where a Christian chapel had been built over the site of a Roman burial place dating back to 1 B.C., when the town was known as Cryptaferrata. Nilus acquired the land, and building began.

Under Bartholomew's rule the monastery acquired the reputation as a centre of learning that it still enjoys, over nine hundred years later. Bartholomew himself was a skilled calligrapher, and much of the monks' time was devoted to the copying of manuscripts. Otherwise, little is known about Bartholomew, and even the date of his death is not certain.

There is a Grottaferrata tradition, which may or may not have some truth in it, concerning Pope Benedict IX, whose grandfather had given the land on which the monastery was built. This pope, who reigned on and off from 1032 to 1048, had an extremely stormy pontificate, and at one stage sold the papal office to his godfather, who reigned from May 1045 to December 1046 as Gregory VI. In 1047, after the brief reign of Clement II and with the help of bribes, he reclaimed the papal office but was finally ejected less than a year later by order of the emperor Henry III (ruled 1039-56). According to the tradition, he came to Grottaferrata, apparently full of remorse, and was welcomed by Bartholomew, who nevertheless made it quite clear that his disorderly life made him unfit to be a priest, let alone pope. Under Bartholomew's influence he became genuinely repentant; he remained at Grottaferrata as a simple monk until he died there in 1055. This account of the link between Bartholomew and Benedict IX first appears in the Life of Bartholomew, possibly written by his third successor, Abbot Luke I. It is not clear how reliable the details are: Benedict was still calling himself pope in 1055; on the other hand, he was certainly buried at Grottaferrata, where he probably also died.

An ancient mosaic representing SS Nilus and Bartholomew can still be seen in the sanctuary of the abbey church, and some of the manuscripts in the abbey library are thought to have been copied by St Bartholomew. Today, the monks concentrate on conserving manuscripts, using modern scientific techniques.

P.G., 127, 476-516; cf. *Anal. Boll.* 61, pp. 202-10. For the resignation of Benedict IX, see H. K. Mann, *Lives of the Popes in the Middle Ages*, 5, p. 292; *O.D.P.*, pp. 142-4. See also S. G. Mercati, *Enciclopedia Italiana*, 6, p. 254; L. Bréhier in *D.H.G.E.*, 6, 1006-7; *Bibl.SS.*, 2, 886-9.

12

ST JOSAPHAT, *Bishop and Martyr* (*c.* 1580-1623)

Josaphat was a great ecumenist three centuries before anyone started talking seriously about ecumenism. He was born Ioann Kuncewycz, probably in 1580, at Wolodymyr (modern Vladimir), in what today is north-western Ukraine. His father was a well-to-do merchant in the town. Ioann went to school in Wolodymyr, but when he was old enough his father had him apprenticed to a merchant in Vilna (now Vilnius, Lithuania). Although he worked hard, he was not especially interested in trade, and he spent his free time learning Church Slavonic so that he could take part more intelligently in the liturgy and recite some of the office each day. He was befriended by Petrus Arcudius, then rector of the Oriental college in Vilna, and by two Jesuits, Valentine Fabricius and Grigory Gruzevsky, all of whom gave him every encouragement. At first the merchant to whom Ioann was apprenticed found this preoccupation with religion unsympathetic. However, the young man was such a good worker that eventually his master offered him a partnership and the hand of one of his daughters in marriage. Ioann, who had already decided to become a monk, refused both offers, and in 1604 he entered the monastery of the Holy Trinity in Vilna.

In October 1595, when Ioann was still in his teens, the Orthodox metropolitan of Kiev, together with five other bishops representative of millions of Ruthenians (Byelorussians and Ukrainians), had gathered in Brest to seek communion with the see of Rome. This action, which led to a long, bitter, and sometimes violent controversy, clearly fired Ioann's imagination. When he entered the monastery, he had persuaded another young man to enter with him. Venyamin Rutsky was a scholar and a convert from Calvinism, who had been ordered by Pope Clement VIII (1592-1605), against his personal wishes, to join the Byzantine rite. Together they began to look at ways of promoting union with Rome and reforming Ruthenian monastic observance, and they were to initiate the movement in Ruthenian monasticism that eventually crystallized as the Order of St Basil, whose members became known in 1932 as the Basilians of St Josaphat.

Ioann, who took the name of Josaphat, was ordained deacon and then priest. He quickly acquired a reputation as a preacher, particularly on the subject of union with Rome, and was known for the extreme austerity of his life. When Rutsky succeeded a man with separatist views as abbot of Holy Trinity, there was a sudden upsurge in the number of men who wished to enter, so Josaphat was taken away from his studies to help found new houses in Poland. Then, in 1614, Rutsky was made metropolitan of Kiev. Josaphat, who succeeded him as abbot of Holy Trinity, took the opportunity of his friend's installation to visit the Monastery of the Caves, near Kiev. This community of 200 monks was somewhat lax in its discipline, but although Josaphat failed to win them round to his point of view on unity and narrowly escaped being thrown into the river Dnieper for his pains, he did succeed, through sheer force of personality, in changing their attitude and increasing their good will.

In 1617 Josaphat himself was ordained bishop of Vitebsk, with right of succession to the aged archbishop of Polotsk. The archbishop died a few months later, and Josaphat had to deal with all the problems of a large and divided eparchy (diocese). The more-religious people, fearing Roman interference in their worship and customs, favoured separation. In addition, churches had been badly neglected, benefices were in the hands of laymen, and monastic standards had deteriorated. Secular priests were marrying two and three times (a married man can be ordained in the Orthodox Church, but he may not remarry if his wife dies). For the next couple of years, helped by monks from his own monastery in Vilna, Josaphat worked hard to get the life of the eparchy back on an even keel. He held synods in all the main towns, published a catechism and made its use obligatory, gave the clergy a code of conduct, and challenged the interference of local landlords in church affairs. At the same time he gave a personal example of dedicated hard work, preaching, administering the sacraments, and visiting the sick and prisoners, even in the remotest hamlets.

Then, in 1620, just as order had been restored, a rival hierarchy of bishops was set up alongside the existing one in the territory affected by the Union of Brest. Josaphat returned from a visit to Warsaw to find that his work was being undermined by a man called Meletius Smotritsky, who had been sent in as archbishop of Polotsk. The nobility, and in some places, including Polotsk itself, the people, remained loyal to Josaphat and union with Rome. But in certain towns, notably Vitebsk, Mogilev, and Orcha, and in the rural areas there was a shift toward Smotritsky, who insisted that Catholicism was not the traditional Christianity of the Ruthenian people.

Unfortunately Josaphat, who stood firm throughout in his support of union with Rome, began to lose his natural allies. The Polish bishops did not back him as enthusiastically as they might because of his uncompromising insistence on the right of the Byzantine clergy and customs to equal treatment with those of Rome. And Leo Sapieha, the Catholic chancellor of Lithuania, fearing the possible political results of the prevailing unrest, listened too readily to dissidents who maintained that Josaphat was himself causing it by his policies. In 1622 he accused Josaphat of resorting to violence in order to maintain the union.

From then on Josaphat was under attack from both sides, but he would not allow this to deter him. At the end of October 1623 he decided to go once again in person to Vitebsk, still a hotbed of anti-Roman feeling; and although he realized that he was placing himself in great danger, he refused to take a military escort. For a fortnight, during which he and his attendants were constantly threatened in the streets, he preached publicly and visited people in their homes.

No doubt Smotritsky's only purpose in stirring up this trouble was to drive his rival from Polotsk. But, as so often happens, his followers took the matter further and plotted to murder Josaphat. On 12 November, falling into a trap set for him, he allowed his attendants to detain a priest called Elias in his house. At a given signal a crowd gathered, demanding that the man be released and the archbishop punished. When Josaphat returned, he let Elias go. But the crowd, still unsatisfied, broke in and started attacking his attendants. He remonstrated with them in words reminiscent of Becket: "My children, what are you doing to my servants? If you have anything against me, here I am. But leave them alone." At this, he was struck on the head with a halberd and then shot; his mangled body was thrown into the river Dvina.

After Josaphat's death, there was a reaction in favour of union with Rome. But the bitter conflict continued, and the dissidents had their own martyr in Bishop Athanasius of Brest, who was killed in 1648. On the other hand, Archbishop Smotritsky was eventually reconciled with Rome. When Josaphat was canonized by Pope Pius IX in 1867, he became the first Eastern-rite saint to have his cause processed by the Congregation of Rites. In 1892 Pope Leo XIII extended his feast to the entire Western Church for 14 November, although the Ukrainians, among others, continued to keep it on 12 November—to which it has now reverted in the West.

Propylaeum, pp. 516-7; A. Guépin, *Un apôtre de l'union des Eglises au dix-septième siècle: Saint Josaphat* (1898); *O.D.S.*, p. 268; *Bibl.SS.*, 6, 545-8. The British Museum has a copy of *Relación verdadera de la Muerte y Martirio de . . . Josafat*, printed in Seville in 1625. See also G. Fini "San Giosafat Kuncewycz, Martire dell'Unione della Chiesa" in *Oekoumenicon* 3 (1963), 62, pp. 420-7; T. Boresky, *Life of St Josaphat, Martyr of the Union* (1955); O. Kozanewyc, *Leben des hl. Josaphat* (1931).

St Nilus the Elder (*c.* 430)

The account of St Nilus accepted by Alban Butler and others is almost certainly a conflation of the lives of two near contemporaries with the same name. The Nilus whose writings have survived in the form of letters and treatises on various religious subjects was most probably a monk from Ancyra in Galatia (modern Ankara). His letters indicate that he was an ascetic man with a deep interior life and that people from every walk of life came to receive spiritual direction from him. In one letter, addressed to a prefect called Olympiodorus, who had just built a church, he makes short shrift of the idea that the walls of the church might be adorned with mosaics of birds, animals, hunting scenes, and so on, as well as of sacred subjects. Olympiodorus is told that he should keep to scenes from the Old and New Testaments and display one cross only, in the sanctuary.

Whether or not this Nilus was a disciple of St John Chrysostom (13 Sept.) is not clear. The legend of the second Nilus, about whom nothing concrete is known, describes him as an official in Constantinople, perhaps a prefect, and a disciple of John Chrysostom. He was married and had two children, but sometime after their birth he was "seized by a great craving after solitude." Eventually he and his wife agreed to withdraw from the world and that he should take his son Theodulus with him. The two went to Mount Sinai, whence, two years later, Theodulus was abducted by Arab raiders. Tracing him to Eleusa, south of Beersheba, Nilus found that a local bishop had bought him from the raiders and given him employment in the church. Both Nilus and Theodulus were ordained by the bishop before they returned to Mount Sinai.

P.G., 79, 583-694. See also K. Heussi, "Untersuchungen zu Nilus dem Asketen" in *Texte und Untersuchungen* (1917); F. Degenhart, *Der hl. Nilus Sinaita* (1915) and *Neue Beitrage zur Nilusforschung* (1918); *D.T.C.*, 11 (1931), 661-74.

St Emilian Cucullatus (574)

San Millán de la Cogolla ("St Emilian with the hood") was a famous early saint of Spain and is one of the country's patrons. What we know of him is based on a Latin Life written some fifty years after his death by St Braulio, bishop of Zaragoza (26 Mar.). His birthplace had been a matter of dispute between Aragon and Castile for centuries—each claiming it for itself. As a boy he watched the sheep, playing as he did so the simple flute that was to become his iconographic symbol. But when he was about twenty he felt called to serve God in a more direct way and went to live under the guidance of a hermit. Eventually he returned home, but so many people made demands on him that he went off again, into the mountains above Burgos. There he remained for forty years—according to tradition on the mountain where the abbey of San Millán was built later—until the bishop of Tarazona insisted that he take Holy Orders and become a parish priest. This was a bad idea from everyone's point of view. Not all the qualities Emilian had developed in his mountain solitude proved useful when it came to running a parish; and he was misunderstood in particular by his fellow clergy, who accused him to the bishop of wasting church property—he had given it away in charity. He was removed from his position, presumably by mutual agreement, and returned, this time with some disciples, to his life of solitude and prayer. He is sometimes described as the first Spanish Benedictine, but this is an anachronism, as the monastery of La Cogolla did not have the Benedictine Rule until long after his time.

For a critical edition of Braulio's Latin Life, see L. Vasquez de Parga (ed.) (1943). See also T. Minguella, *S. Millán de la Cogolla, estudios históricos* (1883); V. de la Fuente, *San Millán, presbítero secular* (1883); M. Gómez in *D.H.G.E.*, 15, 406-12.

St Machar, *Bishop* (Sixth Century)

What little is known about St Machar (or Mochumma) is to be found in the Aberdeen Breviary. What is certain is that he was an Irish missionary and that he came to Scotland with St Columba (9 June). On the other hand, the suggestion that he was the first bishop of Aberdeen is unlikely, although he does seem to have evangelized the isle of Mull and preached to the Picts in the Aberdeen area, where a number of dedications can still be found. According to his legend in the Aberdeen Breviary, Pope Gregory the Great (3 Sept.) appointed him archbishop of Tours for the last years of his life, but there is no reason to believe this. His feast is observed in the Aberdeen diocese, and there are two parishes in the city dedicated to him. Water from St Machar's well was formerly used for baptisms in the cathedral there. There is a fourteenth-century metrical Life in the university library in Cambridge.

K.S.S., pp. 393-4. See also A. S. Ferguson, in *Scottish Gaelic Studies*, 6, pp. 58ff.

St Cunibert, *Bishop (c. 663)*

There are several medieval accounts of St Cunibert's life, but none is very reliable as far as the details are concerned. What is certain is that he was an outstanding bishop and a genuinely holy man. He is said to have been brought up at the court of the Frankish king, Clotaire II (613-29). He was ordained to the priesthood and was made, first, archdeacon of Trier, and then, in about 625, bishop of Cologne. In this capacity his influence was so great that he was referred to as archbishop, though Cologne was not a metropolitan see until the end of the eighth century. Cunibert was also a royal counsellor, and when Clotaire's son, Dagobert I (629-39), made his own four-year-old son, Sigebert, king of Austrasia (the eastern kingdom of Frankish Gaul) in 634, he was appointed one of the boy's guardians. From a letter of St Boniface (5 June), we learn that he had the evangelization of the Frisians much at heart, but his main concern was his diocese, and in his later years he left the court and devoted himself entirely to its welfare. When he died, in about 663, his relics were enshrined in the fine church in Cologne which he himself had founded. He had dedicated it to St Clement (23 Nov.), but it was immediately renamed in his honour.

M. Coens, *Anal. Boll.* 47, pp. 338-67. On the church of St Cunibert, see *Festschrift Anton Ditges gewidmet* (1911); P. Clemen in *Kunstdenkmäler der Rheinprovinz*, 6, pt. 4 (1916), pp. 231-313.

St Cumian, *Abbot (c. 665)*

It is hard to say anything definite about this saint, partly because there is no proper Life in either Latin or Irish, partly because there are several Cumians and they tend to get confused with one another. However, in the *Félire* of Oengus (*c.* 824) under 12 November, we read: "There has been given with wisdom, science and much prudence, to my Cumian of beautiful warfare, the fair tall (*fota*) son of Fiachna." Cuimine Fota, a son of Fiachna, king of West Munster, was born in about 590. He became a monk while he was quite young and presided over the school and district of Clonfert, where he is believed to have been bishop. If he is the Cumian who founded a house at Kilcummin in Co. Offaly, he introduced the Roman computation of Easter into Ireland. Those who opposed him on this account included the abbot of Iona, who rebuked him for abandoning the Celtic computation favoured by St Columba (9 June). In a letter known as the Paschal Epistle, Cumian defended his point of view with reference to synods, Western Church Fathers, and ancient paschal cycles. But despite his learning and his eloquence, the monks of Iona were not convinced. Cumian also wrote a hymn, the last three stanzas of which are included as part of a liturgical office in the Book of Mulling, which belongs to Trinity College, Dublin.

See J. F. Kenney, *Sources for the Early History of Ireland* (1929), 1, pp. 220-1, 324-5. Also J. T. McNeill in *Revue Celtique* (1922/3); L. Gougaud, *Christianity in Celtic Lands* (1932), p. 285 and *passim*.

St Lebuin (*c.* 773)

There are two existing accounts of Lebuin (or Liafwine), both written in the ninth century. An Anglo-Saxon by birth, he became a monk at the monastery founded by St Wilfrid (12 Oct.) in Ripon and eventually a priest. In 754, the year St Boniface (5 June) died, he went over to Frisia, where a number of his compatriots were already working as missionaries. His first act was to visit St Gregory (25 Aug.), Boniface's Frankish co-worker, in Utrecht. Gregory welcomed him warmly and sent him off with St Marchelm (Marculf, 14 July) to the dangerous eastern border territory, an area disputed between the Frisians and Saxons (who were still pagan) and the more or less Christianized Franks. Lebuin is said to have received hospitality from a woman named Abachilda, who, after he had made a large number of converts, collaborated with him in the building of a church on the west bank of the river Ijsel, opposite Deventer. Deventer itself, where he subsequently built a new church and a residence, became the centre of his missionary work. But he made enemies as well as converts, and these enemies, allying themselves with the Westphalian Saxons, burned down his church and scattered his Frisian converts.

Far from being discouraged, Lebuin seems to have been strengthened by this hostility. The ninth-century Life tells how he decided to brave these Saxons when they met for their annual assembly at Marklo, on the river Weser. He entered the assembly, wearing his priestly vestments and carrying a cross and a book of the Gospels. Having cried out to gain their attention, he charged them: "Listen to God who speaks to you by my mouth. Know that the Lord, the maker of the heavens, the earth and all things, is the only true God." And when they stopped to listen, he told them that their own gods were dead and without power, but if they would acknowledge the true Lord of Heaven and receive baptism, this Lord would give them his peace and salvation. On the other hand, if they refused, a prince sent by God would destroy them. Not unnaturally, the Saxons took exception to this, and many cut staves with which to kill him. However, one of their leaders pointed out that if they were ready to show respect to human ambassadors, they should be even readier to show respect to someone whose god was so powerful that he had escaped from their hands. This impressed the assembled Saxons, and Lebuin was allowed to travel freely and preach wherever it suited him. Soon after this he returned to Deventer, where he rebuilt his church and continued his work until he died, sometime before 777. His cult dates back to the Benedictine monasteries of the region in which he lived and worked.

Another Lebuin—of Ghent—appears on the same day in the Roman Martyrology, but historians have concluded that he is a doubling of this Lebuin.

The Life by Hucbald is in *P.L.*, 132, 877-94; the second Life (ed. A. Hofmeister) is in *M.G.H.*, *Scriptores*, 30, pt. 2, pp. 789-95 (Eng. trans. in C. H. Talbot, *Anglo-Saxon Missionaries in Germany*, 1954). See also *Bibl.SS.*, 7, 1163-4; F. Hesterman, *Der hl. Lebuin* (1935); W. Levison, *England and the Continent in the Eighth Century* (1956), pp. 108-10.

St Benedict and Companions, *Martyrs* (1003)

There are two main sources for the history of these martyrs. One is the account by Benedict's friend, St Bruno (or Boniface) of Querfurt (19 June), who, as soon as he heard what had happened to Benedict and his companions, collected evidence from Poland. The other is that of a later writer, Cosmas of Prague. Benedict and Bruno were monks together under the direction of St Romuald (19 June), at a monastery near Ravenna; Benedict also lived there for a while as a hermit. When the emperor, Otto III (996-1002), decided to evangelize the Slavs of Pomerania, Benedict and a number of other monks were sent to do the work. Their first step was to go to the court of Duke Boleslaw I (1025) in western Poland. Here they were generously received by Boleslaw, who provided them with teachers so that they could learn the language, and when they settled at Kazimierz, near Gniezno, he built them a hermitage.

It was in the hermitage at Kazimierz, on 11 November 1003, that Benedict and four others were murdered by pagan robbers. They were immediately venerated as martyrs, and the hermitage became a place of pilgrimage—though their relics were later taken to Olomouc. Their cult was confirmed by Pope Julius II (1503-13) in 1508. The Roman Martyrology refers to "the holy martyred hermits Benedict, John, Matthew, Isaac and Christian who, intent upon the service of God, were grievously troubled by robbers and by them slain with the sword." They are honoured in Poland as the Five Polish Brothers, although they were neither Polish, nor (apart from Matthew and Isaac) brothers, except in the spiritual sense. They are also honoured as "the glory of the Camaldolese Order," despite the fact that they died some years before St Romuald founded Camaldoli.

M.G.H., Scriptores, 15, pp. 716-38; *Bruno von Querfurt* (ed. and trans. H. G. Voigt, 1907). Cosmas of Prague's account is in *P.L.*, 166, 109-13. See also *N.A.*, 8, pp. 365ff.

St Astrik, *Bishop* (c. 1040)

Although it is generally agreed that the first archbishop in Hungary was called Astrik, or Anastasius, there is some uncertainty as to who he actually was. There are three "candidates," all associated with the bishop of Prague, St Adalbert (23 Apr.): Anastasius, the first abbot of Brevnov in Bohemia; Astericus, a priest of the Prague diocese; and Radla, who studied with Adalbert in Magdeburg and was his close friend. The first two may in fact be one person, and on the whole Radla, a

Czech or perhaps a Croat from Bohemia, who is known to have been a monk in Hungary, seems the most likely of the three.

Radla probably received the habit at Brevnov, taking the name Anastasius, of which Astrik is an equivalent. When Adalbert went into exile, having failed to consolidate his position in Prague, Astrik went to help the missionaries who were working among the Magyars. In 997 he is known to have been in the service of the wife of Geza, duke of the Magyars (972-97), and he was almost certainly the first abbot of St Martin's (Pannonhalma), the first church institution in Hungary, founded by Geza. The duke died in 997 and was succeeded by his son, St Stephen (997-1036; 16 Aug.), who was even more zealous for the conversion of the Magyars. Astrik worked hard, both in preaching the gospel and in organizing the church at the institutional level, in which connection Stephen sent him to Rome to consult Pope Silvester II. Soon after his return, in 1001, Stephen was crowned king of Hungary. Astrik was in all likelihood the Astrik who was promoted at this point to be archbishop of the new Hungarian church: when he attended a synod in Frankfurt in 1006, he was described simply as *Ungarorum episcopus*. It seems that his see was probably at Kalocsa, rather than at Esztergom, which eventually became the primatial see, or at Vesprem, the first Hungarian diocese for which there is documentary evidence.

For the remainder of his long life Astrik worked with the king for the conversion of the Magyars and the establishment of the Church throughout the realm. He died in about 1040, shortly after the king himself. Nothing at all is known about his personality, although the fact that St Adalbert had so much affection for him and trusted him so implicitly in itself says something.

On the history of the conversion of Hungary, see F. Dvornik, *The Making of Central and Eastern Europe* (1949); cf. C. Kadlec in *Cambridge Medieval History*, 4, p. 214. See also St Bruno's Life of St Adalbert in *Fontes rerum Bohemicarum* (1871); the Life of St Stephen in *M.G.H., Scriptores*, 11 (cf. 4, pp. 547, 563); *Lexikon für Theologie und Kirche*, 1 (1930), 394.

Bd Rainerius of Arezzo (1304)

There are almost no details available about the life of Rainerius, although there is a manuscript record of the miracles reported at his tomb. He was born in Arezzo into the Mariani family, and as a young man he gave up his career to join the Friars Minor. Miracles were attributed to him during his lifetime, and immediately after his death, which occurred at Borgo San Sepolcro on 1 November 1304, the local municipality—possibly seeing that this could be good for the town for other than purely spiritual reasons—set up an altar in his honour and had a record kept of his miracles. His cult was confirmed in 1802.

AA.SS., Nov., 1, pp.390-402 includes MS record of miracles reported at tomb. See also B. Mazzara, *Leggendario Francescano* (1680), 3, pp. 295-6; Léon. *Auréole Séraphique* (Eng. trans.), 4, pp. 34-5.

Bd John della Pace (*c.* 1332)

The confusion concerning the identity of John (Giovanni) della Pace provides a good example of the way in which in the past a cult could be confirmed on the basis of very little knowledge of the person concerned. When, in 1856, Pope Pius IX approved the celebration of his feast by the Franciscan Order, John della Pace was supposed to have died in the first half of the fifteenth century. However, thanks to the comprehensive researches of A. Barsotti earlier this century, we now know that there were two men in Pisa with the same name and that they became confused. The Giovanni who died in 1433 was a furrier and a married man, who remained such all his life. The other Giovanni, whose feast is celebrated on this day, was a hermit for a while before he founded the Fratelli della Penitenza in Pisa. He died in about 1332. The Fratelli were suppressed in 1782 as part of a reform promoted by the grand duke of Tuscany, Pietro Leopoldo.

A. Barsotti, *Pro Memoria sul B. Giovanni della Pace* (1901); *idem, Un nuovo fiore serafico* (1906). See also *Bibl.SS.*, 6, 859-61. *Anal. Jur. Pont.*, 3 (1858), 378-80.

Bd Gabriel of Ancona (1456)

When the cult of Bd Gabriel was being confirmed in 1753, the fullest account of his life, by his contemporary and fellow-Franciscan, St James of the March (28 Nov.), was found to be missing. However, the main details can be pieced together from the older collections of Franciscan Lives, most of which mention him. He was born Gabriele Ferretti in Ancona, and when he was eighteen he joined the Friars Minor of the Observance (a short-lived independent Franciscan Order set up in 1517, when groups of "observant" friars who lived an austere life in strict fidelity to the Rule were united as a single group with that name). For fifteen years he was a missioner in the March of Ancona, where he gained a reputation for holiness and the gift of miracles. He was then appointed guardian of the Observants in Ancona, but only a few details have survived from this period of his life. Once, he was reported to James for neglecting his duty in some small way. James, looking at the quality of the doer rather than the significance of the deed, told him to accuse and discipline himself before his community. Not only did Gabriel do this quite cheerfully, but he sent James a carpet for his church and a sugar-loaf, as a token of good will. He died in Ancona on 12 November 1456. Pope Pius IX (1846-78), who was born Giovanni Mastai-Ferretti, belonged to another branch of Gabriel's family.

B. Mazzara, *Leggendario Francescano* (1680), 2, pt. 2, pp. 425-7; L. Wadding, *Annales Ordinis Minorum*, 12, 206-14; short sketches by V. M. Ferretti (1754), S. Melchiori (1846). See also Léon, *Auréole Séraphique* (Eng. trans.), 4, pp. 61-6.

13

St Arcadius and Companions, *Martyrs* (437)

There is no independent *passio* of this group of martyrs, but St Prosper of Aquitaine (25 June) gives an account of them in his Chronicle. According to their entry in the Roman Martyrology, their names were Arcadius, Paschasius, Probus, and Eutychian, and they suffered "in Africa"—presumably in the area that today is Tunisia—during "the Vandal persecution." They had refused to accept the teaching of Arius, who denied the divinity of Christ, and were "first proscribed by the Arian king, Gaiseric (428-77), then exiled and treated with atrocious cruelty, and finally slain in various ways." The Martyrology adds that Paulillus, the young brother of Paschasius and Eutychian, also refused to be "turned from the Catholic faith," and was consequently "long beaten with sticks and condemned to the lowest slavery." It seems that the boy died later of exposure. Arcadius was described by Bishop Antoninus Honoratus of Constantine, who wrote to him while he was in prison, as "the standard-bearer of the faith," and we learn from this letter—if this Arcadius was indeed the recipient—that he was married and had a family.

The letter from Bishop Antoninus Honoratus can be found in *P.L.*, 1, 567-70.

St Brice, *Bishop* (444)

All we know about St Brice (or Britius) comes from Sulpicius Severus' Life of St Martin of Tours (12 Nov.) and from popular traditions collected by St Gregory of Tours (17 Nov.). Clearly a volatile and difficult personality, Brice, a native of Turenne, was brought up by Martin at the monastery of Marmoutier. Here he caused so much trouble that Martin only kept him on lest, by dismissing him, he himself might be avoiding a trial sent him by God. His attitude was, "If Christ could tolerate Judas, surely I can put up with Brice." There is one story of how, while he was still a deacon, Brice went round saying Martin was mad. When Martin asked him to justify his words, he denied that he had spoken them, to which Martin replied that he had heard them, adding, "But I have prayed for you, and you shall be bishop of Tours." Brice went off muttering that he had always said the bishop was a fool. Elsewhere, Sulpicius Severus tells how Brice set himself up as a model because he had been brought up at Marmoutier—unlike Martin, who, he pointed out contemptuously, had been brought up in the army camps and was becoming superstitious and foolish in his old age. Suddenly, however, he made a complete *volte-face* and went to Martin to beg his forgiveness, which was never very difficult to obtain. Reading between the lines of Sulpicius' account, which inevitably favours Martin, it seems that Brice was representative of a minority, perhaps in the monastery but certainly in Tours, who regarded Martin as an outsider and found him difficult to deal with.

Martin died in 397 and was indeed succeeded by Brice for what would turn out to be a long and stormy episcopate. A number of attempts—sometimes justified, sometimes not, but always unsuccessful—were made to have him removed. Then in 429 or 430 his enemies accused him of having sexual relations with a woman of the town. He seems to have managed to clear himself—according to Gregory of Tours, by means of a very astonishing miracle—but he was driven from his see and went to Rome to protest his innocence there. The incident seems to have left him somewhat chastened, and he remained for seven years in effective exile in Rome, where he was eventually vindicated by the pope.

When Armentius, who had been administering the diocese of Tours in his absence, died, Brice returned, and for the remaining seven or so years of his life he served his people with genuine apostolic zeal. This was interpreted as his way of making amends for his past faults, and when he died, in 444, he was immediately venerated as a saint. Within twenty-five years his feast was being celebrated in Tours, and his cult spread quickly to England and to Italy because of his connection with St Martin. He was particularly popular in England, featuring in almost all monastic calendars prior to 1100, as well as in the Sarum calendar. Today he is known mainly in connection with the massacre of St Brice's Day, for on 13 November 1002 the English king, Ethelred the Redeless (lacking in foresight, "unready"), ordered the massacre of all Danish settlers in England, thus provoking the invasion led by the Danish king, Sweyn.

Sulpicius Severus' *Vita S. Martini* is in *P.L.*, 20, 159-222; *C.S.E.L.*, 1, pp. 108-216. See also C. Stancliffe, *St Martin and his Hagiographer* (1983); A. Poncelet in *Anal.Boll.* 30, pp. 88-9; H. Delehaye in *Anal.Boll.* 37, pp. 135-6. For letters of Pope Zosimus, see *P.L.*, 20, 650, 663. However, there is a chronological problem here, because Brice is supposed to have been bishop of Tours for thirty-three years before he went to Rome, and Zosimus reigned from 417 to 418.

St Eugenius of Toledo, *Bishop* (657)

There is some confusion in the early episcopal lists of Toledo, which have two men of this name succeeding one another in the see. However, the existence of the first Eugenius, who is described as an astronomer and mathematician, is questionable. His "successor," St Eugenius, was a Spanish Goth who became a monk at Zaragoza. To avoid promotion to the archbishopric of Toledo, he hid in a cemetery but was eventually forced to emerge and to accept episcopal consecration. He was a poet—some of his writings, both in prose and in verse, are still extant—and he is also supposed to have been a good musician who tried to improve the poor standard of church singing, of which he heard all too much. He governed his see with great wisdom, deeply impressing all who came in contact with him, and was succeeded there after his death in 657 by his nephew, St Ildefonsus (23 Jan.). This Eugenius is not to be confused with a Eugenius mentioned by Alban Butler on 15 November, who was probably a martyr and has nothing to do with Spain; or with another Eugenius mentioned in the Roman Martyrology on 17 November, who was a disciple of St Ambrose (7 Dec.).

For the story of the first Eugenius (probably a myth), see *Anal. Boll.* 2. For St Eugenius, see Ildefonsus, *De viris illustribus*, 14, in *P.L.*, 96, 204. His poetry is edited in *M.G.H., Auctores Antiquissimi*, 14. See also *Anal. Boll.* 24, pp. 297-8; J. Madoz in *Revue d'histoire ecclésiastique*, pp. 530-3.

St Maxellendis, *Martyr* (*c.* 670)

After her death an active cult grew up around the relics of St Maxellendis, and she is still venerated in the diocese of Cambrai, where most of the relics were eventually enshrined. According to the surviving account of her life, which dates from the tenth century and of which the details are not to be trusted, she was the daughter of noble parents, Humolin and Ameltrudis, who lived in Caudry, near Cambrai.

As she approached the age of marriage she had many suitors, but her parents favoured a man called Harduin of Solesmes. When she told her father that she did not wish to marry, he replied that it was quite possible to serve God as a wife and mother, and that in fact many saints had done so. She asked for time to think it over, but having dreamed (like many other saints of the early and later Middle Ages) that her resolution was confirmed by an angel, she told Humolin that she was quite determined to become a nun. Since her parents showed equal determination that she should be Harduin's wife and began preparing for the wedding, she took refuge with her nurse at Cateau-Cambresis. Harduin and his friends discovered her hiding place, broke in, and carried her off. She managed to break loose and was running away when Harduin, furious now, struck her with his sword. The force of the blow killed her instantly, and Harduin himself went blind on the spot.

Maxellendis was buried in a nearby church, but so many miracles were reported at her tomb that in about 673 Vindician, bishop of Cambrai, had her relics translated to the church of St-Vaast at Caudry. Harduin, who had asked to be led out to meet the procession, fell on his knees when he reached the coffin, acknowledging his crime and asking God's pardon. His sight was immediately restored. Since their translation to Caudry, the relics (or at least some of them) have been moved several times.

For the *passio*, see J. Ghesquière, *Acta Sanctorum Belgii*, 3, pp. 580-9. See also C. J. Destombes, *Vies des Saints de Cambrai et Arras* (1887), 4, pp. 177-87.

St Kilian of Aubigny (Seventh Century)

Writing in the middle of the ninth century, Hildegaire says that he has a Life of St Kilian in his possession. So, although it dates from relatively late, this Life may nevertheless have some basis in authentic materials. It tells us nothing at all about Kilian's early life except that he was born in Ireland. At some point he went on pilgrimage to Rome, and on his way back he made an extended visit to St Fiacre (1

Sept.), a relative of his, at his hermitage in Brie. While he was still there, St Aubert, bishop of Cambrai (13 Dec.), began looking for missionaries to go to Artois. Kilian was persuaded by St Faro, bishop of Meaux (28 Oct.), to leave the hermitage and undertake this work.

According to one story, told no doubt to confirm a property title, Kilian was passing the house of a nobleman and, being thirsty, asked for something to drink. The man's wife pointed to the nearby river Aisne and told him he could get a drink there, since she had nothing to give him. "May it be as you have said," Kilian replied. When the nobleman returned from hunting and asked for a drink it was discovered that all the barrels, which had been full that morning, were empty. A search party went after Kilian, profuse apologies were made to him, and the barrels were found to be full once more. Kilian eventually made his headquarters at a house in Aubigny owned by the same nobleman. He built a church on a plot of land that was given to him near the river Scarpe, and for the remainder of his life he preached the gospel zealously throughout Artois.

For the Latin Life, see *Anal.Boll.* 20, pp. 431-44; *M.G.H., Scriptores Merov.*, 5; K. Wittstadt, *Sankt Kilian* (1984); P-W. Scheele, *Der Stimme der Iren* (1989); K. Fischung, *Der deutschen Bearbeitungen der Kilianslegende* (1973). See also A. Perret, *Histoire de S. Kilien d'Aubigny* (1920); L. Gougaud, *Les saints irlandais hors d'Irlande* (1936).

St Nicholas I, *Pope* (*c.* 820-67)

When he died on 13 November 867 after a nine-year pontificate, this great man was widely mourned. He quickly acquired the titles of "Saint" and "the Great," and a contemporary wrote of him: "Since the time of blessed Gregory [the Great, 590-604; 3 Sept.], no one comparable with him has been raised to the papal dignity." The same contemporary also provided an insight into his personality: "He gave orders to kings and rulers as though he were lord of the world. To good bishops and priests, to religious lay people, he was kind and gentle and modest; to evildoers he was terrible and stern. It is rightly said that in him God raised up a second Elias."

He was born in about 820 in Rome, where his father was an important official. Pope Sergius II (844-7) attached him to the papal household, where his considerable talents were subsequently used by Popes Leo IV (847-55; 17 July) and Benedict III (855-8). When Benedict died, Nicholas, then only a deacon, was elected as his successor.

As Pope, Nicholas inherited from Leo I (440-61; 10 Nov.), Gelasius I (492-6), and Gregory the Great a strong belief in the primacy of the see of Rome and in the Church's right to be free of State interference, and he devoted all his efforts to putting it into practice. This, however, was easier said than done, given the reality that confronted him. In the West, the Church was in a bad way after the collapse of Charlemagne's empire. The nobility assumed too much power in the appointment and dismissal of bishops, many of whom were young and inexperienced and some of whom were corrupt. Excommunication was used inappropriately as a form of punishment, and contempt for the clergy had led to lack of respect for their office. In particular, Nicholas had to deal with recalcitrant metropolitans such as Hincmar, archbishop of Reims, and John, archbishop of Ravenna, who behaved as though they were in no way accountable to Rome. In one such situation he invoked a document in which the supposed author, St Isidore of Seville (4 Apr.), asserted the authority of the pope over that of synods and metropolitans. Although these so-called False Decretals were in fact written in France in about 850, it is unlikely that Nicholas was aware of their provenance. Those who have accused him of knowing they were false when he used them forget that the forgery came to light only in the fifteenth century.

As a staunch defender of Christian marriage, Nicholas had a moral victory of a kind in the case of Lothair II of Lorraine (855-69). When the king sought to divorce his wife, Theutberga, and remarry, Nicholas stood up not only to him but to the bishops who had gone along with his wishes. They had sanctioned the divorce at a synod in Aachen in 862 and recognized the new marriage at a second synod in Metz in 863. But when two of their number, the archbishops of Cologne and Trier, went to Rome to present the synodal decrees to Nicholas, he asserted his authority by repudiating the decrees and excommunicating the two archbishops for colluding in bigamy. The emperor Louis II took Lothair's side, and for a while Nicholas was forced to take refuge in St Peter's. In the end Lothair had to accept his ruling, and for a time at least he was reconciled with his wife. Nicholas took an equally strong stance when the Frankish king, Charles II le Chauve (840-77), persuaded the Frankish bishops to excommunicate his daughter, Judith, who had married Baudouin of Flanders without his consent. Nicholas intervened to uphold the principle that marriage must be entered into freely.

Things were no calmer in the East, where Nicholas was concerned to maintain the primacy of Rome. In Constantinople the patriarch, Ignatius (23 Oct.), had very recently been removed from his see and replaced by Photius, a talented man but not a priest. The problems this created were to trouble Nicholas throughout his pontificate. He sent representatives to Constantinople, refused to recognize Photius, and appealed to the emperor, Michael III. When his representatives reported in favour of Photius, he preferred a report from Ignatius' supporters and excommunicated Photius, defending his action to the emperor in the name of the primacy of the see of Rome. Meanwhile, Boris, the newly-baptized ruler of the Bulgars, had written to him with a number of questions, to which he responded with what has been described as "a masterpiece of pastoral wisdom and one of the finest documents in the history of the papacy." He also sent missionary bishops in response to a request from the king, and he was therefore understandably disappointed when Boris chose to submit his people to the patriarchate of Constantinople rather than to that of Rome. But Boris' choice may have been determined partly by the fact that Nicholas rebuked him for forcing pagans in his domains to convert to Christianity and suggested that the Bulgars in general might be less superstitious, less ferocious in war, and less inclined to use torture; and partly too by the fact that most of

Bulgaria came within the spiritual jurisdiction of Constantinople anyway. Photius was irritated by what he regarded as interference by Nicholas and held a synod to excommunicate and depose him. Although Nicholas was dead by the time news of this reached Rome, the whole matter undoubtedly hastened the coming division between East and West.

Nicholas believed firmly that all are equal under the law of God and throughout his short reign spoke out fearlessly against injustice and wickedness wherever he saw it. He was a strong and just judge to whom people from outside as well as within Europe turned. But although his responsibilities were to the whole of Christendom, he felt concerned in a very personal way for the people of his own diocese. For example, he had a register drawn up of poor people in Rome who were also disabled and then saw to it that they were fed daily at home, while the able-bodied came to the papal residence. Eventually ill health got the better of him: he admitted to one correspondent that he was in such pain that "not only am I unable to write proper replies to your questions, but I cannot even dictate them, so intensely do I suffer." He died in Rome on 13 November 867 and is described in the *Liber Pontificalis* as "patient and temperate, humble and chaste, beautiful in face and graceful in body.... He was ... the friend of widows and orphans and the champion of all the people." Ironically, as he lay dying he was robbed by one of his officials of money he had set aside for the poor.

O.D.P., pp. 107-8; *Mann*, 3, pp. 1-148; Jules Roy, *St Nicholas I* (Eng. trans. 1901). Nicholas' correspondence is in *P.L.*, 119; *M.G.H., Epistolae*, 6. On the False Decretals, see P. Fournier and G. Le Bras, *Histoires des Collections Canoniques en Occident*, 1 (1931). See also F. Dvornik, *Les Slaves, Byzance et Rome au IXème siècle* (1926); *idem, The Photian Schism* (1948).

St Abbo of Fleury, *Abbot* (1004)

The details of Abbo of Fleury's life were reliably recorded by his contemporary, the Benedictine historian Aimoin (960-1010). One of the most eminent scholars of his time, he was born near Orleans between 945 and 950. As a child he learned grammar, dialectic, and arithmetic at the Benedictine abbey at Fleury-sur-Loire and taught there himself while he was still very young. He went on to study astronomy in Paris and Reims and music in Orleans and then returned to Fleury to become a monk. In 985 he was invited by the bishop of Worcester, St Oswald (28 Feb.), who had been a Benedictine at Fleury himself, to come and direct the school of the recently-founded abbey at Ramsey (now in Cambridgeshire). Abbo spent only two years at Ramsey Abbey, but it was long enough to encourage in the monks he taught an enthusiasm for learning and, more generally, for the monastic reform movement.

When he returned to Fleury in 987, Abbo resumed his own studies, particularly in the fields of philosophy, mathematics, and astronomy. But this peaceful pursuit of learning was not to last for long. In 988 the abbot of Fleury died, and Abbo was elected to succeed him. The election was contested, with repercussions that went beyond the confines of the monastery, but it was eventually settled in Abbo's favour, thanks in part to the intervention of Gerbert of Aurillac, who subsequently became Pope Silvester II (999-1003).

In his role as abbot, Abbo threw himself with great energy into the affairs of the day, so the years that followed were extremely active for him. He came into conflict with the king over the rights of bishops and with the bishop of Orleans over the rights of monasteries, and he was one of the prime movers in the attempt to have the monasteries exempted from episcopal control. He played a prominent part at the synods he attended, and he became involved in negotiations with the pope in the matter of the irregular second marriage of the French king, Robert II (996-1031), with his cousin Berthe.

Abbo's letters indicate that he was much in demand as a restorer of peace to troubled monastic communities. It was while he was on just such a mission in 1004 that he met the violent death for which he was venerated as a martyr. He had gone to restore order in the monastery at La Réole in Gascony, and while he was there an acrimonious quarrel broke out between some of his followers and the monastery servants. He intervened to calm things down but was stabbed as he did so. Although he managed to stagger to his cell, he died shortly afterwards in the arms of one of the monks.

Despite all this activity and the dramatic circumstances of his death, Abbo is best known for his writings—among them the first Life of St Edmund, king and martyr (20 Nov.), which was based on the testimony of Edmund's standard-bearer and which he dedicated to St Dunstan (19 May); and the *Apologeticus*, in which he championed the rights of individuals and groups vis-à-vis those in power. Also, while he was abbot of Fleury the monks copied and studied the *Categories* and *Analytics* of Aristotle.

Aimoin's Life and the letter circulated at the time of Abbo's death are in *AA.SS. O.S.B.*, 6, pt. 1, 32-52. There is no complete edition of Abbo's own works, but see *P.L.*, 139, 417-58, and *Opera Inedita* (ed. A. van der Vyer and R. Raes, 1966). For a modern study, see P. Cousin, *S. Abbon de Fleury, un savant, un pasteur, un martyr* (1954). See also M. Mostert, *The Political Theology of Abbo of Fleury; O.D.S.*, p. 1; "On the Text of Abbo of Fleury's *Quaestiones Grammaticales*" in *P.B.A.*, 10 (1922), pp. 173-80.

St Homobonus (1197)

Homobonus was born in Cremona, in Lombardy, sometime during the first half of the twelfth century. He was the son of a tailor in the town, who gave him his name, which means "good man," when he was baptized. Although he was uneducated in the sense that he never went to school, he learned from his father how to run a business diligently and honestly without compromising himself in any way. When he eventually inherited the business from his father, he looked on it as an employment given him by God and as a means of serving both his family and the wider society of which he was a member. He was married and seems to have had several children, though they and his wife tend to figure in a rather negative light in accounts of his life. This may, of course, have been a hagiographical device to emphasize his virtue, because they were probably concerned to see so much of the family money going to the poor.

Known throughout Cremona for his openhandedness, Homobonus was extraordinarily generous with his time as well as with his money. He would visit people, especially the poor, in their homes, and while doing what he could to meet their temporal needs he would gently encourage them to lead a good life. And when he was about fifty, he decided to give up his business and devote all of his time to charitable works. It was, indeed, his boundless charity that his fellow-citizens noticed above all, though it goes without saying that he was also a man of prayer, which was the context of all he did. On the other hand, he does not seem to have belonged to any of the extreme lay Christian groups, such as the *Humiliati*, which flourished at the time. He was in the habit of going to Mass each evening in the church of S. Egido, and it was there, on 13 November 1197, that he died. During the *Gloria* he stretched out his arms in the form of a cross and fell to the ground. At first people took no notice, thinking it was a manifestation of devotion; but when he failed to stand for the Gospel, they went over to him, only to find that he was dead.

His fellow-citizens immediately honoured him as a saint; and Sicard, the bishop of Cremona, who went to Rome himself to put the case for Homobonus' canonization, wrote in his Chronicle: "In Cremona at that time there was a simple man, extremely faithful and devout, whose name was Homobonus. After his death and through his intercession God gave many miracles to the world." Pope Innocent III (1198-1216) was quickly satisfied by the official inquiry into his life and miracles, and Homobonus was canonized a mere two years later, in 1199. As patron of tailors and clothworkers, his cult spread quickly not only in Italy but also in Germany, where he was known as "Gutman," and in France as well. There are churches dedicated to him in Rome, northern Italy, southern Germany, Spain, and Belgium.

Homobonus is something of a rarity on two counts. First, he was a canonized layman, a canonized entrepreneur and family man at a time when, apart from martyrs and royalty, candidates for canonization were religious "professionals." And second, his cult was approved not only locally but in Rome itself just as the papal reserve became effective. There was nothing extraordinary about his life—his circumstances were those of the majority of people of his time, and, indeed, of any time, but they illustrate well the problems of conscience that face ordinary people who have to work for their living and provide for their families while striving to achieve the Christian ideal. What was extraordinary was the dedicated way in which he lived his life.

See *S. Homoboni civis Cremonensis Vita antiquior* (ed. A. Maini; 1857); G. Belladori, *Il trafficante celeste* (1674). Later accounts by F. Camozzi (1898), D. Bergamaschi (1899), R. Saccani (1938). See also *H.S.S.C.*, 6, pp. 179-84; *Bibl.SS.*, 9, 1173-5. Marco Vida, a sixteenth-century classical poet referred to by Alban Butler as "the Christian Virgil," wrote a poem in honour of Homobonus.

St Didacus (*c.* 1400-63)

Didacus, or Diego, was born of poor parents in the little town of San Nicolás del Puerto, in the diocese of Seville. While still very young he went to stay with a holy priest who was leading an eremitical life near the town. Not only did Didacus imitate the austerities and devotions of his master, but together they cultivated a small garden and made spoons, dishes, and other utensils out of wood. Having lived in this way for some years, Didacus was obliged to return home. He did not stay long, however, but went to the convent of the Friars Minor of the Observance at Arrizafa and received the habit as a lay brother. After his profession he was sent to the Canary Islands, where the Order had a mission. He worked hard, instructing the people and bringing about conversions. Then, in 1445, although he was a lay brother, he was appointed guardian of Fuerteventura, the principal convent in the islands. Four years later he was recalled to Spain, where he lived in a number of friaries in the Seville area.

In 1450 a jubilee was celebrated in Rome. As St Bernardino (20 May) was to be canonized in the course of it, many Franciscans made the journey. Diego accompanied Alonso de Castro, who fell dangerously ill while they were there. The care and compassion with which he looked after his sick companion caught the attention of his superiors, and he was put in charge of the many sick friars who were being accommodated in the convent of Ara Coeli. He was there for three months and is said to have restored some of his patients to health miraculously. He spent the next thirteen years in Spain, first at Salcedo and then at Alcalá, where he was when he fell ill in November 1463. He died peacefully on the 12th, with his brethren gathered round his bed. Several miracles had been attributed to him during his lifetime, and more were to be attributed to his intercession after his death. King Philip II, in gratitude for a miracle worked in favour of his son, urged that Diego be canonized—which he was in 1588. Diego became a very popular saint in the Spanish-speaking world; the extensive iconography includes a portrait by Zurbarán and a cycle of paintings by Murillo, originally in the Franciscan convent in Seville but now distributed in several museums.

See: Mark of Lisbon (Ital. trans., 3, pp. 155ff.), and other Franciscan chroniclers. See also P. Moreno de la Rea, *La Vida del S. Fray Diego* (1602); sketches by Berguin and Chappuis (Fr., 1901) and A. Gioa (Ital., 1907).

Bd Augustina Pietrantoni, *Martyr* (1864-94)

Livia Pietrantoni was born into a poor peasant family at Pozzaglia Sabina, near Rieti, on 27 March 1864. When she was twenty-two she joined the Sisters of Charity of St Jeanne Antide Thouret in Rome. She was clothed on 3 August 1887, taking Augustina as her religious name. For the next two years she worked in various capacities at the Santo Spirito hospital in the city. Then, in the summer of 1889, she started to look after the tuberculosis patients, and by the time she made her religious profession in September 1893, she had contracted the then incurable disease herself. She had much to endure, not only physically as a result of her own illness but spiritually too, as she bore the brunt of her patients' resentment of their lot, a resentment exacerbated by the climate of anti-clericalism which was rampant in Italy at the time.

One of these patients, Giuseppe Romanelli, who was touchier and more violent than the rest, eventually had to be expelled from the hospital because of his aggressive behaviour. Without any evidence at all, he took it into his head that Augustina was responsible for his expulsion, and he started to conduct a vendetta against her. Finally, on 13 November 1894, he entered the hospital through the unguarded main entrance and hid in a recess off one of the passages. As Augustina passed, he stabbed her ferociously seven times. She managed to call for help, but it was too late, and she died shortly afterwards, assuring the distressed superior that she was happy and begging her not to worry.

The people of Rome hailed her as a heroine, not simply because of the manner of her death but equally because of the humble charity, the sincerity and openness, and the fervent spirit of prayer that had characterized her life. She was buried in the Campo Verano, where her body remained until 15 March 1941, when it was taken to the church of the motherhouse of her Congregation. She was beatified by Pope Paul VI (1963-78) on 12 November 1972.

See F. S. Rondina, *Vita e morte di Suor Agostina* (1896); M. Vanti, *Suor Agostina* (1943), which includes an examination of the press coverage of the case.

14

ST LAURENCE O'TOOLE, *Bishop* (1128-80)

Laurence (Lorcán), son of Murtagh Ua Tuathail, was born in Co. Kildare, probably near Castledermot, in 1128. His parents' marriage united the chieftain families of the O'Tooles and the O'Byrnes. In 1138 the king of Leinster, Dermot MacMurrough, raided Murtagh's territory, and Laurence, who was only ten at the time, was taken hostage. He spent the next two years in an isolated and barren area near Ferns, until his father, who heard that he was being badly treated, forced Dermot, with the threat of reprisals, to give the boy up to the bishop of Glendalough. This Dermot did. But when Murtagh arrived to take him home, Laurence told him of his wish to become a monk, so he was left in the care of the bishop.

When he was twenty-five, Laurence was chosen as abbot of Glendalough and avoided becoming bishop only by pointing out that, under canon law, a bishop had to be at least thirty. During the first four months he had more to deal with than the normal duties of an abbot—although he discharged these wisely and justly—because there was a serious famine raging in the surrounding countryside, and the people looked to him for relief. When it was over, he was regarded by those reached by his charity as the saviour of the countryside. But not everyone was so enthusiastic. Outside the abbey he had to deal with the bandits and other dangerous types who infested the Wicklow hills; within, he had to put up with those who tried to destroy his reputation because they resented his integrity and the zeal with which he reproached them for their lax behaviour.

Their attempt seems to have failed, because in 1161, when Gregory, the first archbishop of Dublin, died, Laurence was elected in his place. He was consecrated in Holy Trinity (now known as Christ Church) cathedral by Gelasius, archbishop of Armagh. Laurence's first concern was to reform the diocesan clergy. To this end he imposed on the canons of his cathedral the Rule of the Canons Regular of Arrouaise, an abbey founded in the diocese of Arras in 1090 which had become the model for numerous other houses. Laurence himself wore the religious habit and shared the life of the community as far as he could. He was known in the diocese for his approachability, his extraordinary generosity to the poor, his tireless preaching, and his care for dignity in the liturgy. Once discipline had been restored to the church of Glendalough by his nephew Thomas, who was canonically elected after an unworthy protégé of Dermot had been expelled, Laurence would seek peace from time to time in the cell of St Kevin (3 June), a cave above the Upper Lake.

From 1170 on, Laurence became involved in Anglo-Irish politics. Dermot MacMurrough, who had been driven from Ireland on account of his excesses, was determined to return and sought the help of the English king, Henry II, who was delighted to provide volunteers. Chief among these was Strongbow (Richard de Clare, earl of Pembroke), who landed at Waterford in 1170, overran part of Leinster, and marched on Dublin. Laurence was sent to negotiate with Strongbow, but Dermot's Anglo-Norman allies plundered the city while the discussions were still going on. Laurence then turned to comforting those who had lost members of their families or been raped or maimed themselves, and he generally acted as a source of strength in the midst of danger. With his prize almost within his grasp, Dermot died suddenly, and Strongbow claimed Leinster as Dermot's heir and husband of his daughter (Laurence's niece). The Irish united under their high king, Rory O'Conor; Strongbow shut himself up in Dublin; and Laurence once again acted as negotiator. But the negotiations failed, and Strongbow, in a desperate and final effort, unexpectedly routed the Irish forces.

Fifteen or so years earlier, Henry II had obtained from Pope Adrian IV (Nicholas Breakspear, the only English pope, 1154-9) a Bull authorizing him to go to Ireland in order "to subject its people to the rule of law and to root out therefrom the weeds of vice." In 1171 he went to Dublin, where he received the submission of all the Irish chiefs except those of Connaught, Tyrconnel, and Tyrone. Then in 1172 he convened a synod at Cashel, during which the Irish bishops, who were presented with the papal Bull for the first time, accepted its imposition of clerical celibacy and the Sarum rite (the English form of the Roman liturgy). From then on, Laurence frequently acted as a mediator between Henry and the Irish princes. In 1175, having travelled to Windsor and successfully negotiated a treaty between the English king and Rory O'Conor, he took the opportunity to visit Canterbury, where he was welcomed by the monks at Christ Church and spent the night in prayer at the shrine of St Thomas Becket (29 Dec.). Next day as he prepared to celebrate Mass, a deranged would-be assassin gave him a blow on the head which knocked him out temporarily. He recovered sufficiently to celebrate Mass, and he interceded successfully on the man's behalf when Henry gave an order that he be hanged.

When the Third Lateran Council took place in Rome in 1179, Laurence attended with five other Irish bishops. Before they left England, Henry had obtained from them a promise that they would say nothing that might prejudice his position in Ireland. But this did not prevent Laurence from giving Pope Alexander III a comprehensive account of the state of the church there and making suggestions as to how its problems might be dealt with. The pope, pleased with what he heard, confirmed all the rights of the see of Dublin, gave Laurence jurisdiction over five suffragan dioceses, and appointed him his legate in Ireland. Some of the problems of the Irish church were dealt with later in the same year, 1179, at a council held at Clonfert. Seven "lay" bishops were deposed, the sons of priests or bishops were forbidden to enter the priesthood, and laypeople were forbidden "to have the rule of any church or church matters"—all of which suggests that things had not changed much since St Malachy (3 Nov.) was dealing with similar problems half a century earlier.

Laurence began to exercise his new powers as soon as he returned to Ireland, notably by appointing a Connacht bishop to the see of Armagh and using the papal Bulls to resolve property disputes with Norman settlers near Dublin. Henry, sensing that he might have another Becket in the offing, was angered by this and refused to see Laurence when he visited England to negotiate once again on behalf of Rory O'Conor. Laurence was kept waiting for three weeks in Abingdon, and meanwhile Henry went to Normandy. Laurence followed him and eventually obtained from him leave to return to Dublin. But he was taken ill on the way and, as he approached the abbey of the Canons Regular at Eu, he said: *"Haec requies mea in saeculum saeculi."* He smiled when the abbot asked him whether he had made a will—"God knows I have not a penny in the world"—and it was concern for the welfare of his flock that occupied his mind to the end.

Laurence died on 14 November 1180 and was buried in the crypt of the church of Our Lady at Eu. He was canonized in 1225, and his feast is observed in Ireland, in the diocese of Rouen, and by the Canons Regular of the Lateran.

See C. Plummer, "Vie et Miracles de S. Laurent, archévêque de Dublin" in *Anal.Boll.* 33, pp. 121–86; M. V. Ronan, "St Laurentius, Archbishop of Dublin: Original Testimonies for Canonization" in *I.E.R.* 27, pp. 347–64; 28, pp. 246–56, 467–80, 596–612; *idem*, "St Lorcán Ua Tuathail" in *I.E.R.* 38, pp. 369–86, 486–509; J. Meagher, *St Lorcán Ó Tuathail 1128-1180* (1980). See also A. Gwynn, *The Irish Church in the Eleventh and Twelfth Centuries* (1992); *idem*, "St Laurence O'Toole as Legate in Ireland" in *Anal.Boll.* 68, pp. 223–40; J. F. Doherty, "St Laurence O'Toole and the Anglo–Norman Invasion" in *I.E.R.* 1, pp. 449–77, 600–25; 51, pp. 131–46; R. Sharpe, *Medieval Irish Saints' Lives* (1991); L. Gougaud, *Les saints irlandais hors d'Irlande* (1936), pp. 130–1; J. Hennig, "The Place of the Archdiocese of Dublin in the Hagiographical Tradition of the Continent" in *Reportorium Novum* 1 (1955-6), pp. 45–63.

St Dyfrig, *Bishop (c. 550)*

Dyfrig (in Latin Dubricius) was undoubtedly one of the most important Welsh Christians of the fifth and sixth centuries. However, the information about him that has survived is either not early enough to be relied on or manifestly the stuff of legend. What is certain is that he was active mainly in the Wye valley west of Hereford; and the fact that he was believed to have owned land near Caerleon, the Roman town outside what is now Newport, in Gwent, suggests continuity from Romano-British Christianity. He may well have been born, as is claimed, at Madley, six miles from Hereford. After he had become a monk, his own first foundation was at Henllan, near Ross-on-Wye, in the district of Ergyng or Archenfield, and he had many disciples. From Henllan he is said to have moved up the Wye to Moccas, and he and his disciples founded several churches and monasteries. Other places closely connected with him in this area include Whitchurch and Abbey Dore.

Dyfrig features prominently in the seventh-century Life of St Samson (28 July), which is particularly valuable for the light it throws on his activity outside the Wye valley area. St Illtud (6 Nov.) received the tonsure from him; and in his role as bishop—in this Life he is referred to as *papa*—he is said to have ordained Samson to the priesthood, appointed him abbot, possibly of Caldey (where he himself was supposed to have spent Lent each year and where there is a stone inscription that seems to refer to him), and eventually consecrated him bishop, along with St Deiniol (11 Sept.), who founded the monastery at Bangor Fawr on the Menai Straits. The fact that there are churches dedicated to him in two places as far apart as Gwenddwr, near Builth Wells in Powys, and Porlock in Somerset suggests that he exercised his ministry directly or indirectly in both the west and the south-west. Toward the end of his life he is said to have gone up to Ynys Enlli (Bardsey Island), where he died in about 550.

Far less reliable as sources are the twelfth-century Lives, one version in the *Book of Llandaff* and the other by Benedict of Gloucester. From these we learn that he was a disciple of St Germanus of Auxerre (3 Aug.), which is chronologically unlikely, since Germanus died in 446; and that he persuaded St David (1 Mar.) to attend a synod at Llandewi Brefi and there ceded to him the rank of archbishop and "metropolitan" of Wales, a reflection of twelfth-century concerns. Equally suspect is the assertion that the land he owned near Caerleon (if indeed he did own land near Caerleon) formed a significant part of the territory claimed in the twelfth century by the bishops of Llandaff. Finally, Geoffrey of Monmouth, a writer of historical fiction, makes Dyfrig archbishop of Caerleon and says he crowned Arthur "King of Britain" in Colchester.

In 1120 Dyfrig's relics were taken from Ynys Enlli to the cathedral at Llandaff. He was made one of its four titular saints, which helped to renew his cult. Today his feast is celebrated in the archdiocese of Cardiff and at Caldey Abbey.

O.D.S., pp. 140-1. For the Life by Benedict of Gloucester, see H. Wharton, *Anglia Sacra* (1691), 2, pp. 654-61. See also G. H. Doble, *Lives of the Welsh Saints* (1971); E. G. Bowen, *The Settlements of the Celtic Saints in Wales* (1954), pp. 33-48; S. M. Harris, "Liturgical Commemorations of Welsh Saints: 'St Dyfrig'" in *Faith in Wales*, 19, p. 4. He is the "high saint" in the first part of Tennyson's *Idylls of the King*.

Bd Serapion, *Martyr* (1240)

The long-standing cult of this little-known martyr was approved by Pope Benedict XIII (1724-30) in 1728. He is said to have been born in England in 1179, but there is no real evidence to support this; and the other details of his life, such as they are, come from the records of the Mercedarian Order, which are scanty and unreliable. The story goes that, having been a soldier in the service of Alfonso IX of León (1188-1230), he met St Peter Nolasco (13 May) and joined his newly-founded Mercedarian Order for the redemption of captives. After going in 1229 and 1232 to Algeria, where he ransomed a total of 378 slaves, he went to Britain with the aim of gaining recruits for the Order. This was unsuccessful, partly because he took such a public and uncompromising stand on the misuse of church property that he became *persona non grata* and was more or less driven out. In 1240 he went again to the Moors, first in Murcia and then in Algeria, to obtain the release of some Christian slaves. In Algeria, where he was kept as a hostage for the payment of the balance of the ransom, he took the opportunity to preach to the Muslims, several of whom were converted. This so angered the authorities that he was crucified and then cut to pieces. Pope Benedict XIV (1740-58) added his name to the Roman Martyrology, which also mentions on this day another Serapion who died in the persecution of Decius (249-51).

Prosper Lambertini (Pope Benedict XIV), *De beatificatione et canonizatione*, 2, 24; *Bibl.SS.*, 11, 853-5.

St Nicholas Tavelic and Companions, *Martyrs* (1391)

Nicholas Tavelic was a Franciscan from Sibenik in Dalmatia. After working for twenty years as a missionary in Bosnia among the Patarine heretics (a sect which originated in Milan in the eleventh century and had ideas resembling those of the Albigensians and Cathars), he went with three companions, Déodat de Rodez, Pierre de Narbonne, and Stefano da Cuneo, to preach the gospel in Jerusalem, then held by the Muslims. All four were killed there on the same day, 14 November 1391, in a gesture of hatred toward the Christian faith. Although their cult was not confirmed until 1889, there is evidence that it flourished from the beginning of the fifteenth century. When the four were canonized by Pope Paul VI on 21 June 1970, they became the first canonized martyrs of the Custody of the Holy Land, and Nicholas Tavelic became the first Croat saint.

See A. Crnica, *B. Nicolaus Tavelic thaumaturgus croaticus* (1965); *San Nicolo Tavelic e compagni. Quaderno commemorativo in occasione della canonizzazione dei primi santi della Custodia francescana di Terra Santa* (1970); D. Lasic, "Come Nicolo e i suoi compagni vollero predicare al cadi di Gerusalemme" in *Vita Minorum* 41 (1970), pp. 209-12.

Bd John Liccio (1511)

John (Giovanni) Liccio was born at Caccamo in Sicily in the first half of the fifteenth century. His mother died giving him birth, and his father, whether because he was in a state of shock after his wife's death or because the family was too poor, provided no proper care for the child. Fortunately, a kind neighbour took responsibility for him, otherwise he would certainly have died, and he was subsequently brought up by an aunt. When he was about fifteen, he met Bd Peter Geremia (3 Mar.) in Palermo and was inspired by his example to join the Friars Preachers. He turned out to be a gifted preacher himself and was soon sent to establish a Dominican house in his native town. This was no easy task, as they had to build on some long-abandoned foundations—which, because no one remembered them, were thought to have been provided supernaturally. John was appointed prior there in 1494, and he became widely known for wise governance and his gift of miracles. According to the lessons of the office on his feast-day, he was 111 when he died, in 1511. This, however, is unlikely—even if he was a personal disciple of Peter Geremia, he was probably no more than seventy-five at the time of his death. His cult was approved in 1753.

Monumenta Ord. Praedic. Historica, 14, p. 229-30; Lives by M. Ponte (1853); G. Barreca (1926); J. Procter (ed.), *Short Lives of the Dominican Saints* (1901), pp. 318-21. For a fuller bibliography, see I. Taurisano, *Catalogus Hagiographicus O.P.*

15

ST ALBERT THE GREAT, *Bishop and Doctor* (1206-80)

His contemporaries said of Albert that he was "a man no less than godlike in all knowledge, so that he may fitly be called the wonder and miracle of our age." And it was they who dubbed him "the Great" and referred to him as the "universal doctor." Little is known of his childhood and youth apart from the fact that he came from a wealthy and powerful military family; that he was born in 1206 at Lauingen, the fief on the Danube near Augsburg held by his father; and that he was the eldest son in the family. Sometime prior to 1222 he went to study at the University of Padua, where he came into contact with the Dominican Order. In 1222, despite efforts made by an uncle who lived in Padua to prevent it, he was received by the Dominicans as a postulant. When he heard of it, his father threatened to use force to get him back, but this, too, came to nothing.

By 1228 Albert was teaching in Cologne, and in the course of the next twenty years he supervised studies and taught in Hildesheim, Freiburg-im-Breisgau, Regensburg, Strasbourg, Cologne again, and finally Paris, where he lectured under a master while studying for his own master's degree. In 1248, the year he obtained his degree, the Dominicans opened four new houses of studies, and Albert was sent to be director of the one in Cologne. Among his students for the next four years was a younger member of the Dominican order, one Tommaso d'Aquino, better known to the English-speaking world as Thomas Aquinas (28 Jan.), who was to build so successfully on his master's pioneering achievement.

During this period the Order began to recognize Albert's practical abilities, and in 1254 he was made prior provincial of the Friars Preachers in Germany. In 1256 he went to Paris in that capacity, to attend a general chapter of the Order, which ruled, among other things, that Dominicans at the universities should not be called "master," "doctor," or anything but their own name. This ruling related personally to Albert. Because he himself had already been dubbed "universal doctor," jealous secular professors were showing hostility toward the friars, and the granting of degrees to Thomas Aquinas and the Franciscan Bonaventure of Bagnoreggio (15 July) had been delayed.

Albert went to Rome to defend the mendicant Orders against the criticisms that were being levelled against them, in particular by conservatives like William of St-Amour (*c.* 1200-72), whose tract on the subject was called "On the Dangers of These Present Times." While he was in Rome, he filled the office of master of the sacred palace (the pope's personal theologian and canonist, traditionally a Dominican friar) and preached in the churches of the city. In 1260 Pope Alexander IV

(1254-61) appointed him bishop of Regensburg, a diocese said to be "turned up-side-down in spiritual as well as temporal matters." He worked hard to remedy its many ills, but a more ruthless personality and a different set of skills were needed to deal with the powerful vested interests and entrenched abuses that were plaguing it. After less than two years, to the great relief of the Dominican master general, Bd Humbert of Romans (14 July), who had tried to persuade Alexander IV not to make Albert a bishop in the first place, the new pope, Urban IV (1261-4), accepted Albert's resignation, and he was able to return to the house of studies in Cologne.

Apart from one further interruption in the following year, when he went to help the Franciscan Berthold of Regensburg preach the eighth Crusade in Germany, Albert remained in Cologne teaching and writing until 1274, when he was asked to attend the Second Council of Lyons. Just as he was about to set out for Lyons, news reached him of the death of his disciple and friend, Thomas Aquinas, who was himself on his way to the council when he died. Despite the shock—Aquinas was not yet fifty years old—Albert went to the council and played an active part in its proceedings. In particular, he worked with Peter of Tarentaise (Pope Innocent V: d. 1276; 22 June) and the bishop and classical scholar Guillaume de Moerbeke (*c.* 1215-*c.* 1286) on the important matter of reunion with the Greeks.

Albert's last public appearance probably took place in 1277, when he hurried to Paris to defend Thomas Aquinas' writings, some of which had been seriously attacked by the bishop of Paris, Stephen Tempier, and a number of other theologians. He challenged the university to examine him personally on Thomas' teaching—which was in some sense his own as well—but even so he was unable to prevent the condemnation of certain points. Then, in 1278, he was giving a lecture when his memory suddenly failed him. Over the next two years this loss of memory gradually became more or less complete—today he would be likely to be diagnosed as suffer-ing from Alzheimer's disease or some other form of dementia—and on 15 Novem-ber 1280 he died, suddenly and peacefully, sitting among his brethren in Cologne.

Not for nothing was Albert called "the universal doctor." He had a prodigiously powerful mind and intellectual curiosity to match. Throughout his long years of teaching and administration he always found time to continue his research—in libraries, certainly, but also out in the fields or anywhere else that he could observe natural phenomena at first hand—and his writings, which incidentally contain the sort of biographical reference that is entirely missing from those of Thomas Aquinas, run to nearly forty volumes. At a time when philosophy was understood to include all the main branches of knowledge accessible to the natural powers of the human mind, Albert covered the field. He was particularly fascinated by "the causes that are at work in nature" and is frequently placed alongside Roger Bacon as one of the great natural scientists of his time. He was an authority on physics, astronomy, mineralogy, alchemy (chemistry), and biology. He wrote a treatise on botany, and another on human and animal physiology in which he disposed, on the basis of personal observation, of a number of then current myths (for example, that eagles wrap their eggs in fox skin and leave them to hatch in the sun). As a geographer he explained, among other things, how latitude affects climate, and—two centuries before Columbus—that the earth is spherical. All of this was in addition to the work for which he is principally remembered. As a firm believer in the autonomy of reason and of the role of experience in the life of faith, he set out to show that, far from being in conflict with Christian belief, the teachings of the ancient philosophers, notably Aristotle, can be reconciled with it and used as tools for our understanding of it. And in so doing he created the foundations on which Aquinas built the great edifice of Scholasticism.

In *La Divina Commedia*, Dante places Albert in the fourth sphere of heaven, that of the sun, among the spirits of scholars and wise men; he is seated immediately to the right of St Thomas Aquinas, who introduces him to Dante as his "brother and master." Albert is one of the few saints whose iconography was well developed even before his canonization. The many representations of him in art include an extraordinarily expressive portrait by Tomaso da Modena in the Dominican convent in Treviso and another, similarly expressive, by Justus of Ghent in the ducal palace in Urbino. He stands in the top left-hand corner of *Dominican Beati* in the National Gallery in London—one of three portrayals of him by Fra Angelico (18 Feb.).

Albert was beatified by Pope Gregory XV (1621-3) in 1622, but despite a considerable increase in devotion to him then, especially in Germany, and an appeal from the German bishops in 1927, he was effectively canonized only in 1931, when Pope Pius XI proclaimed him a Doctor of the Church. Albert, the pope said, "is precisely the saint whose example should inspire the present age, which seeks peace so ardently and is so full of hope in its scientific discoveries." He named him patron of students of the natural sciences.

A critical edition of St Albert's works, ed. B. Geyer *et al.*, is in course of publication (1955-). These and the earlier Lives have been thoroughly studied by modern biographers: F. J. Kovach and R. W. Shahan (eds.), *Albert the Great: Commemorative Essays* (1980); G. Meyer and A. Zimmermann (eds.), *Albertus Magnus, Doctor Universalis 1280-1980* (1980); D. H. Madden, *A Chapter in Medieval History* (1969); S. M. Albert, *Albert the Great* (1948); H. Wilms, *Albert the Great* (1933); Thomas M. Schwertner, *St Albert the Great* (1932); A. Garreau, *St Albert le Grand* (1932); H. C. Scheeben, *Albert der Grosse* (1931). See also *Bibl.SS.*, 1, 700-17; J. Quétif and J. Echard, *Scriptores Ordinis Praedicatorum*, 1 (1719); P. de Loë, "De vita et scriptis beati Alberti Magni" in *Anal.Boll.* 19, pp. 257-84; 20, pp. 273-316; 21, pp. 367-71; *Anal.Boll.* 51, pp. 183-90; A. De Libera, *Albert le Grand et la Philosophie* (1990); J. A. Weisheipl (ed.), *Albertus Magnus and the Sciences* (1980). For the iconography, see K. Künstle, *Ikonographie der Heiligen* (1926).

SS Gurias, Samonas, and Abibus, *Martyrs* (Fourth Century)

One of the two principal shrines in Edessa, Syria, was built over the remains of these martyrs, whose originally separate cults eventually merged. There are several Greek variants of their *passio* and a version in Armenian as well as one in Syriac, which seems to be the original. According to this, Gurias (Gurya) and Samonas (Smuna) were arrested during the persecution of Diocletian (284-305). When they refused to sacrifice to the local gods, they were hung up for a while by one hand, with weights attached to their feet, and then thrown into a stinking dungeon. When they emerged after four days, Gurias was already nearly dead, but Samonas was submitted to further torture in an attempt to break his resolve. When this failed, he and Gurias were beheaded. Some time (probably years) later, Abibus (Habib), a deacon from Edessa, managed initially to hide from the persecution of Licinius (308-24) but then gave himself up so that he could die a martyr. The officer in charge gave him a chance to change his mind, but when he refused he was sentenced to be burned. He was accompanied to the place of execution by his mother and other relatives, who, when he was dead, took his body and buried it near those of his friends, Gurias and Samonas. All three are mentioned in the Roman Martyrology, although in two separate entries. They were venerated, curiously, as "avengers of unfulfilled contracts."

The *passio* is in *Biblia Hagiographica Graeca*, 1, 731-6; E. von Dobschütz in *Texte und Untersuchungen*, 37, pt.2. See also: *Bibl.SS.*, 7, 539-43; H. Delehaye, *Les Origines du Culte des Martyrs* (1933); F. C. Burkitt, *Euphemia and the Goth* (1913).

St Didier of Cahors, *Bishop* (655)

Several saints by the name of Didier (Desiderius) are venerated in France. This one, who is also known as Géry, was the son of a nobleman who possessed large estates in the area round Albi. He became a prominent official at the court of King Clotaire of Neustria (584-629), where he met St Arnulf of Metz (18 July) and St Eligius (1 Dec.). When his brother Rusticus, who became a priest and was then consecrated bishop of Cahors, was murdered in 630 (he is venerated as a martyr at Cahors), Didier was elected as his successor, despite the fact that he was still a layman. He proved to be a zealous and effective pastor. From his surviving correspondence it is possible to obtain some idea of the extent of his activities, which were directed toward the temporal as well as the spiritual welfare of his diocese. He was a strong promoter of monasticism, both for men and for women, and he encouraged members of the local nobility to endow religious foundations. He personally endowed one monastery, built three large churches, and directed a convent he had founded; he also seems to have helped to provide an aqueduct for Cahors and contributed to the repair of the city's fortifications. But his main preoccupation was the welfare of his people. Realizing that this depended to a great extent on a respected and educated clergy, he made sure that the priests of the diocese were properly educated and strictly disciplined. He died near Albi in 655 and was buried in Cahors. Miracles were recorded at his tomb.

A late eighth- or early ninth-century Latin Life, with the text of letters and documents of some historical value, is in *M.G.H., Scriptores Merov.*, 4, pp. 547-602; *P.L.*, 87, 219-39.

St Malo, *Bishop* (Sixth-Seventh Century)

There are at least four medieval Lives of St Malo (Machutus, Maclovius, Maclou), who is known principally as the apostle of Brittany. The best known was written toward the end of the ninth century by a deacon named Bili. However, scholars believe there was an earlier Life, which has not survived, on which the others were based. Although these Lives do provide some sort of portrait of this stalwart missionary, there is also much that is unconvincing. He is said, for example, to have set off in search of the Isle of the Blessed and celebrated Easter on the back of a whale, emulating St Brendan (16 May).

According to his medieval hagiographers, Malo was born near Llancarfan in south Wales and educated at the monastery there. When he grew up, he joined the monastic community, but as this was against the wishes of his parents he spent some time in hiding on one of the islands in the Severn Sea (Bristol Channel) in order to get away from them. Once he had been ordained, he decided to leave Britain, possibly because of the plague that ravaged the country in the middle of the sixth century. He crossed to Brittany and, having established his headquarters on the island where the town of Saint-Malo now stands, began to preach the gospel in the neighbourhood of Aleth (Saint-Servan). He built churches, founded monasteries, and did what he could to protect the people from the violence of the local chiefs.

He made many converts as he travelled on horseback from place to place, and he is said to have recited psalms in a loud voice as he went. But he also made enemies and, once the chief who protected him was dead, he was unable to withstand them. With thirty-three other monks, he boarded a ship and, solemnly denouncing the trouble-makers, sailed down the coast. He settled near Saintes, where he remained for some years until a deputation arrived from Aleth, asking him to return. Aleth was suffering from a severe drought, they told him, and this was being attributed to the town's treatment of its bishop. At this point the versions of the story diverge. Some say Malo died before he had a chance to return; others that he did return and that as he arrived there was a heavy fall of rain. According to the second version he did not stay long but died on his way back to Saintes.

The feast of St Malo was celebrated in a number of monasteries in southern England, and his name appears in the calendars of Sarum, York, and Hereford. It has been claimed that the bishops of Winchester encouraged his cult because Gwent and Winchester resemble one another in Latin. Several churches, in Bath and elsewhere, claim to have his relics.

Lives in F. Plaine in *Bulletins et Mémoires de la Soc. archéol. du départment d'Ille-et-Vilaine* (1883), pp. 167-256; A. de la Borderie, *ibid.*, pp. 267-93; F. Lot, "Les diverses rédactions de la vie de St-Malo" in *Mélanges d'histoire bretonne* (1907), pp. 97-206. See also L. Duchesne, "La Vie de St-Malo: Etude critique" in *Revue celtique* 11 (1890), pp. 1-22; A. Poncelet, "Une source de la vie de S. Malo par Bili" in *Anal.Boll.* 24 (1905), pp. 483-6; R. Brown and D. Yerkes, "A Sermon on the Birthday of St Malchus" in *Anal.Boll.* 89, pp. 160-4.

St Fintan of Rheinau (*c.* 879)

What little is known of this Fintan (Findan) is contained in one extant Latin Life. He is said to have been born in Leinster at the beginning of the ninth century, but during one of the Viking raids he was captured and taken off to Orkney. Eventually he managed to escape and, having spent two years under the protection of an unidentified Scottish bishop, travelled to Rome on pilgrimage. On his way back he broke the journey at Rheinau, an island in the Rhine near Schaffhausen, where he was given hospitality by a community of hermits. Instead of returning to Ireland, he remained in Rheinau and joined the community, among whose members he acquired a reputation for holiness. He spent the last twenty-two years of his life as a solitary, refusing even the comfort of a fire in his cell. It is possible that he compiled the *Sacramentary of Zurich*, which contains a calendar of Irish saints. He died in about 879, and his remains were enshrined in Rheinau, where his feast is still celebrated, in 1446.

The Latin Life is in *M. G. H., Scriptores*, 15, pp. 356–60. See also L. Gougaud, *Les saints irlandais hors d'Irlande* (1936), pp. 95-6; D. Pochin Mould, *The Irish Saints* (1964), pp. 173-4.

St Leopold of Austria (1075-1136)

Only a few certain details are known about this prince, who was known as "the Good" and was canonized 350 years after his death by Pope Innocent VIII (1484-92). He was born in 1073 at Gars, near Melk in Lower Austria, and brought up under the influence of St Altman (8 Aug.), the reforming bishop of Passau, who was one of the four south German bishops who stood up to the emperor Henry IV on behalf of Pope Gregory VII (1073-85; 25 May). At the age of twenty-three he succeeded his father as margrave of Austria, and ten years later, in 1106, married Henry IV's daughter, Agnes, already a widow (of Frederick of Hohenstaufen) with two young children. Leopold and Agnes themselves had eighteen children, of whom eleven survived childhood. One of their sons was the historian Otto of Freising, who, while he was abbot of the Cistercian abbey at Morimond in Burgundy, asked his father to found the abbey of Heiligenkreuz in the Wienerwald. This is still active today, as are Leopold's two other foundations: the Augustinian priory at Klosterneuberg, near Vienna, which was influential as a German-speaking centre of the liturgical reform movement in the early decades of this century; and the Benedictine monastery of Mariazell, in Styria, which is still a popular centre of pilgrimage.

Despite the relatively low-key role he played in the tortuous secular and ecclesiastical politics of his time, Leopold, who supported the pope in the investiture struggle, seems to have made enough of a mark to become the preferred candidate of the Bavarians for the imperial crown when his brother-in-law, Henry V, died in 1125. He refused to be nominated, however, preferring to remain margrave of Austria. He died while out hunting in 1136 and was buried at Klosterneuberg, genuinely mourned by his people. He was canonized in 1485 and named patron of Austria in 1683.

The only known medieval Life is in H. Pez, *Scriptores rerum Austriacarum* (1721), 1, pp. 577-92. See also B. A. Egger, German biography (1885, Fr. trans. 1891); V. O. Ludwig, *Die Legende von milden Markgraf Leopold* (1925); essays (ed. S. Wintermayr, 1936); F. Rohrig, *Leopold III der Heilige* (1985).

Bd Lucy of Narni (1476-1544)

Lucy (Lucia) was the eldest of the eleven children of Bartolomeo Brocadelli, treasurer of the commune of Narni in Umbria, and his wife, Gentilina Cassio. She was born in Narni on 13 December 1476 and from an early age was determined to consecrate her life to God. Unfortunately, her guardians—her father died while she was a child—had other ideas for her, and when she was fourteen they tried to betroth her by force. On this occasion she is said to have thrown the ring on the floor, slapped her suitor's face and run from the room. However, in the following year, after some resistance, but on the advice of her confessor—and, she said, of Our Lady, who appeared to her in a vision—she agreed to marry a young man named Pietro di Alessio. But this was a marriage in name only, and after about three years the doubtless bewildered Pietro told her she was free to go and do as she pleased.

Lucy went initially to her mother's house. Then, having received the habit of the Dominican Third Order, she joined communities of regular tertiaries, first in Rome and then in Viterbo. It was while she was in Viterbo, where she remained for three years, that she received the stigmata, along with a physical participation in the passion of Christ which involved actual loss of blood. And as this took place regularly every Wednesday and Friday, it was impossible for her to conceal what was going on. She was examined by the local inquisitor, the master of the sacred palace, a Franciscan bishop, and Pope Alexander VI's personal physician, all of whom came as sceptics and left convinced that the phenomena were genuine. Pietro, too, came to see her and was likewise convinced—he is said to have joined the Friars Minor as a result. Even later, when, as one of her biographers notes, the Franciscans of Mallorca attempted to suppress a picture of her with the stigmata on the ground that Pope Sixtus IV had threatened with excommunication anyone who portrayed someone other than St Francis with the stigmata, the reality of the phenomenon was not questioned.

At this point Lucy became involved in the essentially well-intentioned but nevertheless misguided ambitions of Ercole I, duke of Ferrara. He was a sincere admirer of St Catherine of Siena (29 Apr.), who had died in 1380 and been canonized in 1461, and numbered such contemporary women as Bd Columba da Rieti (20 May) and Bd Osanna of Mantua (20 June) among his friends. When Lucy was brought to his attention he obviously could not resist the idea of a Ferrara-based mystic and, with her assent, obtained the pope's permission to build a convent for her in the city. Great obstacles were placed in the way of her leaving Viterbo, but in the end she was smuggled out of the town in a clothes basket strapped to the back of a mule.

Unfortunately, the project was more or less doomed from the start. Lucy herself was still in her very early twenties and quite lacking in the natural qualities, not to mention the experience, needed in a superior. Ercole d'Este, on the other hand, was a man of large ideas who wanted the new convent, on the building and decoration of which he had spent vast sums of money, to house at least a hundred sisters. To this end he enlisted the help of his son Alfonso's new wife, Lucrezia Borgia, who was undeniably successful in attracting recruits, but not all of them were entirely suitable. This made Lucy's task even harder, and she was soon deposed, her place being taken not by another tertiary but by a Dominican nun, Maria da Parma, whose ambition was to affiliate the entire community to the so-called Second Order.

Then, in 1505, Ercole d'Este died. Deprived of her protector, Lucy, who had hitherto filled the role imposed on her of "fashionable mystic," now lapsed into the total obscurity in which she was to spend the last thirty-nine years of her life. The new prioress treated her with a severity that was nothing short of cruel. Yet these were the years in which Lucy earned her claim to holiness: she was never impatient, and no one ever heard her complain, even when she was ill and left unattended. So complete, in fact, was her self-effacement that when she died on 15 November 1544, the people of Ferrara were astonished to hear that she had been alive all that time. A popular cult developed spontaneously and on such a scale that her body had to be moved to somewhere more public than the convent. Miracles were claimed at her new tomb in the cathedral, and her cult was confirmed in 1710.

G. Marcianese, *Narratione della nascita etc, della b. Lucia di Narni* (1616); Domenico Ponsi, *Vita della beata Lucia di Narni* (1711); L. A. Gandini, *Sulla venuta in Ferrara della beata Lucia da Narni* (1901); Edmund Gardner, *Dukes and Poets in Ferrara* (1904). Ercole d'Este's letter on Lucy's stigmata is in *Spiritualium personarum facta admiratione digna* (1501, a copy of which is in the British Museum).

St Roque González and Companions, *Martyrs* (1628)

The earliest martyrs in the Americas to be beatified suffered in 1628. This is not, of course, to say that there were no martyrs earlier than that in the New World: three Franciscans were killed by Caribs in the Antilles in 1516; massacres soon followed on the mainland; and in 1544 Friar Juan Padilla became the first martyr of North America—it is not certain where he died, but eastern Colorado, western Kansas, and Texas have all been suggested. These earlier martyrs have not been beatified simply because, so far at least, insufficient evidence has come to light concerning the circumstances of their deaths. So the earliest martyrs of America to be beatified were three Jesuits in Paraguay, one of whom, Bd Roque, was American-born.

Roque González y de Santa Cruz was born of noble Spanish parents in the Paraguayan capital, Asunción, in 1576. He was an unusually good boy with a strong religious sensitivity, and everyone seems to have assumed that he would become a priest. When he was twenty-three, he was indeed ordained—albeit unwillingly, since he felt he was very unworthy of the priesthood. Immediately, he began to take an interest in the Indians of Paraguay, going to remote places in order to seek them out and preach Christianity to them. After ten years, wishing to avoid ecclesiastical promotion and have more opportunities for missionary work, he joined the Society of Jesus.

Among the religious Orders in Paraguay, the Jesuits were relative newcomers. The Franciscans had arrived in 1537, followed fairly quickly by the Mercedarians, the Hieronymites, and the Dominicans. The Jesuits came only in 1609, when the governor of Asunción and the local bishop approached them specifically for missionaries. The provincial responded immediately with three pairs of missionaries, who began to set up the communities which came to be known as *reducciones*, "reductions." Seeing themselves not as conquerors and masters of the Indians, as did so many of their fellow-countrymen who came to the Americas, but as trustees and guardians, they aimed to help the Indians become self-sufficient while at the same time converting them to Christianity. In this they were successful until, in the following century, their opposition to Spanish imperialism, to slavery, and to the methods of the Inquisition led to the dissolution of the reductions and the suppression of the Society in Spanish America.

The reductions were independent Indian village communities from which all European settlers were excluded. They had their own political institutions, and only the chief magistrate was appointed by the governor. Their average population was about 3,000, and at their peak there were between thirty and fifty of them. Each was set up in a fertile area on or near a river and according to a basic pattern, round a central *plaza*. On one side would be the church, the priest's house, the cemetery, a house for widows and orphans, a store house, and offices, and on the other three the homes of the Indians. The Jesuits introduced a combination of collective (agriculture) and private (gardens and domestic animals) ownership, and from the sale of the products of domestic industry money was raised to buy items needed by the community. Apart from Christian doctrine, the Indians were taught to read and write and to sing, and any artistic ability was encouraged. Unfortunately, though probably inevitably, things began to fall apart once the Jesuits left, and the reductions were caught up in Spanish-Portuguese border disputes. But while they lasted these settlements were of a quality that left even the sceptical Voltaire impressed: "When the Paraguayan missions left the hands of the Jesuits in 1768, they had arrived at what is perhaps the highest degree of civilization to which it is possible to lead a young people. . . . In those missions, law was respected, morals were pure, a happy brotherliness bound men together, the useful arts and even some of the more graceful sciences flourished, and there was abundance everywhere."

Roque González was involved from the start. He spent nearly twenty years in the reductions, throwing himself wholeheartedly into his work despite hardship, danger, and opposition both from certain Indian tribes and from the colonists. For three years he was in charge of the original reduction, San Ignazio Guazú (founded 1611), named after the founder of the Society of Jesus, St Ignatius of Loyola (31 July), after which he went on to found others. All of these were east of the Paraná and Uruguay rivers, and in the course of his work he reached areas of Latin America where no European had set foot before. A contemporary Spaniard, the governor of Corrientes, testified that he himself was "able to appreciate how much the life which Fr Roque led must have cost him—hunger, cold, exhaustion from travelling on foot, swimming across rivers, wading through bogs, not to mention plaguing insects and the discomforts which no man but a true apostle, who was as holy as this priest was, could have born with such fortitude." As a result of his dedication and of his respect for their way of life, Fr Roque enjoyed extraordinary influence among the Indians. However, toward the end of his life, his work was hampered by the civil authorities, who attempted to use his influence for their own ends. They insisted on having their representatives on each new reduction, and it was not long before the insensitivity and even brutality of the men involved aroused resentment among the Indians, which in turn led to suspicion of all Europeans. The work of the missionaries was seriously undermined.

In 1628 Roque was joined by two Spanish Jesuits, Alonso Rodríguez and Juan de Castillo, both about twenty years younger than himself but experienced missionaries nonetheless. Together the three men founded a reduction near the Ijuhi river, dedicating it in honour of the Assumption. Juan was left in charge, while Roque and Alonso pushed on to Caaró, in what is now the southern tip of Brazil, and established the All Saints reduction.

Here the two men aroused the hostility of a powerful local medicine man, who convinced himself that all Jesuits had to be killed and instigated an attack on the mission. His henchmen arrived as Roque was preparing to hang a small church bell. One of them surprised him from behind, killing him with a single blow to the head with a tomahawk. Hearing the commotion, Alonso came to the door of his hut to see what was going on. The intruders knocked him down and responded to his question, "What are you doing, my sons?" with further blows, which killed him. Before they left, they dragged the bodies to the wooden chapel, which they proceeded to set on fire. It was 15 November 1628. Two days later a similar attack took place on the mission at Ijuhi. Juan was seized and bound, cruelly beaten, and stoned to death. And between then and 20 November three more Jesuits, all of them Spanish, were hunted down and killed: Juan de Fonte, Gerónimo de Morante, and Hernando de Santarén.

Within six months of their martyrdom the first steps were taken toward the beatification of these missionaries, and evidence about what had happened was taken down in writing. This included the testimony of an Indian chief, Guarecupi, who said: "All the Christians among my countrymen loved the Father [Roque] and grieved for his death, because he was the father of us all, and so he was called by the Indians of the Paraná." Unfortunately, the resulting documents were lost, apparently on their way to Rome, which meant that no further progress could be made in the beatification process. Then, about 200 years later, copies of the originals turned up in Argentina, and in 1934 Roque González, Alonso Rodríguez, and Juan de Castillo were declared blessed by Pope Pius XI (1922-39). They were canonized by Pope John Paul II in 1988.

For most of the available evidence, see J. M. Blanco in *Historia documentada de la Vita y gloriosa Muerte de los PP. Roque González. . . .* (1929). See also J. N. Tylenda, *Jesuit Saints and Martyrs* (1985); H. Thurston, S.J., "The first beatified martyr of Spanish America" in *Catholic Historical Review* 20 (1935), pp. 371-83; *N.C.E.*, 6, p. 611. On the reductions of Paraguay, see R. B. Cunninghame Graham, *A Vanished Arcadia* (1924); M. Durán Estragó in E. Dussel (ed.), *The Church in Latin America: 1492-1992* (1992), pp. 351-62; *N.C.E.*, 12, pp. 165-6.

St Raphael Kalinowski (1835-1907)

Jozef, son of Andrey Kalinowski and Jozefa Polonska, was born at Vilna in Russian Poland (now Vilnius, Lithuania) on 1 September 1835. His mother died within a few weeks of his birth, so he was entrusted to the care of her sister Victoria, who later married his father. She too died when he was only nine, and his father, left now with five children, married Sophia Puttkamer, whose mother, Maria Wereszczak, was celebrated in the poetry of the Polish Romantic poet, Adam Mickiewicz. Jozef's early education took place at home, but when he was nine he became a pupil at the College of the Nobility in Vilna, where his father was professor of mathematics. Here he did exceptionally well, graduating when he was seventeen with a gold medal. Although he felt called to the priesthood, he followed his father's advice and decided to go to university first.

For a young Pole at the time, this was not as easy as it might sound. Poland, which then extended to the territory that is now Lithuania, had been occupied by Russia in 1795, and its independent universities had been closed. Any young man who wanted to continue his education had to go to a Russian university. So Jozef enrolled at the Institute of Agronomy in Hory Horki, where he studied zoology, chemistry, agriculture, and apiculture. He did not remain there for long, however. His real enthusiasm was for mathematics and the related sciences, so he transferred to the Academy of Military Engineering in St Petersburg. Having graduated from the latter in 1857 as a lieutenant in the corps of engineers, he was sent in 1858 to supervise the designing and planning of the Kursk-Kiev-Odessa railway line. A letter to his parents written after he had taken up this post suggests that he had just come through some sort of spiritual crisis. "In the complete solitude," he wrote, "in which I live, I have succeeded in developing a strong contemplative life; and honestly, I must emphasize that this working by myself, so far away from other people, has brought about a major change for the better within me. I have recognized the value of our accepted religious beliefs, and have at last returned to them."

When, in 1860, work on the railway was postponed indefinitely, Jozef was transferred to the fortress at Brest-Litovsk, and two years later he was promoted to the rank of captain on the general staff. The three years he spent in Brest-Litovsk were not entirely happy, largely because of the Russian domination and, in particular, the effect this had on the Catholic Church in Poland. But he was not one to give in to discouragement. He founded a small Catholic Sunday school, in which he himself taught, and he limited his personal expenditure in order to have money to spend on the poor.

All this came to an end with the Polish uprising of January 1863. Jozef was too clear-sighted and too familiar with the Russian military not to realize that the enterprise was doomed to failure. But he also realized that by joining the insurgents, the justice of whose cause he recognized, he might be able to encourage some sort of damage limitation. So he resigned from the army, joined the insurgents, and was named minister of war for the Vilna region—a position he accepted on condition that he would not have to pronounce the death sentence on anyone. In fact, he spent the next ten months or so doing what he could to save lives. But he was being watched by the Russians, and less than a year later, on 25 March 1864, he was arrested. Three months later he was condemned to death, but he was so well known and so popular that the Russian authorities, fearing that he might be proclaimed a martyr, commuted the sentence to ten years hard labour. He began the harrowing journey to Siberia—nine months on foot with a long column of others—on 29 June of that year. He captures the bleakness of it all in his memoirs: "Close by Perm [the city where the condemned had to muster before being dispersed] right to the distant east, the immense plain which stretched on either side of the Urals turned into a vast cemetery for tens of thousands of victims, wrenched from the embrace of their mother country. They were swallowed up forever."

In the nine years that Jozef spent in Siberia he was never heard to complain about his own sufferings; he shared what little he had and his words and example were a constant source of strength to his companions. He himself seems to have undergone a profound inward change when, released from work in the salt mines, he took up forced residence in Irkutsk. There he found a friend in a Polish priest, Krzystof Szwernicki, whose parish was the whole of Siberia. Together they taught the children of the residents and prepared them for their First Communion. Meanwhile, under Krzystof's guidance, Jozef began to prepare himself for what he realized now was his true vocation. When he was finally set free in the spring of 1873, his one desire was to enter a monastery.

Perhaps characteristically, Jozef did not take the final decision about this immediately. He went first to visit his family, and his brother George wrote in his diary: "These long years of deprivation have left carved in my brother's face the traces of unspeakable suffering. But what a change in his soul! His appearance spoke of his modesty, his recollection and continual union with God." But one of the conditions of his release was that he would not settle in Lithuania. He could have remained in Poland, but most monasteries and convents had been suppressed. So, sadly, he left his family and set off instead for Paris, where he worked for three years as tutor to Auguste, son of Prince Ladislaw Czartoryski. Then, on 16 July 1877, he left France and went to join the Carmelites at Graz, in Austria.

Having completed his novitiate, and known now by his religious name, Raphael (Rafal), he went first to Györ in Hungary, where he completed his philosophical and theological studies and made his solemn profession. From there he went to Czerna, within the district of Cracow (the only Polish Carmelite monastery to remain open), where he was ordained to the priesthood on 15 January 1882. He was appointed prior at Czerna in the same year and was at various times provincial definitor, prior once again in Czerna and then in Wadowice, and vicar provincial for the Discalced Carmelites nuns. He was particularly gifted as an educator and as a spiritual director. His great ambition was to revitalize completely the Carmelite Order in Poland—and he wanted prayer to be the source and guiding principle of this renewal, just as it was of his own life. It was the authenticity of his prayer that attracted others to him and led to his spending hours in the confessional offering wise and honest guidance. His other great desire was that all Christians might at last reunite under one supreme pastor, and he worked tirelessly for this, even after he had begun to feel his age.

In 1904 Raphael was asked by his superiors to write his memoirs. He embarked on the work, but his health was already failing, and on 15 November 1907 he died in Wadowice. The news spread quickly, and people converged from all over to venerate the man they were already convinced was a saint. Raphael was beatified on 23 June 1983, during the visit to Poland of Pope John Paul II (who was born in Wadowice in May 1920), and canonized on 17 November 1991.

See *A.A.S.*, 44, p. 750; Ambrogio di S. Teresa in *Dizionario Ecclesiastico*, 3, p. 423; J. Galofero, *Al Carmelo attraverso la Siberia* (1960); Monk Matthew, O.D.C. Tert., *Saint from the Salt Mines* (1986); recent material in Polish.

ST MARGARET OF SCOTLAND
Black Greek cross and silver salfire, on blue field.

16

ST MARGARET OF SCOTLAND (*c.* 1045-93)

Margaret, the youngest of four children, was born around 1045, probably in Hungary. Her father, Edward the Atheling, son of Edmund Ironside, king of Wessex (1016), had taken refuge there from Danish rule in England and had married the sister of the Hungarian king. Margaret received a good education in Hungary, and she seems to have had a developed aesthetic sense, which manifested itself in an appreciation of fine books and manuscripts and good taste in clothes. In 1057 her father was called back to England by Edward the Confessor (1042-66; 13 Oct.), who hoped to make him his heir. However, the younger Edward died soon after his arrival in England, leaving the way open for the Normans. After the Conquest it was not safe for Margaret, as one of the few surviving members of the Anglo-Saxon royal family, to remain in England. So she followed her brother, Edgar the Atheling, to Scotland, where she was welcomed at the court of King Malcolm III Canmore (1058-93). Attracted by her beauty and her intelligence, Malcolm married her in about 1070, and they lived very happily together for almost twenty-five years. Of their six sons, three, Edgar, Alexander, and David, who is also venerated as a saint (24 May), ruled in Scotland; and Matilda, one of their two daughters, married the English king, Henry I (1100-35).

It was Matilda who commissioned Turgot, prior of Durham and later bishop of St Andrews, who had also been Margaret's confessor, to write a Life of her mother. His *Vita Margaretae Scotiae reginae* was written between 1104 and 1108, and although it follows the general pattern of such Lives, it benefits from the fact that the author knew his subject so well. According to Turgot, Margaret's influence was considerable, both in private and in public. Life at the Scottish court, which until then had been rather basic and lacking in culture, was transformed by her presence, though some complained that it was becoming too Anglicized. She also promoted reform of the Church in Scotland, helping, for example, to bring local practice in matters such as the observance of Lent and Easter, and abstention from work on Sundays, into line with the practice of the Church of Rome. She was an enthusiastic founder of monasteries, one of her great projects being the revival of the abbey of Iona, while another was the building of Dunfermline as a burial-place for the Scottish royal family. She also arranged for hostels to be built on either side of the Forth River for pilgrims to St Andrews, and she saw to it that they had boats to ferry them across.

Most of her own time, when she was not looking after the needs of her children or of the poor, Margaret spent either in prayer or reading, and she was an accomplished needlewoman. Malcolm, who relied on her constant support and discerning advice, learned also to value her spirit of prayer: he "saw," according to her biographer, "that Christ truly dwelt in her heart. . . . What she rejected, he rejected . . . what she loved, he for love of her loved too." And although he never learned to read, he came to appreciate the beautiful bindings and illuminations of the books from which she read. One or two of her books still survive, including a pocket edition of the Gospels (Bodleian Library, Oxford), an illustrated life of St Cuthbert (20 Mar.), and a Psalter (which may or may not have been hers but which is now owned by University College, Oxford.)

Margaret fell ill, probably with exhaustion as a contributory factor, toward the end of 1093. Just before she died, news came that Malcolm and one of their younger sons had been killed by the army of William II Rufus (1087-1100) at Alnwick. Attempts were made to keep it from her, but she could not be deceived and accepted her loss as the will of God. She died on 16 November 1093 and was buried at Dunfermline with her husband. A cult developed immediately, but it was not confirmed until the thirteenth century, when Pope Innocent IV (1243-54) called for an inquiry into her life and miracles. She was canonized in 1250. Dunfermline was sacked in 1560, but the relics were safely removed. Margaret's body, together with that of Malcolm, was transferred to a chapel in the Escorial, outside Madrid (the head went first to Edinburgh and then to the Jesuits at Douai). In 1673 St Margaret was named a patron of Scotland.

AA.SS., June, 2, pp. 320–40; *Propylaeum*, p. 231. For Turgot's Life, see Symeon of Durham, *Opera*, 1, pp. 234-54; J. Pinkerton, *Lives of the Scottish Saints*, 2 (1889), pp. 159-82; W. M. Metcalfe, *Ancient Lives of Scottish Saints* (1895), pp. 298-321. Modern studies: T. R. Barnett (1926); L. Menzies (2d ed. 1960); D. McRoberts (1960); A. J. Wilson (1993); S. Marwick (1993). See also *Bibl.SS.*, 8, 781-86; *H.S.S.C.*, 6, pp. 206-9; G. W. S. Barrow, "Scottish Rulers and the Religious Orders" in *T.R.H.S.*, 5th ser., 3 (1953), pp. 77-100; *idem*, "From Queen Margaret to David I. Benedictines and Tironians" in *Innes Review* 11 (1960), pp. 22-38; D. Baker, "A 'Nursery of Saints': St Margaret Reconsidered" in *Medieval Women* (1978), pp. 119-42; F. and P. Sharatt, *Écosse Romane* (1985).

SS GERTRUDE THE GREAT (1256-1302) and
MECHTILDIS OF HELFTA (*c.* 1241-98)

The great Benedictine abbey of Helfta was founded in 1234 at Rodarsdorf in Saxony by Burckhards von Mansfeld. In the course of the thirteenth century it produced three of the greatest female spiritual writers in the history of the Church: Mechtild von Magdeburg, who died there; Mechtild von Hackeborn, who spent her entire life there; and Gertrud von Helfta—"the Great"—who did the same. Because there is, in the nature of things, so little to differentiate their lives outwardly and because what commentators like to call "the Helfta style" developed where their writing was concerned, it is not always easy to sort out exactly who wrote what. None of the three was ever formally canonized. However, Gertrude won posthumous recognition when her works were printed in Latin in 1536. Then in 1677 Pope Innocent XI (1676-89) added her name to the Roman Martyrology, and Pope Clement XII (1730–40), at the request of the king of Poland and the duke of Saxony, decreed in 1738 that her feast should be observed throughout the Western Church; she was also named patroness of the West Indies at the request of Philip IV of Spain. Meanwhile, numerous houses of Benedictine nuns are permitted to celebrate the feast of St Mechtildis. St Gertrude's feast has been retained on today's date in the 1969 revision of the Roman Calendar. It therefore seems best to treat Gertrude and Mechtildis (von Hackeborn) together on this day, although in Germany Gertrude is celebrated on 17 November and Mechtildis on the 20th.

When Mechtildis was seven years old, she went with her mother to visit the Benedictine nuns at Rodarsdorf. Her much-loved elder sister (named Gertrud, but not to be confused with the saint), was already a member of the community, and in 1251 she would be elected abbess at the young age of nineteen. Mechtildis begged to be allowed to stay. Her wish was granted, and she became a member, first of the abbey school and then, when she was old enough, of the Benedictine community. Yet it would be wrong to conclude from this that she suffered from narrowness of vision or ignorance of the world. For one thing, she would have gone home frequently during her childhood and adolescence; for another, the education offered to girls in monastery schools could be excellent—as it was at Rodarsdorf and Helfta. We do not know exactly when, but certainly by 1260, she herself was given charge of the children who were sent to the abbey to be educated, a task she combined with her other role as chief chantress, on account of her beautiful singing voice.

In 1258 the community moved from Rodarsdorf to Helfta, also in Saxony and the seat of the Hackeborn family. Three years later, the children in Mechtildis' care were joined by a five-year-old named Gertrude. Nothing is known about her background (she herself strongly hints that she was an orphan), but she was, from all reports, both attractive personally and highly intelligent. There was an immediate rapport between pupil and teacher; and under the care of Mechtildis, who became her novice-mistress after she had made the decision to join the community, Gertrude flourished, becoming among other things an impressive Latin scholar.

When she was twenty-five, Gertrude had a profound spiritual experience, which, as she saw it, effectively divided her life into two—though she makes clear that she did not immediately and irrevocably change. As a result of this experience, "from being a grammarian she became a theologian," turning from the secular writers she had learned to love under Mechtildis' tuition, in order more thoroughly to explore the Bible and the works of the Fathers, notably St Augustine, St Gregory, and St Bernard. Her own writings clearly reflect the influence of her reading—as they do, most significantly, of the liturgy.

A written distillation of Gertrude's experiences was published in five volumes under the title *Legatus divinae pietatis*—though they are commonly referred to as the *Revelations* of St Gertrude. Of these, only the second volume was certainly written entirely by Gertrude herself. The last three, though not written by her, were put together under her guidance, while volume one was compiled posthumously from her notes by those who knew her best. To modern readers, less comfortable than their medieval counterparts with a piety that expresses itself in graphically human terms, her writing can seem emotional and even sentimental. This is only partly cultural, however. It is also a result of the difficulty she has in putting her experience into any sort of words. "I began," she says, "to consider within myself how difficult, not to say impossible, it would be for me to find the right expressions and words for all the things that were said to me, so as to make them intelligible on a human level without danger of scandal." The important thing is that the laden style, in which adjectives and metaphors tumble over one another as they try to convey what it is impossible to convey, is rooted in the liturgy and the scriptures—indeed, most of her mystical experiences took place in the context either of the Mass or of the divine office.

Mechtildis had meanwhile been following the same mystical path as her pupil. When she was fifty, she discovered that Gertrude had been faithfully writing down all her teachings and everything she had told her relating to her own experience. At first this alarmed and upset her, but having prayed about it, she took the view that Gertrude had been inspired by God to do what she did. Together they edited the manuscript, which was published as the *Liber specialis gratiae* (better known as the *Revelations* of St Mechtildis).

For both women the love of Christ, symbolized by his heart, was a recurring theme. In this they anticipated the devotion to the Sacred Heart that was to blossom in France some three centuries later, though they conceived of it in a more broadly Trinitarian context. The attractive thing about their writing is that it is essentially so un-self-regarding in an age when spiritual writers tend to concentrate on the worthlessness of the human person in the presence of God. Gertrude was only too aware of her shortcomings, but she never lost sight of the goodness—love, *pietas*—of God, who accepted her in spite of them:

> I consider that I have profited but little from your gifts, and so I cannot believe that they were meant for me alone, because in your eternal wisdom you cannot be misled. That is why, Giver of Gifts, you who have so freely loaded me with gifts unmerited, I ask you to grant that at least one loving heart reading these pages may be moved to compassion, seeing that through zeal for souls you have permitted such a royal gem to be embedded in the shrine of my heart. May such a one be led to praise and exalt your mercy with hymns of heart and lips. . . . And so you will somehow make good all my deficiencies (*Herald of Divine Love*, 2, 5).

Almost nothing is known of the outwardly uneventful lives of these two saints, apart from the little that can be gleaned from their writings. Mechtildis died on 19 November 1298 at the age of about fifty-seven; Gertrude, who was fifteen years younger but had by then been plagued by ill health for at least ten years, died on 17 November, probably in 1302.

In this century, St Gertrude and St Mechtildis have been best known among Catholics for a series of prayers attributed to them. In fact, these were first published in Cologne at the end of the seventeenth century, and, whatever their merits as prayers, they are certainly not by Gertrude and Mechtildis. On the other hand, a selection of prayers taken from their own works was published in English by Canon John Gray in 1927. Alban Butler described the *Revelations* of St Gertrude as "perhaps the most useful production, next to the writings of St Teresa, with which any female saint has enriched the Church for the nourishing of piety in a contemplative state." It has been suggested by some Dante scholars that Mechtildis is Matelda, *la donna soletta*, who makes a brief appearance toward the end of *Il Purgatorio*; other scholars favour Mechtild von Magdeburg, while yet others dismiss both suggestions.

The *Revelationes Gertrudianae et Mechtildianae* were edited in two volumes by the Benedictines of Solesmes in 1875; for an improved edition, with French translation, see J. Hourlier, A. Schmitt, and P. Doyère (eds.), *Oeuvres Spirituelles*, (*S.C.*, 1967ff.). See also M. Winkworth (ed.), *Gertrude of Helfta, The Herald of Divine Love* (1993); A. Barratt (ed.), *Legatus Divinae Pietatis* (1991); H. Urs von Balthasar (ed.) *Mechtild von Hackeborn, Das Buch von Strömenden Lob* (1955). Lives include G. Dolan (1925); G. Ledos (1901). On Gertrude's influence on the devotional feeling of her age, see E. Michael, *Geschichte des deutschen Volkes vom dreizehnten Jahrhundert*, 3, pp. 174–211; on SS Gertrude and Mechtildis and devotion to the Sacred Heart, see A. Hamon, *Histoire de dévotion au Sacré Coeur*, 2; U. Berlière, *La dévotion au Sacré Coeur dans l'Ordre de St Benoît* (1920); C. Vagaggini, "La dévotion au Sacré Coeur chez sainte Mechtilde (de Hackeborn) et sainte Gertrude" in *Cor Jesu. Commentationes in Literam Encyclicam "Hauriete aquas,"* 2 (1963). See also *Dict.Sp.*, 6 (1967), pp. 331–9; *N.C.E.*, 6, pp. 450ff; *Bibl.SS.*, 6, 277–87; C. Vagaggini, *Theologie der Liturgie* (1959), p. 398; J. A. Moreira de Freitas Carvalho, *Gertrudes de Helfta e Espanha* (1981). On the question of Dante's Matelda, see E. Gardner, *Dante and the Mystics*, p. 269.

ST EDMUND OF ABINGDON, *Bishop* (*c.* 1175-1240)

Edmund, born in about 1175, was the eldest child of Reginald Rich, a merchant of Abingdon, in Berkshire, and his wife Mabel. There is a tradition that at some point in his middle age, while the children were still young, Reginald made sure he had provided for them all and then, with his wife's consent, joined the monastery at Eynsham, where he died a little while later. This may, however, be confusing Reginald with one of his sons—we know that Edmund had one brother and two sisters, but it is more than likely that he had two other brothers and that it was one of these who entered the monastery at Eynsham. What is certain is that the main influence on Edmund and his siblings was that of their formidable mother. Mabel herself lived very austerely, and the children had a strict, not to say rigid, religious upbringing. At the age of twelve Edmund went to Oxford University to study grammar and then, after three years, travelled with his brother Robert to Paris, where he followed the arts course. He returned briefly to visit his mother on her death-bed and to receive her blessing. Then, having settled his two sisters, Margery and Alice, in the Gilbertine monastery at Catesby in Northamptonshire, he went back to Paris to complete his course, faithfully observing "in sometimes trying circumstances" the vow of celibacy he had made while he was at Oxford.

From about 1195 to 1201 he was a member of the arts faculty at Oxford University. Intellectually it was an exciting time. Both in the Muslim and in the Christian world there had been a rediscovery of philosophy, particularly that of Aristotle, and Edmund may well have been the first to teach the logic of Aristotle at Oxford. He soon realized—and in this he was a pioneer of Scholasticism—that the New Learning could be a valuable tool for the understanding and teaching of theology. In 1201 he went to Paris again to study theology. Although there is not much detailed information about this period of his life, it was probably while he was in Paris that he wrote his *Moralities on the Psalms* (which have survived in a single thirteenth-century manuscript) and that he was ordained to the priesthood. When he returned to England, he spent a year with the Augustinian canons at Merton, in Surrey, and then went back to Oxford to lecture in theology. The most likely date for his return to Oxford seems to be 1214, since it was in that year that the papal legate managed to settle a dispute between the university and the civil authorities, after which regular teaching was resumed. In his teaching Edmund emphasized the literal and spiritual senses of the Bible, as well as its historical context, and used this as the springboard for his theological teaching. He always took a personal interest in his pupils, especially those who were either poor or sick.

In 1222 Edmund was invited by Bishop Richard le Poore to become a canon and treasurer of Salisbury cathedral. The office came with a living at nearby Calne, where he had to reside for at least three months of the year. Although this effectively took him away from the academic life of Oxford, he was able to keep his hand in as a teacher by lecturing in the cathedral school in Salisbury, which was supported and developed by Bishop le Poore. As the cathedral was being built at this time, Edmund's duties as treasurer were demanding; and he did not make his own life any easier by his more than generous almsgiving, which, combined with his donation of a quarter of his income to the cathedral building fund, sometimes left him short of funds for part of the year. Whenever he needed to recoup his forces physically or spiritually, he would go to stay with the Cistercians at Stanley Abbey, near Calne, where the abbot, Stephen of Lexington, had been one of his pupils at Oxford. This association with the Cistercians was to be among the most formative of his life.

In 1227 Pope Gregory IX (1227-41) sent him an order to preach the sixth Crusade, giving him the right to receive a stipend from every church in which he did so. Edmund would accept no stipend, but he preached the Crusade with great zeal in a number of places, including Worcester and Leominster. He seems in general to have been a powerful and effective preacher, anxious to warn against multiplying the externals of prayer and drawing each time on the wealth of his own learning and his own interior life. "A hundred thousand persons," he once wrote, "are deceived in multiplying prayers. I would rather say five words devoutly with my heart than five thousand which my soul does not relish with affection and intelligence. Sing to the Lord with understanding: what a man repeats with his mouth, that let him feel in his soul."

In 1233, after three annulled elections, the pope decided to nominate his own candidate for archbishop of Canterbury, and Edmund was chosen to fill the see, which had been vacant since the death of Richard le Grand on 3 August 1231. At first he refused, protesting that he knew nothing of the election (given his scholarly, somewhat reclusive tendencies, he might well have added that in any case he was not the man for the job). But when the bishop of Salisbury exerted his authority and commanded him to accept, he submitted. He was consecrated on 2 April 1234.

Despite his initial reluctance, he turned out to be an outstanding reforming bishop, thanks not least to his considerable personal qualities, which included a warm and affectionate disposition and a gift for mediation combined with meticulous concern for justice, great personal integrity, and moral courage. His success was also due to the calibre of the men who surrounded him. Some of these he inherited from his predecessors, Stephen Langton and Richard le Grand, but he also made appointments of his own. His chancellor was Richard of Wych (3 Apr.), one of his former pupils, who subsequently became bishop of Chichester; also, his brother Robert seems to have remained at his side throughout his life.

The inevitable involvement in politics which his new position brought with it was distasteful to him—he had an instinctive distrust of the court—but he did not shirk it. Indeed, he had not even been consecrated when, shortly after his election, he helped to avert the possibility of civil war by mediating in the dispute between Henry III (1216-72) and his earl marshal, Richard, who was leading a rebellion against the king's method of government. In general, he was courageously outspoken in his relations with Henry, who was happy to use him even while attempting to restrict his jurisdiction. An example of Henry's manoeuvring was his successful effort to obtain the appointment of Cardinal Otto as papal legate. Henry's main aim was to strengthen his position vis-à-vis his own barons in the aftermath of his wedding to Eleonore de Provence. Edmund warned him that the appointment would be the cause of unnecessary trouble, and he proved to be right, as Henry started to play the legate off against him, the bishops, and the barons. On the other hand, Edmund's relations with Cardinal Otto, who was clearly a discreet and tactful man of some integrity, were never as frosty as has sometimes been suggested, largely on the basis of the biased account by Matthew Paris.

While Edmund's problems were not restricted to Henry's interference and his attempts to inhibit the power of the Church, these were always there in the background. In this connection the bishop of Lincoln, Robert Grosseteste, who was himself utterly uncompromising in what he regarded as matters of principle, accused him of being too ready to make sacrifices in order to maintain peace with the king. Meanwhile, from another side, Edmund's authority as archbishop was challenged by the monks of Christ Church, Canterbury, who served the cathedral. They were claiming certain rights and privileges and generally obstructing any plan Edmund might have for change. As his own talents as a mediator failed to resolve the matter, Edmund went in 1237 to Rome to discuss it with Gregory IX. When he returned to England the situation was no better, and after further disagreements and disputes he excommunicated seventeen of the monks. At this point, not all the bishops agreed with the way Edmund had handled the situation. Henry openly opposed him, and Cardinal Otto tried and failed to effect a reconciliation. The result was deadlock, and the matter remained unresolved until after Edmund's death.

The situation came to a head again over Henry's habit of leaving offices and benefices that were in his gift unoccupied in order to benefit from the revenues during the vacancy. In 1239, at great trouble and expense to himself, Edmund obtained from the pope a brief which the metropolitan could present to any cathedral or monastic church where a vacancy had lasted for six months. But Henry managed to persuade the pope to withdraw the brief, and shortly after this, probably in October 1240, Edmund left for the Continent. Many historians, largely on the basis of Matthew Paris' account, have interpreted his departure as voluntary exile on the part of a man whose position had become impossible. But the evidence is against this: it would have been out of character, and it is not mentioned by any other chronicler, although his death and burial are mentioned. What seems most likely is that he had decided to go back to Rome, where the pope had called a general council for early in 1241, and by going early Edmund would have had an opportunity to discuss his problems with him. But he was taken ill on his arrival in France and went to the Cistercian abbey at Pontigny. When it became obvious that it would be unwise for him to risk the journey to Rome—his health apart, the troops of the emperor, Frederick II (1220-50), had invaded the Papal States and were making it difficult for clerics to get there—he decided to return to England. He was taken ill again on the way back and stopped at an Augustinian priory near Soisy. On 16 November he died there, having raised the excommunication on the monks at Canterbury and having sent some of his devotional articles to his brother Robert and to his sisters, Margaret and Alice, in Catesby. He was buried in the abbey church at Pontigny, where his remains have been ever since.

The pope immediately set up a commission to examine Edmund's life and miracles. The findings of the commission, which included among its members Robert Grosseteste and the Franciscan theologian Alexander of Hales, were positive, and Edmund was canonized in 1246—the first Oxford master to be so honoured (St Edmund Hall, one of the colleges of the university, is named after him). When his feast was celebrated for the first time, Henry III presented a vestment of white samite, a chalice, and a donation for candles at the shrine. The canonization aroused great interest in England, and while the popularity of the shrine at Pontigny began to decline toward the end of the thirteenth century, the cult of St Edmund became widespread in England, particularly in Abingdon, where he was born, and in Catesby, where his sisters lived. A collegiate church in Salisbury was dedicated to him, as was an altar in the cathedral there; and other dedications include St Edmund Hall, Oxford, already mentioned, and St Edmund's College, Ware, in Hertfordshire, until 1976 the seminary for the Westminster diocese.

Edmund's writings consist largely of commentaries on the Bible and devotional works. The most famous of all is the *Speculum Ecclesie*. This is a treatise on the way of perfection for monks and nuns—and more specifically a *summa* of the teaching of

Hugh of St Victor on the life of meditation and contemplation. Some eighty medieval manuscripts survive in Middle English and Anglo-Norman as well as Latin, both in England and on the Continent. This suggests that it was widely read at the time, and not just by monks and nuns but by secular priests and laypeople as well. It was once thought that an original form for religious had been adapted for laypeople to produce the text as we now have it, but recent scholarship seems to show that we have it in the form in which Edmund wrote it, with a few minor changes by him or someone else, for the benefit of non-religious.

The *Speculum* offers a simple programme whereby Christians can progress from contemplation of God in creation, through the contemplation of God in scripture, to the contemplation of God in the humanity of Christ and pure contemplation. It reflects the two main influences on Edmund's spirituality, between which he forms a link: the Paris schools and the monastic tradition with its stress on asceticism and personal devotion to the humanity of Christ. It derives its special character from the fact that in writing it Edmund was so influenced by Hugh and Richard of St Victor, who instead of exaggerating the misery of the human condition as the Cistercians tended to do, concentrated on the image of God behind the human sins and weaknesses.

Edmund was writing at a time of transition in the history of religious expression, a transition which is mirrored in the art of the period with its tender, human depiction of religious truths and events. Intense devotion to the humanity of Christ and compassion for his sufferings had been the salient feature of monastic spirituality since the time of St Bernard (*c.* 1090-1153; 20 Aug.) and the early Cistercians and before, but it was only later, through the Franciscan movement, that they came to be part of the spiritual experience of the average Christian layperson. In the *Speculum* Edmund brings the one a bit closer to the other. And just as he had himself come to see that there must be an intimate relation between learning and pastoral work, so he wanted his readers to appreciate the connection between prayer and daily life. In the course of the book, he will offer practical advice:

> If you are well, rise from your bed in the morning and linger not on account of cold or sleep or comfort, for the harder it is for a man to do, the greater shall be his reward if he does it freely. Then should you go to church and devoutly say Matins or quietly hear Mass and all the Hours of the day without chattering.

Or he will help the learner to build up a picture of a scene from the life of Christ:

> The time was in mid-winter, when it was most cold; the hour was at midnight, the hardest hour that is; the place was in mid-ward the street, in a house without walls. In clouts was he wound and as a child was he bound and in a crib before an ox and an ass that lovely lord was laid, for there was no other place empty. And here shalt thou think of the keeping of Mary and her child, and of her spouse Joseph—what joy Jesu sent them.

Or else he will movingly invite the Christian to identify with the sufferings of Christ and his mother:

I know not what I should say here. For if all the sickness of this world and all the sorrow were in the body of one man, and that man might keep as much hurt and anguish and sorrow in his body as all the men of this world might think, it were full little or nought to compare with the sorrow that he suffered for us in one hour of the day. . . . Surely, there is not, nor ever was in this world, pain like to thy pain, O most sweet Jesu. And also though shalt think of our sweet Lady saint Mary, what anguish she had when she stood at the side of her sweetest son. . . .

Several contemporaries, including Robert Rich; Bertrand, abbot of Pontigny; Matthew Paris; Eustace, a monk of Canterbury; and Robert Bacon, an uncle or brother of the more celebrated Roger Bacon, wrote Lives of St Edmund. Four have survived, although it is not entirely clear which should be attributed to whom. For a critical study of the Lives, see C. H. Lawrence, *St Edmund of Abingdon: A Study in Hagiography and History* (1960); *idem, The Life of St Edmund by Matthew Paris* (1996). More modern Lives: B. Ward (1903), M. R. Newbolt (1928). See also C. H. Lawrence, "Edmund of Abingdon" in J. Walsh (ed.), *Pre-Reformation English Spirituality* (1964), pp. 104-20; A. B. Emden, *An Oxford Hall in Medieval Times* (1927); W. A. Pantin, *The English Church in the Fourteenth Century* (1955). For St Edmund's works, see H. P. Forshaw, *Edmund of Abingdon: Speculum Religiosorum and Speculum Ecclesie* (1973); *idem,* "St Edmund's Speculum: A Classic of Victorine Spirituality" in *Archives d'histoire doctrinale et littéraire du Moyen Age,* 39 (1972); M. de la Bigne, *Bibliotheca Patrum et veterum Auctorum Ecclesiasticorum* (1610), 5, pp. 983-1004; C. Horstmann, *Yorkshire Writers: Richard Rolle* (med. Eng. version, 1895), 1, pp. 219-61; H. W. Robbins, *La Merure de Seinte Eglise* (Fr. version, 1925).

St Eucherius of Lyons, *Bishop* (*c.* 449)

There is no formal Life of St Eucherius, who was the most famous churchman connected with Lyons after St Irenaeus (28 June). However, he does merit a brief mention in Gennadius' *De viris illustribus,* and other information can be gleaned from his own writings. He was born into a successful Gallo-Roman family and married a woman named Galla, by whom he had two sons, Salonius and Veranus. He sent his sons to be educated at the recently-founded monastery on what became known as the Ile St-Honorat, the smaller of the two Iles de Lérins. Both eventually became bishops, one of Vence, the other of Geneva, and both were venerated as saints.

After a time Eucherius himself joined the monastery of Lérins—as is so often the case, the sources do not relate what happened to his wife—and in his own lifetime he and St Honoratus (16 Jan.), its abbot and founder, were described by St John Cassian (23 July) as "the two models of that house of saints." Eucherius did not remain in the monastery, however, but went off to the neighbouring island, now known as Ste-Marguerite, in search of greater solitude. While he was there he wrote a book in praise of the solitary life, which he dedicated to St Hilary of Arles (5 May), and a letter to his cousin, Valerian, whom he urged to resist the transitory enjoyments of this world and to make God his only concern. "I have seen," he warns him, "men raised to the highest point of worldly honour and riches. Fortune seemed to be in their pay. . . . Their prosperity in all things outdid their very desires. But in a moment they disappeared. Their vast possessions were fled and the masters themselves were no more." He seems in general to have been an enthusiastic letter writer: one recipient described his letters as "sparing in words but full of doctrine, easy to read but perfect in their instruction." Another letter of his is an important document in the history of St Maurice and the Theban Legion (22 Sept.). However, not all the works attributed to him came from his pen.

At a certain point, probably in 434, Eucherius was forced out of his retirement to become bishop of Lyons. He was to prove an admirable pastor—learned but intellectually humble, an eloquent preacher and tireless in works of charity—and was responsible for the foundation of several churches and religious houses. St Paulinus of Nola (22 June) and St Sidonius (21 Aug.) were among those, along with St Honoratus and St Hilary of Arles, who sought his friendship and spoke of him with great respect. He died in about 449.

St Eucherius' writings are in *P.L.*, 1; *Vienna Corpus Scrip. eccles. lat..* See also Tillemont, 15, pp. 126-36, 848-57; *D.T.C.*, 5, 1452-4; O. Bardenhewer, *Geschichte der altkirchlichen Literatur*, 4, pp. 561-70.

St Afan, *Bishop* (Sixth Century)

In the churchyard of Llanafan Fawr, up in the hills a few miles north-west of Builth Wells in Powys, there is an ancient tombstone which bears the inscription: *Hic Iacet Sanctus Avanus Episcopus*—"Here lies St Afan the Bishop." The existence of this stone is the sole justification for mentioning Afan here at all, since nothing whatsoever is known about his life. The lettering on the stone is said, probably reliably, to date from the end of the thirteenth century at the earliest; but Afan certainly lived long before that. Some identify him with Afan Buellt (of Builth), a member of the house of Cunedda and a relative of St David (1 Mar.), who lived during the early part of the sixth century and was the leading holy man of the area. According to the legend, he was put to death by Irish raiders.

The church is mentioned by Gerald of Wales in his *Journey through Wales* (1, 1), in connection with "the castellan of Radnor castle." During the reign of Henry I, this man spent the night there with his hounds, "which was a foolish and irreverent thing to do." According to Gerald, who, it should be remembered, was drumming up support for the Crusades, the man woke up next morning to find himself blind and his dogs mad. Eventually, after living for a time in "tedium and darkness," he went to Jerusalem on pilgrimage—"for he did not wish to allow his spiritual light to be extinguished as his eyes had been." There, he was armed, helped onto a horse and led to the field of battle, where "he charged forward in the front line, but was immediately struck by a blow from a sword and so ended his life with honour." All of which tells us something about twelfth-century religious ideas and recruiting methods, but nothing, unfortunately, about St Afan.

See T. Jones, *History of Brecknock*, 2, pp. 225-6; Gerald of Wales, *The Journey through Wales* (trans. L. Thorpe, 1980), pp. 77-8.

St Agnes of Assisi (1253)

Caterina Offreduccio was the younger sister of Chiara (St Clare of Assisi, 11 Aug.). She was only about fifteen when she followed Clare, who had left the family home to become a nun under the direction of Francesco Bernardone (St Francis of Assisi, 4 Oct.). As their permanent house at San Damiano was still being built, the two were taken in at the Benedictine convent of Sant' Angelo di Panzo, on the slopes of Monte Subasio, near Assisi. While they were there, Caterina's relatives were said to have used every means, including violence, to get her to leave again. The *Chronica XXIV Generalium*, which describes what happened, describes also alleged miracles by which they were thwarted, although none of this is mentioned in Pope Alexander IV's Bull of canonization of Clare. Caterina duly received the habit from Francis, who gave her the name Agnes, and she was sent with her sister to San Damiano.

Eight or so years later, in 1220, Francis decided to establish a new convent of Poor Clares at Monticelli, outside Florence, and Agnes was sent there as its first abbess—a touching letter she wrote to Clare at this time still survives. Agnes is said to have supervised the foundations at, among other places, Mantua, Padua, and Venice, and she steadfastly supported her sister in her long struggle for the privilege of complete poverty. She was still in Monticelli in August 1253 when she received a call from Assisi to say that Clare was dying. She arrived in time to see her sister, who predicted that she, Agnes, would soon follow her. In fact, Agnes died on 16 November in that same year. She was buried initially at San Damiano, but in 1260 her body was laid alongside that of her sister in the newly-built church of Santa Chiara in Assisi. Miracles were reported at her tomb, and in 1752 the Franciscans received permission from Pope Benedict XIV (1740-58) to celebrate her feast.

For the account in *Chronica XXIV Generalium*, see *Anal. Fran.*, 3 (1897), pp. 173-82. St Agnes is also mentioned in the early volumes of L. Wadding's *Annales Ordinis Minorum*. See also *Bibl.SS.*, 1, 369-70; F. Casolini in *Chiara d'Assisi, rassegna del protomonastero* (1954), pp. 6-12; G. Hourdin, *François, Claire et les autres* (1984); M. Bartoli, *Clare of Assisi* (1989).

Bd Edward Osbaldeston, *Martyr* (1594)

Relatively little is known about Edward Osbaldeston. He was born near Blackburn in Lancashire, but his parents sent him to the English College at Douai for his education. He went on to study there for the priesthood and was ordained in 1585. On 27 April 1589 he returned to England and for several years carried out his ministry on his own home ground. On 30 September 1594 (the feast of St Jerome, and significant to Edward as the anniversary of the day on which he celebrated his first Mass), he was betrayed by a former Roman Catholic priest, surnamed Clark, who handed him over to the authorities. He was tried in York and, having been condemned to death for high treason under the Act Against Jesuits, Seminary Priests and Other Suchlike Disobedient Subjects (1585), was executed on 16 November 1594. He is one of the Eighty-five Martyrs of England, Scotland, and Wales (22 Nov.), who were beatified in 1987.

See *M.M.P.*, pp. 208-10; B. C. Foley, *The Eighty-five Blessed Martyrs* (1987); *N.C.E.*, 9, pp. 319-32.

ST ELIZABETH OF HUNGARY (over page)
Three gold crowns, on brown field.

17

ST ELIZABETH OF HUNGARY (1207-31)

Elizabeth, who was born in Bratislava in 1207, was the daughter of Andrew II of Hungary (1205-35) and his wife, Gertrude of Andechs-Meran. When she was about four years old, she was betrothed to Ludwig, the eldest son of Hermann I, *Landgraf* of Thuringia, and sent to the Thuringian court at Wartburg, near Eisenach, to be brought up with her future husband. Although she was treated unkindly by some members of the court, who no doubt envied her striking good looks, her goodness, and her warm and generous personality, Ludwig's affection only increased, developing into genuine love as she grew older. In 1221, when he was twenty-one and had succeeded his father as *Landgraf*, and she was fourteen, their marriage was solemnized. Attempts had been made to persuade him to send her back to Hungary, but he insisted that he would rather forfeit a mountain of gold than give her up. Ludwig, who is venerated in Germany as a saint (11 Sept.), although his cult has never been confirmed, seems to have had personal qualities to equal hers, and their brief marriage was outstandingly happy. They had three children, Hermann, who died when he was nineteen; Sofia, who married the duke of Brabant; and Bd Gertrude (13 Aug.), who became abbess at Altenburg.

Ludwig accepted Elizabeth's need for a simple and mortified life, and he did nothing to hinder her long periods of prayer or her works of charity. Her extraordinary generosity was sometimes criticized by others as extravagance. In 1225, for example, when their part of Germany was hit by a famine, she used all her available funds and distributed her entire store of corn to help those most affected. To the people of his household who complained to him about this, Ludwig replied that at least she had not alienated any of his domains and added, typically: "As for her charities, they will bring upon us divine blessings. We shall not want as long as we let her relieve the poor as she does." Indeed, one of the most famous stories used to illustrate Elizabeth's charity tells as much about Ludwig's own sensitivity as it does about her. One day, she placed a dying leper in the bed she shared with her husband. When he was told about this, Ludwig rushed angrily into the room and tore off the bedclothes. "But at that instant," according to Elizabeth's biographer, Dietrich of Apolda, "Almighty God opened the eyes of his soul, and instead of a leper he saw the figure of the crucified Christ stretched upon the bed." (Unfortunately later biographers turned this simple description of inner understanding and growth into a material apparition, so that Leopold is said physically to have seen "a bleeding crucifix with out-stretched arms.")

Because the castle at Wartburg was situated on a very steep hill, Elizabeth built a

144

hospital at the bottom, where she was regularly to be found feeding the patients or making their beds. And then there were the children, especially orphans, to whom she never refused help, and the poor who came daily to her gate for food. But she was shrewd as well as generous, and for those who were capable of it she would provide suitable work rather than food or money.

In 1227 Ludwig decided to go to Apulia to join the emperor, Frederick II, who was drumming up support for a new Crusade. Elizabeth, "in great pain and grief" at the thought of the coming separation, rode out for a day with him. But Ludwig never reached the Holy Land. He contracted the plague at Otranto, and by 11 September of the same year he was dead. The news reached Wartburg in October, but Elizabeth, who was still only twenty and had just given birth to her second daughter, misunderstood what her mother-in-law was saying and thought Ludwig had been imprisoned. When the truth dawned on her she was utterly heart-broken. "The world is dead to me," she cried, "and all that was joyous in the world"—and for a while, quite unable to contain her grief, wandered about the castle weeping uncontrollably.

What happened next is not entirely clear. One account has it that Elizabeth's brother-in-law, Henry, while acting as regent for her infant son, was anxious to seize power for himself. He drove her from Wartburg with her children and two attendants that same winter, and they suffered severe hardship until Elizabeth's aunt Matilda, who was abbess of Kitzingen, took them in. However, according to another version, Elizabeth left Wartburg voluntarily, which would have been entirely consistent with her desire to live at the level of ordinary people and with her feeling that the rich live off the backs of the poor. In either case, she did go to Kitzingen, where she left Sofia in the care of the nuns before going on herself to Bamberg, where her uncle, Eckembert, was bishop. He put his castle at Pottenstein at her disposal and started to entertain ambitious plans for her remarriage. But Elizabeth refused: before Ludwig left for the Crusade, they had exchanged promises never to marry again. Once Ludwig's body had been solemnly buried in the abbey church at Rheinhardsbrunn and provision had been made for her family, she went instead to the Franciscan church at Eisenach and, on Good Friday 1228, received the habit and cord of the Third Order of St Francis.

As *Landgräfin* of Thuringia, Elizabeth had found that there was a limit to the ways in which she could put her love of poverty into action. Now, having seen her children provided for, and after one or two false starts, she settled just outside Marburg in a small house built to her own design. To this house she attached a hospice for the sick, the poor, and the old, and it was to the care of these that she now devoted herself. Some biographers see a complete break between Elizabeth as she was as a child and then as a wife and mother, and Elizabeth the widow and ascetic, and they criticize her for leaving her children. It is impossible to know what went on in her mind, but she may not have wanted them to suffer hardship; and it may be that the fact that she herself was sent away from her parents at a very young age made it easier for her to do the same herself.

A major and, it has to be said, dubious influence on her life from now on was the fanatical ascetic, Konrad of Marburg, who became her confessor in 1225. Ludwig had shared the high opinion that the pope, Gregory IX (1227-41), and others had of Konrad and had allowed Elizabeth to make a promise of obedience to him. However, from this distance in time it is impossible to escape the conclusion that, whatever his intentions—and there is no reason to question his zeal—this severe and domineering, not to say sadistic, man, whose experience of success was as an inquisitor of heretics, was quite unsuited to direct a young woman as warm-hearted, spontaneous, and impressionable as Elizabeth.

It is true that in some ways he acted as a necessary brake on her enthusiasm. He would not allow her, for example, to divest herself definitively of everything, to give away more than a certain amount at a time, or to risk infection from leprosy and other diseases. But overall his aim was to break her will so that, as he saw it, she might live entirely according to the will of God. The methods he adopted were at times decidedly cruel. For example, he deprived her of the company of two much-loved ladies-in-waiting, one of whom had been with her since her childhood and was no doubt loved by her as a surrogate mother, and he replaced them with two "harsh females" who were unfamiliar to her. These women would report back to Konrad on her slightest infringements of his detailed commands, and he was known to slap her face or strike her with a "long thick rod" by way of punishment. The truth is that Konrad simply did not recognize the source of her unfettered generosity, and it is a measure of her mental health and the strength of her personality that she retained her sense of humour and did not crumble under his régime. Once, referring to his disciplinary methods, she compared herself with the sedge that is flattened by the waters of the stream during the flood season but springs back again, straight and unharmed, once the rains have passed.

A Magyar nobleman who arrived in Marburg and asked to be directed to her residence was shocked to find Elizabeth dressed in plain grey and seated at a spinning wheel in the hospice. He urged her to return with him to her father's court, but she refused, insisting that her children, her poor, and her husband's grave were in Thuringia and that she would remain there for the rest of her life. That was to be all too short. She worked unstintingly in her hospice and in the homes of the poor, and despite ill health continued to practise great personal austerity. But she had not been in Marburg for two years before her health gave way. She was only twenty-four years old when she died, in the evening of 17 November 1231. Her body lay in state in the hospice chapel, and it was here that she was buried. Miracles were soon being reported at her intercession, and Konrad immediately began to collect statements about her sanctity. He did not live to see it, but she was canonized only four years later by Pope Gregory IX. In 1236 her relics were taken, in the presence of Frederick II and of a great gathering of people from all over Europe, to the church of St Elizabeth, built by her brother-in-law, in Marburg. Here her shrine remained a popular focus of pilgrimage until 1539, when a Lutheran *Landgraf* of Hesse had her relics removed—to a still-unknown destination.

From the moment she died artists started portraying Elizabeth either as a queen or else as a Franciscan tertiary. Scenes from her life can be seen in the stained-glass windows of the church in Marburg and in nineteenth-century frescoes in Wartburg Castle. Simone Martini (1344) painted her on the wall of the lower church of the basilica of St Francis in Assisi; she appears in the front row of *Forerunners of Christ with Saints and Martyrs* by Bd Fra Angelico (*c.* 1395-1455; 18 Feb.) in the National Gallery in London; and there are powerful representations by Piero della Francesca (1416?-92) in the Pinacoteca in Perugia and by Jan van Eyck (1441) in the Frick Collection in New York City. A late fifteenth- or early sixteenth-century screen in the church at Tor Brian in Devon, where she is depicted holding a double crown, shows that her popularity went far beyond the confines of her adopted country. She also appears in a modern stained-glass window at Eversley in Hampshire.

Early Lives by Dietrich of Apolda (ed. H. Canisius, *Antiquae Lectiones*, 5, pp. 147-217); Caesarius of Heisterbach (ed. A. Huyskens in *Annales des historischen Vereins für den Niederrhein*, 86, pp. 1-59); Konrad of Marburg (ed. A. Huyskens in *Quellenstudien zur Geschichte der hl. Elisabeth Landgräfin von Thuringen* [1908], pp. 110-40). Other important contemporary material: *Libellus de dictis IV ancillarum* (summary of depositions of ladies-in-waiting in *N.A.*, 34 [1908], pp. 437-502), Konrad of Marburg's letters to the pope, and other documents sent to Rome at the time of Elizabeth's canonization. Modern biographies: J. Ancelet-Hustache (1946; Eng. trans. 1963); *Sankt Elisabeth, Furstin, Dienerin, Heilige* (1981). See also *H.S.S.C.*, 6, pp. 124-32; *Bibl.SS.*, 4, 1110-23; *Anal.Boll.* 27, pp. 493-7; 28, pp. 333-5; and especially I. Coudenhove, *The Nature of Sanctity* (1932).

ST HUGH OF LINCOLN, *Bishop* (*c.* 1140-1200)

Hugh (Hugues) was born in about 1140 at Avallon in the kingdom of Burgundy, where his father, Guillaume, a distinguished soldier, was the local landowner. His mother, Anne, died when he was eight years old, and from then on he was educated in the Augustinian priory at Villard-Benoît—to which his father also withdrew at the same time. When he was only fifteen, Hugh made his profession as an Augustinian canon, and as soon as he was ordained deacon at the age of nineteen, he began to gain a reputation as a preacher. Soon he was placed in charge of a small dependency of his priory, at Saint-Maximin, and it was while he was there that he went with his prior to visit the great monastery founded in 1084 by St Bruno (6 Oct.) in La Grande-Chartreuse *massif* north of Grenoble.

This visit changed Hugh's life. He was immediately drawn by the silence of the place and its isolated position as well as by the dedication of the monks. Despite the alarming picture painted by the prior of the rigours of Carthusian life, and the fact that his own superior exacted a promise from him that he would not leave Villard-Benoît, Hugh, who on mature reflection decided that the promise had been made under severe emotional stress, returned to La Grande-Chartreuse when he was about twenty-five and received the Carthusian habit.

Of the next ten years of his life we know little, although his biographer provides one tiny but vivid detail: squirrels and many species of bird were attracted to the small garden outside his cell, and the hold he seemed to have over them was like that of his younger contemporary, St Francis of Assisi (4 Oct.). When he had been at the monastery for ten years he was appointed procurator, an office he filled for the next seven years. It was his task to welcome visitors to the monastery, and among those he is known to have cared for personally was St Peter of Tarentaise (8 May), who visited La Grande-Chartreuse in his old age.

At this point Hugh's life took another change of direction. As part of his reparation for the murder, some ten years earlier, of St Thomas Becket (29 Dec.), the English king, Henry II (1154-89), had founded the first Carthusian house in England, at Witham in Somerset. The first two priors were not up to the task in hand, and under their rule the enterprise had failed dismally. So Henry, who had been told about Hugh by a French nobleman, sent the bishop of Bath over to La Grande-Chartreuse to invite him to come and set the new foundation on its feet. Hugh laid the matter before the Carthusian chapter, which, after some debate, agreed that he should accompany the bishop back to England.

When Hugh reached Witham he found not only that building had not even begun, but that no attempt had been made to provide for or compensate those whose lands and tenements had been requisitioned to make room for the monks. The first thing he did was to insist that they be compensated, and he refused to take up his office until this had been done "to the last penny." There was only one further hitch, when, with the buildings almost completed, Henry fell down on his payment of the bills; but with Hugh's tact the matter was soon put right, and the first English charterhouse was at last in being. During the early stages the monastery had acquired not a few enemies, but Hugh's humility and his evident integrity won them round, and it was soon attracting suitable candidates. Indeed, Hugh's reputation was such that people—including the king, who had a deep regard for him and was a regular visitor—came long distances to seek his advice.

One matter on which Hugh did not hesitate to express an opinion was Henry's practice of keeping sees vacant in order to draw their revenues. A particularly scandalous example was Lincoln, which, apart from one eighteen-month period, was without a bishop for nearly eighteen years. Eventually, in 1186, the dean and chapter were told to elect a new one, and under heavy pressure from the king, Hugh was chosen. His decision not to accept on the ground that the election was not canonical was overruled by the prior of La Grande-Chartreuse, and leaving Witham, he went to rule the largest diocese in England, stretching from the Humber to the Thames.

Not surprisingly, the diocese was in dire need of reform. So Hugh gathered round him a group of educated and committed priests and with characteristic energy set about rekindling the spirit of faith among his people, restoring discipline among the clergy, and reintroducing a pattern of communal worship. He himself set an example of hard work, travelling tirelessly throughout the diocese to perform his pastoral duties. His attitude to the acceptance of fees by the clergy was uncompromising: he even refused an honorarium to the archdeacon of Canterbury, who enthroned him at Lincoln. He was also responsible for the restoration and extension of the cathedral, which he found in ruins (it had been seriously damaged by an earthquake in 1185), and he sometimes contributed to the work with his own hands. It was still unfinished when he died, but part of the existing choir and transepts are his, and he left his final instructions with the master-builder, Geoffrey de Noiers. Indeed, the entire cathedral apart from the Angel Choir and part of the west transept were in the main designed by him.

But much of Hugh's success must have been due to his contemplative spirit (once a year he would retire to Witham for a while to refresh his monastic roots) and to his engaging personality. He was reputed to be the most learned monk in Britain, but according to his biographer, Adam, a monk of Eynsham who served as his chaplain, he was also full of fun and good conversation and was of a most cheerful, responsive, and enthusiastic disposition. He was particularly fond of children and babies, and there are several charming stories in the Life which illustrate this trait.

Another salient characteristic was his fearless concern for justice. During the third Crusade (1189-92), for example, there was a nasty epidemic of anti-Semitism in England, amounting to persecution. In Stamford and in Northampton, as well as in Lincoln, Hugh, alone and unarmed, faced an armed and vicious mob, and managed somehow to lower the temperature and persuade the rioters to spare their intended victims. The same lightness of touch was apparent in his relations with three successive kings—Henry II, Richard I (1189-99), and John (1199-1216)—all of whom regarded him as a friend. If he felt one of them had overstepped the limit in some way, he was not afraid to say so. In 1197, for example, Richard I wanted the bishops as well as the barons to subsidize his war with the French king, Philippe II Auguste (1180-1223). Hugh refused, on the ground that his see was liable to assist only in home defence. When his one supporter, Bishop Herbert of Salisbury, had all his goods confiscated, Hugh rebuked the king to his face for this and other acts of oppression, and he carried the day. Richard himself once said of Hugh that "if all the prelates of the Church were like him, there is not a king in Christendom who would dare to raise his head in the presence of a bishop."

Shortly after his coronation, John sent Hugh to France to witness the signing of the treaty of Le Goulet. While he was there, he visited his old home at La Grande-Chartreuse, as well as the great abbeys of Cluny and Cîteaux, and was everywhere received with affection and respect. But he was already prey to the disease that would kill him, and on his return he went to pray at the shrine of St Thomas in Canterbury. His condition did not improve, however, and instead of attending a national council in London he was forced to retire to bed in his house in the Old Temple, Holborn (now Lincoln's Inn). Having received the sacrament of the sick on the nineteenth anniversary of his episcopal consecration, he lingered patiently, in great pain for almost two months. He died on 16 November 1200. His body was taken on a sort of triumphal progress to Lincoln, where it was buried in the cathedral amid genuine and universal grief. The congregation represented all the phases and aspects of his life: fourteen bishops, in addition to the archbishop of

Canterbury (his opposition to whom Hugh never abandoned); 100 abbots; one archbishop from Ireland and another from Dalmatia; a prince, Gruffydd ap Rhys, from Wales; William the Lion, king of Scotland (1165-1214); John, king of England, and the people of Lincoln—not to mention representatives of the Jewish ghetto in London, who mourned the loss of a "true servant of the great God" and their protector. He was canonized in 1220 by Pope Honorius III (1216-27)—the first Carthusian to be so honoured, although the request for his canonization came not from the Carthusians but from the English king and bishops.

After 1339, when charterhouses throughout Europe began to celebrate Hugh's feast as one of the highest rank, interest in him began to spread from England to Flanders, France, Italy, the Rhineland, and Spain. But the centre of veneration remained Lincoln. In 1280 his relics were translated to a new shrine in the cathedral there, and pilgrims came from far and wide until the Reformation, when the shrine was dismantled. Attempts were made in 1887 and again in 1956 to find the body, but without success, and all that outwardly remains is Hugh's white linen stole, which used to be at La Grande-Chartreuse but is now in the charterhouse at Parkminster, in West Sussex. The events of his funeral are depicted in the rose window known as the Dean's Eye in Lincoln Cathedral, and there are at least two extant portraits. One, in the Paris charterhouse, was particularly venerated by mothers with sick children; the other, by Francisco de Zurbarán, is in Cadiz. In this Hugh is represented with a chalice with the infant Jesus on it, a reference to an occasion when, just before one of his clashes with Richard I, Hugh was strengthened by a young priest who told him that as he, Hugh, had held up the host for veneration during the Mass, he himself had had a vision of Jesus as a tiny child. Hugh's other emblem is a swan, because, according to Gerald of Wales, one of the swans at his manor at Stow would feed from his hand, follow him about and keep guard over his bed.

Lives by D. H. Farmer (1985); R.M. Woolley (1927); H. Thurston (1898). See also D. L. Douie and D. H. Farmer, *Magna Vita S. Hugonis* (1985); H. Mayr-Harting (ed.), *St Hugh of Lincoln* (1985); R. M. Loomis, *Gerald of Wales's Life of Hugh of Avalon* (1985); C. Gorton, *Metrical Life of St Hugh* (1986). For the canonization report, see D. H. Farmer in *Lincs. Arch. and Archaeol. Soc. Papers*, 6 (1986), pp. 86-117. See also D. Knowles, *The Monastic Orders in England* (1963), pp. 375-91; C. R. Cheney, *Hubert Walter* (1967); *Bibl.SS.*, 12, 775-8.

St Dionysius of Alexandria, *Bishop* (265)

Most of what we know of Dionysius comes from Eusebius and from extracts of his letters preserved by Eusebius. Called "the Great" by St Basil (2 Jan.) and other Greek writers and "Teacher of the Catholic Church" by St Athanasius (2 May), he was born of pagan parents toward the end of the second century and educated in Alexandria. When he became a Christian, he enrolled in the school of Origen (*c.* 183-*c.* 252), of which he eventually became director for two years (231-2). In 247 he was chosen to be bishop of Alexandria. Not long after this a persecution instigated by a pagan prophet in the city was raised against Christians, only to be reinforced in

249 by the edict of Decius (249-51), on the authority of which troops were sent to arrest Dionysius. In the confusion that followed, Dionysius was eventually rescued, put on a donkey, and sent off to a safe place in the Libyan desert. He ruled the church of Alexandria from the desert, where he stayed, with two companions, until the persecution was over.

Back in Alexandria, he had to deal with the schism of Novatian, who took a very hard line against those who weakened under persecution and offered sacrifice to the pagan gods. Novatian had set himself up as pope over the head of the validly-elected incumbent, Pope Cornelius (251-3; 16 Sept.), and wrote asking Dionysius for support. Dionysius' reply is uncompromising: "You ought to have suffered all things rather than have caused a schism in the Church. To die in defence of its unity would be as glorious as laying down one's life for its faith; in my opinion, more glorious, because here the safety of the whole Church is concerned. If you bring your brethren back to union, your fault will be forgotten. If you cannot gain others, at least save your own soul." Dionysius also exchanged several letters on the subject with Bishop Fabius of Antioch, who favoured the rigorist position.

Shortly after this Alexandria was struck by the plague, which lasted for several years and claimed a large number of lives. Dionysius wrote an account of its terrors, in which, possibly generalizing somewhat, he praised the selflessness of the Christians in contrast with what he saw as the selfishness of the pagans. He was a keen interpreter of the scriptures as well as an enthusiastic denouncer of dogmatic error, and many of his writings date from this period. He used arguments against St John's authorship of the book of *Revelation* that were revived by some critics earlier in this century; and he took part in a debate about the validity of baptism by heretics in which he tended to think that such baptisms were not valid. Still, he followed the guidelines set down by Pope Stephen I (254-7; 2 Aug.), who took the opposite view. At one point, the tireless bishop was forced to defend his own opinions. In denouncing the views of some followers of Sabellianism, which denied any distinction between the persons of the Trinity, he expressed views that were denounced in their turn to Pope Dionysius (259-69; 26 Dec.). However, he managed satisfactorily to explain his teaching.

When the persecution started up again in 257 under Valerian (253-9), the prefect of Egypt attempted to persuade Dionysius and some of his priests to sacrifice to the "protector" gods of the empire. The attempt failed, and they were banished to Kephro in Libya. Dionysius used the time he spent there to preach the gospel to the local people. When he returned to his see in 260, Alexandria was in a state of upheaval: rioting and violence of every sort were the order of the day, and the plague had returned, adding to the havoc and confusion. He governed his diocese "with great wisdom and sanctity" for another five years, until he died in 265.

Eusebius devotes much attention to him; for refs, see the Pengiun Classics ed., p. 362. For Dionysius' writings, see C. L. Feltoe, ed. (1904, 1918). See also: O. Bardenhewer, *Geschichte der altkirchlichen Literatur*, 2, pp. 206-37; *J.T.S.* 25, pp. 364-77; H. Delehaye, *Les passions des martyrs...* (1921), pp. 429-35; P. S. Miller, *Studies in Dionysius the Great of Alexandria* (1933).

St Gregory the Wonderworker, *Bishop* (*c.* 213–*c.* 270)

Given his importance as a link between the age of the martyrs and the age of the Cappadocian fathers, there is curiously little material written by or about this saint, whose alleged miracles earned him the title *Thaumaturgus*, or Wonderworker. He was born at Neocaesarea in Pontus into a distinguished pagan family and given the name Theodore (it is not clear at exactly what point he became known as Gregory). When he was fourteen, his father died, but he continued his education, which was preparing him for a career in the law. A few years later he and his brother, Athenodorus, who subsequently became a bishop and suffered for his faith, accompanied their sister when she went to join her husband at Caesarea in Palestine.

In Caesarea, the two young men had the good fortune to come into contact with Origen, who had opened a school there a short while before. Origen immediately recognized their potential, both intellectual and personal, while they, on their side, were fascinated by his style and the content of his teaching. Both enrolled without further ado, abandoning their original plan to go to law school in Beirut. In his own account of his relations with Origen, Gregory says that he and Athenodorus were attracted to him as much by the example of his life as by his teaching. With him they studied the works of the poets and philosophers, learning to weigh up what these had to say about God and to discern what was true and was what false. Above all, he taught them that human reason alone can never attain certain knowledge of the truths of religion, and it was through his influence that they were converted to Christianity. After their conversion they continued to study under Origen until about 238, when they returned to Neocaesarea. Before they left, Gregory thanked Origen and celebrated his wisdom in a public address which throws interesting light on Origen's teaching methods. Also extant is a letter from Origen to Gregory, in which he calls Gregory his respected son and urges him to use his talents in the service of God, borrowing from non-Christian philosophy whatever might serve that purpose.

Gregory returned to Neocaesarea with the intention of practising law. However, he had not been there long when he was appointed bishop—despite the fact that there were only seventeen Christians in the town. Unfortunately, very few details of his long episcopate have come down to us: although St Gregory of Nyssa (10 Jan.) supplies a good deal of information about the deeds that earned Gregory the title *Thaumaturgus*, much of it is clearly legendary. What is certain, on the other hand, is that Neocaesarea was a prosperous, heavily-populated city, with its fair share of crime and immorality, and that Gregory applied himself with great zeal to his task, for which he received an extraordinary power to work miracles. St Basil the Great (2 Jan.), who, like his brother Gregory of Nyssa, learned what he knew of Gregory *Thaumaturgus* from their grandmother, St Macrina the Elder (14 Jan.), spoke of the "formidable power over evil spirits" that Gregory possessed "through the cooperation of the Spirit," adding: "He altered the course of rivers in the name of Christ; he dried up a lake that was a cause of dissension between two brothers; and his foretelling of the future made him equal with the other prophets. . . . Such were his signs and wonders that both friends and enemies of the truth looked on him as another Moses." When, in 1738, Pope Clement XII (1730–40) decided to add St Gertrude to the Western Calendar, he was confronted with the fact that she died on the same day, 17 November, as Gregory *Thaumaturgus*. Referring to the latter's miraculous removal of a great stone—which in the *Dialogues* of Gregory the Great becomes a mountain—Clement decreed that a saint who moved mountains should not himself be moved, and assigned St Gertrude to 15 November. But Basil also mentions Gregory's more mundane virtues—his zeal, his spirit of prayer, his simplicity and love of truth, and his lack of anger and bitterness.

On the day he took possession of his see, Gregory, having accepted the hospitality of a locally influential man named Musonius, immediately went out to preach. By nightfall he had the makings of a small congregation, and early the next morning, the word clearly having gone round, the doors were crowded with sick people, whom he cured physically as well as spiritually. Eventually his converts became so numerous that, with their help in the form of money or labour, he was able to build a church for their use. What is more, over the years he seems to have earned widespread respect for his wisdom and tact and was called on to advise in civil as well as religious matters. And toward the end of his life, he was present at the first synod of Antioch (265), where he defended the orthodox faith against the heretical bishop of Antioch, Paul of Samosata.

But there were difficulties as well as successes. In 250 the persecution of Decius (241-51) broke out. Gregory took a very pragmatic view of the situation and advised his flock to hide rather than expose themselves to the risk of losing their lives for their faith. He himself went into the desert with one of his converts, a former pagan priest who was by then his deacon. Informed that he was on a particular mountain, the authorities are said to have sent soldiers to apprehend him, but the men returned saying they could see nothing but two trees. The informer then went himself, found that the "trees" were Gregory and his deacon at prayer, and judging their escape to be miraculous, became a Christian. When the persecution was over—Decius died in 251—the area was attacked first by the plague and then by the Goths on one of their periodic raids into Roman territory. Both added to the sum of Gregory's responsibilities, and it is hardly surprising that he left so little in the way of written works. He does, however, refer to his episcopal cares and duties in a canonical letter written during the barbarian raids, one of the few authentic manuscripts of his that survives. Among other things he mentions one of his more original missionary methods: the organization of secular entertainments in connection with the annual commemoration of the martyrs. These were designed to attract pagans as well as to popularize religious gatherings among Christians.

There is no record of how successfully these achieved their end, but shortly before his death Gregory asked how many pagans still remained in the city. Seventeen, he was told—the number of Christians there had been when he arrived. Having prayed for the conversion of the seventeen and for the perseverance of those who already believed, he asked his friends not to procure a special burial-place for him when he died. He had lived as a pilgrim in this world, he said, and wished to be buried as one. For unexplained reasons his body was eventually taken to a Byzantine monastery in Calabria, where a considerable local cult developed. He is invoked especially in times of flood or earthquake.

For St Gregory's writings, see H. Crouzel (ed.) in *S.C.* (1969); F. Froidevaux, "Le symbole de Saint Grégoire le Thaumaturge" in *Recherches de Sciences Religieuses* 19 (1929), pp. 193-247. Gregory of Nyssa's panegyric is in *P.G.*, 46, 893-958. See also A. Poncelet, "La vie latine de S. Grégoire le Thaumaturge" in *Anal. Boll.* 1, pp. 132-60; W. Telfer, "The Cultus of St Gregory Thaumaturgus" in *Harvard Theological Review* 29 (1936), pp. 225-344; *N.C.E.*, 6, pp. 797-8.

SS Alphaeus and Zachaeus, *Martyrs* (303)

All we know about these two martyrs is recorded by Eusebius in his *Martyrs of Palestine*. From him we learn that as the games for celebrating the twentieth year of Diocletian's reign drew near, the governor of Palestine sought and obtained the emperor's pardon for all criminals. However, this also happened to be the first year of Diocletian's general persecution of Christians, who were therefore not included in the general amnesty. Zachaeus, a deacon at Gadara, east of the Jordan, was arrested at this time, tortured, and thrown into prison. Here he was placed in the stocks in such a way that his body was nearly torn apart, but he endured his situation very cheerfully, praising God at all times. It was not long before he was joined by Alphaeus, who, although he came originally from Eleutheropolis, was a lector in the church of Caesarea. When the persecution began he had encouraged other Christians to remain faithful. He was arraigned before the prefect, whom he baffled with his answers during a first examination, and thrown into prison. After a second court appearance, during which he was severely beaten, he was cast into the same cell as Zachaeus. Appearing once again before the prefect, both were condemned to death. They were beheaded together on 17 November 303.

See Eusebius, *Martyrs of Palestine*, 1, p. 5; also *C.M.H.*, pp. 604-5.

SS Acisclus and Victoria, *Martyrs* (? Fourth Century)

The medieval *passio* of these two saints is no more than a pious fiction, and there seems to be no real evidence at all for the existence of Victoria. Acisclus, on the other hand, was a genuine martyr: he is mentioned by Prudentius and in the *Hieronymianum* under 18 November—with the curious note, "on this day roses are gathered." His name appears in an early sixth-century Spanish inscription referring to relics, and both were once regarded as sufficiently important to warrant a proper office in the Mozarabic liturgy. There is, however, no agreement within 100 years or more as to when they lived and died, though tradition has it that they suffered in the persecution of Diocletian (284-305). In his *Memorial of the Saints*, St Eulogius (11 Mar.) says they were a brother and sister from Córdoba. Having been denounced as Christians, they were imprisoned and tortured in an attempt to get them to apostatize. When they stood firm, they were taken to the amphitheatre, where Acisclus was beheaded and Victoria pierced with arrows. Their bodies were buried by a wealthy woman, named Minciana, in the grounds of her country house. Eventually a church was built on the spot, and many of the martyrs of the Arab persecution were buried there. The basilica of St-Sernin in Toulouse claims some of the relics of Acisclus and Victoria.

For the medieval *passio*, see Florez, *España sagrada*, 10, pp. 485-91. For the Spanish inscription, see J. Vives, *Inscripciones cristianas de la España romana y visigoda* (1942), no. 316.

St Anianus of Orleans, *Bishop* (453)

There are two extant Latin Lives of this saint, both of which are late in date and unreliable. It seems, however, that Anianus (or Aignan) was born in Vienne into a noble family and that he lived there for some time as a hermit. Then, attracted by the reputation of Evurtius, the local bishop, he went to Orleans, where Evurtius ordained him to the priesthood. This was how things remained until Evurtius, toward the end of his life, decided to resign his see. He called an assembly for the election of his successor, and the lot, drawn by a child, fell on Anianus. To make sure that there could be no mistake it was confirmed by *sortes biblicae* (a practice, prevalent from the fourth to the ninth century, whereby randomly chosen biblical or literary texts were used to elect a bishop or make some other decision of ecclesiastical importance). When he came to take possession of his cathedral, Anianus is said to have followed the custom of the time and asked the prison governor to release all those currently in custody. At first the governor refused, but then he had a close brush with death which he took as a warning from God, and he did as the bishop had asked.

In 451, Orleans was threatened by the Huns, under their leader, Attila. Like many another bishop of the period in a similar situation, Anianus was the one who took the initiative, organizing the defences and encouraging the people. He appealed urgently to the powerful Roman general Flavius Aetius (396-454) to come to their help, but Aetius was slow to move, and the Huns took the city. As they left with their booty and captives, however, they found themselves facing the oncoming troops of Aetius, who eventually defeated them at the battle of the Catalaunian Plains, near Durocatalaunum (modern Châlons-sur-Marne). Gregory of Tours describes the relief of Orleans in some detail, attributing it to Anianus. Anianus died two years later at an advanced age. His relics are venerated in the church in Orleans that bears his name.

For the better of the two Latin Lives (ed. B. Krusch), see *M.G.H., Scriptores rerum merov.*, 3, pp. 104-17. See also Gregory of Tours, *History of the Franks* (ed. L. Thorpe, 1974), 2, 7, pp. 116-7; C. Duhan, *Vie de St Aignan* (1877); P. Barbier, *Vie de S. Aignan* (1912); L. Duchesne, *Fastes Episcopaux*, 2, p. 460; *Bibl.SS.*, 1, 1258-9.

St Gregory of Tours, *Bishop* (539-94)

Georgius Florentius, who later took the name Gregory, was the best-known early bishop of Tours after St Martin (11 Nov.). He was born at Clermont-Ferrand in 539 of a distinguished Auvergnat family. His great-grandfather was St Gregory of Langres (4 Jan.), and his uncle, to whose care he was entrusted on the death of his father, was St Gallus of Clermont (1 July). When Gallus died in his turn while Gregory was in his early teens, the boy contracted a serious illness, during which he began to think seriously of dedicating his life to God. Once recovered, he went to study scripture under St Avitus I (5 Feb.), at the time a priest in Clermont, and was ordained deacon in 563. Then, in 573, at the request of Sigebert I, king of Austrasia (561-75), and of the people of Tours, he was appointed to succeed St Euphronius as bishop there.

Merovingian Gaul was an unsettled and violent place. When Clovis (481-511), who had converted to Christianity in 496, died in 511, the Frankish kingdom was divided among his four sons. It came together again briefly under Clotaire I (511-61), only to be divided up once more for Clotaire's four sons. Like so many bishops of the period, Gregory was unable to isolate himself from the politics of the day. When his episcopate began, two of Clotaire's sons, Sigebert I and Chilperic of Neustria (561-84), were at war with one another, and Tours was a particularly troubled diocese. In such circumstances it was not easy for a bishop to maintain his integrity. Nevertheless, despite the inevitable violence and intrigues associated with court life and the fact that he was frequently called upon to undertake diplomatic missions on behalf of the king, Gregory was never anything but his own man. When Chilperic's son, Meroveus, angered his father by marrying his uncle Sigebert's widow, Brunhild, Gregory gave Meroveus sanctuary and was the only bishop to support his fellow-bishop, Praetextatus of Rouen (24 Feb.), who had conducted the marriage ceremony. And though it could have improved their generally strained relationship, Gregory could not bring himself to pretend that King Chilperic was a good theologian, in spite of the fact that the king thought himself to be such.

But this is not the aspect of his own life and work that Gregory chose to dwell on at the end of his great *Historia Francorum*. He wanted to be remembered instead for what he achieved in his role as a pastor and for his writings. As bishop he worked hard to revitalize the life of the diocese, and during his episcopate there was a flowering of faith and works of charity, and many who had lapsed or turned to heresy were reconciled to the Church. He rebuilt and enlarged the cathedral, which had been destroyed by fire, and he restored a number of smaller churches, including that of St Martin. He encouraged devotion to Mary at a time when such devotion was in its infancy, and he is known to have believed in her Assumption. He was widely revered for his humility, his charity, and his generosity toward his enemies, and his writings reveal him as a shrewd and humorous observer of the human scene.

It is, of course, for his writings that he is best remembered. From them we learn most of what we know about him as well as about sixth-century Gaul, and they are an extraordinary achievement. This man was responsible for a huge diocese. His primary task was to defend and interpret faith and morals; but he was also expected to visit monasteries and convents, found schools, look after the fabric of church property, and administer the Church's not inconsiderable estates—all of which he seems to have done with distinction. Yet he found time to write a number of books on the lives and miracles of the saints, including *De Gloria Martyrum* and *De Gloria Confessorum*; individual Lives of St Martin and St Julian (28 Aug.); a commentary on the psalms; and the ambitious ten-volume history of the Franks. This, like most of his books, is thought to have been a work in progress throughout his episcopate, as he constantly made additions and introduced cross-references.

When Gregory died in 594, he was buried in the cathedral in Tours, where, over a century later, St Ouen (24 Aug.) built a worthy tomb for him beside that of St Martin. Here, according to an early biographer, St Odo of Cluny (18 Nov.), miracles were recorded. Unfortunately, this tomb was destroyed by the Vikings in the ninth century and, having been restored in the eleventh century, by the Huguenots in 1562.

For Gregory's works, see *M.G.H., Scriptores rerum meroving.*, 1; *P.L.*, 71; O. M. Dalton (trans.), *History of the Franks* (1927, rp. 1971); W. C. MacDermott (trans.), selected minor works (1949); E. James, *Gregory of Tours: Life of the Fathers* (1985). Biographical works include J. Verdon, *Grégoire de Tours, "le père de l'Histoire de France"* (1989); G. Vinay, *San Gregorio di Tours* (1940). See also J. M. Wallace Hadrill, *The Frankish Church* (1983); Harman Grisewood in *Saints and Ourselves* (1953), pp. 25-40; P. Brown, *The Cult of the Saints* (1981); *idem*, "Relics and Social Status in the Age of Gregory of Tours" in *Society and the Holy in Late Antiquity* (1982); H. Delehaye, "Les recueils antiques des miracles des saints" in *Anal. Boll.* 43, pp. 305-25.

St Hilda of Whitby, *Abbess* (614-80)

The cult of St Hilda (Hild) must have been recognized almost immediately after her death, because her name appears in the calendar of St Willibrord (7 Nov.), which was written as early as the beginning of the eighth century. She was one of the daughters of Hereric, a nephew of St Edwin, king of Northumbria (12 Oct.), who was living in exile with his family in a British enclave of Elmet (in what today is North Yorkshire). When she was thirteen, she was baptized, with Edwin, by St Paulinus, the archbishop of York (10 Oct.). For the next twenty years she lived, as Bede put it, "most nobly in the secular state," and then decided formally to consecrate her life to God. Her initial plan was to go to the kingdom of East Anglia, where her cousin Anna was king, travel from there to Chelles, in France, and join the monastic community of which her sister Hereswitha was already a member. She was forestalled by St Aidan, bishop of Lindisfarne (8 Oct.), who persuaded her to return to Northumbria.

She lived briefly on a small plot of land given her by Aidan on the banks of the river Wear. Soon, however, she was elected to succeed Heiu as abbess of the double monastery at Hartlepool. Such double monasteries of monks and nuns, who sang the office together in church but otherwise lived entirely separately, with the abbess

157

in supreme charge except in strictly spiritual matters, were not uncommon at the time. Her task here was to reorganize the life of the community, and this she did on the basis of a Rule derived from Irish sources—possibly that of St Columbanus (21 Nov.)—which differed in certain respects from the Rules followed in the Frankish Church and the rest of Christendom.

Nine or ten years later, in 657, Hilda was transferred to Streaneshalch (later Whitby), either to reform an existing double monastery or to found a new one—it is not clear which, but the significant thing is the success with which she did it. She was a fervent believer in the importance of education, especially, though not exclusively, of the clergy. Within the monastery, reading and study of scripture were encouraged, as was the study of Latin language and literature, and there was soon an established library. Bede, whose *Ecclesiastical History* is the source of virtually all we know about Hilda, observes that "she obliged those who were under her direction to attend much to reading the Holy Scriptures and to exercise themselves freely in works of righteousness in order that many there might be found fit for ecclesiastical duties and to minister at the altar." As it happens, several of her monks became bishops, including St John of Beverley (7 May).

Hilda's personal prestige and her influence extended beyond the confines of the monastery. Bede tells us that "not only ordinary people, but even kings and princes sometimes asked and accepted her advice." She encouraged the Anglo-Saxon poet Caedmon (11 Feb.), who was a cowherd for the monastery and eventually joined it, to write poetry in the vernacular on Christian themes. And it was probably due to her reputation, as well as to the suitability of the place, that the abbey at Whitby was chosen as the site of the famous synod of 663–4, which was convened to decide the date of Easter.

At least that was the immediate issue—a debate between those who favoured the Irish method of calculating the date and those, headed by the archbishop of York, St Wilfrid (12 Oct.), and backed by the Northumbrian king, Oswiu, who favoured the Roman method. But behind this discussion lay a long-standing tension between the Celtic churches, which had developed rather independently, and the rest, which followed the lead of Rome. Hilda and the members of her community, with their Celtic Rule, not surprisingly supported the Celtic method of calculating the date of Easter, but in the end the Roman method was endorsed by the majority. Hilda fully accepted the decision. Fifteen years later, however, when the archbishop of Canterbury, St Theodore (19 Sept.), made a somewhat arbitrary decision to divide Wilfrid's diocese, the confines of which at that stage were those of the kingdom of Northumbria, she sided with Theodore against Wilfrid. This was no doubt because it genuinely seemed a good idea and because two of the new bishops, St Bosa (9 Mar.) and St John of Beverley, were monks of Whitby, but it has been suggested that she also saw it as a way to even the score with Wilfrid.

For the last seven years of her life Hilda suffered from a chronic illness. We do not know what the condition was, but what is certain is that she did not allow it to prevent her from carrying out her duties, particularly those that involved teaching.

She died in 680, probably on 17 November. According to Bede, a nun called Begu in the daughter-house at Hackness, thirteen miles away, heard the passing bell in a dream and saw Hilda's soul departing for heaven. She alerted her sisters, and they were already in church praying for Hilda when brothers from the monastery at Whitby arrived at dawn with the news.

After Hilda's death Roman, as opposed to Irish, thinking predominated at Whitby. This was largely due to the influence of St Enfleda (24 Nov.) and St Elfleda (8 Feb.), daughter and grand-daughter of St Edwin. Both joined the monastery while Hilda was abbess, and each served a term as abbess. The abbey itself was destroyed by the Danes in about 800. The supposed relics of St Hilda were removed, but it is not clear to where, since both Glastonbury and Gloucester claimed to hold them. Her cult was strongest in the north of England, where no less than fourteen churches, including eleven in Yorkshire and two in Durham, were dedicated to her. Her feast was also solemnized at Evesham, on account of its involvement when Whitby was refounded as an abbey in the eleventh century.

Bede, *H.E.*, 4, p. 23; *Catologus Sanctorum Pausantium in Anglia* (under Glastonbury); A. Warin, *Hilda* (1989); P. Hunter Blair, *The World of Bede* (1970), pp. 145-8; H. Mayr-Harting, *The Coming of Christianity to Anglo-Saxon England* (1972), pp. 150-2.

Bd Salome, *Abbess (c. 1211-68)*

Salome was the daughter of Leszek the Fair, prince of Cracow. It is difficult to date accurately the early events of her life, since the sources differ quite considerably. It seems certain, however, that when she was three, the bishop of Cracow, Bd Vincent Kadlubek (8 Mar.), was commissioned to take her to the court of King Andrew II of Hungary (1205-35). Leszek had arranged a marriage between her and Andrew's son, Kálmán, who was six at the time; with such royal marriages, it was not uncommon at the time for the girl to grow up at the court of her future father-in-law. The two children were crowned and "ruled" over Halicz for about three years, until it was occupied by a Ruthenian prince, Mstislav, who took them prisoner. During their captivity, when Salome was about nine, they are said to have made a joint vow of chastity. They were released when the Hungarians recovered Halicz, and eventually the marriage was solemnized.

After this, Salome seems to have lived a somewhat ascetic life, becoming a Franciscan tertiary and doing her best to make her court a model of Christian life. Kálmán governed Dalmatia and Slavonia until he died in a battle against the Tartars in 1241. For about a year after his death Salome remained at the court, where she involved herself in good works, but in 1242 she returned to Poland. She was a particularly generous benefactress of the Friars Minor, and with the help of her brother Boleslaw she founded a convent of Poor Clares at Sandomierz in 1245. She entered this convent herself and was eventually elected abbess. She died on 17 November 1268, and her remains were taken to the Franciscan church in Cracow. Pope Clement X (1670-6) approved her cult in 1672.

For a medieval Life, see *Monumenta Poloniae Historica*, 4, pp. 776-96. See also L. Wadding, *Annales Ord. Min.*, 3, pp. 353-5; 4, pp. 284-5; Léon, *Auréole Séraphique* (Eng. trans.), 4, pp. 71-4.

Bd Joan of Signa (*c.* 1245-1307)

Apart from what we learn, particularly about her miracles, from an anonymous Latin Life written in about 1390, very few details have come down to us about Joan (Giovanna da Signa). She was born about 1245 into a peasant family at Signa, a village on the Arno near Florence, and from an early age she was sent out to mind the sheep and goats. Taking advantage of the long hours they spent out in the fields, she would gather other shepherds around her and talk to them in simple language about the truths of faith. Many were persuaded, as much by her example as by her words, and some saw the supernatural at work in her ability to keep dry in wet weather, though this was more likely due to the simple expedient of sheltering under a large tree with dense foliage. When she was twenty-three, possibly inspired by what she had heard of Bd Verdiana of Castelfiorentino (16 Feb), who died about the time of her own birth, Giovanna went to live as a hermit on the banks of the Arno. For the next forty years she welcomed all (and they were many) who came from the surrounding area to consult her or to obtain healing for their sick, and she had a great reputation for miracles. A cult developed as soon as she died on 9 November 1307, and this was greatly enhanced in 1348, when the sudden cessation of an epidemic was attributed to her intercession. It was confirmed in 1798 by Pope Pius VI (1775-99). The Franciscans, the Augustinians, the Carmelites, and the Vallombrosian monks claim a connection with Joan, but the Bollandists take the view that there is insufficient evidence to connect her with any one Order.

For the Latin Life, see *Archivum Franciscanum Historicum*, 10 (1917), pp. 367-86; *AA.SS.*, Nov., 4, p. 280. See also Léon, *Auréole Séraphique* (Eng. trans.), 4, pp. 160-4; *Vies des Saints*, 11, p. 286.

Bd Elizabeth the Good (1386-1420)

We are relatively well informed about Bd Elizabeth thanks to her confessor, Konrad Kugelin, who wrote a Life in German, the original of which has been preserved. She was one of the last of the medieval women mystics, most of them connected with one or other of the mendicant Orders, who were remarkable for their extreme austerity, visions and visitations, and abnormal physical phenomena. (Bd Alpais [3 Nov.] and Bd Christina of Stommeln [6 Nov.] are two other examples.) In many cases the facts as presented are so extreme—particularly where abstention from food is concerned—that questions need to be asked, not about the integrity of the person involved, but about the motives of those most closely associated with her, who might have had an interest in cultivating a following.

Elizabeth (Elisabetha) was born to a poor couple, Johannes and Anna Achler, at Waldsee in Württemberg, on 25 November 1386. From her earliest childhood she was known, because of her innocence and her sweet nature, as *die gute Betha*—good little Bessie. When she was fourteen, her confessor, Fr Kugelin, who remained her spiritual director all her life, suggested that she become a Franciscan tertiary. She followed his advice and took lodgings with a woman weaver in order to learn her trade. There she remained for three years, at which point Fr Kugelin placed her with a community of four other tertiaries at Reute, near Waldsee. Here she did the cooking—at which she appears to have been more proficient than she was at weaving.

According to Fr Kugelin, she was notable both for the diabolical manifestations that frequently punctuated her otherwise uneventful life and for long periods of abstinence from food. On one occasion things were found to be missing from the house, only to appear at last under Elizabeth's bed. She had not put them there and believed this was the work of the devil, but she accepted the penance imposed on her by her sisters, who, perhaps understandably, came to distrust her. She was also said to have been granted visions of heaven and purgatory, frequent ecstasies, a miraculous Communion, and, from time to time, the stigmata of Christ's passion, including the marks of the crown of thorns and the scourging, which bled copiously and were extremely painful. And she is said to have lived for years on far less than the minimum amount of food needed to keep a human being alive. She died on 25 November 1420, attended by Fr Kugelin. Her cult was approved by Pope Clement XIII (1758-69) in 1766, and her shrine at Reute is still a place of pilgrimage.

For Konrad Kugelin's Life (ed. A. Berlinger), see *Alemannia*, 9 (1881), pp. 275-92; 10 (1882), pp. 81-109, 128-37. See also Nidermayer, *Die selige gute Betha von Reute* (1766); P. Lechner, *Leben der sel. Elisabetha Bona von Reute* (1854); A. Baier, *Der sel. gute Betha von Reute* (1920); K. Bihlmeyer in *Festgabe Philipp Strauch* (1932), pp. 96-109. On fasting saints, see Rudolph M. Bell, *Holy Anorexia* (1985); Walter Vandereycken, *From Fasting Saints to Anorexic Girls* (1994).

ST HUGH OF LINCOLN (pp. 147-50)
Silver swan (said to have been a pet) on blue field.

18

ST PHILIPPINE DUCHESNE (1769-1852)

Rose-Philippine Duchesne was born at Grenoble on 29 August 1769. On both sides her background was prosperous and secure: her father, Pierre-François Duchesne, was a prominent lawyer and politician; her mother, Rose-Euphrosine Périer, was the daughter of a successful merchant. Philippine was the second of their six children, but she was effectively the eldest, because an older sister died in infancy. The wider world of her childhood was unsettled as France lurched toward the Revolution, but she herself grew up in a happy atmosphere surrounded by a large extended family. She became particularly close to her cousin Joséphine Périer, who was to remain her lifelong friend and correspondent. Her strong, imperious personality was quick to manifest itself, as was her innate seriousness; and despite the comfort of her home life, she was well aware of the inequalities of life and that others were not so fortunate. She was unusually well educated for her time, going to school with the Visitation nuns at Ste-Marie-d'En-haut and sharing her cousins' tutor. She developed an early enthusiasm for history, and her interest in the missionary life, particularly in America, was sparked by a visiting Jesuit who had worked in Louisiana and had stories to tell about the Indians.

When she was seventeen, Philippine told her parents, who were already looking around for a husband for her, that she intended to become a nun. After some initial opposition, her father allowed her to join the community at Ste-Marie-d'En-haut, although eighteen months later he refused permission for her profession on the grounds that the future for France looked too uncertain. In this he was only too right. By 1789 the Revolution was gathering momentum, and in 1791 the Visitation nuns were expelled from Grenoble. Philippine returned to her family, and for the duration of the Revolution she concerned herself with the care of the sick, the needs of prisoners, and above all, the education of children.

In 1801 the Vatican, in the person of Pope Pius VII (1800-23), signed a concordat with Napoleon. This brought to an end ten years of conflict between the Church and the Revolution, and it reinstated Catholicism as the established church in France. Philippine now gained possession of the former convent buildings at Ste-Marie-d'En-haut, in the hope that she would be able to re-establish the Visitation community there. But the undertaking was fraught with difficulties, and by 21 August 1802 (feast of the foundress of the Order of the Visitation, St Jane Frances de Chantal), Philippine and one other Sister were left alone in the convent. Accepting the inevitable, she decided to offer the buildings and herself to Madeleine Sophie Barat (25 May), who had recently opened, in Amiens, the first house of the

Society of the Sacred Heart. Mother Barat welcomed the proposal, and on 31 December 1804 Philippine and four others were admitted as postulants. Less than a year later, Philippine was professed.

Early in 1806 the abbot of La Trappe, Dom Augustin de Lestrange, who in 1803 had sent the first Cistercian monks to North America, visited Ste-Marie-d'En-haut. It was a period when the frontiers were still being pushed back in the United States, and Philippine's youthful desire to go there as a missionary was rekindled. However, although Mother Barat approved in principle, Philippine had to wait for another twelve years, during which she prepared herself spiritually and acquired some of the administrational and practical skills she would need. Then, in late 1816, Bishop William Dubourg of Louisiana, who was looking for nuns to work in his diocese, was encouraged by Mother Barat's brother Louis to start thinking in terms of Philippine. When the matter was put to her, Mother Barat hesitated but was eventually won round. There was a bad moment in 1817 when Bishop Dubourg returned to find that she had changed her mind, but in the end, thanks to Philippine's impetuous enthusiasm, it was decided that five Sisters of the Sacred Heart, with Philippine as their superior, would go to Louisiana. They left Paris on 8 February 1818, and set sail from Bordeaux on 21 March.

The journey was long and trying, and they did not reach New Orleans until 29 May. Even then they did not stop to rest, but immediately made their way up the Mississippi to St Louis, then a town of about 6,000 inhabitants, in what is now Missouri. Bishop Dubourg welcomed them and found them the log cabin at St Charles, on the Missouri River, which was to be their first house on American soil. *(See map on p. 169.)* Here they lost no time in opening the first free school west of the Mississippi, for the children of the poor. The white population—French, English, Creole, and other—was predominantly Catholic. Many of them were bilingual (the nuns themselves had started studying English while they were still in France and it was to prove a real disadvantage for Philippine that she never really mastered the language), but they were poor and in other respects ignorant. And the Indians were not the "docile and innocent savages" Philippine had dreamed of teaching. On the contrary: "The women are idle and given to drink as much as the men." All in all, this first year was a hard one, and toward the end of 1819, in bitterly cold weather, they moved to a three-storey brick house Bishop Dubourg had found for them at Florissant, nearer to St Louis. Philippine's first act was to erect a small shrine to St John Francis Regis (16 June), a French Jesuit missionary to the poor to whom she had a great devotion and to whom she had once made a vow, promising that, in return for some favour, she would always have an oratory or altar in his honour in any convent she lived in.

The larger space gave Philippine the idea of starting a novitiate. Bishop Dubourg was not too sure this would succeed, given the differences between French and American attitudes. However, a young woman named Mary Layton joined as a lay sister, and on 22 November 1820 she became the first American to receive the habit of the Society of the Sacred Heart. Encouraged by the opening of the novitiate and the progress of the school, Philippine began to make plans for the future. She never really became reconciled to the idiosyncrasies of American culture—to an egalitarian society that had slavery built into it—but she mellowed as she aged, becoming more realistic about her own limitations, and her enthusiasm seemed unending. She wrote to Mother Barat in 1821: "I thought I had reached the height of my ambition, but I am burning with desire to go to Peru. However, I am more reasonable than I was in France when I used to pester you with my vain aspirations."

In that same year, 1821, the second house of the Society was opened in Grand Coteau, Louisiana, about 150 miles west of New Orleans. The journey Philippine made to visit Grand Coteau was probably the worst of her life—four weeks there by steamboat on the Mississippi River and nine weeks back, during which an outbreak of yellow fever on board left her nursing the sadly neglected sick, until she too fell ill and had to be put ashore at Natchez. Back in Florissant she was beset by problems, especially in relation to the school, which was threatened by financial difficulties and the slanders of hostile outsiders. Just when things looked at their worst and there were only five pupils left, help arrived in the shape of Jesuits from Maryland. With their encouragement, Philippine opened new houses in St Michael's, near New Orleans, in 1826 and in St Louis itself in 1827, and in the following year she reopened the house in St Charles.

Despite these signs of success, for the next ten years hardship, disappointments, and ill-health left Philippine in a state of chronic fatigue and wishing she could resign the responsible office she had never wanted in the first place. Her wish was finally granted in 1840, not by Mother Barat but by Mother Elizabeth Galitzin, the assistant general of the Society, an imperious woman not unlike the younger Philippine. During a visitation of the American houses, Mother Galitzin, by accepting the resignation without demur, managed to give Philippine, who was already seventy-one, the impression that she had somehow failed in the trust assigned to her. It is hard to exaggerate the pain the apparent rejection in this caused her, given all she had endured so readily in terms of loneliness, distance from her closest friends, and trying to come to terms with a new language and culture.

But, ever realistic, she went to live at the St Louis house, and trying to put the past behind her, she turned her attention to the Indians, for whose sake she had wanted to come to America in the first place. She was one of four Sisters who, at the request of Fr Peter De Smet, S.J., went to set up a school for the Potawatomi Indians at Sugar Creek, in Kansas. Unfortunately, it was too late: she had found English difficult, but the Potawatomi language was impossible, and the hardships of the life were too much for her failing strength. Her superiors recalled her and she left without complaint.

Her last years were spent at St Charles. Here she had to look on as houses she had founded were threatened with dissolution. For about four years she lost her greatest support when, for reasons that still have not been fully explained, she stopped getting letters from Mother Barat. The breakdown in communication probably began in 1843 with a simple misunderstanding over the closure of one of the schools, but in a sense the cause is irrelevant. To Philippine, who already felt that by failing to keep her vow to St John Francis Regis (Mother Galitzin had removed his picture during her visitation and replaced it with one of the Sacred Heart) she was somehow responsible for all the misfortunes, the silence was a source of enormous pain. Fortunately someone alerted Mother Barat to this, and in 1847 she not only wrote but with great sensitivity had one of Philippine's nieces, who had joined the Society of the Sacred Heart, deliver it in person.

When Philippine died on 18 November 1852 at the age of eighty-three, a contemporary said of her: "She was the St Francis of Assisi of the Society. Everything in and about her was stamped with the seal of a crucified life." She was buried in the chapel of the convent in St Charles, where her austere shrine remains. A plan to build a larger church in her honour came to nothing, which is probably just as well, for as one of her biographers points out, she would not have wanted the attention and would have deplored the expense. Philippine Duchesne was beatified by Pope Pius XII (1939-58) in 1940 and canonized by Pope John Paul II in 1988.

There are Lives by M. Baumard (Eng. trans. 1879), M. Erskine (1926); M. Symon (1926); C. M. Mooney (1990). See also C. Collins, M. A. Guste, A. Thompson (eds.), *Philippine Duchesne R.S.C.J.: A Collection* (1988); M. Williams, *The Society of the Sacred Heart of Jesus: History of a Spirit 1800-1975* (1978); L. Callan, *The Society of the Sacred Heart in America* (1937); M. K. Richardson, *Redskin Trail* (1952); *O.D.S.*, p. 137; *Bibl.SS.*, 4, 847.

St Romanus of Antioch, *Martyr* (304)

Romanus died at Antioch during the persecution of Diocletian (284-305). However, because he was born in Palestine, Eusebius, who is the point of departure for our knowledge of him, included him in his account of the martyrs of Palestine. He is also the subject of a panegyric by St John Chrysostom (13 Sept.), and Prudentius (6 Apr.) wrote a poem in his honour.

He was a deacon of the church of Caesarea, and when the persecution broke out, he went about urging his fellow Christians to stand firm. Seeing some who were about to sacrifice to the pagan gods out of fear, he called out to warn them against it. He was arrested immediately, scourged, and taken before the judge, who, we are told, condemned him to be burned alive. When the fire was put out by a heavy rainstorm, the emperor, who happened to be in Antioch, ordered that his tongue be pulled out by the roots. But Romanus still spoke, praising God, so he was placed in the stocks for some time and then strangled in prison. Prudentius mentions, without naming him, a seven-year-old boy who, encouraged by Romanus, acknowledged the Christian God and was beheaded. Eusebius says nothing about him, but he is mentioned with Romanus in the Roman Martyrology, where his name is given as Barula. It seems most likely that he was a Syrian martyr called Baralaha or Barlaam, who, through some juxtaposition in an ancient list, became connected with Romanus.

See Eusebius, *De Martyribus Palestinae*, 2; *C.M.H.*, pp. 605-6; *Anal.Boll.* 22, pp. 129-45; 38, pp. 241-84; 50, pp. 241-83.

St Mawes, *Bishop* (? Fifth Century)

Judging by the number of churches dedicated in his honour, St Mawes (Maudez, Maudetus) was the most popular saint in Brittany after St Ivo (19 May). And tradition identifies him as the patron of a Cornish fishing village, St Mawes-in-Roseland, near Falmouth, though exactly how the chapel and well there came to bear his name is not clear. Yet very little is known about him, and the two medieval lives that have come down to us are of little historical value. His name is British, and there is topographical evidence to support the theory that he was closely associated with St Budoc (8 Dec.) and that both were monks from Wales who went as missionaries to Cornwall and to Brittany, where they founded monasteries and were somehow connected with Dol. But according to a separate tradition Mawes was an Irishman who went to Brittany during the reign of Childebert I (511-88) and settled there with a few disciples on an island, Ile Modez, off the coast of the Pays de Léon, which he cleared of snakes and vermin by setting fire to the grass (he is invoked against snake-bite, headache, and worms). In both Brittany and Cornwall tradition made him a monk who spent much time teaching his disciples in the open air. According to Leland, he was a bishop in Brittany. His relics were venerated in a number of places, including Lesneven, Quimper, Tréguier, and especially Bourges, where, it was claimed, his body was taken during the Norse invasions of the tenth century. In the twelfth century, Alain, count of Penthièvre and Goëlo, is said to have obtained the relics and given them to the abbey of Beauport, which he had founded for the Premonstratensians in the diocese of Saint-Brieuc. The name of St Mawes appears in tenth-century Breton litanies.

See G. H. Doble, *The Saints of Cornwall*, 3 (1964), pp. 57-73. Also F. Duine, *Memento* (1918), pp. 97-9; L. Gougaud, *Les saints irlandais hors d'Irlande* (1936), pp. 135-9.

St Odo of Cluny, *Abbot* (*c.* 880-942)

Odo was the son of Abbo (or Ebles), lord of Déols, on the Poitou-Lorraine border, and his wife Hildegarde. He was born in Tours in about 880 and was brought up first in the household of Foulques II, count of Anjou, and then in that of Guillaume le Pieux, duke of Aquitaine, who was later to found the abbey of Cluny. He had begun to train for a military career, but when he was about nineteen he suffered some unspecified illness and was forced to abandon the idea. He returned instead to Tours, where he received the tonsure in the church of St Martin. He did not stay in Tours, however, but spent the next few years studying in Paris and Reims, where he also devoted much of his time to his great love, music. Returning eventually to Tours, he became a canon of St Martin's church and one day picked up the *Rule of St Benedict* for the first time. Feeling that his life fell far short of the ideal it put forward, he made up his mind to become a monk and went to the monastery of Baume-les-Messieurs, where the reform of the great abbot, St Benedict of Aniane (11 Feb.), was scrupulously observed. Here, in 909, he received the habit from the abbot, Berno (13 Jan.).

On 11 September of that same year, Guillaume d'Aquitaine gave Berno a property at Cluny, in Burgundy, a few miles north-west of Mâcon, for use as a Benedictine monastery. The subsequent history of this monastery and the extraordinary influence it exerted on the monasticism of western Europe from the middle of the tenth century to the beginning of the twelfth, when it could count at least 1000 dependencies, were determined not least by two significant clauses in the act of foundation: Guillaume renounced any rights he might have had as founder; and the abbey was placed under the direct protection of the Holy See—so becoming independent not only of the temporal power but of the spiritual power in the person of the local bishop as well.

Although it began life unobtrusively as a reformed abbey following the Rule of St Benedict (11 July), Cluny soon became the centre of a reform which spelled the end of lay domination of the monasteries and inspired reform in other countries as well as France. Berno, who left Odo in charge of the monastery school at Baume and went to Cluny as its first abbot, brought a number of monasteries into line with the Cluniac ideal. But Odo, who succeeded Berno as abbot in 927, bringing with him about 100 books to form the basis of a great library, was the one who consolidated and extended the reform. The principle behind it—careful observance of the letter and above all of the spirit of the Rule—was clear, although in its simple insistence on personal poverty, total celibacy, and obedience it was greatly at variance with prevailing practice among the clergy. Odo nevertheless enforced it firmly, and many monasteries, attracted by its very simplicity and idealism, became dependencies of Cluny. Among the best known, those at Fleury-sur-Loire, which was to have considerable influence in England, and Bourg-Dieu were ruled directly from Cluny, while others as far afield as Pavia, Monte Cassino, Naples, and Salerno absorbed the spirit of the Cluniac reforms. In 931, Odo obtained a significant privilege from the pope: Cluny could introduce reform in any monastery at that monastery's request, and Cluny could accept monks from non-reforming monasteries. In fact, Cluny would not have been able to push its reforms forward without the constant support it received from Rome.

In 936 Odo was called to Rome by Pope Leo VII (936-9), who wanted him to mediate in a dispute between Hugues de Provence, king of Italy (926-48), and Alberic, so-called Patrician of the Romans (932-54). Odo, who was much respected by Hugues, achieved at least temporary success by negotiating a marriage between the latter's daughter and Alberic's son. But the peace did not last, and Odo went to Rome twice more to sort things out. Since, on his travels, he was always ready to preach the principles of monastic reform, the abbey at San Paolo *fuori le mura* grasped the opportunity afforded by his presence to return to the "apostolical way."

Two incidents recounted by his biographer throw light on Odo's personality and style. When he first went to the monastery at Fleury, the monks, who resented this attempt to jolt them out of their lax ways, went to meet him armed with swords and stones, and some even threatened to kill him if he crossed the threshold. Odo talked gently to them, gave them three days to cool down, and then rode up to the entrance on a donkey as if nothing had happened. "They received him like a father and his escort had nothing to do but go away." On another occasion, a peasant who said the monks of San Paolo *fuori le mura* owed him money attempted to kill Odo by hurling a stone at him. Odo paid him the money and thought no more about it until he heard Alberic had sentenced the man to lose his right hand for attempted murder. He went immediately to the prince and got the sentence annulled, and the man was freed.

In 942 Odo went to Rome once more, and on his way back called in at the monastery of St-Julien in Tours. He fell ill after attending the celebrations for the feast of St Martin (11 Nov.) and died a week later, on 18 November. One of his last acts was to compose a hymn, still extant, in honour of St Martin. He had always found time in his busy life to write, and surviving works include a second hymn and twelve metrical antiphons for St Martin, three books of moral essays, a Life of St Gerald of Aurillac (13 Oct.), and an epic poem on the redemption. He is also said to have written several books of music, but these have not survived (and those that bear his name are not his).

For the Life by John of Cluny, see *P.L.*, 133, 105-845; *AA.SS.*, *O.S.B.*, 5, 150-99. Modern lives include: G. Sitwell, *St Odo of Cluny* (1958, with trans. of John of Cluny's Life and of Odo's Life of Gerald of Aurillac); R. Oursel, *Les Saints Abbés de Cluny* (1960). See also: *H.S.S.C.*, 5, pp. 97-108; *Bibl.SS.*, 9, 1101-4; *O.D.S.*, pp. 362-3; L.M. Smith, *The Early History of the Movement of Cluny* (1925); J. Leclercq, "Pour une histoire de la vie de Cluny" in *R.H.E.* 57 (1962), pp. 385-408, 783-812; *idem*, "St Odon et son idéal" in *Témoins de la Spiritualité Occidentale*, 2 (1965), pp. 127-35; N. Hunt, *Cluny under St Hugh* (1967); H. E. J. Cowdrey, *The Cluniacs and the Gregorian Reform* (1970).

Bd Caroline Kozka, *Martyr* (1898-1914)

Caroline (Karolina) Kozka was born at Wal-Ruda, near Tarnow in Poland, on 2 August 1898. She was the fourth of the eleven children of a poor agricultural worker, Jan Kozka, and his wife, Maria Borzecka. Her spiritual development was very much shaped by the context of her life—a large family, a close rural community, and an active local church. She grew up in a household where daily prayer, frequent Mass, and devotion to the Sacred Heart and Our Lady were the norm and which was always open to any relative or neighbour who wished to visit. As a young teenager she devoted much of her spare time to her numerous brothers and sisters. But encouraged by her parish priest, Fr Ladislaw Mendrala, she also played an active part in the life the parish, finding time to teach the catechism to the children of the neighbourhood and to visit the old and the sick.

On 18 November 1914, exactly six months after her confirmation and three months after the beginning of the First World War, she was accosted by a Russian soldier who forced her into a nearby forest and killed her as she struggled to safeguard her virginity. Her body, which was not recovered until 4 December, was buried on 6 December in the parish cemetery, and word of her martyrdom spread quickly. Four years later, on 18 June 1916, a monument in her honour was placed near the church at Zabawa, while a cross was set up in the forest to mark the spot where she died. In the following year, once again on 18 November, her relics were taken to a tomb built especially for them next to the parish church. Caroline was beatified by Pope John Paul II in 1987.

See: H. Szuman, "Sp. Karolina Kozka 16-letnia bohaterka" in *Nasz Przwodnik* (1917); P. Wezykowna, *Karolina Kozka in Nasze pisemko* (1932); K.J. Bialobok, "Karolina Kozka S.B." in *Hagiographia Polska*, pp. 895–982; Beaudoin, *Index processuum beatificationis*, p. 242.

The south-eastern United States

Places associated with St Philippine Duchesne, pp. 162–5

19

St Barlaam, *Martyr* (? Fourth Century)

It seems likely that this Barlaam was the real person behind the "Barula" mentioned in connection with St Romanus (18 Nov.). His *acta* as they have come down to us are spurious, but he is the subject of a panegyric by St John Chrysostom (13 Sept.). According to the legend, Barlaam was a labourer in a village near Antioch. His persistent confession of Christ provoked the authorities, who imprisoned him. When his case eventually came to trial, the judge mocked his rough manners and appearance, although he had to admire his constancy. Various tortures were devised in an attempt to break Barlaam's resolve, but none succeeded. Finally, he was forced to hold a handful of incense and red-hot coals over the sacrificial flames on the altar. Had he shaken them off into the flames he would have been said to have offered sacrifice, so he kept his hand out till the flesh burned off. Whatever the actual timing and circumstances of his martyrdom, it took place not in Caesarea in Cappodocia as the Roman Martyrology states but in Antioch, where a church is dedicated to him.

See H. Delehaye in *Anal. Boll.* 22, pp. 129-45; 38, pp. 241-84; 50, pp. 241-83.

St Nerses, *Bishop,* and Other Martyrs (Fourth Century)

What we know of this martyr and his companions comes from a Life which has survived in a Syriac text with a Latin translation. According to this account, Nerses, bishop of Sahgerd, and his disciple Joseph were arrested during the fourth year of the persecution decreed by the Persian king, Sapor II. The king happened to be in Sahgerd at the time, so he had the prisoners brought before him. Touched by the old man and his young companion, he begged Nerses to consider his own safety and worship the sun as required. Nerses refused, telling the king that he had been a Christian since his infancy and that he would not betray his faith now that he was over eighty. Realizing his efforts were useless, the king had the men led to a place of execution, where they were beheaded. The same account mentions the martyrdom of several others, among them a eunuch from the royal palace who refused to sacrifice, which took place at about the same time.

For the Syriac text, Latin trans., and numerous bibliographical references, see *AA.SS.*, Nov., 4, under 10 Nov.

St Nerses I, *Martyr* (*c.* 330–*c.* 373)

St Nerses I, *katholikos* of the Armenians, was the first of several Armenian saints of this name. He was born into a princely family in about 330 and received his early education at home. After a while he was sent to Caesarea in Cappadocia, the rugged area north of the Taurus mountains, where he came under the influence of St Basil (2 Jan.). It was in Caesarea that he married Sahaktucht, daughter of Prince Vardan Mamikonian, by whom he had one son, Sahak (Isaac). When his wife died three years after their marriage, Nerses became an official at the court of the Armenian king, Tiran, and was admitted to Holy Orders (Christianity had been adopted in 300 as the established religion in Armenia, which thus became the first Christian state).

Asked to reinstate the *katholikos*, or principal bishop of the Armenian church, Tiran's devious successor, Arshak, chose Nerses. Nerses refused but, still much against his will, he accepted in 363, when he was elected by the Armenian bishops. Once installed, he set about his task with zeal and earned a reputation as a strong reformer—a reputation inherited by his son and successor, St Isaac (9 Sept.). It was a time of growth for the Armenian church, as Nerses founded new monasteries, built hostels for the poor, and set up the first hostels for lepers. In 365 he convened a national synod at Astishat, his aim being to bring better discipline to his church. However, besides encouraging monasticism and the building of hospitals, he introduced canonical legislation on the Greek model, which infuriated Arshak. When Arshak murdered his nephew Gnel and Gnel's wife, Nerses refused to come to court, so Arshak banished him and appointed another bishop in his place.

Shortly afterwards, Arshak was killed in battle against the Persians. Nerses returned, but only to find that the new king, Arshak's son Pap, was worse than his father. When Nerses refused him entry to his church until he mended his ways, Pap, understandably if unjustifiably enraged, feigned repentance, invited Nerses to dine with him, and had him poisoned. Nerses, who is referred to as "the Great," has been venerated as a martyr ever since, and his name occurs in the Canon of the Armenian liturgy. He was buried in the church of the village of Erzerum (Tuil), which was a place of pilgrimage until the time of the Arab invasions.

See *Bibl.SS.*, 9, 742-5; J. Mecerian, *Histoire et institutions de l'église arménienne* (1965); L. Kogyan, *L'Eglise Arménienne* (1961), pp. 113-9; F. Tournebize, *Histoire politique et religieuse de l'Arménie* (1901), pp. 63-8. See also *Anal.Boll.* 39, pp. 65-9; G. Messina and O. Markwart in *Orientalia christiana* 27 (1932), pp. 141-236.

Bd Salvator Lilli and Companions, *Martyrs* (1895)

Salvatore was the son of Vincenzo and Annunziata Lilli. He was born on 19 June 1853 in Cappadocia, a village in the Apennines east of Avezzano. In 1870, aged seventeen, he joined the Franciscans, making his vows on 6 August 1871 at the friary of Nazzano, near Rome. When the religious Orders were suppressed by the Italian government in 1873, Salvator went off to Palestine with the idea of remaining there as a missionary. He lived first at the friary in Bethlehem, where he completed his philosophical studies and made his solemn profession, and then in Jerusalem, where he studied theology and was ordained to the priesthood on 6 April 1878. He spent another two years in Jerusalem, serving the churches of St Saviour and the Holy Sepulchre, at the end of which he was sent to Marasc in Armenia.

For the next fifteen years Marasc was the scene of his tireless and effective apostolate. He seems to have been a compelling preacher, and the friary chapel was soon full, as people returned to the practice of their faith. But his influence was felt beyond the confines of this chapel. On the practical level, he established two villages and several work schemes, using money donated to the church to buy land and the tools needed to work it. He was particularly active during the cholera epidemic that broke out in Marasc in November 1891, managing to care for the sick, in places single-handedly, for almost six weeks, without catching the disease himself. Meanwhile, his other great contribution was to repair the rather strained relations between the church and Marasc's most prominent citizens, some of whom were themselves Catholics.

In 1894 Salvatore was sent as parish priest and superior to the Franciscan house in Mujukderesi. He had not been there a year when he found himself caught up in the violent political unrest which had been spreading throughout the country since 1890. As Armenian Catholics were being massacred in large numbers, friends tried repeatedly to persuade him to take refuge outside Turkey. He resolutely refused, insisting that the shepherd's place is with his sheep. Finally, and inevitably, he was arrested, on 22 November 1895, and taken with a number of his parishioners, most of them simple peasants, to Marasc. According to an eyewitness, they were given several opportunities to deny their Catholic faith and accept Islam. When they refused, they were brutally bayoneted to death, after which their bodies were burned. They were beatified by Pope John Paul II on 3 October 1982.

B. Spila, *Memorie storiche della provincia riformata romana*, 2 (1896), pp. 70-84; G. C. Guzzo, *Vita e martirio dei servi di Dio p. Salvatore Lilli O.F.M. e compagni* (1942); S. Lilli, *Vita del padre Salvatore Lilli da Cappadocia O.F.M.* (1949).

ST EDMUND
Gold crown and arrows, on blue field.

20

ST EDMUND, *King and Martyr* (841-869)

Edmund's origins are obscure, but it seems he was of Saxon parentage and was brought up as a Christian. Sometime before 865, and according to some accounts as early as Christmas day 855, when he was only fourteen, the East Angles chose him as their king. He was regarded as both a wise and successful ruler and a good man. But in 866 the Great Army of the Vikings, under Ingvar, began the invasion that was to culminate in the imposition of Danelaw from Northumbria to the Thames estuary. Only Wessex and Mercia escaped, thanks to Alfred the Great (871–99), who managed, not without reverses, to repel their advance and shortly afterwards became king of the West Saxons. In 869, having crossed the Humber and taken York, the Danes marched south plundering and burning as they went, through Mercia and into East Anglia, where they took up winter quarters at Thetford. The *Anglo-Saxon Chronicle* tells what happened next: "And that winter Edmund fought against them, and the Danish men got the victory and slew the king, and subdued all that land and destroyed all the monasteries that they came to."

That brief, unadorned statement includes all that is historically certain about Edmund's death. But what it does not say is exactly why, where, and how he died. As a Christian patriot-king, symbol of resistance to the Viking invaders, Edmund immediately became the object of a cult, which, encouraged by Alfred no doubt for his own purposes, would develop to make him a national patron, but the details tended to be blurred. According to Abbo of Fleury (13 Nov.), whose account does include some uninventable detail, Ingvar would have preferred to reign with Edmund rather than kill him, but Edmund was prepared neither to renounce his Christian faith nor to rule as Ingvar's vassal, and he lost his life as a result. What is not clear is whether he died fighting or was murdered after the battle. One account has it that he soon realized that his army was no match for the Danes, and he retreated toward his castle at Framlingham. When he rejected the terms offered by Ingvar, he was overtaken near Hoxne and captured by the river Waveney (or, in another version, in the church at Hoxne). For a second time Ingvar stated his terms. Again Edmund rejected them, declaring that his faith was more precious to him than his life, which he would never purchase by offending God. So, in what sounds like some sort of ritual killing, Ingvar had him tied to a tree, and after he had been scourged the soldiers fired arrows at him, deftly so as not to kill him, until his whole body was covered with arrows—this touch may have been taken from accounts of the martyrdom of St Sebastian (20 Jan). He was then taken down and beheaded, so that his body could not get repose. Another tradition names Hellesdon, Suffolk, as the place where he died and says he was buried in a small wooden church nearby. This is the more likely, as Hellesdon is very near to Bury St Edmunds.

Whatever the truth of the details, sometime between 903 and 915 Edmund's body was found to be incorrupt and immediately translated to Boedricsworth (later Bury St Edmunds). In 925 Athelstan, king of Wessex and Mercia (924-39), founded a small community of two priests and four deacons to look after the shrine. In 1010 another Viking invasion made it necessary to move the relics to the church of St Gregory, near St Paul's cathedral in London, and here they remained until it was safe to return them to Bury three years later.

By now the cult, based on the ideals of heroism, independence, and holiness, was beginning to flourish. Witness to this are the numerous East Anglian coins that have been found dating from the ninth century and apparently issued by the local Scandinavian ruler: they bear the inscription, *Sc Eadmund rex*. Sometime between 985 and 987 Abbo of Fleury, who at the time was living at Ramsey, wrote at the request of St Dunstan (19 May) a Life based on the recollections of Edmund's armour-bearer, whom he had met at the court of Athelstan (924-39). Then, in about 1020, the Benedictine abbey of St Edmundsbury was founded by Knut (1016-35), who, as part of his attempt to reconcile Danes and Anglo-Saxons, endowed it with significant land grants and a charter of jurisdiction over the town that by then surrounded it.

The body of St Edmund, which was brought to the abbey in 1095, became its principal relic. By this time the feast of St Edmund was appearing on monastic calendars, particularly throughout southern England (in the thirteenth century it was a holyday of obligation), and in the end sixty or more churches were dedicated to him. In 1198 the body was re-enshrined after a fire, an episode powerfully described by Jocelin de Brakelond in his Chronicle.

The subsequent history of the relics is uncertain. French soldiers claimed that they had removed them to France after the Battle of Lincoln in 1217, and there is some documentary evidence for this. But the claim, first formulated in the fifteenth century, that relics in the cathedral of St-Sernin in Toulouse were those of St Edmund, was eventually rejected at the beginning of the twentieth. When he was building Westminster Cathedral, Cardinal Manning asked the archbishop of Toulouse for some of the St-Sernin relics and a token collection was duly sent. Later, the request of the third archbishop of Westminster, Cardinal Vaughan, for the whole body, was refused, but Cardinal Vaughan appealed to Pope Leo XIII (1878-1903), and the relics were eventually sent to England. In the end, however, they were not enshrined in the cathedral because a number of scholars, including M. R. James, claimed convincingly that they were not authentic. The true relics, they maintained, had remained in Bury until the Reformation, when they were re-buried in a place unknown. Modern scientific methods have subsequently shown that the Toulouse relics came from not one but several bodies, as seems to be the case with not a few medieval shrines.

The life and death of St Edmund have been a rich source of inspiration for artists. Perhaps the best-known work is the so-called *Wilton Diptych* (National Gallery, London), in which Edmund, recognizable by the arrow he is holding, stands alongside St Edward the Confessor (13 Oct.) and St John the Baptist (24 June, 29 Aug.) on the left-hand panel. The Morgan Library in New York City possesses an illustrated Life (MS 736), written at Bury in about 1130; while in the British Library there is a verse Life (MS Harley 2278), written and illustrated by John Lydgate, one of the Benedictines of Bury. Paintings other than the *Wilton Diptych* include one in the *Albani Psalter* and another in the *Queen Mary Psalter*, a number of French images from the seventeenth and eighteenth centuries, ten screen paintings in East Anglia, and mural paintings in churches in other parts of England. Edmund's emblem is an arrow, although he is sometimes shown with the wolf that is supposed to have guarded his head after his death.

See *Anglo-Saxon Chronicle*, 870; Life by Abbo of Fleury and later legends, in T. Arnold (ed.), *Memorials of St Edmund's Abbey*, 1 (*R.S.*, 1890), pp. 3-209; Life by Aelfric, in W.W. Skeat (ed.), *Lives of the Saints*, 2 (E.E.T.S., 1909), pp. 958-64. See also Lord Francis Hervey, *Corolla S. Eadmundi* (1907); *idem, The History of King Edmund the Martyr and of the Early Years of His Abbey* (1929); B. Houghton, *St Edmund: King and Martyr* (1970); M. Winterbottom (ed.), *Three Lives of English Saints* (1972); S. J. Ridyard, *The Royal Saints of Anglo-Saxon England* (1988). On the growth of the legend, see G. Loomis, "The growth of the St Edmund Legend" in *Harvard Studies and Notes in Phil. and Lit.* 14 (1932), pp. 83-113; D. Whitelock, "Fact and Fiction in the Legend of St Edmund" in *Proc. Suffolk Inst. of Archaeology*, 31 (1969), pp. 217-33; A. Gransden, "The Legends and Traditions Concerning the Origins of the Abbey of Bury St Edmunds" in *E.H.R.* 99 (1985), pp. 1-24. On the iconography, see G. F. Warner, *The Queen Mary Psalter* (1912); O. Pacht, F. Wormald and C. R. Dodwell, *The St Albans Psalter* (1960); R. M. Thomson, "Two Versions of a Saint's Life from St Edmund's Abbey" in *Revue Bénédictine* 84 (1974), pp. 383-408. On the Viking presence see A. P. Smith, *Scandinavian Kings in the British Isles, 850-80* (1977), pp. 201-13. On the Toulouse relics: D. H. Farmer, "New Light on the Cult of St Edmund of East Anglia," paper read at E.B.C. History Symposium, 1994; R. O'Neil, *Cardinal Herbert Vaughan* (1995), pp. 368-70.

St Dasius, *Martyr* (?303)

When the Greek *acta* of St Dasius were published in 1897, they aroused great interest, but opinions varied as to their authenticity. Some accepted the story as an accurate narrative; others took it for an elaborate moral tale built on the simple fact of a martyr's beheading. The story is that thirty days before the winter festival known as the Saturnalia, it was the custom in the Roman army to elect a "lord of misrule." The person chosen led the revels, which frequently became excessive, and then, at the end, was sacrificed to Kronos. In 303, the garrison at Durostorum (now Silistria, Bulgaria) chose a soldier called Dasius. As a Christian he refused to take part, arguing that he would have to die either way and that he would prefer to die in a good cause rather than in a bad one. He was brought before the legate, who reminded him of his duty as a soldier and urged him either to renounce his faith or to go through the form of offering sacrifice before the images of the emperors. When Dasius refused to alter his position he was sentenced to death by beheading. His alleged relics are preserved in Ancona, where they are supposed to have been taken in the second half of the sixth century, perhaps to save them from the Avars.

For the Greek *acta* see *Anal.Boll.* 16, pp. 5-11. See also H. Delehaye, "Commentarius perpetuus in Martyrorum Hieronymianum," in *AA.SS.*, Nov., 2, pt.2, pp. 609-10. On the Ancona inscription, see G. Mercati, *Rendiconti dell'accademia pontificia di archeologia*, 4, pp. 59-71.

St Bernward, *Bishop* (*c.* 960-1022)

Bernward was born into the Saxon nobility in about 960. His parents died when he was still a small child, and his uncle, Bishop Volkmar of Utrecht, who assumed responsibility for him, sent him to the cathedral school at Hildesheim for his education. He completed his studies in Mainz, where he was ordained to the priesthood by the archbishop, St Willigis (23 Feb.). Initially he refused to accept any office, since his time was taken up with the care of his uncle; but when the old man died, in 987, he became an imperial chaplain and tutor to the child-emperor, Otto III (983-1002; crowned 996), over whose career he had a strong, though some would say insufficiently strong, influence. Six years later he was appointed bishop of Hildesheim, where he proved to be a wise, able, and energetic pastor. He organized a system of deaneries in the diocese, held an annual synod, and in addition to his ecclesiastical activities, is known to have built castles as defences against the invading Danes and Slavs. He was responsible for the great church and monastery of Sankt Michael, and as a great lover of ecclesiastical art, he used the opportunities afforded by his office to encourage and promote good workmen. According to Thangmar, his biographer and former teacher, Bernward himself was a talented painter and metalworker, and he spent as much time as he could spare on both. Several very beautiful pieces of metalwork in Hildesheim are attributed to him, most notably the bronze doors at Sankt Michael.

Unfortunately, the relative peace of Bernward's thirty-year episcopate was disturbed by a dispute with the archbishop of Mainz, which had begun under his predecessor. Willigis claimed episcopal rights in the great convent at Gandersheim, which was in the diocese of Hildesheim, and he was encouraged in this by the abbess Sophie, sister of the emperor Otto III (996-1002), who egged him on even after Bernward had called her to order. The dispute continued for about seven years, well after the Holy See had pronounced in favour of Bernward, who remained calm and dignified throughout. Eventually, Willigis submitted, apologizing publicly for his wilfulness and lack of judgment. Bernward died on 20 November 1022, having assumed the Benedictine habit not long before. He was canonized in 1193 and is the patron of goldsmiths.

For Thangmar's Life, see *M.G.H.*, *Scriptores*, 4, pp. 754-82; *P.L.*, 140, 393-436. See also *Der hl. Bernwards von Hildesheim Kunstwerke* (1922); F. J. Tschan, *St Bernward of Hildesheim: His Life and Times* (3 vols., 1942-52); *Bibl.SS.*, 3, 82-5; *N.C.E.*, 2, p. 354.

Bd Mary Fortunata Viti (1827-1922)

Anna Felice, third of the nine children of Luigi Viti and Anna Bono, was born on 10 February 1827 at the family house in Veroli, south-east of Rome. Her father ran a fairly successful business out of a factory in nearby Frosinone, but when Anna was in her early teens the family was dealt a double blow. Luigi lost or was defrauded of his money and the business failed, and almost at the same time his wife died. He was so stunned by his losses that he became completely apathetic and unable to cope with his large family. Anna not only became "mother" to her brothers and sisters but "father" too, in the sense that she went into service with a nearby family in order to earn money for them all to live on.

She was courted for a while by a wealthy young man from Alatri, but on 21 March 1851, having decided definitely not to marry him, she entered the Benedictine convent in Veroli as a lay sister, taking the name of Maria Fortunata. For nearly seventy-two years, sometimes as assistant infirmarian, sometimes as portress, she did no more than live out the Benedictine ideal of prayer and work based on charity. Her Christocentric piety, expressed in the idiom of the period, was influenced for circumstantial reasons by Passionist and Capuchin spirituality, but she was essentially a Benedictine. She died on 20 November 1922 and was beatified on 8 October 1967 by Pope Paul VI (1963-78), who spoke of her "greatness and littleness."

See A. Sarra, *Potenza e carità di Dio, Beata Maria Fortunata Viti* (1967); *Bibl.SS.*, 12, 1242.

THE BLESSED VIRGIN (over page)
Fleur-de-lys, used as a symbol of the B.V.M.
because of its derivation from the lily (virginity and purity).

21

THE PRESENTATION OF THE BLESSED VIRGIN MARY

Jewish parents were obliged under the law to dedicate their first-born sons to God, and this eventually took place in a ceremony in the Temple. There was no similar obligation regarding girls, but the mother had to perform certain rituals after the birth, and it may well have been customary to bring girls to the Temple anyway. In the popular mind, this feast has always been associated with the story that appears in a number of the apocryphal gospels. This tells how, when she was three years old, Mary was taken by her parents to the Temple in Jerusalem and left there to be educated. According to the account in the *Protoevangelium of James*, Joachim suggested that they take her there when she was only two but agreed with Anne that she should wait until she was three, "in order that [she] may not seek for father or mother." The *Protoevangelium* continues:

> And the child was three years old ... and they went up into the Temple of the Lord, and the priest received her and kissed her and blessed her, saying, "The Lord has magnified thy name in all generations. In thee, on the last of the days, the Lord will manifest his redemption to the sons of Israel." And he set her down upon the third step of the altar, and the Lord God sent grace upon her; and she danced with her feet and all the house of Israel loved her. And her parents went down marvelling, and praising the Lord God because the child had not turned back. And Mary was in the temple of the Lord as if she were a dove that dwelt there.

However, nowhere in the liturgy of the Roman Church is there any indication that this is the event celebrated by today's feast, which is not in fact a very ancient one. On the grounds that it is listed for 21 November in the Greek synaxaries, which date from the tenth century, it is thought to have originated in the East, probably in the eighth century. Here it was known as the Entrance of the All-Holy Mother of God into the Temple, and it was probably connected with the commemoration of the dedication of the basilica of St Mary the New in Jerusalem in 543.

General acceptance in the Western Calendar came slowly. The feast was observed first and then only sporadically in England, from the eleventh century. In the Canterbury Cathedral Benedictional of the period, a "*Benedictio de praesentatione sanctae Mariae*" is listed between the feast of St Martin on 11 November and that of St Cecilia on the 22nd. But it then fell into disuse, only to re-emerge toward the end of the fourteenth century. Pope Sixtus IV (1471-84) built it into the Roman Breviary, and it was finally given a place in the Universal Calendar by Sixtus V

(1585-90) in 1585, though only after it had been removed from the Breviary for a while by Pope Pius V (1565-72; 30 April), who in 1568 took exception to a crudely-worded sequence in a Mass dating from 1505. The Presentation of Mary has been a popular subject among artists such as Giotto, Ghirlandaio, Titian, and Tintoretto, to name only a few. Titian (1486-1576), while at the height of his powers, produced the huge *Presentation of the Virgin in the Temple*, in the Accademia in Venice, executed for the Scuola della Carità in 1538-8..

See *Horae* (Christ's Coll., Cambridge, MS 6); *Leofric Collectar*, 2, p. 509. For the 1505 sequence, see Henry Bradshaw Society reprint of 1474 *Missale Romanum*, 2, pp. 251-3. See also S. Beissel, *Verehung Marias in Deutschland*, 1, p. 306; B. H. Cowper (ed. and trans.), *The Apocryphal Gospels and Other Documents Relating to the History of Christ* (1897); M. J. Kishpaugh, *The Feast of the Presentation of the Virgin Mary in the Temple* (Dissertation, Cath. Univ. of America, 1941); E. Campana, *Maria nel culto cattolico*, 1 (1943), pp. 207-14; N. Chirat, *Mélanges* (1945), pp. 127-43; *N.C.E.*, 11, pp. 758-9.

St Gelasius I, *Pope* (496)

Gelasius reigned for only five years, but he was one of the most energetic and effective of the early popes, "famous all over the world," as one contemporary put it, "for his learning and holiness." Little is known about his early life. Although of African descent, he was born in Rome and in due course became a valued assistant and adviser to Pope Felix II (483-92; 1 Mar.). He succeeded Felix in 492 and was immediately confronted with problems on two fronts: a difficult political situation—Arian kings ruling throughout the former Western empire, and Italy at war as Theodoric the Ostrogoth laid siege to King Oadacer in Ravenna—and the aftermath of the Acacian schism. (This was a by-product of the Monophysite controversy, Monophysitism being the doctrine, condemned in 451 at the Council of Chalcedon, that Jesus Christ had only one nature.)

As far as the second problem was concerned, Acacius himself was already dead, and the patriarch of Constantinople, Euphemius, was anxious to heal the breach. Gelasius, however, took the view that communion could not be restored until the *Henotikon*—a compromise document upheld by the Byzantine emperor, Anastasius I (491-518), which concurred with some of Acacius' Monophysite teachings—was definitively repudiated. His repeated insistence that the excommunication of Acacius, regarded as uncanonical in the East, had been justified, alienated the emperor and drove the Eastern bishops to suggest that his attitude was threatening the unity of the Church. In view of this he finally reinstated one of the bishops excommunicated by his equally uncompromising predecessor.

Gelasius is thought to have been a prolific writer, although from his total output only about 100 letters and fragments of letters and a number of theological treatises have survived. As his letters show, he was a staunch supporter of the See of Peter. He set out its prerogatives and was probably the first pope to be referred to as "vicar of Christ." Most significantly, there is a passage in a letter to Anastasius in which he spells out the right relationship between religious and secular authority—

what he described as the "consecrated authority of the bishops" and the "royal power." Each, he said, is independent in its own sphere, although, as the channel through which the temporal is saved, the spiritual is inherently superior. Although a contemporary priest claimed that he compiled a sacramentary, the so-called *Gelasian Sacramentary* dates from a later period and is definitely not his.

Gelasius emerges from the Acacian controversy as a somewhat harsh and inflexible personality, but there was clearly another side to him. He is known, for example, to have enjoyed a lasting friendship with Theodoric. And then there is the account of Dionysius Exiguus, written fifty years at the most after Gelasius' death. Based on conversations with the dead pope's disciples, it mentions his humility, his desire to serve rather than to rule, his spirit of prayer, and his great generosity to the poor: he believed that bishops have a duty to devote a quarter of their income to charity. Gelasius died in 496.

See *Liber Pontificalis* (ed. L. Duchesne). 1, pp. 254–7. Gelasius's letters are in A. Thiel, *Epistolae Romanorum Pontificum genuinae a S. Hilaro usque ad Pelagium II*, 1 (1858), pp. 285–613. See also *O.D.P.*, pp. 47–9; J. Chapin in *N.C.E.*, 6, pp. 315ff.; A. K. Ziegler, "Pope Gelasius I and His Teaching on the Relation of Church and State" in *Catholic Historical Review* 27 (1942), pp. 412–37; B. Capelle, "L'oeuvre liturgique de S. Gelase" in *J.T.S.* 2 (1951), pp. 129–44.

St Albert of Louvain, *Bishop and Martyr* (*c.* 1166–92)

Albert de Louvain had the misfortune to become involved in the struggle between two noble houses—Brabant and Hainaut—for possession of the influential see of Liège, whose occupant always wielded considerable political influence throughout the twelfth century. Born in about 1166, he was the son of Godefroi III, duke of Brabant, and his wife Marguerite. He was brought up at his father's castle on a hill at Louvain, now known as Mont-César, where there is a well-known Benedictine abbey. The boy was early marked out for a career in the Church and at the age of only twelve was made a canon of Liège. However, when he was twenty-one, he renounced this benefice and asked his family enemy, Baudouin V, count of Hainaut, to accept him as a knight—presumably because he wished to take part in the forthcoming Crusade. Baudouin agreed and made him a member of his own entourage. What happened next is rather curious. Although Albert was one of those who "took the cross" when the papal legate preached the Crusade in Liège a few months later, he rejoined the ranks of the clergy at the same time, received back his canonry, and never went to the East. In 1188, still only a subdeacon, he was appointed archdeacon of Brabant.

In 1191 the bishop of Liège died. Two men, Albert of Louvain and Albert of Rethel (each an archdeacon, neither a priest), were suggested as possible successors. Albert of Rethel was a cousin of Baudouin de Hainaut and uncle of Constance, the wife of the emperor, Henry VI. Albert of Louvain, clearly the more suitable candidate, was elected by a large majority of the canons, but Albert of Rethel appealed to the emperor. When the case was heard at Worms, the emperor would rule in favour of neither and announced that he had given the see of Liège to Lothar, provost of Bonn. Albert of Louvain quietly informed him that his own election was valid, rebuked him for interfering in church matters, and gave notice of his intention to appeal to the Holy See. He then set out for Rome, disguised as a servant because he realized the emperor's men would try to intercept him.

Albert of Louvain's election was declared valid by Pope Celestine III (1191-8). But on his return he could not take possession of his see because Lothar was still in residence, and because the archbishop of Cologne was too old and ill, and too fearful of the emperor, to ordain and consecrate him. Celestine had foreseen this, however, and Albert was finally ordained priest and bishop by the archbishop of Reims.

While Albert was in Reims, news came that the emperor was in Liège and had vowed to exterminate him and his followers. Albert's uncle was prepared to fight on his behalf, but Albert said he preferred exile to war and would remain for the time being in Reims. On 24 November 1192, when he had been there for nearly ten weeks, he decided to visit the abbey of St-Rémi, outside the walls. On the way, as he was going through a narrow pass, he was set upon and murdered by a party of German knights. The people of Reims were horrified, and Albert was buried with great honour in the cathedral. Henry was forced to do penance, and Lothar, who was excommunicated, fled the city.

In 1612 what were believed to be St Albert's relics were moved from Reims to the church of the Carmelite convent in Brussels. But in 1919, while Reims cathedral was being cleared of debris from the German bombardment, a tomb supposed to be that of Odalric, a tenth-century archbishop, was opened up. Examination of the contents aroused suspicions, and in 1921 a panel of experts reached the unanimous conclusion that these were St Albert's remains and that those of Odalric were in Brussels. On 18 November of the same year the remains of Odalric were taken back to Reims, while a promise made 300 years before was honoured and those of St Albert were solemnly returned to Belgium. A substantial relic was later detached and sent back to Reims.

Reliable contemporary life in *M.G.H., Scriptores*, 25, pp. 137-68. See also *Bibl.SS.*, 1, 691-2; J. B. David, *Histoire de St Albert de Louvain* (1848); E. Moreau, *St Albert de Louvain* (1946). On the identification of the relics, see *Anal.Boll.* 40, pp. 155-70.

Bd Mary Siedliska, *Foundress* (1842-1902)

Franciszka Siedliska was born on 12 November 1842 of well-to-do landowning parents, Adolf Siedliski and Cecilia Morawska, at Roszkowa Wola in Poland. She inherited from her mother the ill health which was to dog her throughout her life, but she had many gifts to compensate for this. She was highly intelligent as well as sensitive, with a particular warmth that made her very approachable. But she also shared her father's quick temper, which led to stormy scenes between them when she was growing up. The Siedliskis made little effort to educate Franciszka and her younger brother, Adam, in the Faith. She was baptized a week after her birth, but in Poland in those days Catholicism generally had more to do with patriotism and nationalism than with spirituality and religious practice. However, they gave them a good education in other ways. Adam went to the Jesuit college in Metz, while excellent tutors were laid on at home for Franciszka.

Franciszka's first religious experience occurred when, as a child of about nine, she prayed in desperation before a picture of Our Lady of Czestochowa that her mother, then critically ill, would not die. But her formal introduction to the Faith was through a Capuchin friar, Leander Lendzian, whom she met at her grandparents' home in Warsaw and who was to play an important role throughout her life. He prepared her for her First Communion and Confirmation in 1855, which was the year in which she first thought of dedicating her life to God. The next few years were difficult. For a while she went along with Adolf's plans to introduce her to society, but the strain of this, followed by the hostility of her family once she admitted her true ambition, made her—and her mother—seriously ill. Adolf's concern overcame his anger. He accompanied his wife and daughter to Italy on a roundabout journey which took them to Bavaria, France, and Switzerland, leaving Franciszka greatly enriched spiritually and intellectually. While they were in Cannes he finally, if sorrowfully, agreed to let her follow her vocation.

After several more years, during which she strove for self-knowledge and self-mastery under Fr Leander's direction, she came to understand that her vocation was to found a new religious Order. In 1873 she asked Pope Pius IX (1846-78) to approve the Congregation of the Holy Family of Nazareth, whose members would "offer their prayers, works and their entire life for the Church and the Holy Father, and imitate the hidden life and the virtues of the Holy Family." The pope gave his approval on 1 October 1873, and Franciszka, now Mother Mary of Jesus the Good Shepherd, having eliminated other possibilities, including Poland, decided that the first house should be in Rome. She bought a suitable site in via Machiavelli, and on the first Sunday of Advent 1875 the Congregation was officially founded.

Mother Mary began immediately to work on the Rule, which was finally to be approved by Pope Pius X (1903-14; 26 Aug.) on 2 August 1909. In her concern to stress the primacy of the spirit over the letter, she had a vision that, like those of some other nineteenth-century foundresses, was ahead of its time. True charity, she insisted, does not compel or restrict, and no Rule should do so either. "In Nazareth," she wrote to Fr Antoni Lechert, a priest whom she had consulted while travelling in 1863 and who helped and advised during the early years of the Congregation, "there should be freedom of conscience, the liberty of the children of God, regard for the psyche of the sisters, their temperament, and their natural disposition." Her great concern was for the welfare of the family and any work undertaken by the Sisters had this in mind. In Rome they began immediately to care for neglected and abandoned children, teach religion to young people, prepare couples for marriage, and organize discussion groups for young women. These and similar works were undertaken by the Sisters wherever they happened to be.

The first house outside Rome was established in Cracow in 1881, and by 1894 there were four houses in Poland. The first American house opened in Chicago in 1885; and in 1891, Mother Mary managed to overcome the misgivings of the archbishop of Paris, Cardinal François Richard, who objected to her lack of funds, and Sisters were sent to educate the daughters of Polish immigrants there. Such was the demand that a request in 1893 from the archbishop of Westminster, Cardinal Herbert Vaughan, for Sisters to work among the poor Poles in London, could not be fulfilled until 1895, despite the urgent need.

When Mother Mary died on 21 November 1902, she was mourned not only by her Sisters, who felt they had lost a loving mother as well as a firm and honest leader, but by the many who depended on her or whose respect she had won. She was beatified by Pope John Paul II on 23 April 1989. The cause of eleven Sisters of the Holy Family of Nazareth who were shot by the Nazis in north-eastern Poland on 1 August 1943 is also going forward. They offered their lives in the place of a number of local married men and fathers of families who had been arrested and condemned to death.

See Inez Strzalkowska C.F.S.N., *Blessed Mary of Jesus the Good Shepherd* (1989); recent material in Polish.

ST CECILIA (over page)
Gold harp with silver strings, on blue field.

22

ST CECILIA, *Martyr* (?Third Century)

Throughout the centuries Cecilia has remained one of the best-loved saints in the Church's Calendar. This long-standing cult, which includes a mention in the Roman Canon, testifies to the fact of her martyrdom. Yet the *passio* that tells her story dates from the fifth century, and it is unfortunately neither reliable nor even indisputably based on authentic materials.

According to this legend, she was born of a patrician family in Rome and brought up as a Christian. She wished to consecrate her life to God, but her father betrothed her to another patrician, Valerian, who was a pagan. On the day of the wedding, Cecilia sat apart, singing to God "in her heart" and praying for help. Once they were alone, she told Valerian her "secret": that she was watched over by an angel of God, at whose hands he would suffer if he tried to consummate the marriage, but that he too would see the angel if he came to believe in the one, true God and accept baptism. Valerian, convinced by her sincerity, went off to find Bishop Urban (Pope Urban I; 222-30) among the poor, near the third milestone on the Appian way, and was baptized. When he returned, he found standing at Cecilia's side an angel, who placed on each of their heads a crown of flowers. Soon after this, Valerian's brother Tiburtius arrived. At first he was incredulous at what Cecilia told him about Jesus, but soon he too was on his way to find Bishop Urban and ask for baptism.

From then on, the two young men spent their time doing good works; they were eventually arrested for burying the bodies of those who had been martyred. Neither would recant under cross-examination. The prefect, who at first wanted to give them further time to reflect on their decision, was then convinced that this would merely enable them to distribute their belongings, thus depriving the State of the opportunity to confiscate them, and so they were condemned to death. Together with an official called Maximus, who was converted to Christianity by the example of their courage, they were beheaded at Pagus Triopus, a few miles from Rome, and Cecilia buried their bodies.

Officials were now sent to persuade Cecilia to offer sacrifice to the pagan gods, but she converted them to Christianity instead. And before any further steps were taken, Urban had the opportunity to baptize some 400 people who had gathered at her house. One of them, named Gordian, established it as a church, which Urban subsequently dedicated in her name. Eventually Cecilia was called before the tribunal, and when she would not recant she was sentenced to be suffocated in her own bathroom. This did not work, despite the enormous quantities of wood that were piled into the furnace, so a soldier was sent to behead her. He failed to finish his task and she lingered for three days, during which she formally made her house over to Urban. She was buried in the catacomb of San Callisto, next to the papal crypt.

Unfortunately, there is no contemporary or near-contemporary evidence—nothing in the fourth-century *Depositio martyrum*, nothing in the works of writers who were otherwise particularly interested in the martyrs—to support this popular fifth-century account. The most likely explanation is that the legend grew up to explain the dedication of a church founded in the Trastevere district of Rome by a woman named Cecilia. On the other hand, although nothing is known about them beyond the fact that they died as martyrs and were buried in the catacomb of Praetextatus, Valerian and Tiburtius (14 April) do seem to have been identifiable historical figures.

Early in the ninth century Pope St Paschal I (817-24; 11 Feb.) had the supposed relics of St Cecilia moved, with those of SS Valerian, Tiburtius, and Maximus, from the catacomb of Praetextatus (where, rather than in the catacomb of San Callisto, he had been instructed in a dream to find them) to the church of Santa Cecilia in Trastevere. In the course of some restoration work in 1599, the relics of the four had to be reinterred. St Cecilia's body was allegedly still incorrupt, and although it disintegrated quickly on contact with the air, the sculptor Stefano Maderno (*c.* 1576-1636) had time to make the life-size statue which lies beneath one of the altars in the church. A replica occupies the recess in the catacomb of San Callisto where her body was originally supposed to have been buried.

While modern scholars discuss whether or not Cecilia existed and question the assertion that her body was found intact in the position in which Maderno sculpted it, she survives in the popular imagination and is best known as the patron saint of music and musicians. This is probably the result of a medieval misreading of the *passio*: there she is said to have sung "in her heart" as the musicians played at her wedding, but later the words "in her heart" were omitted, and from then on she was shown playing the organ and singing aloud. Be that as it may, she was chosen as patron when the Accademia della Musica was founded in Rome in 1584. Poets and musicians have felt inspired to write in her honour—among them Purcell, Dryden, Handel, Pope, and Britten, who set Auden's *Hymn to St Cecilia* to music. Her legend appears as the Second Nun's Tale in Chaucer's *Canterbury Tales*, and she appears frequently in religious paintings—for example, she is shown with her floral crown in Fra Angelico's *Forerunners of Christ with Saints and Martyrs*, while in another picture in the National Gallery in London, Pietro da Cortona depicts her with her organ and carrying the palm of martyrdom, as does Raphael in a painting which hangs in Bologna. She can be seen in the mosaics in the church of S. Apollinare Nuovo in Ravenna, in frescoes in the catacomb of San Callisto and in the church of Santa Maria Antiqua in Rome, and in the stained-glass windows of the cathedral in Bourges.

See H. Delehaye, *Etude sur le légendier romain* (1936), pp. 73-96. See also V. L. Kennedy, *The Saints of the Canon of the Mass (Studi di Antiquità Cristiana* 14, 1938); *Vies des saints*, 11 (1954), pp. 731-59; *D.A.C.L.*, 2, 2712-38; *Bibl.SS.*, 3, 1064-86. For the iconography, see K. Künstle, *Ikonographie*, 2, pp. 146-50.

SS Philemon and Apphia, *Martyrs* (First Century)

Philemon, a citizen of Colossae in Phrygia and a friend and convert of St Paul (25 Jan., 29 June), was the recipient of the shortest and most touchingly personal of all Paul's Epistles. In this letter, which is the source of all we know about Philemon, Paul addresses him as "our beloved fellow-worker," which suggests that Philemon took an active part in the life of the Church after his conversion. Paul also refers to the fact that he and his wife, Apphia, offered their home as a meeting place for the Christians of Colossae. Most of the letter, however, is an appeal to Philemon's generosity of spirit, which Paul seems to feel he can rely on. One of Philemon's slaves, Onesimus, has run away, possibly having stolen something before he left, and made his way to Paul, who is in prison. Assuring him that Onesimus, whose name means "Useful," has undergone a complete change of heart and been baptized ("Formerly he was useless to you, but now he is indeed useful, to you and to me"), Paul begs Philemon, not from a sense of obligation but as a spontaneous act of kindness, to take his slave back—and since he is now "much more than a slave," to welcome him as he would welcome Paul, as "a beloved brother."

There is no historical record of what happened next, but tradition has it that Philemon forgave Onesimus, gave him his freedom, and took him on as a fellow-worker in the spreading of the gospel. According to different legends, Philemon became bishop of Colossae, or of Gaza, and was martyred in Ephesus, or Colossae. The Roman Martyrology sums up the story that is accepted in the East: "When, under the Emperor Nero, the gentiles broke into the church on the feast of Diana at Colossae in Phrygia, and the rest fled, Philemon and Apphia were taken. By command of the governor Artoclis they were scourged and then buried in a pit up to the waist, where they were overwhelmed with stones."

See St Paul, *Letter to Philemon*; also *Synaxarium Constantinopolitanum* (ed. H. Delehaye), 247-8; J. Knox, *Philemon among the Letters of St Paul* (1935, 1960); P. Benoît in *Dictionnaire de la Bible* (1966), 1204-11.

The Eighty-five Blessed Martyrs of England, Scotland, and Wales

These eighty-five men and women suffered for their adherence to Roman Catholicism during the persecutions of the sixteenth and seventeenth centuries. They were arrested (and in most cases tortured), tried, and executed because they refused to accept certain statutes enacted under Henry VIII and Elizabeth I and ratified in subsequent reigns. These had to do with the royal supremacy, with going abroad to study for the priesthood and returning to do pastoral work and celebrate the Mass, and with the harbouring of priests. The first of the eighty-five was executed at Tyburn, in London, in 1584, and the last, an Irish Franciscan, was hanged in Wales in 1679. The majority—sixty-three—were priests, while the twenty-two laypeople came from all walks of life. The eighty-five were, in alphabetical order: John Adams, Thomas Atkinson, Edward Bamber, George Beesley, Arthur Bell, Thomas Belson, Robert Bickerdike, Alexander Blake, Marmaduke Bowes, John Bretton, Thomas Bullaker, Edward Burden, Roger Cadwallader, William Carter, Alexander Crow, William Davies, Robert Dibdale, George Douglas, Robert Drury, Edmund Duke, George Errington, Roger Filcock, John Fingley, Matthew Flathers, Richard Flower, Nicholas Garlick, William Gibson, Ralph Grimston, Robert Grissold, John Hambley, Robert Hardesty, George Haydock, Henry Heath, Richard Hill, John Hogg, Richard Holiday, Nicholas Horner, Thomas Hunt, Thurstan Hunt, Francis Ingleby, William Knight, Joseph Lambton, William Lampley, John Lowe, Robert Ludlam, Charles Meehan, Robert Middleton, George Nichols, John Norton, Robert Nutter, Edward Osbaldeston, Anthony Page, Thomas Palaster, William Pike, Thomas Pilcher, Thomas Pormont, Nicholas Postgate, Humphrey Pritchard, Christopher Robinson, Stephen Rowsham, John Sandys, Richard Sargeant, Montford Scott, Richard Simpson, Peter Snow, William Southerne, William Spenser, Thomas Sprott, John Sugar, Robert Sutton, Edmund Syke, John Talbot, Hugh Taylor, William Thomson, Robert Thorpe, John Thules, Edward Thwing, Thomas Watkinson, Henry Webley, Christopher Wharton, Thomas Whitaker, John Woodcock, Nicholas Woodfen, Roger Wrenno, Richard Yaxley. They were beatified on 22 November 1987. (See "BB Martyrs of England and Wales," 4 May, and "The Forty Martyrs of England and Wales," 25 Oct., for historical accounts of the persecution, and individual entries under dates of death.)

ST CLEMENT OF ROME (over page)
Gold anchor on blue field.

23

ST CLEMENT OF ROME, *Pope* (*c.* 100)

Clement was bishop of Rome at the end of the first century. There is one tradition that puts him fourth in line, while another, apparently dating back to Tertullian (*c.* 160–*c.* 225), has him as Peter's immediate successor. In most second-century lists, however, he comes third in line, and this is the order most widely accepted today. His importance is as a witness to the life of the Church in the first generation after the apostles. St Irenaeus (*c.* 130–200; 28 June), writing in the middle of the second century, presents him as someone who associated with the apostles and absorbed their teaching; Origen (*c.* 254) called him a "disciple of the apostles"—in fact, scholars debate as to whether or not he was the Clement mentioned by St Paul in his letter to the Philippians (4:3), to which the simple answer seems to be that it is possible.

It is as the author of an *Epistle to the Corinthians* that Clement is primarily known. Written between 95 and 98 and surviving as a complete text, this is a most significant document. We do not know exactly what the dissensions that prompted it were about, but it is the earliest surviving record of intervention by the church of Rome in the affairs of another church. Interestingly, there is no suggestion that the intervention was sought; it seems to have come as a genuine manifestation of solicitude on the part of the Roman church for the church in Corinth. Although the letter is from Clement, he writes, with great lightness of touch, as from the church of Rome as a whole, urging reconciliation and acceptance of the tradition of the apostles. He is credited with the authorship of other writings, including a second epistle to the Corinthians, but these are probably not his.

One tradition, almost certainly not reliable, identifies Clement of Rome with the consul Titus Flavius Clemens, a cousin of the emperor Domitian (81-96), who was executed for atheism—that is to say, adopting Jewish practices—in 95 or 96. He might, though, have been a freedman in the consul's household. Another tradition, popular in the Middle Ages, makes him a martyr, but this is unlikely. There is a colourful *passio*, but this dates from the fourth century as do the earliest inscriptions, and writers such as Clement of Alexandria, Eusebius, and Origen do not mention it.

According to this *passio*, Clement was exiled to the Crimea, where he worked in the mines and was eventually killed by being thrown into the sea with an anchor round his neck; angels made him a grave on the sea bed, and this was revealed once a year when the tide was unusually low. In the ninth century SS Cyril and Methodius (14 Feb.), apostles to the Slavs, claimed they had recovered both the relics, which they pieced together, and the anchor. The relics were taken to Rome and buried in the church of San Clemente. (This archaeologically fascinating church was built on the site of a third-century pastoral centre, the *titulus Clementis*, which had itself developed from a place of worship in the house of a man called Clement—possibly, though probably not, the saint.) In this church there are some ninth-century frescoes depicting the legend of St Clement.

See: J. B. Lightfoot, *Apostolic Fathers*, 1 (1890), pp. 148-200; K. Lake, *The Apostolic Fathers* (1930); A. Jaubert (ed.), *Clément de Rome, Epître aux Corinthiens* (1971); J. Colson, *Clément de Rome* (1994). See also *H.S.S.C.*, 2, pp. 108-13; *C.M.H.*, pp. 615-6; H. Delehaye, *Etude sur le Légendier Romain* (1936), pp. 96-116; *D.H.G.E.*, 12, 1089-93; L. Boyle, *St Clement's Rome* (pamphlet, 1960). On the church of San Clemente, see S. G. A. Luff, *The Christian's Guide to Rome* (n.e. 1990), pp. 99-105.

ST COLUMBANUS, *Abbot (c. 543-615)*

Columbanus (Columban), one of the greatest of the Irish missionary monks of the sixth and seventh centuries, was born in Leinster, probably of a noble family. He received a good education: from his own works it is clear that he was familiar not only with the Bible, but with the Latin Fathers and pagan Latin authors such as Seneca, Horace, Virgil, and Ovid. According to Jonas, his earliest biographer, his education was interrupted during his adolescence, when he was distracted by the attractions of the opposite sex, and in particular by the temptation presented by what Jonas described as certain *lascivae puellae*. Apparently on the advice of a woman hermit, who counselled him simply to turn his back on what he could not otherwise avoid, but totally against the wishes of his mother, he became a monk. He went first to learn from one of St Finnian's (12 Dec.) disciples, Sinell, who lived on Cluain Inis, an island in Lough Erne, and from there to the great monastic foundation at Bangor, where his master was St Comgall (10 May). According to Jonas, he stayed here for "many years," possibly teaching in the monastic school, and it was probably not until about 590 that he set sail with twelve companions for Gaul. The *deorad De*—one who goes into voluntary exile for the love of God and to spread the gospel—was a familiar figure in the Celtic church at this time, and Columbanus was one of the most influential of them all.

The situation he found in Gaul was not encouraging. The repartition of the kingdom of the Franks after the death of Clotaire I in 561 had led to a period of internal conflict and general civil unrest. This, combined with a general laxity among the clergy, meant that religion was at a rather low ebb. The Irish monks, undaunted, began immediately to preach to the people and to encourage them by their example. Their reputation reached the king of Burgundy, Gontran (561-92), who gave Columbanus a plot of land with a disused Roman fort on it at Annegray in the Vosges. Here Columbanus founded his first monastery; when, because of the numbers who wished to join him, it became too small, he built another at nearby Luxeuil, and eventually a third at Fontes (now Fontaine).

The essence of Columbanus' Rule was love of God and love of neighbour; for the

189

rest he enjoined what he himself had been taught in Ireland, and he observed the Irish date for Easter, despite the fact that the Roman practice had been in use in Gaul from the beginning of the fifth century. The Rule was accompanied by a Penitential, in which Columbanus prescribed penances for even the slightest of faults. It was in fact in the austerity, even harshness, of its discipline that Celtic monasticism differed most from Benedictine monasticism, which eventually superseded it.

More significantly, Celtic practice in general differed from the practice of the rest of the Frankish church. Columbanus and his monks had been peacefully pursuing their strenuous way of life for twelve years when they began to sense hostility from the Frankish bishops, who no doubt resented the independence of these newcomers. Columbanus was told to appear before a synod so that he could give an account of his Celtic practice. Seeing no reason to obey—he regarded the Frankish bishops as negligent and their clergy as lax—he refused to go. But because the bishops had focussed their attack on the date of Easter, he wrote them a letter in which he described himself as "a poor stranger in these parts for the cause of Christ" and humbly begged them to leave him and his monks in peace. He also hinted that there might be more important things to worry about than the date of Easter. As the bishops were not to be fobbed off so easily, he wrote also to the pope—initially Gregory I (590-604; 3 Sept.) and then, later, Boniface IV (608-14). On both occasions he confirmed his loyalty to the See of Peter, explained Irish customs, and asked the pope to confirm them. The matter was left like this until a few years later, when the bishop of Lyons renewed the attack. Columbanus, who could be extremely blunt and outspoken, wrote again, this time to the Synod of Chalons-sur-Saône, appealing for tolerance and asking that his monks simply be allowed to live according to the tradition with which they were familiar.

Meanwhile trouble was brewing on another front. The king of Burgundy, Theodoric II, had a certain respect for Columbanus and used to discuss things with him. But when Columbanus reproved him for keeping concubines instead of marrying and refused to bless his illegitimate children, Theodoric and his grandmother, Brunhild, the redoubtable widow of Clovis' son Sigebert, were seriously provoked— she not least because she realized that a lawful wife would be queen, and hence a threat to her own position. Columbanus made matters worse for himself by adhering to the Irish rather than the Frankish custom and refusing Brunhild entry to his monastery—as indeed he refused entry to any woman or layman. Brunhild stirred up trouble between Theodoric and Columbanus, with the result that in 610 the latter was ordered to leave the country with those of his original Irish companions who had survived.

Columbanus penned a now-famous letter to the monks left behind at Luxeuil— Montalembert said it contained "some of the finest and grandest words ever produced by the Christian genius"—and then embarked. But almost immediately the ship ran into a storm and was forced back to port. Avoiding Burgundy, the monks went to the court of the Austrasian king, Theodebert II, at Metz, where they were well received. But because of their vigorous methods and perhaps excessive zeal, they were not so well received by the people in the neighbourhood of Zurich and of Bregenz, where they mainly preached. So when Austrasia and Burgundy went to war and Theodebert was defeated, Columbanus decided the time had come to move further afield.

Although he was about seventy years old by now, he made the journey across the Alps with his monks and went to Milan, where he was kindly received by Agilulf, the Arian king of the Lombards, whose wife, Theodelinda, and their three children were Catholics, although out of tune with the Holy See on the matter of the Three Chapters. These writings of Theodore of Mopsuestia and two others were condemned in 553 at the Council of Constantinople on the grounds that they favoured Nestorianism, but the bishops of Istria and some in Lombardy defended them with such passion that they were prepared to break off communion with the pope. Agilulf and his wife persuaded Columbanus to step in and write to Pope Boniface IV in defence of the Three Chapters. Unfortunately Columbanus knew next to nothing about either the documents or the circumstances in which they had been written. His letter makes clear his great devotion to the Holy See and his desire for unity in the faith, but it is not a particularly useful contribution to the debate about the Three Chapters. To do him justice, Columbanus seems to be aware of this and asks, not without humour, "*Quis poterit glabrum audire?*"—"Who could listen to a greenhorn?"

Meanwhile, Agilulf had given Columbanus some land at Bobbio, in an Apennine valley between Genoa and Piacenza. Here Columbanus made the last of his monastic foundations. Despite his age, he even sometimes helped with the building work. By now all he wanted was to retire and prepare for death. So when Clotaire II of Neustria, under whom the Frankish kingdom had once again been reunited since the death of Theodoric in 613, invited him to return, Columbanus refused. He did, though, ask the king to look kindly on the monks of Luxeuil. Shortly after this, on 23 November 615, he died. He was buried in Bobbio.

As "a monastery of the Benedictine Congregation of St-Vanne," Luxeuil flourished until the French Revolution put an end to its long history. Bobbio, which housed one of the greatest libraries of the Middle Ages, declined from the fifteenth century onward and was finally suppressed by the French in 1803, but the dispersal of the library was already begun in the sixteenth century. In addition to the Rule and the Penitential, Columbanus's own writings consist mainly of letters and a handful of poems. The quality of the thought and style is consistently high and is epitomized in *Epistola IV*, to the monks at Luxeuil—an extraordinary mixture ("love does not keep order, hence my message is confused") of theology, spiritual advice and moving self-revelation, reminiscent of St Paul in his more personal moments:

> I wanted to write you a tearful letter; but for the reason that I know your heart, I have simply mentioned necessary duties, hard of themselves and difficult, and have used another style, preferring to check than to encourage tears. So my speech has been outwardly made smooth, and grief is shut up within. See, the

tears flow, but it is better to check the fountain; for it is no part of a brave soldier to lament in battle. . . . Now as I write a messenger has reached me, saying that the ship is ready for me in which I shall be borne unwilling to my country; but if I escape, there is no guard to prevent it; for they seem to desire this, that I escape. If I am cast into the sea like Jonah, who himself is also called Columba in Hebrew, pray that someone may take the place of the whale to bring me back in safe concealment by a happy voyage, to restore your Jonah to the land he longs for.

For the Life by Jonas, a monk of Bobbio, see *Ionae Vitae Sanctorum Columbani*, Vedasti, Johannis (1905), pp. 1-294; B. Krusch in *M.G.H., Scriptores rerum merov.*, 4 (1902), pp. 1-156; 7 (1920), pp. 822-7; D. C. Munro (ed.), *The Life of St Columban, by the Monk Jonas* (1993). Other biographies: G. Metlake, *The Life and Writings of St Columbanus* (1914); M. M. Dubois, *Un Pionnier de la civilisation occidentale* (1950; Eng. trans. 1961); F. McManus, *Saint Columban* (1963); J. F. Kenney, *San Colombano e la sua opera in Italia* (1953); T. O'Fiaich, *Columbanus* (1974). For the writings, see G. M. S. Walker, *Sancti Columbani Opera* (1957); J. Laporte. *Le Pénitentiel de S. Columban* (1958); *M.G.H., Epistolae*, 3, pp. 154-90. See also: *H.S.S.C.*, 4, pp. 112-21; L. Bieler, *Ireland: Harbinger of the Middle Ages* (1963), pp. 25-94; M. Brennan and H. B. Clarke, *Columbanus and Merovingian Monasticism* (1981); R. Sharpe, *Medieval Irish Saints' Lives* (1991); L. Gougaud, *Les saints irlandais hors d'Irlande* (1936), pp. 51-62; T. M. Charles Edwards, "The Social Background to Irish Peregrinatio" in *Celtica* 11 (1976), pp. 43-69; A. Maestri, *Il culto di San Colombano in Italia* (1955); P. Grosjean, "Débuts de la controverse pascale chez les Celtes" in *Anal. Boll.* 64 (1946), pp. 200-15.

St Amphilochius, *Bishop* (339-400)

The principal source of information about St Amphilochius is his correspondence with two close friends, St Gregory of Nazianzen, whose cousin he was, and St Basil (both 2 Jan.). Amphilochius was born in Cappadocia and as a young man taught rhetoric in Constantinople. He was still young when he got into some sort of financial difficulty and abandoned the city for a place near Nazianzus, where he could live a quiet life while caring for his elderly father. A small insight into his life at this time is provided by a letter from Gregory, who seems to have supplied him with corn in return for vegetables from his garden.

In 374, when he was about thirty-five, Amphilochius was appointed bishop of Iconium. Aware of what this would entail, he accepted with great reluctance, and when his father complained to Gregory that he was going to miss his son's care, Gregory replied that he had had no hand in the appointment, and in any case he was going to feel the loss of Amphilochius' company himself. Basil, who may well have been responsible for the appointment, wrote to encourage his friend, urging him to lead others, not to be led by them. Amphilochius frequently consulted Basil—it was for him that Basil wrote his treatise on the Holy Spirit—and preached the panegyric at his funeral.

Ever zealous in the cause of orthodoxy, in 376 Amphilochius held a council at Iconium to condemn the Macedonian heresy, which denied the divinity of the Holy Spirit, and he was present when it was condemned at the Council of Constantinople in 381. He also urged the emperor, Theodosius I (379-95), to forbid Arians to hold their assemblies. At first Theodosius refused on the grounds that such a measure would be unnecessarily severe, but Amphilochius eventually coaxed him into passing a law which made it illegal for Arians to meet publicly or privately. He equally vigorously opposed the teaching of the Messalians, an illuminist and Manichean sect which believed that prayer alone is the essence of religion; and in 394 he presided over a synod at Sida in Pamphylia, where it was condemned. Amphilochius was described by Gregory as a herald of truth and a bishop beyond reproach, and his father affirmed that sick people had been healed by his prayers.

Two short Greek biographies in *P.G.*, 39, 13-26; 116, 956-70. See also K. Holl, *Amphilochius von Ikonium* (1904); G. Ficker, *Amphilochiana* (1906); O. Bardenhewer, *Altkirkliche Literatur*, 3, pp. 220-8; *D.H.G.*, 2, pp. 1346-8; *D.C.B.*, 1, pp. 103-7; *Bibl.SS.*, 1, 1182-3.

St Gregory of Girgenti, *Bishop* (*c.* 603)

This St Gregory is usually identified with the St Gregory Agrigentinus referred to in the letters of Pope Gregory the Great (590-604; 3 Sept.). However, a Life written allegedly soon after his death by Leontius, a monk of St Sabas in Rome, is not reliable, and there is still no agreement about the chronology of his life. According to Leontius, Gregory was born near Girgenti (Agrigentum) in Sicily and educated by the local bishop, St Potamion. He went on a pilgrimage to Palestine, where he spent four years studying at different monasteries and was eventually ordained deacon in Jerusalem. From there he went to Antioch and Constantinople, and he soon gained a reputation as one of the holiest and wisest men of his age. Eventually he reached Rome, where the pope appointed him bishop of Girgenti. He returned to Sicily, and almost immediately his zeal for discipline gained him enemies. An attempt was made to tarnish his reputation by planting in his house a prostitute, who was duly "discovered." He was summoned to Rome but had no trouble in clearing himself and went back to his see. Gregory is best remembered today as the author of a Greek commentary on the book of Ecclesiastes. He is mentioned in the Roman Martyrology, and his feast is kept in Greek churches of the Byzantine rite, to which he belonged.

For Leontius's Life, see *P.G.*, 98, 549-716; cf. *P.G.*, 116, 190-269. See also *D.C.B.*, 2, pp. 776-7; O. Bardenhewer, *Geschichte der altkirchlichen Literatur*, 5, pp. 105-7; L. T. White in *American Historical Review* 42 (1936), pp. 1-21.

St Trond (*c.* 630-*c.* 692)

The Life of St Trond (Trudo), compiled less than a century after his death by Donatus, a deacon of the church in Metz, is relatively reliable. Trond, whose parents were Franks, is venerated as the apostle of the area of Brabant known as Hasbaye. Having decided early on to enter the service of the Church, he was sent by St Remaclus (3 Sept.), a missionary bishop, to the cathedral school at Metz. There he studied theology and scripture, and he was eventually ordained by St

Clodulf (8 June). Once back in his own district, Trond preached to the pagans, of whom there were still many in the seventh century. He built a church with a monastery attached, on his own estate—which gave its name to present-day Saint-Trond, between Louvain and Tongres. Trond also founded a convent near Bruges. After he died, in about 692, miracles were reported at his tomb, which became a place of pilgrimage.

Donatus' Life is in *M.G.H., Scriptores merov.*, 6. See also L. van der Essen, *Etude critique sur les saints mérovingiens* (1907), pp. 91-6; M. Coens, *Anal.Boll.* 72, pp. 85-133. St Trond is also mentioned in the early Wissenburg text of the *Hieronymianum*.

Bd Michael Pro, *Martyr* (1891-1927)

Michael (Miguel) Pro Juárez was born in Guadalupe, in the state of Zacatecas, Mexico, on 13 January 1891. One of the ten children of Miguel Pro and Josefina Juárez, he had a comfortable and happy childhood, during which he absorbed the example of his parents' strong and living faith. The one disadvantage seems to have been that his father's job as a mining engineer took him from place to place, and the family was frequently uprooted. Perhaps to give him greater stability, perhaps simply because it provided a good education, Michael was sent, at the age of ten, to the Jesuit college of San José in Mexico City. He had not been there long, however, when an illness from which he was to suffer throughout his life first began to show itself. He returned home and was sent to continue his education at the college of Acuna de Santillo. But this too was short-lived. His parents discovered that the college authorities were attempting to put anti-Catholic ideas into the head of their child and removed him immediately. After this they decided that he could get all the education he needed from private tutors.

When Michael was fifteen, his formal education, such as it was, came to an end. He went next to work as his father's secretary in the Department of Mines (a role which gave him the opportunity to demonstrate his considerable administrative skills), making use of his free time to do charitable work among the poor and the sick. Not long after this he experienced some sort of spiritual crisis. Enormously popular on account of his sunny disposition and deep sensitivity, he seems himself to have felt there was something missing, but without knowing which direction to take. Things clarified for him when one of his much-loved sisters left home to become a nun, and on 10 August 1911 he entered the novitiate of the Mexican province of the Society of Jesus at El Llano, in Michoacán. Two years later, on 15 August 1913, he made his simple perpetual vows, and he remained at El Llano to continue his studies. As he had had no sustained education, studying did not come easily to him, but he approached the situation with his customary courage and determination.

Meanwhile, the political situation in Mexico had been deteriorating. A rebel general, Venustiano Carranza, and a bandit, Pancho Villa, rival opponents of the dictator Porfirio Díaz (ruled 1876-1910), had made the Catholic Church one of their particular targets. When a group of Carranza's men ransacked the main building of the novitiate and burned the library, the community was forced to disperse. With the other student priests, Michael escaped across the border into Texas and travelled on to Los Gatos, California, where he remained for one year. From 1915 he spent five years studying classics and philosophy in Granada (Spain), two doing his master's degree in Granada (Nicaragua), and four studying theology in Sarria (Spain) and Enghien (Belgium). It was in Enghien, on 30 August 1925, that he was finally ordained to the priesthood. The months that followed were difficult for him. His illness flared up again, which meant that he had to undergo a number of painful operations, and then he received news that his mother had died. But he refused to allow his pain and grief to become a burden to others, concealing them instead behind his customary cheerfulness.

On 8 July 1926 Michael returned to Mexico, and more precisely to the Jesuit house in Mexico City. He had scarcely arrived, however, when the government passed laws which made it illegal to hold religious services in Mexican churches, thus opening up the way for more persecution and provoking the mass resistance movement of *Cristeros*. Michael went to live with his family, which had moved to Mexico City, and he carried on a clandestine ministry. In so doing he was placing himself in great danger, as there was always the possibility that the police might turn up at one or other of the Communion stations he set up throughout the city. But he managed somehow to celebrate the Eucharist, hear confessions, and administer the other sacraments, as well as to conduct retreats, especially for workers, and organize care for the poor. In all this he drew strength from the time he spent each day in prayer, offering himself to God on behalf of his country, and not least from his brothers Humberto and Roberto, who among other things were helping to print and distribute literature for the League for the Defence of Religious Freedom.

Finally, on 18 November 1927, he was arrested, along with his two brothers. And although he had at no time taken part in or supported armed action against the government, the authorities accused him not only of having done so but also of being the mastermind behind an attempt made a few days previously on the life of the president-elect, General Alvaro Obregón. (The bomb that wounded the general was in a car that had belonged to one of Michael's brothers until he sold it about a week before the event). There was not a shred of evidence to suggest that Michael or his brothers had had anything at all to do with it, but having arrested them, General Obregón decided to use Michael in particular as an example to all Catholics—even when Luis Segura, the person responsible, gave himself up. There was no trial, indeed nothing approaching a judicial procedure. On 23 November Miguel was simply taken out and shot to death by a firing squad in the presence of a large group of people brought together by the government. As he stood waiting for the order to shoot, he raised his arms in the form of a cross and said firmly: "*Viva Cristo Rey*"—the slogan of the *Cristeros*. Humberto, too, was executed, but Roberto was spared at the last minute.

The government may nevertheless have failed in its attempt to frighten Catholics. Twenty thousand people are said to have attended Michael's burial, and news of his death travelled immediately round the world. He was soon one of the best known and most venerated martyrs of modern times. If his cause was not introduced until 1952, this was because of the difficult political situation in Mexico and for no other reason. He was beatified on 25 September 1988.

See: A. Dragon, *Pour le Christ Roi. Le Père Pro de la Compagnie de Jésus* (1958); F. Royer, *Padre Pro Mexican Hero* (1963); A. Dragon, *Vie intime du Père Pro* (1943). See also *Positio super Introductione Causae* (1950); *Positio super Martyrio* (1968); J. N. Tylenda, *Jesuit Saints and Martyrs* (1984). On the religious persecution in Mexico 1925-9, see Anon., *La lucha de los Católicos Mejicanos, por un Amigo de Méjico* (1927); A. P. Moctezuma, *El conflicto religioso de 1926. Sus orígenes. Su desarrollo. Su solución* (1960); M. A. Puente, "The Church in Mexico" in E. Dussel (ed.), *The Church in Latin America, 1492-1992* (1992), pp. 222ff.

24

St Chrysogonus, *Martyr* (? *c.* 304)

Although Chrysogonus is one of the martyrs mentioned in Eucharistic Prayer I for the Roman rite of the Mass, almost nothing is known about him apart from the fact that he seems to have suffered at Aquileia. He was venerated in northern Italy, but his cult was introduced also in Rome, where the titular church of San Crisogono in Trastevere is mentioned in 499, and referred to again as *titulus Sancti Crisogoni* in 521. The story of St Chrysogonus occupies the first part of the *Passio Sanctae Anastasiae* (25 Dec.), where he is described as a Roman official who became Anastasia's spiritual father, continuing to correspond with her from prison until he was condemned and beheaded at Aquileia during the persecution of Diocletian. This should probably be regarded as a hagiographical fiction. It has been suggested that the house in Rome which became the church of San Crisogono may have belonged to a man of that name, and that once this was mistaken for a dedication to St Chrysogonus a legend was invented to identify him with the real martyr who suffered at Aquileia.

The Latin text of the *Passio Sanctae Anastasiae* is in H. Delehaye, *Etudes sur le légendier romain* (1936), pp. 221-49. See also *C.M.H.*, pp. 618-9; J. P. Kirsch, *Die römischen Titelkirchen im Altertum*, pp. 108-13; M. Mesnard, *La basilique de Saint-Chrysogone à Rome* (1935); S. G. A. Luff, *The Christian's Guide to Rome* (n.e. 1990), pp. 150-1.

St Colman of Cloyne, *Bishop* (*c.* 530-*c.* 606)

There is a dearth of biographical material about this Irish saint, who was born in Munster in the first half of the sixth century. He was a gifted poet and became royal bard (which meant chronicler and genealogist as well as poet laureate) at Cashel. It was not until he was nearly fifty that he became a Christian. The story of his conversion is that St Brendan (16 May) came to Cashel to settle a dispute about the royal succession, and while he was there the relics of St Ailbhe (12 Sept.) were found. The bard was involved with the discovery, after which Brendan, declaring that hands that had touched such holy relics should not remain the hands of a pagan, baptized him and gave him the name Colman—an extraordinarily common one in the early Irish church. Colman became a priest and then a bishop, preaching in Limerick and also in the eastern parts of Cork. He is believed to have founded two churches, one at Cloyne, where he is venerated as the first bishop, and another at Kilmaclenine. The remains of a church can be seen in both places, and there seems to have been a holy well at Cloyne. St Colman is mentioned in the *Félire* of Oengus under 24 November.

See: R. Thurneysen, "Colman mac Lenene und Senchan Torpeist" in *Zeitschrift für celtische Philologie* 19 (1933), pp. 193-209; D. Pochin Mould, *The Irish Saints* (1964), pp. 84-5; R. Sharpe, *Medieval Irish Saints' Lives* (1991).

St Enfleda, *Abbess* (*c*. 704)

Enfleda was the daughter of the Northumbrian king, Edwin (616-33), and a Kentish princess, Ethelburga. She was baptized by St Paulinus (644; 10 Oct.), the first bishop of York, on Pentecost Sunday 626. When her father was killed at the Battle of Hatfield Chase on 12 October 633, she went with her mother and Paulinus to Kent. In 642, she returned to Northumbria, married King Oswiu of Bernicia (641-70) in the hope that this would permanently unite the two strands of the Northumbrian monarchy, and she became an influential protector of Christianity. In 651, when Oswiu murdered his cousin Oswin (20 Aug.), she persuaded him to found the monastery at Gilling in reparation. Although she had been brought up in the Celtic tradition, she supported St Wilfrid (12 Oct.) and the Roman method of computing in the Easter controversy. It was the largely the fact that Oswiu initially supported the Celts, which meant that Easter was celebrated twice in the royal household, that brought the matter to a head and led to the convening of the Synod of Whitby (663-4). In recognition of her zeal and of her support in the Easter controversy, Pope Vitalian (657-72) sent her a gold cross allegedly made from St Peter's chains.

When Oswiu died in 670, Enfleda joined the abbey at Whitby, where St Hilda (17 Nov.) was still ruling as abbess. Enfleda eventually became abbess herself—as later did her daughter St Elfleda (8 Feb.)—and under her rule the monastery became increasingly Rome-oriented. Oswiu was buried at Whitby, and Enfleda had her father's relics brought there for burial in the chapel of St Gregory. She died in about 704 and was buried with Oswiu. Unfortunately all trace of an early cult was destroyed by the Danes, though according to William of Malmesbury her relics were taken to Glastonbury, along with those of other Northumbrian saints.

See Bede, *H.E.*, 2, 9, 20; 3, 15, 24-5, 29; 5, 19. See also: *O.D.S.*, p. 158; *Bibl.SS.*, 4, 1208-9; R. Stanton, *A Menology of England and Wales* (1892).

Bd Mary Anna Sala (1829-91)

Mary (Maria) Anna Sala was born at Brivio, an old village on the banks of the Adda, near Lecco, on 21 April 1829. Her parents, Giovanni and Giovannina Sala, had eight children, of whom she was the fifth, and the home was a particularly happy one. Giovanni, a hard-working and deeply religious man, earned a good living in the timber trade, and he was active in his local church. Both parents were keenly aware of their responsibility to pass their faith on to their children, while making sure that each was educated according to his or her particular gifts. Mary Anna was very receptive in both respects. In 1842, she went to a boarding school recently opened at Vimercate by the Sisters of St Marcellina, leaving four years later with a teaching diploma and a strong desire to join the Congregation. She was unable to do so immediately—her mother was ill, and her father had just been defrauded of his all money—but having helped to support the family through this crisis, she finally entered in February 1848, and she made her profession on 13 September 1852.

For the remaining forty years of her life she taught in the schools of the Congregation in Cernusco, Milan, Genoa, and Chambéry and lived in simple fidelity to its Rule. She was a successful and popular teacher: her pupils, who appreciated her directness and the strength behind her gentleness, found her understanding and helpful, and many treasured the letters she wrote to them. She worked tirelessly for her pupils (one of whom would eventually be the mother of Pope Paul VI (1963–78), wishing them to become strong in faith as well as learning, and she never found it easy to move from one convent to another, because it meant leaving them—and her Sisters in religion—behind. In a letter to one of her superiors she describes quite openly the sense of loss it gave her in human terms, but she adds: "I have read my letter again and realize that you may think I am not happy here; that is not true; I feel sorry at having left you all, but God is good to me."

In about 1883 she was diagnosed as having throat cancer. Never one to allow her sufferings to become a burden to other people, she continued to teach and take part in community life as usual until the autumn of 1891, when she was forced to retire to the infirmary. She died, after a fortnight of terrible suffering, on 24 November 1891. Nuns and pupils alike spread news of her holiness, but it was not until 1920, when her body was exhumed and found to be intact, that the cause for her beatification was introduced. Mary Anna Sala was beatified on 26 October 1980.

See Institute of St Marcellina, *Blessed Maria Anna Sala.*

25

St Moses of Rome, *Martyr* (251)

The information we have about Moses is by and large contemporary and trustworthy. Most of it comes from the letters of St Cyprian (16 Sept.), the third-century bishop of Carthage, other sources being Pope St Cornelius (16 Sept.) and the *Catalogus Liberianus*. Cyprian records that Moses, who was possibly of Jewish origin, was a priest in Rome and the leader of a group of priests who were the first Christians to die for their faith in the persecution of Decius (249-51). Moses and his fellow-priests exchanged regular letters of encouragement with Cyprian and the clergy of Carthage, and they formed a united front against Novatian, who had himself consecrated Bishop of Rome in opposition to the rightful pope, Cornelius, when the latter began readmitting to the Church people who had apostatized under pressure during the persecution. (Novatian took the view that the Church had no power to forgive in such cases or in a number of others.) After Moses and his companions had been in prison for almost a year—eleven months and eleven days, according to the *Catalogus Liberianus*—Moses died, probably in the first months of 251, and he was immediately hailed as a martyr. For some reason, Cardinal Baronius put him in November in the Roman Martyrology.

Cyprian's letters are in *C.S.E.L.*, 3, pp. 544-7, 557-65, 576-9, 627. See also Eusebius, 6, 3, n.20; *Liber Pontificalis* (ed. L. Duchesne), 1, pp. 148-50; Tillemont, 3, 4; *D.C.B.*, 3, pp. 948-9.

St Mercurius, *Martyr* (date unknown)

St Mercurius, like St Mennas (11 Nov.) and St George (23 Apr.), is one of the so-called warrior saints who were so popular in the East. Like the others, he was undoubtedly a real person who died for his faith; but his various *acta*, which have much in common with theirs, as with those of other martyrs, are all versions of a pious romance. According to the legend, he was the son of a Scythian officer at Rome and was himself a successful soldier who had risen to the rank of *primicerius*. When the city was threatened by the Goths during the reign of the emperor Decius (249-51), Mercurius encouraged the emperor and, armed with a sword given him by an angel, led the imperial troops to a great victory. Noticing that Mercurius was absent from the sacrifices to the gods which traditionally followed such a victory, Decius sent for him to find out why. When Mercurius flung down his military cloak and belt, insisting that he would not deny Christ, Decius, who was afraid of arousing the anger of the people of Rome, had him taken to Caesarea in Cappadocia, where he was tortured and beheaded.

Later a new element was added to the legend, which made St Mercurius even more famous. He was invoked by St Basil (2 Jan.) 113 years later for help against Julian the Apostate (361-3). According to the Alexandrian Synaxary, the warrior saint appeared in the heavens girt with a sword and brandishing a spear, with which he killed the infidel emperor. He is also said to have appeared at Antioch, with St George and St Demetrius (8 Oct.), to the soldiers of the first Crusade. In art, Mercurius is always shown in military gear, most frequently in the act of killing Julian the Apostate. In Egypt, where many churches are dedicated to him, he is known as Abu Sayfayn, "the father of swords," on account of the weapons with which he is always represented.

See H. Delehaye, *Les légendes grecques des saints militaires* (1909); E. Wallis Budge, *Miscellaneous Coptic texts* (1915); S. Binon, *Essai sur le cycle de St Mercure* (1937); *idem., Documents grecs inédits relatifs à S. Mercure de Césarée* (1937).

26

St Peter of Alexandria, *Bishop and Martyr* (311)

Although the *passio* of St Peter is thoroughly unreliable, he is mentioned several times by Eusebius, who describes him as an excellent teacher of the Christian religion and a great bishop. We do not know when or where Peter was born, but we do know that in 300 he succeeded St Theonas as bishop of Alexandria and that he governed that church for nearly twelve years. For the last nine of these he had to endure the persecution of the emperor Diocletian (284-305) and his successors. As a bishop he was renowned for the support he gave to his persecuted fellow-Christians. Inevitably, not all managed to stand firm under torture, so Peter, whose jurisdiction extended to all the churches of Egypt as well as to those of the Thebaid and Libya, drew up instructions for the treatment of those who had denied their faith but wished to be reconciled—instructions that were later adopted by the entire Eastern Church.

Eventually Peter himself was forced to go into hiding. During his absence from Alexandria—and at a time when all its energies were needed to withstand the persecution—the church in Egypt was rent by a schism. The exact circumstances are uncertain. It seems, however, that Meletius, bishop of Antioch, took it upon himself to exercise Peter's metropolitan functions and in particular to ordain priests in sees where the incumbent was in hiding. To justify his actions he spread lies about Peter and accused him of being too lenient toward the lapsed. And since he refused to stand down, Peter had no option but to excommunicate him. Meanwhile, Peter continued to administer his church and care for his people, until at last he was able to return to the city. But the persecution was renewed almost immediately by Maximinus Daia (308-13). In 311 Peter was seized unexpectedly and executed without charge or trial. In Egypt he is known as "the seal and complement of the persecution," because he was the last martyr to be put to death by public authority at Alexandria. He is also known as "he who passed out through the wall"—a reference to the legend that when he realized that the authorities would be prepared to massacre the huge crowd of Christians who had gathered in protest outside the prison where he was held and were blocking the way for the executioners, Peter suggested to the commandant that they make a breach in the wall under cover of dark, so that the executioners could enter unseen by the crowd.

Eusebius, *H.E.*, 7-9. The supposed *passio* is in *C.M.H.*, pp. 620-1. See also: Tillemont, 5, pp. 755-7; O. Bardenhewer, *Geschichte der altkirchlichen Literatur*, 2, pp. 203-11; *D.T.C.*, 12, 1802-4; *Anal.Boll.* 67, pp. 117-30; *D.C.B.*, 4, pp. 331-2.

St Siricius, *Pope* (399)

Little is known about Siricius as a person, though he is thought to have been born in Rome and to have been a member of the Roman clergy from the time of Pope Liberius (352-66). He was unanimously elected pope in 384, when Pope St Damasus I (366-84; 11 Dec.), one of whose deacons he had been, died. St Jerome (30 Sept.), doubtless out of pique because he was not chosen to be a counsellor under Siricius as he had been under Damasus, makes Siricius out to be an insignificant, rather simple person, but the reality was somewhat different. He fulfilled his charge as bishop with great energy, and it was he who issued the first papal decretals—documents which detail the law in order to acknowledge or create it. Because of the criticisms of St Jerome and also of St Paulinus of Nola (22 June), Siricius was left out of the 1584 edition of the Roman Martyrology, but his name was added in 1748 by Pope Benedict XIV (1740-58). His entry describes him as "distinguished for his learning, piety and zeal for religion, for condemning various heretics and for strengthening ecclesiastical discipline by very salutary decrees."

"Various heretics" refers to two in particular: Jovinian, a monk who questioned the value of virginity and denied that Mary remained a virgin after the birth of Christ, and the bishop of Naissus (Sardica), Bonosus, who supported Jovinian's point of view and said that Mary bore children to Joseph after the birth of Jesus. The "salutary decrees" include a letter to Himerius, bishop of Tarragona, which highlights the authority of the Bishop of Rome and is the earliest papal decretal to have survived intact. Sent also to the church in Africa, it includes various provisions, including one forbidding married priests and deacons to sleep with their wives—the first known enforcement by the Roman see of priestly celibacy. It was Siricius who supported St Martin of Tours (11 Nov.) when he defended the right of the heretic Priscillian to be judged by the Church rather than by the emperor. And it was Siricius who consecrated the basilica of San Paolo *fuori le mura* after its enlargement by the emperor, Theodosius I; his name is still to be seen on a pillar that survived the fire of 1823. Siricius died on 26 November 399 and was buried in the basilica of San Silvestro, near the cemetery of Priscilla.

See Jerome, *Epistolae,* 127, 9; Paulinus of Nola, *Epistolae,* 5, 14; *Liber Pontificalis* (ed. L. Duchesne), 1, pp. 217-8. See also E. Caspar, *Geschichte des Papsttums,* 1 (1930), pp. 257ff.; *O.D.P.,* pp. 35-6; *D.C.B.,* 4, pp. 696-702; *N.C.E.,* 13, p. 258; *D.T.C.,* 14, 2171-4.

St Basolus, *Bishop* (*c.* 620)

According to the three short Latin Lives that survive, Basolus (or Basle) was born in Limoges in the middle of the sixth century. He started his career in the army, but after a few years felt called to the religious life. In search of guidance, he made a pilgrimage to the shrine of St Remigius (13 Jan.) in Reims and was sent by the archbishop to the nearby monastery of Verzy. He was outstandingly faithful to the spirit as well as to the letter of the Rule; but after a while he realized that he needed more solitude. With the agreement of the abbot, he moved to an isolated cell at the top of a nearby hill. Here he remained for the rest of his life, attracting several disciples, including St Sindulf, who is named with him in the Roman Martyrology. Numerous miracles were attributed to Basolus. According to one story (told, with variations, of several saints, no doubt to perpetuate the idea that a particular piece of land was sacred and should remain in the hands of the Church), the count of Champagne, out hunting in the vicinity, ran a wild boar in the direction of Basolus' cell. When the animal took refuge in the folds of the monk's habit, the dogs stopped dead and refused to come nearer. So impressed was the count that he made Basolus a present of a large tract of land.

Of the three short Latin Lives, one is in *AA.SS. O.S.B.*, 2, 61-2, one in *M.G.H., Scriptores*, 13, pp. 449-51, and one in *P.L.*, 137, 643-58. See also E. Quentelot, *St Basle et le monastère de Verzy* (1892).

St Conrad of Constance, *Bishop* (975)

There is an unsatisfactory biography of St Conrad, written about a century after his death by Udalschalk of Maissach, but apart from this no dependable account of his life survives. From such reliable sources of information as do exist, we know that he was born into the powerful Guelf family and that his father, Count Heinrich von Altdorf, founded the still-surviving abbey of Weingarten. As a second son, Konrad was sent to the cathedral school in Constance for his education, and he was eventually ordained priest. He was made provost of the cathedral almost immediately, and in 934, when the bishop died, he was chosen to succeed him. One of his champions was the bishop of Augsburg, St Ulrich (4 July), and a close friendship grew up between the two men. Konrad, who had made a vow of poverty, resolved the problem of what to do with his inherited estates by giving them to his brother in exchange for other land near Constance. This he made over to the diocese and to the poor, having first built and endowed three new churches, in honour of St Maurice (22 Sept.), St John the Evangelist (27 Dec.), and St Paul (25 Jan., 29 June), and restored many old ones. Finally, we know that he made the pilgrimage to Jerusalem three times, at a time when it was commonly made once.

In art, Konrad is usually represented with a chalice and a spider. The legend is that he was celebrating Mass one Easter Sunday, when a large spider dropped into the chalice. Out of respect for the Sacrament, and ignoring the commonly-held belief of the time that all or most spiders are poisonous, he swallowed it without doing himself any harm. He died in 975 and was canonized in 1123.

Udalschalk of Maissach's biography is in *M.G.H., Scriptores*, 4, pp. 430-60. See also J. Mayer, *Der hl. Konrad* (1898); Grober and Merk, *Das St Konrads Jubilaeum* (1923); O. Künstle, *Ikonographie*, 2, pp. 385-8.

St Nikon "Metanoiete" (998)

St Nikon's life is relatively well documented. There is a long Greek Life, which was also translated into Latin and is of considerable historical interest, and a document that is said to be his spiritual testament. Nikon was born in Pontus (in present-day Turkey). While he was still a young man, he left home and went to a monastery known as Khrysopetro, where he spent twelve years living a life of prayer and penance. However, his spiritual conferences were so effective that his superiors decided to send him out to preach. So he went as a missionary to Crete, which Byzantium had recovered from the Arabs in 960, and there brought back to the Christian faith many who had converted to Islam. His name comes from his habit of prefacing every sermon with the injunction: "*Metanoiete!*"—"Repent!" Having spent a number of years in Crete, he went on to Sparta, where he built three churches and a monastery, and to other parts of Greece. His teaching was said to have been confirmed by miracles. He died in a monastery in Peloponnesus on 26 November 998 and appears in both the Roman and Greek martyrologies.

The Latin translation of the Life is in Martène and Durand, *Amplissima collectio*, 6, pp. 837-87. See also Prince Max of Savoy, *Das christliche Hellas* (1919), pp. 129-33; *Vies des Saints*, 11, pp. 895, 900; *Bibl.SS.*, 9, 897-8; *D.T.C.*, 11, 655-7.

Bd Pontius of Faucigny, *Abbot* (1178)

Not much is known about Bd Pontius (Ponce), but he was greatly venerated by St Francis de Sales (24 Jan.), who opened his tomb in 1620 to examine the relics and removed some of them. Pope Leo XIII (1878-1903) confirmed his cult in 1896. Pontius was born into the Savoyard nobility. When he was twenty he became a Canon Regular at the abbey of Abondance in Chablais, the Constitutions of which he rewrote, bringing them into line with the Rule of St Augustine. Then, in 1144, he founded another house at Sixt, where he spent the next twenty-eight years—the last seventeen of them as abbot, after Pope Adrian IV raised Sixt to the status of abbey in 1155. He then returned to Abondance as abbot but resigned soon afterwards and died in retirement at Sixt on 26 November 1178. He was buried in the abbey church, and his cult was confirmed in 1896.

See L. Albert, *Le bx Ponce de Faucigny*; Mercier, "L'abbaye et la vallée d'Abondance" in *Mémoires et documents de l'Académie salésienne*, 8 (1885), pp. 1-308; *D.H.G.E.*, 1, 147, 151; *Vies des Saints*, 11, pp. 881-2.

St Silvester Gozzolini, *Abbot* (*c.* 1177-1267)

A comprehensive and apparently reliable Life of St Silvester was written within fifteen years of his death by a contemporary, Andrea di Giacomo. Silvestro Gozzolini was born at Osimo, south of Ancona, in about 1177. He was sent to read law in Bologna and Padua, but much to the fury of his father, who is said to have refused to speak to him for ten years, he soon abandoned his legal studies in favour of scripture and theology. Back in Osimo, he accepted a substantial benefice and proceeded to work with great zeal among the people, until he came into conflict with the local bishop. The latter was, not surprisingly, angry when Silvester took it upon himself to rebuke him for his disedifying lifestyle, and he threatened to strip him of his benefice. Had he carried out his threat, it would not have worried Silvester, who had for some time felt drawn to the contemplative life.

Finally, in 1227, when he was fifty, Silvester resigned his benefice and withdrew to a lonely spot some thirty miles from Osimo. He lived there in great poverty and discomfort until the local landlord gave him another plot of land, but this proved too damp, so he moved again. Finally, in 1231, having decided to establish a monastery for the disciples who were gathering around him, he went to Monte Fano, near Fabriano, and built on the remains of an ancient pagan temple. He chose for his monks the Rule of St Benedict (11 July) in its most austere form, and for the next thirty-six years he governed with great wisdom. The Order of St Benedict of Monte Fano was approved by Pope Innocent IV (1243-7) in 1247, although because of their extreme stress on certain points, especially poverty, and way the Congregation was organized, the Silvestrian Benedictines, of which a few houses still exist, have never been recognized as part of the Benedictine Confederation.

When Silvester died in 1267 at the age of ninety, no fewer than eleven monasteries recognized his jurisdiction. Miracles were reported at his tomb, and in 1275 his relics were enshrined in the church at Monte Fano. Pope Clement VIII (1592-1605) added his name to the Roman Martyrology in 1598, and on 19 August 1890 Pope Leo XIII extended his feast to the whole Western Church.

The Latin Life is in C. S. Franceschini, *Vita di Silvestro Abate* (1772). See also Amadeo Bolzonetti, *Il Monte Fano e un grande anacoreta; Ricordi storici* (1906).

St Elzéar (*c.* 1285-1323) and Bd Delphina (*c.* 1285-1360)

Elzéar of Sabran was born in his father's castle at Ansouis in Provence and educated at the abbey of Saint-Victor, where his uncle, Guillaume de Sabran, was abbot. He was betrothed while still young to an orphan, Delphina (in French Delphine) de Glandèves, heiress to the lord of Puy-Michel, and they were married when both were about sixteen. After some hesitation Elzéar agreed to Delphina's request, prompted, it is said, by a Franciscan friar, that they should live as brother and sister, and they seem to have enjoyed a very harmonious and mutually supportive marriage. When at the age of twenty-three Elzéar inherited his father's titles and estates he found himself confronted with opposition from various quarters. This he countered with a combination of gentle firmness and patient diplomacy, for which he was criticized by friends who insisted that "with the wicked" he should "play the lion." Elzéar would not change his methods, however, and almost invariably won the good will of his enemies in the end. In about 1317 they went to Naples, Delphina as lady-in-waiting to Sanchia, the wife of King Robert (1309-43), and Elzéar as tutor to their son Charles. His effectiveness in this role led eventually to his appointment as justiciar in the southern Abruzzi. In 1323 the king sent him to Paris to ask the French king, Philip V, to give his daughter, Mary of Valois, in marriage to Charles. When he had fulfilled his commission he was taken ill and after a few days died on 27 September in the arms of the Franciscan friar who had been his confessor. He was canonized in 1369 by Pope Bd Urban V (1362-70; 19 Dec.), who as Guillaume de Grimoard had been his godson. Delphina, who survived her husband by thirty-seven years, returned to Provence after Sanchia's death. Having given away all she could to the poor, she lived as a recluse, first at Cabrières and then at Apt. During her last years she suffered a painful illness with great patience. When she died on 26 November 1360 she was buried with her husband at Apt. According to an old tradition both were members of the Third Order of St Francis; they are therefore particularly venerated by the Franciscans.

There is interesting material in *AA.SS.*, Sept., 7. See also P. Girard, *Saint Elzéar et la B. Delphine de Signe* (1912); a good popular account by G. Duhamlet (1944).

Bd James of Mantua, *Bishop* (1338)

A brief Life of James (Giacomo) was published in Rome when his cult was confirmed in 1859. Otherwise few details have survived. While he was a young Dominican, his combined talents and goodness caught the attention of the master general, Niccolò Boccasini, who chose him as his companion and adviser—a role James continued to fill when Niccolò became a cardinal in 1298. In 1303, when Niccolò was elected pope as Benedict XI (7 July), James was sent to his native Mantua as bishop. Discharging his pastoral duties with wisdom and considerable energy, he remained there, probably until he died on 19 November 1338. Apart from a brief period immediately after his death, during which he was venerated as a saint, he seems to have been forgotten until his tomb was accidentally broken open in 1483 and his body was found to be intact. This and reports of miracles led to another brief period of popularity. Then he was forgotten again until 1604, when the body was again found to be intact, and the bishop of Mantua publicly encouraged his cult.

Analecta Juris Pontificii, 4 (1860), 1896-7. See also A. Touron, *Hommes illustres O.P.*, 2, pp. 134-6; F. Ughelli, *Italia Sacra*, 1, 938; J. Procter, O.P. (ed.), *Short Lives of the Dominican Saints* (1901), pp. 337-9.

BB Hugh Taylor and Marmaduke Bowes, *Martyrs* (1585)

Born in Durham, Hugh Taylor went to study for the priesthood at the English College in Reims. He was ordained in 1584 and sent immediately to work on the English mission. He had been back scarcely a year when Marmaduke Bowes, "of Angram Grange, near Appleton, in Cleveland," a Catholic who had conformed outwardly to the new religious statutes, either entertained him in his home or gave him a drink at the door. Shortly after this, Marmaduke heard that Hugh had been arrested, and he went to York assizes to see what he could do to free him. As a result of his efforts, he too was thrown into prison. The two men were hanged, drawn, and quartered at York on 26 November 1585. They were the first to suffer under a new statute, the Act Against Jesuits, Seminary Priests and Other Suchlike Disobedient Subjects, which made it high treason for any priest ordained since the first day of the reign of Elizabeth I (1558-1603) to return to or remain in England and Wales, and for anyone else to harbour such a priest, knowing that that was what he was. Both are included among the Eighty-five Martyrs of England, Scotland, and Wales (22 Nov.).

M.M.P., p. 106; B. C. Foley, *The Eighty-five Blessed Martyrs* (1987); *N.C.E.*, 9, pp. 319-332.

St Leonard of Port Maurice (1676-1751)

Paolo Girolamo Casanova was born at Porto Maurizio on the Italian Riviera on 20 December 1676. When he was thirteen, his father, a master mariner, entrusted the boy to the care of a wealthy uncle in Rome. This uncle sent Paolo to the Jesuit college in the city, where he studied literature and philosophy. He also began to realize that he had a religious vocation—though to the Order of Friars Minor rather than to the Society of Jesus. His uncle, who wanted him to become a physician, objected and eventually turned him out of the house. Fortunately, Paolo managed to find a home with another relative, Leonardo Ponzetti, with whom he stayed until he received his father's unconditional permission to become a friar. He was clothed at the Franciscan novitiate at Ponticelli in 1697, taking the name Leonardo as an expression of gratitude to Ponzetti. Having completed his studies at the friary of San Bonaventura in Rome, he was ordained in 1702. This friary was the principal house of the *Riformella*, an offshoot of the strict *Riformati* branch of the Franciscans, and Leonard was to practise throughout his life the ideal of active missionary work combined with austerity and solitude to which he was introduced there. His great ambition had been to go abroad as a missionary, but he contracted tuberculosis shortly after his ordination, while he was teaching philosophy at San Bonaventura, and was told that Italy would be his mission.

In 1709, Leonard was sent with a group of friars to San Francesco del Monte in Florence, a friary that had been presented to the *Riformella* by the grand duke, Cosimo III de' Medici. The Franciscan standard of poverty was re-introduced, and the community began to increase in number. Soon the friary was an important religious centre, from which Leonard and the other friars went off to preach through-out Tuscany. Eventually, Leonard was appointed guardian of San Francesco del Monte. One parish priest wrote of this work there: "God alone knows all the good he has done here. His preaching has touched the hearts of all. . . . All the confessors in town have had to work hard." One of his first acts was to establish a hermitage at Incontro, in the mountains nearby, where the friars could withdraw for a while in turn twice a year to live alone and simply, while they refuelled themselves spiritually.

Florence was Leonard's base for many years, but as time went on he was increas-ingly asked to preach elsewhere. His first mission to Rome was too long for Duke Cosimo, who sent a ship to the Tiber to fetch him back; but in 1736 he went to Rome for good, as guardian of San Bonaventura. He held this office for a year, during which he found time to preach, with some effect, to the soldiers, sailors, convicts, and galley slaves in the port of Civitavecchia. Once released from office, he branched out to places as far afield as Umbria, Genoa, and the Marches, often attracting such huge crowds that he had to move out of the church and preach in the open air. One of his favourite "preaching aids" was the Stations of the Cross, and that devotion's abiding popularity is largely due to him. He also encouraged exposition of the Blessed Sacrament and devotion to the Sacred Heart and to Our Lady, none of which was as widespread then as it became later. He was particularly keen that the Immaculate Conception should be defined as a dogma of faith, and he suggested that the mind of the Church be sounded on the matter without an ecumenical council—as it was a century later. Leonard also found time, in the midst of all this activity, to act as spiritual director to a number of individuals. These included Clementina Sobieska, the wife of James Edward Stuart, the Old Pretender—whom the Italians recognized as James III of England.

In 1744 Pope Benedict XIV (1740-58), who had a high regard for Leonard, sent him, with the agreement of the island's ruler, the doge of Genoa, to Corsica, where religion was neglected and order in general had broken down. Of all Leonard's missionary tasks, this was the one he found most difficult. He was received with a certain amount of hostility, as some people assumed he was an agent of the doge in disguise. It was certainly true that the mission had a political aspect, since the trouble was largely an expression of opposition to the domination of Genoa. But Leonard persevered with his preaching, despite the fact that many men would turn up carrying guns, and he could say in one of his many letters: "In every parish we meet with the most formidable feuds, but peace and quiet generally come out on top in the end. However, unless the administration of justice gets strong enough to stamp out these vendettas, the good we are doing can be only transitory. . . . During these years of war the people have had no instruction whatsoever. . . . When I have an opportunity to meet the bishops I shall tell them what I think. . . . Though the work is so exacting, the harvest is abundant."

But Leonard was now sixty-eight and the fatigue, the intrigues, and the constant need to be vigilant began to affect his health. By the end of six months he was so ill that a ship was sent from Genoa to take him home, and his assessment of the state of affairs in Corsica was confirmed in a letter from the pope, who wrote: "The Corsicans have got worse than ever since the mission, so it is not thought advisable that you should go back there." Once recovered, he continued to preach and to give retreats to nuns and laypeople, especially in preparation for the jubilee of 1750. In that year he achieved one of his great ambitions when the pope gave him permission to set up the Stations of the Cross in the Colosseum.

In the spring of the following year he set off—in a carriage, as ordered by the pope, rather than on foot—to preach in Lucca and other places, but his energy was failing, and this, combined with the hostility or indifference he met with in some places, meant that these late missions were relatively unsuccessful. Early in November, knowing his work was done, he set out for Rome. The carriage broke down in Spoleto, so he continued on foot, arriving at San Bonaventura in the early evening of 26 November. He was carried to bed and given the last sacraments; at nine o'clock an affectionate message arrived from the pope, and by midnight he was dead. Apart from the legacy of his preaching, he left behind several devotional treatises and the *Resolutions*, which tell as much about him as about their subject; and then there are his surviving letters. Leonard was beatified in 1796 and canonized in 1867. His striking death mask is in the church of San Bonaventura in Rome.

There are Lives by G. da Masserano (1796; Eng. trans. 1852), S. di Ormea (1851), L. de Chérancé (1903), F. M. Pecheco (1963). For St Leonard's works, see B. Innocenti (ed., 1915, 1929); C. Ortolani da Pesaro (ed., 1927). See also articles in *Archivum Franciscanum Historicum*; Léon, *Auréole Séraphique* (Eng. trans.), 4, pp. 98-112; *Bibl.SS.*, 7, 1208-21.

27

St James Intercisus, *Martyr* (*c.* 421)

James is the best-known victim of the second great persecution in Persia, which began in about 420. According to the *passio*, much of which is clearly the stuff of legend, he was a close associate of King Yazdigerd I (399-420). When the latter, provoked by an over-zealous bishop named Abdias, declared war on the Christian religion, James preferred to go through the motions of abandoning his faith rather than lose the friendship of the king. This greatly distressed his wife and his mother, who, when Yazdigerd died, wrote to reproach and warn him. Greatly moved by their letter, he began to repent of what he had done, no longer appearing at court, renouncing his honours, and publicly rebuking himself.

James was eventually summoned by the new king, Bahram V, who accused him of ingratitude and threatened a lingering death. Failing to move him, he condemned him to be stretched out, so that his limbs could be cut off joint by joint—*Intercisus* means "cut-to-pieces." People turned out *en masse* to watch this novel form of execution, while the Christian minority prayed for James' perseverance. Having once again refused the attempts of the executioners to persuade him to dissemble his religion, James remained cheerful throughout his terrible ordeal, until one of the executioners finally severed his head from his body. The event is depicted in a miniature in the Menology of Basil II in the Vatican Library, and in several churches, especially in eastern Europe.

For the Syriac text of the *passio* (ed. P. Bedjan) see *Acta martyrum et sanctorum* (1890-7); for a German translation, see *Bibliothek der Kirchenvater*, 22, pp. 150-62. See also S. E. Assemani, *Acta sanctorum martyrum orientalium et occidentalium,* 1, pp. 242-58; P. Devos, *Anal.Boll.* 76, pp. 157-210; 72, pp. 213-56.

St Secundinus, *Bishop* (447)

Secundinus (in Irish, Sechnall) was one of the three *seniores* sent from Gaul in 439 to help St Patrick (17 Mar.). Information about him is scarce and contradictory. There is a medieval Latin Life, now in the Royal Library of Belgium, and he is mentioned in various annals and in Lives of St Patrick. According to the *Annals of Ulster*, he was already a bishop when he arrived in Ireland in 439 and was seventy-two when he died in 447. In part at least, this contradicts Tirechan (*c.* 700), who said Secundinus was consecrated by Patrick once he reached Ireland. The traditional view is that he was one of Patrick's auxiliary bishops and died before him. In some of the old lists his name appears immediately after Patrick's in the see of Armagh, but it is doubtful that he was ever bishop of Armagh. The *Tripartite Life of Patrick* says Patrick left Secundinus in charge of Armagh when he went to Rome, which is probably how the confusion, if there is one, arose.

Secundinus is best remembered as a hymn-writer, and in particular as the author of *Audite, omnes amantes Deum*, the earliest known Latin hymn written in Ireland. Composed in honour of Patrick, it has twenty-three verses, the initial letters of which are alphabetical, and was regarded as a "preserver," for use in an emergency. The beautiful Irish Communion hymn, *Sancti, venite, Christi corpus sumite*, is also attributed to Secundinus, but this is less likely: the *Bangor Antiphonary*, in which it is found, simply refers to it as "the hymn when the priests communicate."

The Latin Life is in *Anal.Boll.* 60, pp. 26-34; references in *Tripartite Life of St Patrick, Lebar Brecc*, etc. See also Bernard and Atkinson, *The Irish Liber Hymnorum*, 2, p. 96; F. E. Warren, *The Antiphonary of Bangor*, 2, p. 44; R. Sharpe, *Medieval Irish Saints' Lives* (1991); J. F. Kenney, *Sources for the Early History of Ireland.* 1, pp. 250-60; E. MacNeill, *St Patrick* (1934); *Bibl.SS.*, 11, 805-7.

St Maximus of Riez, *Bishop* (*c.* 460)

Information about St Maximus comes from two sources: a eulogy, probably written by Faustus, his successor as bishop of Riez, and a Life by Dynamius, a patrician contemporary. Maximus was born near Digne, in Provence. His Christian parents brought him up to cherish his faith, and no one was surprised when, as a young man, he applied to the monastery of Lérins and was received by the founder and abbot, St Honoratus (16 Jan.). In 426, when Honoratus was made bishop of Arles, Maximus succeeded him as abbot. St Sidonius (21 Aug.) speaks of his good influence on the monastery and of his reputation for miracles, which attracted crowds from the mainland. He managed successfully to foil the attempts of the clergy and people of Fréjus to make him their bishop by hiding for some days in a nearby forest. But his efforts to avoid becoming bishop of Riez by escaping in a boat were not so successful. Eventually he submitted, and he was received enthusiastically by the clergy and people. As his parents had originally come from Riez, he was regarded as a citizen. As bishop, he continued to observe the monastic rule as far as he could, retaining the same love of poverty, the same spirit of prayer, and the same humility for which he had been known at Lérins.

For Faustus's eulogy, see the works of Eusebius of Emesa; for Dynamius' Life, see *P.L.*, 80, 30-40. See also L. Duchesne, *Fastes Épiscopaux*, 1, pp. 283-4.

St Congar, *Abbot* (Sixth Century)

The question of the life and identity of St Congar (Cungar, or Cyngar) is somewhat confused, since there is at least one Welsh saint of that name and one Breton, and the sources are incomplete. Added to that, the Life cobbled together in Wells in the twelfth century relies heavily on hagiography and folklore. However, this Congar probably came as a missionary from south Wales to the Devon and Somerset region of south-west England, where he established one monastery in a marshy area near

Congresbury, the town in Somerset that now bears his name, and possibly others. Later, perhaps fleeing before the Saxons, he is supposed to have returned to Wales and founded a church near Cardiff. Welsh legend has it that, as an old man, he accompanied his "cousin" St Cybi (8 Nov.) to Ireland and followed him from there to Anglesey, where he is honoured at Llangefni. But this may refer to another Congar, as may the Breton tradition that he died at St-Congard in Morbihan, one of the many place-names in the region that incorporate the name. The matter is further complicated by the fact that a twelfth-century Life identifies him with St Decuman (Doccuin, Docco). Congar's name is mentioned in an eleventh-century litany from Winchester, and a number of medieval wills contain bequests for candles at his shrine.

See G. H. Doble, *The Saints of Cornwall,* 5, p. 3–29; "St Congar" in *Antiquity* 19 (1945), pp. 32–43; P. Grosjean, "Cyngar Sant" in *Anal.Boll.* 4, pp. 100–20; J. A. Robinson, "A Fragment of the Life of St Cungar" in *J.T.S.* 20, pp. 97–108; *idem,* "The Lives of St Congar and St Gildas," *loc. cit.,* 23, pp. 15–22; *idem,* "St Congar and St Decuman," *loc. cit.,* 29, pp. 137–40. See also *O.D.S.,* p. 110; *AA.SS.,* Nov., 3, pp. 403-7.

St Virgil of Salzburg, *Bishop* (784)

The most reliable source of information about St Virgil (Feargal, or Ferghil) is an epitaph by Alcuin. There is a twelfth-century Life, but this is less reliable, partly because of its later date. Virgil was an Irish monk, possibly educated at Colbroney by St Samthann (18 Dec.) and possibly, as the Annals of the Four Masters and the Annals of Ulster claim, abbot of Aghaboe. In about 723 he set off, *pro amore Christi,* for the Continent and perhaps even for the Holy Land—another example of medieval monastic *peregrinatio.* On his way through France, where he spent two years, he met and was befriended by Pépin the Short, who in 751 was to become king of all the Franks. His next stop was Bavaria, then a Frankish dependency, where Pépin sent him to make peace with Duke Odilo, the leader of a failed uprising. At this point he seems to have abandoned his pilgrimage. Duke Odilo appointed him abbot of St Peter's monastery in Salzburg and administrator of that diocese. As he was not a bishop—out of humility according to some but more probably because St Boniface (5 June), archbishop of Mainz and papal legate in Germany, who in any case did not approve of itinerant bishops, was annoyed at not being consulted by Odilo and blocked the appointment—he co-opted an Irish bishop to perform exclusively episcopal functions, until he was finally consecrated himself.

That, however, was not until after Boniface, with whom Virgil came into conflict on a number of occasions, died in 754. On the first, Virgil had ruled that it made no difference to the sacrament when a priest who was completely ignorant of Latin mispronounced the words of baptism. Boniface disapproved and appealed to the pope, St Zacharias (741-52; 15 Mar.), who confirmed Virgil's ruling. Things came to a head again later when Boniface once again denounced Virgil to the Holy See for his cosmological ideas—he was alleged to have taught that there is another world below this one, and another human race. What Virgil in fact taught is not entirely clear. Was he, as Boniface no doubt suspected, endorsing the existence of the fairy world of Irish folklore, or had he understood, ahead of his time, that the world is round and that there are people in the antipodes? The pope took the line that, if he was in any way denying the unity of the human race and therefore the universality of the redemption, he should be excommunicated by a synod; otherwise he should be left alone. As there is not a shred of evidence that he was tried, let alone condemned, for his views, and as he was eventually consecrated bishop, we may assume that the dispute was essentially about the "Roman" and the "Irish" ways of doing things.

During his time in Salzburg Virgil built the first cathedral, consecrating it in 774 and enshrining there the body of St Rupert (27 Mar.), the founder of the see. As well as being a man of vast culture, with a great interest in mathematics and the sciences in particular, he was very active pastorally. When two Slav dukes of Carinthia whom he had baptized asked him for missionaries, he not only sent some Benedictines but went to preach there himself. He became ill soon after his return from this preaching expedition, died on 27 November 784, and was buried in the cathedral. This was destroyed by fire in 1167, but his remains were found and re-enshrined, with those of St Rupert, under the main altar of the new cathedral. He was canonized by Pope Gregory IX (1227-41) in 1233; his feast is kept in Ireland as well as in parts of central Europe, where he is venerated as the apostle of the Slovenes.

Alcuin's epitaph is in *M.G.H., Poetae Latinae*, 1, p. 340; the Life is in *M.G.H., Scriptores*, 9, pp. 86–95. See also L. Gougaud, *Les saints irlandais hors d'Irlande* (1936), pp. 170-2; F. S. Betton, *St Boniface and St Virgil* (Benedictine Historical Monographs, 1927); P. Grosjean, "Virgile de Salzbourg en Irlande," *Anal.Boll.* 78, pp. 92-123; H. van der Linden, "Virgile de Salzbourg et les théories cosmographiques au VIIIe siècle," *Bulletins de l'Académie royale de Belgique, Classe des Lettres* (1914), pp. 163-87; *Bibl.SS.*, 12, 1206-8; *O.D.S.*, pp. 482-3.

St Fergus, *Bishop* (?Eighth Century)

The name Fergus is a common one in Irish hagiography. What we know of this St Fergus comes from the Aberdeen Breviary, but that little is confirmed by the existence of local dedications and place-names. Fergus, known in his own country, Ireland, as "the Pict," went as a missionary bishop to Scotland. He is believed to have settled in Strathearn (Strogeth), building one church there and two others at Blackford and Dolpatrick, all of which he dedicated to St Patrick (17 Mar.). From Strathearn he moved on to Caithness, and from there to Buchan, and finally to Glamis, where he died, and where a cave and a well bear his name. It is possible that this Fergus is the *Fergustus episcopus Scotiae Pictus*, who was present at the Council of Rome, convened by Pope Gregory II (715-31; 11 Feb.) in 721. After his death, Fergus' relics were kept in Glamis for several centuries, until, under the Scottish king, James IV (1488-1513), the abbot of Scone exhumed the body and then, having made the tomb more splendid, returned it minus the head. In the British Museum there is a reliquary which, according to the inscription, contains some of Fergus' relics.

See *K.S.S.*, pp. 336–8; *D.C.B.*, 2, pp. 505–6; *Bibl.SS.*, 5, 630–1; R. I. Best and H. J. Lawlor (eds.), *The Martyrology of Tallaght* (1931), p. 69.

Bd Bernardino of Fossa (1420-1503)

Bernardino Amici was born at Fossa, in the Abruzzi, in 1420. His early education took place at nearby Aquila, where his namesake, the great Franciscan St Bernardino of Siena (20 May), was buried, and from there he went on to Perugia to study law. A few years later he, like another namesake, Bd Bernardino of Feltre (28 Sept.), was attracted to the Friars Minor of the Observance during a Lenten mission preached by St James of the March (28 Nov.). He received the habit in Perugia in 1445, and after his ordination he became well known in Italy as a preacher. He was also superior provincial in his own area from 1454 to 1460 and from 1472 to 1475. In 1464 he was sent to Dalmatia and Bosnia, where differences of nationality were causing tension among the friars. This peace-making mission bore fruit, and Bernardino succeeded in uniting the various elements into a single province. When he returned to Italy, the pope wished to appoint him to the see of Aquila but accepted his plea that he be allowed to continue his work as a simple friar. Among his writings are a Life of St Bernardino of Siena and a historical *Chronicle of the Friars Minor of the Observance*. He died at the Franciscan friary of San Giuliano, near Aquila, on 27 November 1503. His cult was approved by Pope Leo XII (1823-9) in 1828.

See the memoir by Antonio Amici (great-nephew); short biography by Ugo de Pescocostanza (1872); Léon, *Auréole Séraphique* (Eng. trans.), 4, pp. 42-4; *Bibl.SS.*, 1, 1005-6.

Bd Humilis of Bisignano (*c.* 1582-1637)

Humilis was born at Bisignano in Calabria and baptized with the name Luca. He was earning his living as a farm labourer when, in his late teens, he resolved to become a Franciscan. However, it was not until 1609 that he was accepted as a lay brother by the Friars Minor of the Observance in Bisignano; he was given the name Humilis at his clothing. As it turned out this was a most appropriate name. He remained humble, despite the gift of miracles and the fact that men more learned than he came from all over to consult him. Eventually Pope Gregory XV (1621-3) sent for him, and although Gregory died while he was in Rome, his successor, Urban VIII (1623-44), persuaded Humilis to remain at his side. But the Roman climate did not suit him. He was taken ill and after a while returned to Bisignano, where he continued to live humbly and devoutly, until he died on 26 November 1637. He was beatified in 1882.

See *Acta Ordinis Fratrum Minorum ad ordinem quoque modo pertinentia*, 29 (1910); B. Mazzara, *Leggendario Francescano* (1680), 2, pt. 2, pp. 554-72; Life by A. da Vicenza (1872); Léon, *Auréole séraphique* (Eng. trans.), 4, pp. 154-6.

28

St Stephen the Younger, *Martyr* (764)

Stephen, one of the most famous martyrs of the Iconoclast persecution, was born in Constantinople sometime early in the eighth century. When he was fifteen his parents placed him in the monastery of St Auxentius, near Chalcedon, where his job was to fetch the daily provisions for the monastery. On the death of his father he returned to Constantinople, sold his share of the estate, and gave the proceeds to the poor. He then took his mother and one of his sisters—the other was already a nun—to Bithynia, where he found them and himself a home in a monastery. When the abbot died, Stephen, who was still only thirty, was chosen to replace him. The monastery consisted of a number of small cells scattered across a mountainside, with a cave at the summit for the abbot. Here Stephen lived, combining prayer with copying books and making nets, until, at the age of forty-two, he resigned as abbot and withdrew to a remote cell where he could neither stand nor lie with ease.

At this time the Iconoclast emperor, Constantine V Copronymus (741-75), was targeting monks in particular in his war against holy images. Aware of Stephen's enormous influence, he was anxious to get him to subscribe to a decree passed by the Iconoclast bishops in 754. When Stephen refused, the emperor sent soldiers to drag him from his cell and from then on used various means, including false accusations and entrapment, in an attempt to discredit him. Eventually, when Stephen challenged bishops loyal to the emperor on the subject of holy images, he was banished to the island of Proconnesus in the Propontis (now the Sea of Marmara). Two years later he was brought back to a prison in Constantinople and almost immediately arraigned before the emperor, who asked him whether a person who trampled on Christ's image trampled on Christ. No, Stephen replied; but then he produced a coin and asked how someone who trampled on the emperor's image should be treated. When the emperor expressed indignation that anyone should even think of such a thing, Stephen asked him why, if treading on the emperor's image was so great a crime, it was all right to burn that of Christ. With that, the emperor commanded that he be scourged. When this failed to kill him, the emperor was heard to say: "Will no one rid me of this monk?" At which point some of those who overheard him went off and dragged Stephen through the streets by his feet until eventually he was clubbed to death. The Roman Martyrology mentions, along with Stephen, other monks who suffered at the same time.

A Greek Life by Stephen, "deacon of Constantinople," is in *P.G.*, 100, 1069-86. See also B. Hermann, *Verborgene Heilege des griechischen Ostens* (1931).

St Simeon Metaphrastes (*c.* 1000)

Although a Life of Simeon Metaphrastes (the Recorder) by Michael Psellos appeared less than a century after his death, little certain information about him has survived. He is known principally as a compiler of the legends of the saints in the menologies of the Byzantine Church—though unlike Bd Ado of Vienne (16 Dec.) and Bd James of Voragine (13 July), who performed the same function in the Western Church, he was not a priest. According to Psellos he was a *logothete*, or sort of secretary of state, and he undertook his work on the saints at the request of the emperor, probably Constantine VII Porphyrogenitus (913-55). Today he is identified with Simeon the Logothete, who lived in the tenth century and wrote a chronicle.

As for Simeon's collection of legends, there is some uncertainty as to where he got his material, and he has been variously accused of wholesale fabrication and childish credulity. But more recent scholars have vindicated his reputation on the ground that he did not invent the sometimes absurd stories he tells but was simply setting them down in writing. How far he believed them is another matter. His collection of legends was translated into Latin and published in Venice in the mid-sixteenth century. His feast is kept on 28 November in the Orthodox Church, but there has been no cult in the West.

The Life and legends are in *P.G.*, 104-6, 109. See also *Anal.Boll.* 16, pp. 312-29; 17, pp. 448-52; *American Ecclesiastical Review* 23 (1900), pp. 113-20; *Catholic Encyclopaedia*, 10, pp. 225-6; *D.A.C.L.*, 11, 420-6.

St James of the March (1394-1476)

Domenico Gangali, the second youngest of the nineteen children of Antonio Gangali and Antonia o Tonna, was born in 1394 at Monteprandone in the March of Ancona—hence the designation *della Marca*. The family was poor, and when he was still only six or seven Domenico was given the task of looking after the sheep. He had not been doing it for long when he was severely frightened by a wolf, about which his brothers teased him so badly that he either was sent or ran away to a relative in Offida. This turned out to be his lucky break. The relative had him educated, first in Offida, then in Ascoli, and eventually in Perugia; he then went to Florence, where he taught in the house of a gentleman. In 1416 he was accepted by the Friars Minor in Assisi and took the religious name of James (Giacomo or Jacobo). After his novitiate he went first to Fiesole to study under Bernardino of Siena (20 May) and then to Perugia to read law. As soon as he was ordained, in about 1323, he began his long career as a vehement and effective preacher, initially in Tuscany, Umbria, and the March of Ancona, later in Bohemia, Germany, Hungary, and Poland as well. He was extremely austere, setting aside only three hours for sleep, inflicting severe penances on himself, wearing only a threadbare habit, and making his own copies of the books he needed for his work.

James did much of his work in partnership with St John Capistrano (23 Oct.), who had studied with him under Bernardino of Siena. In 1426 Pope Martin V (1417-31) appointed both men to conduct an inquisition against the *Fraticelli* (a collective name for several deviant Franciscan groups in Italy at the time). The two carried out their mandate with such severity—not only were thirty-six houses of the *Fraticelli* destroyed and their inmates dispersed, but a number of individuals were burned at the stake—that some of the bishops strongly protested. But James was also capable of less violent methods. At the Council of Basle (1431) he took part in the successful attempt to conciliate some of the more moderate Hussites by conceding Communion under both kinds, while at the Council of Florence he was one of those who helped to bring members of the Orthodox Church back into communion with Rome. And later he took part, as an Observant Franciscan, in efforts to settle the differences between the Observants and the Conventuals—though unfortunately the compromise solution he put forward was acceptable to neither side. He was also much in favour of the so-called *montes pietatis* (charitable pawnshops designed to enable the poor to borrow money at reasonable rates), which were later to be reorganized and popularized by Bd Bernardino of Feltre (28 Sept.).

When James Capistrano died in 1456, James was sent to take his place as papal legate in Hungary, a post he held for four years. On his return to Italy he was offered the see of Milan, but he did not accept it, preferring to continue as a preacher. His preaching was based on the Bible, with references to the works of theologians and moralists, to the Latin classics, and to Dante—he knew the *Divina Commedia* by heart and would quote passages from it in his sermons. In 1462, while preaching at Brescia on Easter Monday, he voiced a theological opinion about the blood of Christ and as a result became a pawn in the rivalry between the Franciscans and the Dominicans. He was cited by the local inquisition (the inquisitor was a Dominican) but refused to appear, and when the matter was pursued, he appealed to Rome. This led to a full-scale disputation before Pope Pius II (1458-64). Although in the end no decision was given, and silence was imposed on both sides, the incident overshadowed the remainder of James' life. He went to Naples in 1473 and died there on 28 November 1476. He was buried in the church of Santa Maria Nuova and was canonized in 1726. A portrait by Crivelli, who presents him as a gaunt figure with a powerful inner presence, hangs in the Louvre, and in a contemporary painting by Nicola di Maestro Antonio, now in the Ashmolean Museum, Oxford, he is shown holding a crucifix.

For authentic memoir by St James' friend and travelling companion, Venanzio da Fabriano (ed. T. Somigli), see *Archivum Franciscanum Historicum*, 17 (1924), pp. 378-414. For more recent material, see U. Picciafuoco, *San Giacomo della Marca* (1976); S. Candela, *San Giacomo della Marca* (1962); G. Caselli, *Studi su S. Giacomo della Marca* (2 vols., 1926); D. Pacetti, many articles on aspects of St James' life and works in *Studi Franciscani*. See also *Bibl.SS.*, 6, 388-402; *N.C.E.*, 7, pp. 811-2.

Bd James Thompson, *Martyr* (1582)

James was a native of York, in which city he spent most of his life. In 1580 he went to Reims to study for the priesthood but was forced to return to England a year later, when his health broke down. However, thanks to a special dispensation, he was ordained before he left France and therefore qualified to work on the English mission. This he did for about a year, under the name of Hudson, until he was arrested and brought before the Council of the North. He immediately acknowledged that he was a priest—causing some surprise, since his short absence from the city had scarcely been noticed—and was sent for trial. Some details of this, and of his imprisonment and death, are still extant. Asked at his trial whether he would take up arms against the pope should the latter invade England, he replied that when the time came he would show himself a true patriot; but when asked if he would fight against the pope "now," he said he would not. He spent three months in prison, for part of the time in irons and with common criminals. Then on 28 November 1582 he was hanged in the Knavesmire, York. Before mounting the scaffold he spoke to the crowd, protesting his loyalty to the queen; then, as he climbed the steps, he turned and said: "I have forgotten one thing. I pray you all to bear witness that I die in the Catholic faith." As he hung there choking, people were astonished to see him make the sign of the cross.

See: *M.M.P.*, pp. 70-2; *N.C.E.*, 9, pp. 319-32.

Bd Christopher Wharton, *Martyr* (1600)

Christopher Wharton is one of the many martyrs of the Elizabethan period who came from Yorkshire. Born at Middleton in the West Riding, he went to Trinity College, Oxford, where he obtained the degree of master of arts and was for a while a fellow. A convert to Roman Catholicism, he soon abandoned his fellowship and went over to study for the priesthood at the English College in Douai, which had been founded in 1569 by William, later Cardinal, Allen. Christopher was ordained on 31 March 1584, and by 1586 he was an active member of the English mission. The circumstances of his arrest are unknown, except that it took place in the house of a Mrs Eleanor Hunt, who was apprehended at the same time for harbouring a priest—the Act Against Jesuits, Seminary Priests and Other Suchlike Disobedient Subjects (1585) made it as much an offence to harbour a priest as to work as one. Both were in prison in York Castle in 1599. Wharton was tried at the Lent Assizes in York in 1600. Having failed in an attempt to persuade his judges that he was ordained before the beginning of Elizabeth's reign, and having refused the bribes offered him if he would conform, he died at York on 28 March 1600. He is one of the Eighty-five Martyrs of England, Scotland and Wales (see 22 Nov.)

B. C. Foley, *The Eighty-five Blessed Martyrs* (1987).

St Joseph Pignatelli (1737-1811)

A member of the Spanish branch of a noble Neapolitan family, Joseph (José) was born in Zaragoza in 1737. He was the seventh of the eight children of Don Antonio Pignatelli and his wife, Doña Maria Francisca, who died when he was only four. He was brought up by a sister, but when his father died too, his brothers sent him to be educated by the Jesuits. At the age of sixteen he joined the Society of Jesus in Tarragona, but he returned after his ordination to work in his native city.

Four years later, in 1767, the Society, which had already been suppressed in France and Portugal, was banned from Spain by Carlos III (1759-88), who feared its independence. As members of the Spanish nobility, Joseph and his brother Nicolás, also a Jesuit, were told they could remain in Spain provided they left the Order, but both refused. Initially, the Spanish Jesuits found a home in Corsica, but they were expelled from there too when the French occupied the island in 1768. Joseph managed to find a place for them, as well as for Jesuits from Mexico and Peru, in Ferrara, where things went well as long as Pope Clement XIII (1758-69), a great defender of the Society, was alive. But he died in 1769 and in 1773 his successor, Clement XIV (1769-74), yielding to pressure from the monarchs of France, Portugal, and Spain, suppressed the Society altogether. The measure was purely administrative—the papal Bull was careful not to say that the charges brought had been proven—but its effect was to secularize about 23,000 religious. Commenting on it at Joseph's beatification ceremony, Pope Pius XI (1922-39) said: "It is a sad page of history, as everyone agrees."

For the next twenty years Joseph lived mainly in Bologna, where he studied, collected books and manuscripts relating to the history of the Society of Jesus, and supported his fellow-Jesuits—many of whom were in grave want—both materially and spiritually. Meanwhile, in Russia, the empress, Catherine II (ruled 1762-96), had refused to allow the bishops to promulgate the brief of suppression, so, with the agreement of the Holy See, the Society continued to exist there. In 1792 the duke of Parma invited three Italian Jesuits then resident in Russia to open a house in his state. Joseph was anxious to be involved in this venture but unwilling to act without authority. However, once the duke had obtained for him the guarded approval of Pope Pius VI (1775-99), he renewed his vows privately and in 1797 was put in charge. Two years later, with verbal permission from the pope, he organized an informal novitiate at Colorno, just north of Parma. From here the students went to Russia to make their profession, a practice that became canonical in 1801, when Pope Pius VII (1800-23) formally approved the Jesuit province there.

Joseph's tireless work for the revival of the Society was rewarded in 1804 when it was re-established in the kingdom of Naples, he himself being appointed provincial. The Fathers had to disperse again when the French invaded in 1805, but most were able to go to Palermo (the resulting Sicilian province became the mother of the modern Irish province). Joseph himself went to Rome, where he became provincial for Italy. A generous gift from his sister enabled him to restore the Sardinian province and to re-lay the foundations of the Society in Rome, Tivoli, and Orvieto.

Thanks to his prudence none of the gains made was lost during the period of the French occupation and the exile of Pius VII; and in 1814 his ultimate objective, the complete restoration of the Society, was realized. He did not live to see it, as he died in Rome on 11 November 1811, but Pius XI nevertheless described him as "the chief link between the Society that had been and the Society that was to be . . . the restorer of the Jesuits." He was buried in the church of San Pantaleo, in the little street where he died, not far from the Colosseum, and his death mask is preserved in the room of St Ignatius at the Jesuit generalate in Rome. He was canonized in 1954.

Biographies by A. Moncon (1833); G. Boero (1856); J. Nonell (1893-4): the latter is the most complete and includes some of the saint's letters. More modern biographies: P. Zurbitu (Span., 1933), C. Beccari (Ital., 1933), J. March (Span., 1935), D. A. Hanly (Eng., 1932). See also *Bibl.SS.*, 6, 1333-7.

St Catherine Labouré (1806-76)

Zoë Labouré was born on 2 May 1806. She was the eighth of the ten children of a French yeoman farmer, Pierre Labouré, and his wife, Madeleine Goutard, who lived at Fain-les-Moutiers in the Côte d'Or. She was the only member of her large family who did not go to school, and she never learned properly to read and write. When she was only eight her mother died, and not long after this she inherited from her sister Louise, who left home to become a Sister of Charity, the combined role of housekeeper and helper to her father. From the age of fourteen she felt called to the religious life herself, but her father was opposed to the idea and, in order to distract her, sent her to Paris to be a waitress in a café belonging to one of her brothers. This had no effect on her, so in 1830 M. Labouré gave in and allowed her to join the Sisters of Charity of St Vincent de Paul at Châtillon-sur-Seine. She took the name Catherine, and once her postulancy was over she was sent to the convent in the rue du Bac in Paris.

She arrived four days before the relics of St Vincent de Paul (27 Sept.) were transferred from the cathedral of Notre-Dame to the Lazarist church on the rue de Sèvres, and on the evening of the opening day of the festivities she had the first of the visions for which she was to become famous. Three more visions took place in mid-July, and then, on 27 November, Our Lady appeared to her standing on a globe, with shafts of light streaming from her hands and the words "O Mary, conceived free from sin, pray for us who have recourse to thee" surrounding the image. When Our Lady turned round, Catherine saw a capital M with a cross above it and below it two hearts (one thorn-crowned, one pierced with a sword). Catherine seemed to hear a voice telling her to have what she saw struck as a medal and promising that those who wore the medal with devotion would receive great graces at the intercession of Mary. The visions continued until September 1831.

Catherine confided in her confessor, M. Aladel, who, after thorough investigations, obtained permission from the archbishop of Paris to have the medal struck. The first 1,500 of what came to be known as the "miraculous medal" (because of its origin rather than its properties) were issued in June 1832. In 1834, M. Aladel published a *Notice historique sur l'origine et les effets de la Médaille Miraculeuse*, 130,000 copies of which were sold in six years, with translations into seven languages, including Chinese. When in 1836 the archbishop of Paris ordered an enquiry into the alleged visions, Catherine could not be persuaded to appear—she had taken such precautions to keep herself unknown and did not want to lose that anonymity now. So the tribunal went on without her, coming down, in the end, in favour of the authenticity of the visions.

The popularity of the medal increased daily, particularly after the conversion, in 1842, of an Alsatian Jew, Alphonse Ratisbonne. Having reluctantly agreed to wear it, he had a vision of Our Lady in the same form, became a Christian, and went on to become a priest and to found the Congregation of Notre-Dame de Sion and the Fathers of Zion.

Alphonse Ratisbonne's vision was subjected to canonical inquiry, and the reports of this, as well as of the archbishop of Paris' inquiry into Catherine's visions, were used in Catherine's beatification process. Almost nothing is recorded about her personal life. From 1831 until her death on 31 December 1876, she lived unobtrusively in the convent at Enghien-Reuilly—as portress, or minding the poultry, or looking after the old people in the hospice. Her superiors spoke of her as "rather insignificant," "matter-of-fact and unexcitable," "cold, almost apathetic." Not until eight months before her death would she speak to anyone other than her confessor about the graces she had received, and then only to her superior, Sister Dufès. But there was an outburst of popular veneration at her funeral, and a twelve-year-old child, crippled from birth, was reported to have been cured at her grave soon afterwards. Catherine Labouré was canonized in 1947. Her relics remain in the chapel of the convent in the rue du Bac, where she had her visions.

See J. I. Dirvin, *St Catherine Labouré of the Miraculous Medal* (1984); C. Yves, *La vie secrète de Catherine Labouré* (1948); G. Fullerton, *Life and Visions of a Sister of Charity* (1880); other biographies in Eng. trans.: E. Crapez (1920), E. Cassinari (1934). See also *O.D.S.*, p. 286; *N.C.E.*, 8, pp. 301-2; *Bibl.SS.* 3, 1045-7.

29

St Saturninus of Toulouse, *Bishop and Martyr* (?Third Century)

The story of Saturninus (or Sernin) is important because it touches indirectly on many of the problems associated with the origins of the church in Gaul. His name is African, and although little is known about him before he became a bishop, he is venerated as a missionary and as the first bishop of Toulouse. He is supposed to have preached on both sides of the Pyrenees, and according to Venantius Fortunatus he converted a great number of idol-worshippers by his preaching. St Sidonius Apollinaris (21 Aug.) also pays tribute to him, while St Gregory of Tours (17 Nov.) refers to him more than once and was clearly familiar with the text of his *passio*.

According to the author of the *passio*, which was written before the seventh century, he would gather his flock together in a small church in Toulouse, which was separated from his own house by the chief temple in the city. People came to consult the oracles in this temple; but for some time they had been silent, and this was attributed to the presence of a Christian bishop. So, seizing Saturninus one day as he was passing, the temple priests dragged him into the temple and told him that he must either offer sacrifice to the offended gods or propitiate them with his own blood. Saturninus replied: "I worship only one God and to him I am ready to offer a sacrifice of praise. Your gods are evil and are more pleased with the sacrifice of your souls than with those of your bullocks. How can I fear them who, as you acknowledge, tremble before a Christian?" Enraged by this, the priests tied his feet to a bull, which they then goaded into running violently down the hill until the bishop's skull was broken and his brains were dashed out. When the cord broke, what remained of the body was left outside the city gates, where it was collected by two women, who hid it in a ditch. Later the relics were enshrined in what is now the great basilica of St-Sernin. A church built near the place where the bull stopped is called the Taur. Later, other legends, that he was sent to Gaul by Pope St Clement, or even by the apostles, were woven around him.

The iconographical evidence suggests that his cult was widespread in southern France and northern Spain from the third century: apart from the basilica in Toulouse, there are several churches dedicated to him on the pilgrim route to Compostela. Painted cycles of his life include a thirteenth-century one now in the Museo del Arte Catalán in Barcelona and another, painted in the sixteenth century for the church of St Saturninus in Tours by Jacques de Semblançay, which can be seen in the museum in Angers. St Saturninus' iconographical symbol is a bull.

L. Duchesne, *Fastes Episcopaux*, 1, pp. 26, 306-7; *Bibl.SS.*, 11, 673-81.

St Saturninus, *Martyr* (*c.* 308)

What information we have about this Saturninus is found in the *passio* of Pope St Marcellus I (306–8; 16 Jan.). This is not entirely reliable, but it says he was a Christian who was condemned to transport sand for the construction of the baths of Diocletian during the period when Maximinus Daia (308–13) came back from Africa. Pope St Damasus (366–84; 11 Dec.) says he was a priest who came to Rome from Carthage. The Roman Martyrology adds further details. He suffered at Rome, on the Salarian Way, during the persecution of Maximian (306–8), with a younger man, a deacon called Sisinnius. Before they were beheaded Saturninus and Sisinnius spent some time in prison, where they were given too little to eat as a way of weakening them. Finally they were stretched on the rack, scourged, and beheaded. Saturninus was buried in the cemetery of Thraso on the via Salaria Nova. A basilica there, which was said to have been dedicated to St Saturninus, burned down during the papacy of Felix IV (526–30); according to the *Liber Pontificalis*, it was rebuilt and restored during the reigns of Adrian I (772–95) and Gregory IV (827–44).

AA.SS., Jan, 2, pp. 5–7, 12; *C.M.H.*, pp. 626–7; *Anal.Boll.* 5, pp. 340; 8, pp. 125–35.

BB George Errington, William Gibson, and William Knight, *Martyrs* (1596)

In the first volume of his *Memoirs of Missionary Priests*, Challoner observes that 1596 was the first year since 1580 in which no priest died "in this kingdom" for his faith. He records, however, the deaths of three Catholic laymen who were tried for high treason at the end of that November. "These were George Errington, gentleman, born at Herst, in Northumberland; William Knight, son of Leonard Knight, a wealthy yeoman of South Duffield, in the parish of Hemingborough in Yorkshire; William Gibson, yeoman, born near Ripon in the same county." All three were betrayed by a Protestant minister who showed an interest in returning to Roman Catholicism, won their trust, and then handed them over to the authorities. They were charged with "persuading to popery," tried, and executed at York on 29 November 1596. All three are included among the Eighty-five Martyrs of England, Scotland, and Wales (see 22 Nov.).

M.M.P., pp. 229–30; B. C. Foley, *The Eighty-five Blessed Martyrs* (1987).

BB Dionysius and Redemptus, *Martyrs* (1638)

Pierre, the first of the ten children of a couple surnamed Berthelot, was born at Honfleur in Normandy in 1600. When he was nineteen, the boy sailed for the East Indies in a French ship, the *Espérance*. The ship was captured and burned by Dutch privateers, but Pierre managed to escape. After trading for some years on his own, he entered the Portuguese service at Malacca and, first as a pilot, then as a cartographer, took part in several expeditions. In 1635, while he was in Goa, he met the prior of the Discalced Carmelites, who encouraged him to join the Order. This he did, taking the name Dionysius. He had not been professed for long when the Portuguese viceroy asked him to act as pilot for an embassy he was sending to Sumatra. The Carmelites agreed, ordained Dionysius immediately so that he could serve as chaplain as well, and gave him a companion in the person of a lay brother, Redemptus, who as Tomás Rodríguez da Cunha had been a soldier in India before he joined the Carmelites. No sooner had they reached Achin (Sumatra) than the ambassador and his suite were seized and imprisoned by the Sumatrans. Several of the party were killed, including the two friars, neither of whom was prepared to apostatize. As soon as the news reached Goa, the prior began to collect evidence with a view to introducing the cause of their beatification. In fact they were not beatified until 1900. There are some meticulously worked maps—*tabulae maritimae*—in the British Museum which are said to be the work of Dionysius.

João do Sacramento, *Chronica de Carmelitas Descalcos*, 2 (1721), pp. 798-813. See also Thomas de Jésus, *Les bx Denis de la Nativité et Rédempt de la Croix* (1900); P. Gonthier, *Vie admirable de Pierre Berthelot* (1917); *Etudes Carmélitaines* (1912), pp. 426-42; (1913), pp. 215-27, 387-97; *Bibl.SS.*, 4, 648-50.

St Francis of Lucera (1681-1742)

Donato Antonio Giovanni Fasani—known to all as Giovanniello—was born at Lucera in Puglia in 1681, the son of Giuseppe Fasani and Isabella Della Monaca. When he was only ten, his father, a farm labourer, died, and his mother married again. Her new husband, Francesco Farinacci, took seriously his responsibilities toward her children, and he sent the boy to be educated by the Friars Minor Conventual in Lucera. Giovanni soon felt called to join the Order, and when he was fifteen he was clothed at the novitiate on Monte Gargano, taking the names Francesco Antonio. Over the next nine years he pursued his studies in various places while leading an exemplary religious life, and he was finally ordained at Assisi in 1705. Two years later, having gained a doctorate in theology, he went as lecturer in philosophy to the Conventuals' college in Lucera.

Lucera was to be Francis' headquarters for the rest of his life. Although he filled a variety of posts, including that of minister provincial of the province of Sant' Angelo, from the moment he became a master of theology he was known in Lucera as Padre Maestro, and people used to say of him: "If you want to see St Francis, watch Padre Maestro." From the start he made his mark as a preacher and teacher, his main aim being to make himself "understood by all"; he also wrote a handful of books for preachers. Another particular concern was the welfare of prisoners, who were kept in appalling conditions. (His biographer quotes Gladstone, who, even 100 years later, was harshly critical of the state of Neapolitan prisons.) He also started a Christmas custom of collecting for the poor, and people constantly came to him for help, which he never refused, even if the request seemed impossible.

Francis' great devotion was to Mary in her Immaculate Conception, and he celebrated a public novena each year before the feast on 8 December. Some time before the novena began in 1742, when he seemed to be in good health, he confided to a companion, Fr Lodovico Gioca, that he would die shortly, and that Fr Lodovico would not long survive him. Francis died on the first day of the novena, 29 November 1742, and Fr Lodovico survived him by no more than two months. Francis was canonized on 13 April 1986.

Italian biographies by T. M. Vigilanti (1848), L. Berardini (1951), G. Stano (1951; Eng. trans.: R. Huber, 1951): the latter includes two interesting portraits. See also *Bibl.SS.*, 5, 468–70.

ST ANDREW (over page)
Silver saltire on blue field.

30

ST ANDREW, *Apostle* (First Century)

Andrew came from Bethsaida, a Galilean town on the shore of Lake Genesareth, where he worked as a fisherman together with his brother Simon Peter. According to St John's Gospel (1:35-42), he was a disciple of John the Baptist (24 June) and was present when John pointed out a man who had been baptized the day before: "Behold, the Lamb of God." Intrigued, he and another of John's disciples followed the man and spent the rest of the day with him. Early the next morning, Andrew met Simon. "We have found the Messiah," he told him, and took him to Jesus, who gave him the name Peter. St Mark's Gospel (1:16-20) gives a quite different version of events, which is picked up in the Gospels of St Matthew (4:18-22) and St Luke (5:1-11)—although here Andrew is not mentioned by name. According to this version, Andrew and Simon were called personally by Jesus while they were out fishing. In the Greek tradition, Andrew is referred to as the *"protoclete,"* or "first-called."

However it was that he met him, Andrew, along with his brother, followed Jesus, and when Jesus chose twelve of his disciples to be apostles, Andrew was among them. He is always named among the first four in the New Testament lists of the apostles; but more than that, he is one of the small group of the Twelve who are more than mere names and was obviously regarded as a leader. He is mentioned individually on two occasions—both in relation to the apostle Philip: it was he who pointed out the boy with the five loaves and two fishes before the feeding of the five thousand (John 6:8-10); and when Jesus and the apostles were in Jerusalem for what was to be Jesus's last Passover, it was he who told Jesus that there were Greeks who wished to speak to him (John 12:20-2).

Little is known about Andrew's subsequent apostolate, since most of the sources that mention him are apocryphal. However, Eusebius says he preached in Scythia, while according to Theodoret he went to Greece—a view favoured by St Gregory Nazianzen (2 Jan.), who specifies Epirus, and St Jerome (30 Sept.), who specifies Achaia. An early medieval forgery claimed that he founded the see of Byzantium, later Constantinople (presumably to encourage the view that the church there was of apostolic origin, like those of Rome, Alexandria, and Antioch). Although Andrew's supposed relics were taken from Patras in Greece to the church of the Apostles in Constantinople sometime during the reign of Constantius II (ruled 337-61), the truth is that the first-known bishop of Byzantium was St Metrophanes (4 June), early in the fourth century.

Equally obscure are the facts about his death. The apocryphal *passio* says he was crucified at Patras in Achaia, adding that he was bound, not nailed, to the cross and that he preached from it for two days until he died. The idea that his cross was saltire (or X-shaped) was first expressed at Autun in the tenth century and did not become common until the fourteenth. In 356 or 357, for prestige purposes (Rome had the relics of at least one apostle, so it would enhance Constantinople's position to have the same), his supposed relics were taken by the emperor Constantius II (337-61) to the church of the Apostles in Constantinople. However, when the city was captured by the Crusaders in 1204, they were removed and given to the cathedral at Amalfi in Italy; the head was brought to Rome in 1461 or 1462, and it remained at the Vatican until Pope Paul VI (1963-78) returned it to Constantinople.

The feast of St Andrew was universal in the West from the sixth century, and from a very early date churches were dedicated to him, especially in France, Italy, and England, where Hexham and Rochester are the earliest. The popularity of the St Andrew legend is also indicated by the Anglo-Saxon poem *Andreas*, which is based on it.

Andrew is one of the several patron saints of Russia, a country he never visited, although there is a valueless tradition that he preached there, travelling as far as Kiev. There is no suggestion that he preached in Scotland, of which he is also the patron. The legend there is that a certain St Regulus (or Rule), who had charge of St Andrew's relics during the fourth century, was told by an angel to take the relics and go to a place that would be indicated to him. Regulus duly set off in a north-westerly direction "towards the ends of the earth" and was finally stopped by the angel when he reached what is now St Andrews in Scotland. There he built a church to house the relics, became its first bishop, and spent the next thirty years evangelizing the people. The legend, which exists in several conflicting versions, is the basis for the choice of St Andrew as patron of Scotland. He is also a patron of Greece and of fishermen, sailors, and (curiously) spinsters.

In art, Andrew is most frequently shown with a book—see *St Andrew and St Thomas* by Gian Lorenzo Bernini (1598-1680) in the National Gallery in London, or *St Andrew* by Simone Martini (1344) in the Metropolitan Museum in New York. When he is shown with a cross it is normally a Latin cross (as in the panel of a diptych by Carlo Crivelli, also in the National Gallery), though in paintings from the fourteenth century onward it is not unusual to see him with the saltire cross— popularly know as St Andrew's cross and now incorporated into the Union Jack to represent Scotland. *The Crucifixion with Saints* by the Master of Lieborn, also in the National Gallery, shows this cross.

For the *passio* see M. Bonnet, "Acta Andreae Apostoli" in *Anal. Boll.* 12, pp. 309-78; 13, pp. 309-78. See also *Bibl. SS.*, 1, 1094-1113; J. Flamion, *Les Actes apocryphes de l'apôtre André* (1911); M. R. James, *The Apocryphal New Testament* (1924); E. Mâle, *Les saints compagnons du Christ* (1957); F. Dvornik, *The Idea of Apostolicity and the Legend of the Apostle Andrew* (1958); *O.D.S.*, pp. 20-1. For the connection with Scotland, see W. Skene, *Celtic Scotland* (1876), pp. 296-9; *K.S.S.*, pp. 436-40.

ST CUTHBERT MAYNE, *Martyr* (1544-77)

In the early days of the penal laws a legal distinction was made between "Marian" priests, who had been ordained in England, and "seminary" priests, ordained at the English College founded in 1568 at Douai. Cuthbert Mayne, who was born at Youlston near Barnstaple in 1544, was the first "seminary" priest to die for his faith.

Cuthbert was brought up as a member of the Church of England by his uncle, a former Catholic priest, and educated at Barnstaple Grammar School. Thanks to his uncle's influence, he was given the living of Huntshaw parish when he was only seventeen, and two years later he was ordained priest in the Anglican Church. While at Oxford, where he went next to read for an arts degree at St Alban's Hall (later Merton College), he met two Catholics, Dr Gregory Martin and Edmund Campion, who at that time was still a Protestant. In their company he soon became convinced of the truth of Roman Catholicism, and although he held back initially for fear of losing his living and his appointments, he was soon corresponding on the subject with the other two men, who had by this time gone over to Douai. Unfortunately, one of the letters fell into the hands of the bishop of London, who sent a pursuivant to round up all those whose names appeared in it. Cuthbert was away at the time, but the incident made up his mind for him. He rejected Protestantism and in 1573 was accepted at Douai. In April 1576, having been ordained to the priesthood and taken a bachelor's degree in theology, he was sent back to England with John Payne (2 Apr.).

He returned to the west country, to Probus near Totnes, where, in the guise of estate steward, he entered the household of Francis Tregian of Golden Manor. Little is known of his ministry to recusants in the area, but suspicions were aroused, and on 8 June 1577 Golden Manor was raided by 100 armed men led by the high sheriff of Cornwall, Richard Grenville. Most of the household were arrested, including Cuthbert, whose papers were in order, but who was found to have an *agnus dei* round his neck. He was taken to Launceston Castle, where he was chained to the bedpost in a filthy prison cell. At the Michaelmas assizes he was charged with a number of offences in contravention of the Act of Supremacy, found guilty of treason, and condemned to death. The trial attracted more than the usual amount of attention, partly because Cuthbert was the first seminary priest to be tried but also because the evidence was purely circumstantial, and one of the judges, Mr Jeffreys, was not at all satisfied with the outcome. Grenville had effectively bullied the jury into returning a verdict of guilty, and Jeffreys asked for a review of the case. However, although the weight of opinion was on his side, the Privy Council decided to let the conviction stand "as a terror to the papists" and a warning to priests coming from abroad.

On 29 November, the day before he was due to be executed, Cuthbert was told that he would go free if he took the Oath of Supremacy. In response, he took a Bible, kissed it and said: "The queen neither ever was nor is nor ever shall be the head of the Church of England." On the 30th he was taken on a sledge to Launceston marketplace, where he asked for but was refused permission to address the crowd. When the authorities tried to get him to implicate Francis Tregian and his brother-in-law, Sir John Arundell, Cuthbert replied: "I know nothing of them except that they are good and pious men; and of the things laid to my charge no one but myself has any knowledge." After that they hanged him, but he was probably already unconscious when they cut him down alive to carry out the savage ritual of drawing and quartering.

Cuthbert was canonized by Pope Paul VI (1963-78) in 1970, as one of the Forty Martyrs of England and Wales (25 Oct.). There is a contemporary portrait of him in the Ashmolean Museum in Oxford; and a substantial relic of his skull, recovered from Launceston where it was displayed, is now at the Carmelite convent in Lanherne in Cornwall. Francis Tregian, for his part, had his lands confiscated and spent nearly thirty years in prison because of his association with Cuthbert Mayne. When he died in Lisbon in 1608, miracles were associated with his relics.

See *M.M.P.*, pp. 1-6; W. Allen, *A Briefe Historie of the Glorious Martyrdom of Twelve Reverend Priests* (1582; 1908); E. S. Knox in B. Camm, *Lives of the English Martyrs*, 2 (1914), pp. 204-21. See also R. A. McElroy, *Bd Cuthbert Mayne* (1929); P. A. Boyan and G. R. Lamb, *Francis Tregian* (1955); *N.C.E.*, 9, pp. 520-1.

SS Sapor and Isaac, *Bishops and Martyrs* (339)

An account in Syriac of the martyrdom of these two bishops was first published in the eighteenth century. According to this, Sapor and Isaac were active in Persia during the reign of King Sapor II, a time when there was widespread suspicion that Christians were in league with the Roman emperors against their own country. Profession of the national religion, Mazdeism, was made a test of loyalty, and Persian Christians who failed to pass it were savagely persecuted. Sapor and Isaac were among the first to be arrested, for building churches and making converts.

Together with three others, Mahanes, Abraham, and Simeon, they were brought before the king, who asked them why they refused to obey his laws, given that he, who was of divine descent, still sacrificed to the sun. They replied: "We acknowledge one God, and him alone we worship." Sapor added: "We confess only one God, who made all things, and Jesus Christ, born of him." The king ordered that he be struck in the mouth, which was done with such force that his teeth were knocked out, and then he was beaten with clubs until many of his bones were broken. Isaac, who appeared next, remained equally steadfast and was taken off to be stoned to death. When Sapor, now in prison, heard of Isaac's death he gave thanks to God, and himself died two days later from his wounds. To be certain that he really was dead, the king had his head cut off, and then had the remaining three put to death in equally brutal ways.

For the Syriac account of the martyrdom, see P. Bedjan, *Acta martyrum et sanctorum*, 2 (1891). See also S. E. Assemani, *Acta sanctorum martyrum orientalium et occidentalium*, 1, pp. 225-30.

Bd Frederick of Regensburg (1329)

Almost nothing is known about Frederick apart from what is told in a short, conventional biography, which was published in 1615. He was born of poor parents in Regensburg, where he eventually joined the Augustinian hermits as a lay brother. He was employed principally as a carpenter, and it was his job also to chop wood for fuel: he used to thank God that there was any job for which he seemed suited. Accounts exist of various marvels connected with him, including one of his having received Communion at the hands of an angel. All the evidence—the appearance of his name in calendars, the special location of his tomb, and the designation Blessed—suggest that he was highly regarded by his contemporaries. He died on 30 November 1329.

AA.SS., Nov., 1, pp. 496–8. For short biography, with engraving, see M. Rader, *Bavaria Sancta* (1702), 1, p. 298.

Bd Andrew of Antioch (*c.* 1268-*c.* 1348)

Andrew was born in Antioch in about 1268—the year in which the power of the Crusaders in Syria was finally broken by the Sultan Bibars. Andrew was descended from Prince Bohemund III of the Latin kingdom of Antioch (1163-1201), and therefore from the Norman adventurer Robert Guiscard (1015-85), who had succeeded in establishing Norman rule in Sicily. Having joined the community of Augustinian Canons that had been formed to serve the basilica of the Holy Sepulchre in Jerusalem, he was appointed keybearer by the Latin patriarch. This meant that he had charge of the key to the holy sepulchre, though the office was in fact a merely honorary one, since the Saracens had retaken possession of Jerusalem about twenty-five years before Andrew was born. The canons were not driven out, but the keys were handed over to two Muslim families, descendants of whom are said to be the official doorkeepers still. Toward the end of his life, Andrew was sent on a mission to Europe, his task being to visit the houses of his Order and collect funds for the maintenance of the community in Jerusalem. He travelled to Sicily, Italy, Poland, and France, and it was at Annecy, in Savoy, that he died in about 1348. He had a great reputation for holiness, and his cult was recognized in 1360, when his relics were placed in a shrine. St Francis de Sales had a strong devotion to him and bore witness to miracles that were reported at his tomb.

See: *D.H.G.E.*, 2, 1632-3; *Bibl.SS.*, 1, 1113, 1117.

Bd Alexander Crow, *Martyr* (1586/7)

Alexander Crow was born at South Duffield or Howden in the South Riding of Yorkshire. He began his adult life as a shoemaker but in his late twenties went to the English College at Douai to study for the priesthood. After his ordination in 1584 he returned to England and was active in the north. In 1586 (or 87—there is some disagreement about the year), he was arrested in South Duffield, on his way to baptize a child, and taken to York. There he was tried and condemned to death under the 1585 Act against Jesuits, Seminary Priests and Other Suchlike Disobedient Subjets, which made it a treasonable offence for a subject of the queen to return from abroad as a minister of religion. According to the account of his life and death that favours 1587 for the date of the latter, he went through a severe spiritual crisis during his last night in prison and was tempted to commit suicide in his cell. However, he persevered in prayer and eventually "the monster disappeared," leaving him "full of consolation." He was hanged, drawn, and quartered in York on 30 November, and he is one of the Eighty-five Martyrs of England, Scotland, and Wales (see 22 Nov.) who were beatified in 1987.

See *M.M.P.*, pp. 125-9; B. C. Foley, *The Eighty-Five Blessed Martyrs* (1987).

Consultant Editors

REV. PHILIP CARAMAN, S.J. Author of numerous biographies of saints and chief promoter of the cause of the Forty English Martyrs (canonized in 1970). Consultant on English Martyrs.

DAVID HUGH FARMER. Former Reader in history at the University of Reading. Author of *St Hugh of Lincoln* and other biographical studies of saints. Author of *The Oxford Dictionary of Saints*. General consultant editor.

JOHN HARWOOD Librarian of the Missionary Institute in London and course lecturer on the Orthodox churches. Consultant on Eastern and Orthodox saints.

DOM ERIC HOLLAS, O.S.B. Monk of St John's Abbey, Collegeville, Minnesota and director of the Hill Monastic Manuscript Library in Collegeville, where he also teaches theology at St John's University. General consultant, U.S.A.

PROF. KATHLEEN JONES, Emeritus Professor of Social Policy at the University of York. Author of many books and articles on social policy and mental illness. Honorary Fellow of the Royal College of Psychiatrists. Translator of *The Poems of St John of the Cross* (1993). Consultant on social history and abnormal behaviour.

DOM DANIEL REES, O.S.B. Monk of Downside Abbey and librarian of the monastery library. Bibliographical consultant.

DR RICHARD SHARPE. Reader in diplomatic history at the University of Oxford. Author of *Medieval Irish Saints' Lives* (1991), *Adomnán of Iona. Life of St Columba* (1995), and numerous articles on Celtic saints. Consultant on this subject.

REV. AYLWARD SHORTER, W.F. Long experience of African Missions and author of many books on the subject. Former President of Missionary Institute, London, now Principal of Tangaza College, Nairobi. Consultant on missionary saints.

DOM ALBERIC STACPOOLE, O.S.B. Monk of Ampleforth Abbey. Fellow of the Royal Historical Society. Secretary of the Ecumenical Society of Our Lady. Editor of several works, including *Vatican II by Those Who Were There* (1985). Engaged on a study of St Anslem. Consultant on feasts of Our Lady.

DOM HENRY WANSBROUGH, O.S.B. Monk of Ampleforth Abbey, currently Master of St Benet's Hall, Oxford, and member of the Pontifical Biblical Commission. Author of numerous works on scripture and Editor of the *New Jerusalem Bible* (1985). Consultant on New Testament saints.

SR BENEDICTA WARD. Anglican religious. Lecturer at Oxford Institute of Medieval History. Author of numerous works on hagiography, spirituality, and mysticism. Consultant on Middle Ages and age of Bede.

232